Legal Code of Relig Rights

This volume presents a systematic collection of the various international legal sources that define the rights of religious minorities.

In a time of increasing tensions around religious minorities, this volume presents a systematic collection of international and European documents on the protection and promotion of religious minorities' rights. The code includes documents from the United Nations, the Council of Europe, the Organization for Security and Co-operation in Europe, and the European Union. An index system connects the various sources and norms and emphasises the strengths and the weaknesses in the legal frameworks of international and European institutions. While allowing for further research on the historical and conceptual development in the area, the code provides the reader with a new, easily accessible tool facilitating experts and actors who wish to improve the knowledge and protection of religious minorities.

This book will be an invaluable resource for students, academics, and researchers interested in law and religion, international law, public law, and human rights law. The code is also a powerful tool for minorities themselves and for advocates of their rights.

Daniele Ferrari is a researcher in Law and Religion at the University of Siena, Italy.

ICLARS Series on Law and Religion

Series Editors:
Silvio Ferrari,
University of Milan, Italy, Russell Sandberg, Cardiff University, UK
Pieter Coertzen,
University of Stellenbosch, South Africa
W. Cole Durham, Jr.,
Brigham Young University, USA
Tahir Mahmood,
Amity International University, India

The *ICLARS Series on Law and Religion* is a new series designed to provide a forum for the rapidly expanding field of research in law and religion. The series is published in association with the International Consortium for Law and Religion Studies, an international network of scholars and experts of law and religion founded in 2007 with the aim of providing a place where information, data and opinions can easily be exchanged among members and made available to the broader scientific community. The series aims to become a primary source for students and scholars while presenting authors with a valuable means to reach a wide and growing readership.

Other titles in this series:

The Transition of Religion to Culture in Law and Public Discourse
Lori Beaman

Religious Minorities, Islam and the Law
International Human Rights and Islamic Law in Indonesia
Al Khanif

The Internal Law of Religions
Introduction to a Comparative Discipline
Burkhard Josef Berkmann
Translated by David E. Orton

Legal Code of Religious Minority Rights
Sources in International and European Law
Daniele Ferrari

Law, Religion, and Freedom
Conceptualizing a Common Right
Edited by W. Cole Durham, Jr., Javier Martínez-Torrón, and Donlu Thayer

For more information about this series, please visit: www.routledge.com/ICLARS-Series-on-Law-and-Religion/book-series/ICLARS

Legal Code of Religious Minority Rights
Sources in International and European Law

Daniele Ferrari

LONDON AND NEW YORK

First published 2022
by Routledge
2 Park Square, Milton Park, Abingdon, Oxon OX14 4RN

and by Routledge
605 Third Avenue, New York, NY 10158

Routledge is an imprint of the Taylor & Francis Group, an informa business

© 2022 Daniele Ferrari

The right of Daniele Ferrari to be identified as author of this work has been asserted by them in accordance with sections 77 and 78 of the Copyright, Designs and Patents Act 1988.

All rights reserved. No part of this book may be reprinted or reproduced or utilised in any form or by any electronic, mechanical, or other means, now known or hereafter invented, including photocopying and recording, or in any information storage or retrieval system, without permission in writing from the publishers.

Trademark notice: Product or corporate names may be trademarks or registered trademarks, and are used only for identification and explanation without intent to infringe.

British Library Cataloguing-in-Publication Data
A catalogue record for this book is available from the British Library

Library of Congress Cataloging-in-Publication Data
Names: Ferrari, Daniele, author.
Title: Legal code of religious minority rights : sources in international and European law / Daniele Ferrari.
Description: New York : Routledge, 2021. | Series: Iclars series on law and religion | Includes bibliographical references and index.
Identifiers: LCCN 2021007135 (print) | LCCN 2021007136 (ebook) | ISBN 9780367858445 (hardback) | ISBN 9780367655099 (paperback) | ISBN 9781003015369 (ebook)
Subjects: LCSH: Religious minorities—Legal status, laws, etc. | Religious minorities—Civil rights. | Religious minorities—Legal status, laws, etc.—European Union countries.
Classification: LCC K3242 .F47 2021 (print) | LCC K3242 (ebook) | DDC 342.08/52—dc23
LC record available at https://lccn.loc.gov/2021007135
LC ebook record available at https://lccn.loc.gov/2021007136

ISBN: 978-0-367-85844-5 (hbk)
ISBN: 978-0-367-65509-9 (pbk)
ISBN: 978-1-003-01536-9 (ebk)

Typeset in Galliard
by Apex CoVantage, LLC

This book has been produced in the context of the research project of the University of Siena on religious diversity in Europe funded by the Italian Ministry of Research (PRIN 2017).

Contents

Introduction 1

Law reading guides 25

I   **United Nations** 27
Section 1   27
International Covenant on Civil and Political Rights 27
Optional Protocol to the International Covenant on Civil and Political Rights 29
A. Legal definition 32
   A.1. Francesco Capotorti (Special Rapporteur of the Sub-Commission on Prevention of Discrimination and Protection of Minorities), Study on the Rights of Persons Belonging to Ethnic, Religious and Linguistic Minorities *(ST/HR(05)/H852/no.5), 1979.* 32
    Chapter I. The concept of a minority 32
   A.2. Jules Deschênes (Special Rapporteur of the Sub-Commission on Prevention of Discrimination and Protection of Minorities), Proposal concerning a definition of the term "minority" *(E/CN.4/Sub.2/1985/31), 1985.* 41
    Introduction 41
   A.3. UN Human Rights Committee (HRC), CCPR General Comment No. 23: Article 27 (Rights of Minorities) *(CCPR/C/21/Rev.1/Add.5), 8 April 1994.* 52
   A.4. Office of the High Commissioner for human rights (OHCHR), Minority Rights: International Standards and Guidance for Implementation *(HR/PUB/10/3), 2010.* 53
    I. Definitions 53

A.5. *Forum on Minority Issues*, Recommendations of the Forum on Minority Issues at its Sixth Session: Guaranteeing the Rights of Religious Minorities *(A/HRC/25/66), 26 and 27 November 2013.* 57
A.6. *UN Office of the High Commissioner for Human Rights (OHCHR)*, The inclusion of religious minorities in consultative and decision-making bodies, *2014.* 57
    Who are religious minorities? 57
A.7. *Fernand de Varennes (Special Rapporteur on Minority Issues)*, Report of the Special Rapporteur on Minority Issues *(A/74/160), 15 July 2019.* 57
    IV. Conclusions and recommendations 57
A.8. *Fernand de Varennes (Special rapporteur on minority issues)*, Report of the Special Rapporteur on Minority Issues, Effective Promotion of the Declaration on the Rights of Persons Belonging to National or Ethnic, Religious and Linguistic Minorities *(A/75/211), 21 July 2020.* 58
    3. Religious or belief minorities 58
B. Right to profess and practise religion or belief 59
  B.1. *Francesco Capotorti (Special Rapporteur of the Sub-Commission on Prevention of Discrimination and Protection of Minorities)*, Study on the Rights of Persons Belonging to Ethnic, Religious and Linguistic Minorities *(ST/HR(05)/H852/no.5), 1979.* 59
    IV. Application of the principles set forth in Article 27 of the International Covenant on Civil and Political Rights 59
  B.2. *UN Human Rights Committee (HRC)*, CCPR General Comment No. 22: Article 18 (Freedom of Thought, Conscience or Religion) *(CCPR/C/21/Rev.1/Add.4), 30 July 1993.* 69
  B.3. *UN Human Rights Committee (HRC)*, CCPR General Comment No. 23: Article 27 (Rights of Minorities) *(CCPR/C/21/Rev.1/Add.5), 8 April 1994.* 70
  B.4. *UN Human Rights Committee (HRC)*, Sister Immaculate Joseph and 80 Teaching Sisters of the Holy Cross of the Third Order of Saint Francis in Menzingen of Sri Lanka v. Sri Lanka *(CCPR/C/85/D/1249/2004), communication no. 1249/2004, 4 April 2001.* 74
    Factual background 74
    The complaint 75

The State party's submissions on admissibility and merits 77
Authors' comments on the State party's submissions 78
Issues and proceedings before the Committee 79
Consideration of the merits 80
B.5. UN Human Rights Committee (HRC), Gareth Anver Prince v. South Africa *(CCPR/C/91/D/1474/2006), Communication No. 1474/2006, 14 November 2007.* 82
Facts as presented by the author 83
The complaint 84
The State party's submission on admissibility and merits 85
Issues and proceedings before the Committee 89
C. Non-discrimination 92
C.1. Francesco Capotorti (Special Rapporteur of the Sub-Commission on Prevention of Discrimination and Protection of Minorities), Study on the Rights of Persons Belonging to Ethnic, Religious and Linguistic Minorities *(ST/HR(05)/H852/no.5), 1979.* 92
III. The position of persons belonging to ethnic, religious and linguistic minorities in the society in which they live 92
C.2. UN Human Rights Committee (HRC), General Comment No. 22: The Right to Freedom of Thought, Conscience and Religion: Art. 18 *(CCPR/C/21/Rev.1/ Add.4), 30 July 1993.* 94
C.3. UN Human Rights Committee (HRC), CCPR General Comment No. 23: Article 27 (Rights of Minorities) *(CCPR/C/21/Rev.1/Add.5), 8 April 1994.* 95
C.4. UN Human Rights Committee (HRC), Fatima Anderson v. Denmark *(CCPR/C/99/D/1868/2009), Communication No. 1868/2009, 7 September 2010.* 96
Decision on admissibility 96
The facts as presented by the author 96
The complaint 97
The state party's observations on the admissibility and merits of the communication 98
Issues and proceedings before the Committee 99
C.5. UN Office of the High Commissioner for human rights (OHCHR), Minority Rights: International Standards and Guidance for Implementation *(HR/PUB/10/3), 2010.* 100
C. Equality and non-discrimination 101
D. Right to culture 104

D.1. *UN Human Rights Committee (HRC), CCPR General Comment No. 23: Article 27 (Rights of Minorities) (CCPR/C/21/Rev.1/Add.5), 8 April 1994.* 104
E. *Right to education* 105
E.1. *Francesco Capotorti (Special Rapporteur of the Sub-Commission on Prevention of Discrimination and Protection of Minorities), Study on the Rights of Persons Belonging to Ethnic, Religious and Linguistic Minorities (ST/HR(05)/H852/no.5), 1979.* 105

Section 2 109
Convention relating to the Status of Refugees 109
  Protocol relating to the status of refugees 112
A. *Right to asylum* 115
  A.1. *UN Refugee Agency (UNHCR), Guidelines on International Protection: "Membership of a particular social group" within the context of Article 1A(2) of the 1951 Convention and/or its 1967 Protocol relating to the Status of Refugees (HCR/GIP/02/02), 7 May 2002.* 115
    B. *UNHCR's definition* 115
    Relevance of size 116
  A.2. *UN Refugee Agency (UNHCR), Guidelines on International Protection: Religion-Based Refugee Claims under Article 1A(2) of the 1951 Convention and/or the 1967 Protocol relating to the Status of Refugees (HCR/GIP/04/06), 28 April 2004.* 117
    I. *Introduction* 117
    II. *Substantive analysis* 118

Section 3 121
Convention on the elimination of all forms of discrimination against women 121
A. *Discrimination against minority women* 122
  A.1. *Committee on the Elimination of Discrimination against Women (CEDAW), Concluding Comments of the Committee on the Elimination of Discrimination Against Women: Greece (CEDAW/C/GRC/CO/6), 2007.* 122
  A.2. *UN Human Rights Council (HRC), Freedom of religion or belief. Report of the Special Rapporteur on freedom of religion or belief (A/HRC/43/48), 27 February 2020.* 123

Section 4 125
Convention on the rights of the child 125

A. *Right to education* 126
    A.1. Office of the High Commissioner for Human Rights, Promoting and Protecting Minority Rights. A Guide for Advocates *(HR/PUB/12/7), 2012.* 126
        Minority children 126
        Basic education and gender equality 126
B. *Right to maintain religion or belief* 127
    B.1. Special Rapporteur on freedom of religion or belief – Independent Expert on minority issues – Special Rapporteur on the sale of children, child prostitution and child pornography – Special Rapporteur on trafficking in persons, especially women and children – Chair-Rapporteur of the Working Group on the issue of discrimination against women in law and in practice – Special Rapporteur on violence against women, its causes and consequences, Special procedures of the Human Rights Council, Communication 29 May 2013 – Iraq *(IRQ 2/2013).* 127

Section 5 131
Declaration on the Rights of Persons Belonging to National or Ethnic, Religious and Linguistic Minorities 131
A. *Right to existence* 134
    A.1. UN Commission on Human Rights, Sub-Commission on the Promotion and Protection of Human Rights, Commentary of the Working Group on Minorities to the United Nations Declaration on the Rights of Persons Belonging to National or Ethnic, Religious and Linguistic Minorities *(E/CN.4/Sub.2/AC.5/2005/2), 4 April 2005.* 134
    A.2. UN Office of the High Commissioner for human rights (OHCHR), Minority Rights: International Standards and Guidance for Implementation *(HR/PUB/10/3), 2010.* 136
        B. *Promotion and protection of the identity of minorities* 136
    A.3. Forum on Minority Issues, Note by the Independent Expert on minority issues, Rita Izsák, on guaranteeing the rights of religious minorities *(A/HRC/FMI/2013/2), 3 October 2013.* 136
        III. *Legal framework* 136
B. *Right to culture* 137

B.1. *UN Commission on Human Rights, Sub-Commission on the Promotion and Protection of Human Rights,* Commentary of the Working Group on Minorities to the United Nations Declaration on the Rights of Persons Belonging to National or Ethnic, Religious and Linguistic Minorities *(E/CN.4/Sub.2/AC.5/2005/2), 4 April 2005.* 137

C. *Right to profess and practise religion or belief* 138

C.1. *UN Commission on Human Rights, Sub-Commission on the Promotion and Protection of Human Rights,* Commentary of the Working Group on Minorities to the United Nations Declaration on the Rights of Persons Belonging to National or Ethnic, Religious and Linguistic Minorities *(E/CN.4/Sub.2/AC.5/2005/2), 4 April 2005.* 138

III. *Interpretation of and comments on the title and the individual articles* 139

The title and scope of the Declaration 139

D. *Right to participation* 140

D.1. *UN Commission on Human Rights, Sub-Commission on the Promotion and Protection of Human Rights,* Commentary of the Working Group on Minorities to the United Nations Declaration on the Rights of Persons Belonging to National or Ethnic, Religious and Linguistic Minorities *(E/CN.4/Sub.2/AC.5/2005/2), 4 April 2005.* 140

D.2. *UN Human Rights Council (HRC),* Recommendations of the second session of the Forum on Minority Issues on minorities and effective political participation *(A/HRC/13/25), 12 and 13 November 2009.* 143

I. *Introduction* 143

II. *Recommendations* 143

D.3. *Office of the High Commissioner for human rights,* Minority Rights: International Standards and Guidance for Implementation *(HR/PUB/10/3), 2010.* 150

D. *Effective and meaningful participation* 150

D.4. *UN Office of the High Commissioner for Human Rights (OHCHR),* The inclusion of religious minorities in consultative and decision-making bodies, *2014.* 151

Why should religious minorities participate in decision-making? 151

*How the participation of religious minorities facilitates
conflict prevention?* 152
*Participation in consultative and decision-making bodies:
positive measures* 152
*Obstacles hindering religious minorities' participation
in consultative structures* 152
E. Right to association 153
E.1. *UN Commission on Human Rights, Sub-Commission
on the Promotion and Protection of Human Rights,*
Commentary of the Working Group on Minorities
to the United Nations Declaration on the Rights of
Persons Belonging to National or Ethnic, Religious and
Linguistic Minorities *(E/CN.4/Sub.2/AC.5/2005/2),
4 April 2005.* 153
E.2. *UN Office of the High Commissioner for Human Rights,*
Minority Rights: International Standards and Guidance
for Implementation *(HR/PUB/10/3), 2010.* 153
*C. Identifying priorities to address the situation of
minorities* 154
F. Non-discrimination 154
F.1. *High Commissioner for Human Rights (OHCHR),*
Promoting and Protecting Minority Rights. A Guide
for Advocates *(HR/PUB/12/7), 2012.* 154
*Part one – minority rights focus in the United
Nations* 154
F.2. *Forum on Minority Issues,* Note by the Independent
Expert on minority issues, Rita Izsák, on guaranteeing
the rights of religious minorities *(A/HRC/FMI/2013/2),
3 October 2013.* 156
III. Legal framework 156
F.3. *UN Secretary General,* Guidance note of the Secretary
General on racial discrimination and protection
of minorities, *March 2013.* 156
II. Normative and conceptual foundations 157
III. Guiding principles for effective UN action 158

2 **Council of Europe** 161
Section 1 161
European Convention on Human Rights 161
Protocols 1. Enforcement of certain Rights and Freedoms not
included in Section I of the Convention 162
A. Right to profess and practise religion or belief 162

xii Contents

      A.1. *European Courts of Human Rights, Case of* Serif
         c. Greece *(Application no. 38.178/97), 14 March 2000.* 162
         The facts 162
         The Law 167
   B. *Right to free self-identification* 173
      B.1. *European Courts of Human Rights, GC, Case
         of* Molla Sali c. Greece *(Application no. 20.452/14),
         19 December 2018.* 173
         The facts 173
         3. The Court's assessment 178
         II. Application of Article 41 of the Convention 186
Section 2 188
*Framework Convention for the Protection of National
   Minorities* 188
   A. *Right to profess and practise religion or belief* 189
      A.1. *Advisory Committee on the Framework Convention
         for the protection of national minorities,* Compilation
         of Opinions of the Advisory Committee relating to
         Article 8 of the Framework Convention for the Protection
         of National Minorities (3rd cycle), *13 May 2016.* 189
         Present situation 189
         Recommendation 191
   B. *Right to association* 191
      B.1. *Advisory Committee on the Framework Convention for the
         protection of national minorities,* Compilation of Opinions
         of the Advisory Committee relating to Article 8 of the
         Framework Convention for the Protection of National
         Minorities (3rd cycle), *13 May 2016.* 191
         Present situation 191
         Recommendations 192
   C. *Right to education* 193
      C.1. *Advisory Committee on the Framework Convention
         for the protection of national minorities,* Compilation
         of Opinions of the Advisory Committee relating to Article 8
         of the Framework Convention for the Protection
         of National Minorities (4th cycle), *18 September 2017.* 193
         Present situation 193
         Recommendation 194

3. **Organization for Security and Co-operation in Europe (OSCE)**   195
   Section 1 195
   *Conference for Security and Co-operation in Europe, Helsinki
      Decisions, 10 July 1992* 195

Conference on Security and Co-operation in Europe, Budapest Summit Declaration, 21 December 1994 195
A. Definition of national minorities 196
   A.1. *Office of the OSCE High Commissioner on National Minorities,* The Ljubljana Guidelines on Integration of Diverse Societies, *7 November 2012.* 196
      Introduction 196
B. Right to profess and practise religion or belief 197
   B.1. *OSCE Office for Democratic Institutions and Human Rights (ODIHR),* Guidelines on the Legal Personality of Religious or Belief Communities, *2014.* 197
      Part 1. *The freedom of religion or belief and permissible restrictions in general* 197
      II. *The freedom to manifest religion or belief in community with others* 199
C. Right to legal personality 201
   C.1. *OSCE Office for Democratic Institutions and Human Rights (ODIHR),* Guidelines on the Legal Personality of Religious or Belief Communities, *2014.* 201
D. Right to education 202
   D.1. *OSCE High Commissioner on National Minorities (HCNM),* The Hague Recommendations regarding the Education Rights of National Minorities & Explanatory Note, *October 1996.* 202
      General introduction 202
      The spirit of international instruments 204
      Public and private institutions 204
      Minority education at primary and secondary levels 205
      Minority education in vocational schools 206
   D.2. *OSCE-ODIHR, Advisory Council of Experts on Freedom of religion or Belief,* Toledo Guiding Principles on Teaching about Religions and Beliefs in Public Schools, *2007.* 206
      Minority rights 206
E. Right to participation 207
   E.1. *Office of the OSCE High Commissioner on National Minorities,* The Ljubljana Guidelines on Integration of Diverse Societies, *7 November 2012.* 207
      c. Participation in cultural and religious life 208
F. Right to access to justice 209
   F.1. *OSCE High Commissioner on National Minorities,* The Graz Recommendations on Access to Justice and National Minorities, *November 2017.* 209

xiv Contents

    Introduction 209
  G. *Right to access to media 213*
    G.1. *Office of the OSCE High Commissioner on National Minorities,* The Tallinn Guidelines on National Minorities and the Media in the Digital Age & Explanatory Note, *February 2019. 213*
    Introduction 213
    The Tallinn Guidelines on National Minorities and the Media in the Digital Age *215*

4 European Union   223
Section 1 223
Charter of Fundamental Rights of the European Union 223
Treaty on European Union 224
Treaty on the functioning of the European Union 224
A. *Non-discrimination 225*
  A.1. *European Parliament's Committee on Civil Liberties, Justice and Home Affairs,* Towards a comprehensive EU protection system for minorities, *August 2017. 225*
    Non-discrimination is the first and traditional EU approach to minority protection 228
    The second approach is that of minority rights 229
    Religious minorities 233
B. *Right to profess and practise religion or belief 233*
  B.1. *Council of the European Union,* EU Guidelines on the promotion and protection of freedom of religion or belief, *24 June 2013. 233*
    I. Introduction 233
    II. Operational guidelines 236
  B. *Priority areas of action 237*
Section 2 239
Charter of Fundamental Rights of the European Union 239
Treaty on the functioning of the European Union 240
A. *Right to Asylum 244*
  A.1. *European Asylum Support Office (EASO),* country guidance Afghanistan, *June 2019. 244*
    Common analysis 244
    COI summary 245
    Risk analysis 245

Nexus to a reason for persecution 245
Common analysis 246
COI summary 246
Risk analysis 246
Nexus to a reason for persecution 246

Chronological index of institutional documents and judgements	247
Chronological index of legal sources	251
Index of rights and principles	253
Bibliography	258
Name index	260
Subject index	262

Detailed Contents

Introduction   1
   I. The genealogy of the notion of religious minority in international and European law: Introductory remarks 1
   II. Origin 2
   III. Implementation 5
      a) New legal sources 7
      b) Social groups 9
      c) Foreigners 11
      d) The principle of non-discrimination 12
   IV. Synergy 14
      a) The explicit synergy 15
      b) The implicit synergy 17
   V. Conclusion 21

Law reading guides   25

I   United Nations   27
   Section 1 27
   International Covenant on Civil and Political Rights 27
   Optional Protocol to the International Covenant on Civil and Political Rights 29
   A. *Legal definition* 32
      A.1. Francesco Capotorti (Special Rapporteur of the Sub-Commission on Prevention of Discrimination and Protection of Minorities), **Study on the Rights of Persons Belonging to Ethnic, Religious and Linguistic Minorities** (ST/HR(05)/H852/no.5), 1979. 32
      Chapter I. The concept of a minority 32
      A. Analysis of the concept of a minority 32

B. *The question of official recognition by States of ethnic, religious or linguistic minorities within their population* 39

A.2. *Jules Deschênes (Special Rapporteur of the Sub-Commission on Prevention of Discrimination and Protection of Minorities)*, Proposal concerning a definition of the term "minority" *(E/CN.4/Sub.2/1985/31), 1985.* 41
   Introduction 41
   I. *Elimination of non-problems* 42
      A. *The question of indigenous populations* 42
      B. *The question of resident aliens* 42
      C. *Relationship between groups and their members* 43
   II. *Isolation of the variables of the minority concept* 43
      A. *The will of the minority to survive* 44
      B. *The number of members of the minority* 44
   III. *Identification of the constants in the concept of minority* 46
      A. *National minorities* 46
      B. *Judicial opinions* 47
      C. *Quasi-judicial opinions* 50
   Human Rights Committee 50
      D. *Doctrinal opinions* 50
      E. *Observations by Governments* 51
   IV. *Conclusion: a definition of minority* 51

A.3. *UN Human Rights Committee (HRC)*, CCPR General Comment No. 23: Article 27 (Rights of Minorities) *(CCPR/C/21/Rev.1/Add.5), 8 April 1994.* 52

A.4. *Office of the High Commissioner for human rights (OHCHR)*, Minority Rights: International Standards and Guidance for Implementation *(HR/PUB/10/3), 2010.* 53
   I. *Definitions* 53
      A. *Who are minorities under international law?* 53
      B. *Are indigenous peoples considered to be minorities?* 54
      C. *Do minority rights apply to non-citizens?* 55
      D. *What is the relationship between minorities, non-citizens and stateless persons?* 56

A.5. *Forum on Minority Issues*, Recommendations of the Forum on Minority Issues at its Sixth Session: Guaranteeing the Rights of Religious Minorities *(A/HRC/25/66), 26 and 27 November 2013.* 57

Detailed Contents xix

    A.6. UN Office of the High Commissioner for Human Rights (OHCHR), The inclusion of religious minorities in consultative and decision-making bodies, *2014.* 57
        Who are religious minorities? 57
    A.7. Fernand de Varennes (Special Rapporteur on Minority Issues), Report of the Special Rapporteur on Minority Issues *(A/74/160), 15 July 2019.* 57
        IV. Conclusions and recommendations 57
    A.8. Fernand de Varennes (Special rapporteur on minority issues), Report of the Special Rapporteur on Minority Issues, Effective Promotion of the Declaration on the Rights of Persons Belonging to National or Ethnic, Religious and Linguistic Minorities *(A/75/211), 21 July 2020.* 58
        3. *Religious or belief minorities* 58
B. Right to profess and practise religion or belief 59
    B.1. Francesco Capotorti (Special Rapporteur of the Sub-Commission on Prevention of Discrimination and Protection of Minorities), Study on the Rights of Persons Belonging to Ethnic, Religious and Linguistic Minorities *(ST/HR(05)/H852/no.5), 1979.* 59
        IV. Application of the principles set forth in Article 27 of the International Covenant on Civil and Political Rights 59
            B. The right of persons belonging to religious minorities to profess and practise their own religion 59
            Celebration of marriage 62
            Other matters of personal status 63
            Observance of religious holidays 64
            Conscientious objection to military service 65
            Taking of an oath 65
    B.2. UN Human Rights Committee (HRC), CCPR General Comment No. 22: Article 18 (Freedom of Thought, Conscience or Religion) *(CCPR/C/21/Rev.1/Add.4), 30 July 1993.* 69
    B.3. UN Human Rights Committee (HRC), CCPR General Comment No. 23: Article 27 (Rights of Minorities) *(CCPR/C/21/Rev.1/Add.5), 8 April 1994.* 70
    B.4. UN Human Rights Committee (HRC), Sister Immaculate Joseph and 80 Teaching Sisters of the Holy Cross of the Third Order of Saint Francis in Menzingen of Sri Lanka v. Sri Lanka *(CCPR/C/85/D/1249/2004), communication no. 1249/2004, 4 April 2001.* 74

    Factual background 74
    The complaint 75
    The State party's submissions on admissibility and
     merits 77
    Authors' comments on the State party's submissions 78
    Issues and proceedings before the Committee 79
     Consideration of admissibility 79
    Consideration of the merits 80
  B.5. UN Human Rights Committee (HRC), Gareth Anver
   Prince v. South Africa *(CCPR/C/91/D/1474/2006)*,
   Communication No. 1474/2006, 14 November 2007. 82
   Facts as presented by the author 83
   The complaint 84
   The State party's submission on admissibility and merits 85
   Issues and proceedings before the Committee 89
    Consideration of admissibility 89
    Consideration of merits 91
C. Non-discrimination 92
  C.1. Francesco Capotorti (Special Rapporteur of the
   Sub-Commission on Prevention of Discrimination and
   Protection of Minorities), Study on the Rights of Persons
   Belonging to Ethnic, Religious and Linguistic Minorities
   (ST/HR(05)/H852/no.5), 1979. 92
    III. The position of persons belonging to ethnic, religious and
     linguistic minorities in the society in which they live 92
  C.2. UN Human Rights Committee (HRC), General
   Comment No. 22: The Right to Freedom of Thought,
   Conscience and Religion: Art. 18 *(CCPR/C/21/Rev.1/*
   Add.4), 30 July 1993. 94
  C.3. UN Human Rights Committee (HRC), CCPR General
   Comment No. 23: Article 27 (Rights of Minorities)
   (CCPR/C/21/Rev.1/Add.5), 8 April 1994. 95
  C.4. UN Human Rights Committee (HRC), Fatima
   Anderson v. Denmark *(CCPR/C/99/D/1868/2009)*,
   Communication No. 1868/2009, 7 September 2010. 96
   Decision on admissibility 96
   The facts as presented by the author 96
   The complaint 97
   The state party's observations on the admissibility and merits
    of the communication 98
   Issues and proceedings before the Committee 99
    Consideration of admissibility 99

C.5. *UN Office of the High Commissioner for human rights
(OHCHR)*, Minority Rights: International Standards
and Guidance for Implementation *(HR/PUB/10/3),
2010.* 100
    C. *Equality and non-discrimination* 101
D. *Right to culture* 104
    D.1. *UN Human Rights Committee (HRC)*, CCPR General
Comment No. 23: Article 27 (Rights of Minorities)
(CCPR/C/21/Rev.1/Add.5), 8 April 1994. 104
E. *Right to education* 105
    E.1. *Francesco Capotorti (Special Rapporteur of the
Sub-Commission on Prevention of Discrimination and
Protection of Minorities)*, Study on the Rights of Persons
Belonging to Ethnic, Religious and Linguistic Minorities
(ST/HR(05)/H852/no.5), 1979. 105

Section 2 109
    Convention relating to the Status of Refugees 109
    Definition of the term "refugee" 109
    Non-discrimination 111
    Religion 111
        Protocol relating to the status of refugees 112
    General provision 112
    *Co-operation of the national authorities with the United
Nations* 112
    Information on national legislation 113
    Settlement of disputes 113
    Accession 113
    Federal clause 113
    Reservations and declarations 114
    Entry into protocol 114
    Denunciation 115
    *Notifications by the Secretary-General of the United
Nations* 115
    *Deposit in the Archives of the Secretariat of the United
Nations* 115
A. *Right to asylum* 115
    A.1. *UN Refugee Agency (UNHCR)*, Guidelines on
International Protection: "Membership of a particular
social group" within the context of Article 1A(2)
of the 1951 Convention and/or its 1967 Protocol
relating to the Status of Refugees *(HCR/GIP/02/02),
7 May 2002.* 115

  B. *UNHCR's definition* 115
  Relevance of size 116
 A.2. *UN Refugee Agency (UNHCR), Guidelines on International Protection: Religion-Based Refugee Claims under Article 1A(2) of the 1951 Convention and/or the 1967 Protocol relating to the Status of Refugees (HCR/GIP/04/06), 28 April 2004.* 117
  I. *Introduction* 117
  II. *Substantive analysis* 118
   A. *Defining "religion"* 118
   B. *Well-founded fear of persecution* 119
    a) *General* 119

Section 3 121

Convention on the elimination of all forms of discrimination against women 121

Part I 121

A. Discrimination against minority women 122
 A.1. *Committee on the Elimination of Discrimination against Women (CEDAW), Concluding Comments of the Committee on the Elimination of Discrimination Against Women: Greece (CEDAW/C/GRC/CO/6), 2007.* 122
 A.2. *UN Human Rights Council (HRC), Freedom of religion or belief. Report of the Special Rapporteur on freedom of religion or belief (A/HRC/43/48), 27 February 2020.* 123

Section 4 125

Convention on the rights of the child 125

A. Right to education 126
 A.1. *Office of the High Commissioner for Human Rights, Promoting and Protecting Minority Rights. A Guide for Advocates (HR/PUB/12/7), 2012.* 126
  Minority children 126
  Basic education and gender equality 126

B. Right to maintain religion or belief 127
 B.1. *Special Rapporteur on freedom of religion or belief – Independent Expert on minority issues – Special Rapporteur on the sale of children, child prostitution and child pornography – Special Rapporteur on trafficking in persons, especially women and children – Chair-Rapporteur of the Working Group on the issue of discrimination against*

women in law and in practice – *Special Rapporteur on violence against women, its causes and consequences,* Special procedures of the Human Rights Council, Communication 29 May 2013 – Iraq *(IRQ 2/ 2013). 127*

Section 5 *131*
Declaration on the Rights of Persons Belonging to National or Ethnic, Religious and Linguistic Minorities *131*
A. Right to existence *134*
    A.1. *UN Commission on Human Rights, Sub-Commission on the Promotion and Protection of Human Rights,* Commentary of the Working Group on Minorities to the United Nations Declaration on the Rights of Persons Belonging to National or Ethnic, Religious and Linguistic Minorities *(E/CN.4/Sub.2/AC.5/2005/2), 4 April 2005. 134*
    A.2. *UN Office of the High Commissioner for human rights (OHCHR),* Minority Rights: International Standards and Guidance for Implementation *(HR/PUB/10/3), 2010. 136*
        B. *Promotion and protection of the identity of minorities 136*
    A.3. *Forum on Minority Issues,* Note by the Independent Expert on minority issues, Rita Izsák, on guaranteeing the rights of religious minorities *(A/HRC/FMI/2013/2), 3 October 2013. 136*
    III. *Legal framework 136*
        A. *Protection of the existence of and prevention of violence against religious minorities 137*
        B. *Promotion and protection of the identity of religious minorities 137*
B. Right to culture *137*
    B.1. *UN Commission on Human Rights, Sub-Commission on the Promotion and Protection of Human Rights,* Commentary of the Working Group on Minorities to the United Nations Declaration on the Rights of Persons Belonging to National or Ethnic, Religious and Linguistic Minorities *(E/CN.4/Sub.2/AC.5/2005/2), 4 April 2005. 137*
C. Right to profess and practise religion or belief *138*

       C.1. UN Commission on Human Rights, Sub-Commission on the Promotion and Protection of Human Rights, Commentary of the Working Group on Minorities to the United Nations Declaration on the Rights of Persons Belonging to National or Ethnic, Religious and Linguistic Minorities *(E/CN.4/Sub.2/AC.5/2005/2), 4 April 2005.* 138
           III. *Interpretation of and comments on the title and the individual articles* 139
              The title and scope of the Declaration 139
           IV. *Framing questions for action* 139
              A. *Does the situation of persons belonging to religious minorities require particular attention?* 139
   D. *Right to participation* 140
       D.1. UN Commission on Human Rights, Sub-Commission on the Promotion and Protection of Human Rights, Commentary of the Working Group on Minorities to the United Nations Declaration on the Rights of Persons Belonging to National or Ethnic, Religious and Linguistic Minorities *(E/CN.4/Sub.2/AC.5/2005/2), 4 April 2005.* 140
       D.2. UN Human Rights Council (HRC), Recommendations of the second session of the Forum on Minority Issues on minorities and effective political participation *(A/HRC/13/25), 12 and 13 November 2009.* 143
          I. *Introduction* 143
          II. *Recommendations* 143
              A. *Governments (national, regional, local) and parliaments* 143
              B. *Political parties* 146
              C. *National human rights institutions* 147
              D. *Civil society* 147
              E. *United Nations human rights mechanisms* 148
              F. *The international community and United Nations agencies* 148
              G. *The media* 149
       D.3. Office of the High Commissioner for human rights, Minority Rights: International Standards and Guidance for Implementation *(HR/PUB/10/3), 2010.* 150
          D. *Effective and meaningful participation* 150

D.4. *UN Office of the High Commissioner for Human Rights (OHCHR)*, The inclusion of religious minorities in consultative and decision-making bodies, *2014. 151*
   Why should religious minorities participate in decision-making? 151
   How the participation of religious minorities facilitates conflict prevention? 152
   Participation in consultative and decision-making bodies: positive measures 152
   Obstacles hindering religious minorities' participation in consultative structures 152
E. *Right to association 153*
  E.1. *UN Commission on Human Rights, Sub-Commission on the Promotion and Protection of Human Rights*, Commentary of the Working Group on Minorities to the United Nations Declaration on the Rights of Persons Belonging to National or Ethnic, Religious and Linguistic Minorities *(E/CN.4/Sub.2/AC.5/2005/2), 4 April 2005. 153*
  E.2. *UN Office of the High Commissioner for Human Rights,* Minority Rights: International Standards and Guidance for Implementation *(HR/PUB/10/3), 2010. 153*
      C. Identifying priorities to address the situation of minorities 154
F. *Non-discrimination 154*
  F.1. *High Commissioner for Human Rights (OHCHR),* Promoting and Protecting Minority Rights. A Guide for Advocates *(HR/PUB/12/7), 2012. 154*
   Part one – minority rights focus in the United Nations 154
     Chapter I – Overview: development of minority rights in international law 154
     The United Nations 154
   Chapter II – The Office of the United Nations High Commissioner for Human Rights 155
  F.2. *Forum on Minority Issues,* Note by the Independent Expert on minority issues, Rita Izsák, on guaranteeing the rights of religious minorities *(A/HRC/FMI/2013/2), 3 October 2013. 156*
     III. Legal framework 156

xxvi   Detailed Contents

    F.3. *UN Secretary General,* Guidance note of the Secretary General on racial discrimination and protection of minorities, *March 2013.* 156
      II. *Normative and conceptual foundations* 157
      III. *Guiding principles for effective UN action* 158
        1. *Ensure coordinated engagement of all three pillars* 158
        2. *Pursue a human rights-based approach* 158
        3. *Address multiple and intersecting forms of discrimination* 159
        4. *Apply a gender perspective* 160

2 Council of Europe   161
Section 1 161
European Convention on Human Rights 161
Protocols 1. Enforcement of certain Rights and Freedoms not included in Section I of the Convention 162
A. Right to profess and practise religion or belief 162
    A.1. European Courts of Human Rights, Case of Serif c. Greece *(Application no. 38.178/97), 14 March 2000.* 162
    The facts 162
      I. *The circumstances of the case* 162
        A. *The background of the case* 162
        B. *The criminal proceedings against the applicant* 163
      II. *Relevant law and practice* 165
        A. *International treaties* 165
        B. *The legislation on the muftis* 166
        C. *Legislative decrees under Article 44 § 1 of the Constitution* 166
        D. *Articles 175 and 176 of the Criminal Code* 167
        E. *The legislation on ministers of "known religions"* 167
    The Law 167
      I. *Alleged violation of Article 9 of the Convention* 167
        A. *Existence of an interference* 168
        B. *"Prescribed by law"* 168
        C. *Legitimate aim* 169
        D. *"Necessary in a democratic society"* 169
      II. *Alleged violation of Article 10 of the Convention* 172
      III. *Application of Article 41 of the Convention* 172
        A. *Damage* 172
        B. *Costs and expenses* 173
        C. *Default interest* 173

B. Right to free self-identification *173*
  B.1. European Courts of Human Rights, GC, Case of
    Molla Sali c. Greece *(Application no. 20.452/14),*
    19 December 2018. 173
    The facts 173
    I. The circumstances of the case 173
      A. Proceedings in the Rodopi Court of First Instance 174
      B. Proceedings in the Thrace Court of Appeal 175
      C. Proceedings in the Court of Cassation 175
      D. Proceedings in the Court of Appeal following remittal
        of the case 176
      E. Proceedings in the Court of Cassation concerning
        the Court of Appeal's judgment after remittal of the
        case 177
      F. Proceedings in the Istanbul Civil Court of First
        Instance 178
    3. The Court's assessment 178
      (a) Preliminary remarks and method followed 178
      (b) Applicability of Article 14 of the Convention read in
        conjunction with Article 1 of Protocol No. 1 179
        (i) General principles 179
        (ii) Application of those principles in the present
          case 180
      (c) Compliance with Article 14 of the Convention read in
        conjunction with Article 1 of Protocol No. 1 180
        (i) General principles 180
        (ii) Application of those principles to the present
          case 181
        (a) Whether there was an analogous or relevantly similar
          situation and a difference in treatment 181
        (b) Whether the difference in treatment was justified 182
    II. Application of Article 41 of the Convention 186
Section 2 *188*
Framework Convention for the Protection of National
  Minorities 188
A. *Right to profess and practise religion or belief 189*
  A.1. *Advisory Committee on the Framework Convention*
    for the protection of national minorities, Compilation
    of Opinions of the Advisory Committee relating to
    Article 8 of the Framework Convention for the
    Protection of National Minorities (3rd cycle),
    13 May 2016. 189

    Present situation 189
    Recommendation 191
  B. Right to association 191
    B.1. *Advisory Committee on the Framework Convention for the protection of national minorities*, Compilation of Opinions of the Advisory Committee relating to Article 8 of the Framework Convention for the Protection of National Minorities (3rd cycle), *13 May 2016.* 191
      Present situation 191
      Recommendations 192
  C. Right to education 193
    C.1. *Advisory Committee on the Framework Convention for the protection of national minorities*, Compilation of Opinions of the Advisory Committee relating to Article 8 of the Framework Convention for the Protection of National Minorities (4th cycle), *18 September 2017.* 193
      Present situation 193
      Recommendation 194

3 Organization for Security and Co-operation in Europe (OSCE) 195

Section 1 195
Conference for Security and Co-operation in Europe, Helsinki Decisions, 10 July 1992 195
Conference on Security and Co-operation in Europe, Budapest Summit Declaration, 21 December 1994 195
  A. Definition of national minorities 196
    A.1. *Office of the OSCE High Commissioner on National Minorities*, The Ljubljana Guidelines on Integration of Diverse Societies, *7 November 2012.* 196
      Introduction 196
  B. Right to profess and practise religion or belief 197
    B.1. *OSCE Office for Democratic Institutions and Human Rights (ODIHR)*, Guidelines on the Legal Personality of Religious or Belief Communities, *2014.* 197
      Part 1. The freedom of religion or belief and permissible restrictions in general 197
      II. The freedom to manifest religion or belief in community with others 199
  C. Right to legal personality 201
    C.1. *OSCE Office for Democratic Institutions and Human Rights (ODIHR)*, Guidelines on the Legal Personality of Religious or Belief Communities, *2014.* 201

D. Right to education 202
   D.1. OSCE High Commissioner on National Minorities (HCNM), The Hague Recommendations regarding the Education Rights of National Minorities & Explanatory Note, *October 1996.* 202
   General introduction 202
   The spirit of international instruments 204
   Public and private institutions 204
   Minority education at primary and secondary levels 205
   Minority education in vocational schools 206
   D.2. OSCE-ODIHR, *Advisory Council of Experts on Freedom of religion or Belief,* Toledo Guiding Principles on Teaching about Religions and Beliefs in Public Schools, *2007.* 206
   Minority rights 206
E. Right to participation 207
   E.1. *Office of the OSCE High Commissioner on National Minorities,* The Ljubljana Guidelines on Integration of Diverse Societies, *7 November 2012.* 207
   c. Participation in cultural and religious life 208
F. Right to access to justice 209
   F.1. OSCE High Commissioner on National Minorities, The Graz Recommendations on Access to Justice and National Minorities, *November 2017.* 209
   Introduction 209
      ii. Imprisonment 213
G. Right to access to media 213
   G.1. *Office of the OSCE High Commissioner on National Minorities,* The Tallinn Guidelines on National Minorities and the Media in the Digital Age & Explanatory Note, *February 2019.* 213
   Introduction 213
   The Tallinn Guidelines on National Minorities and the Media in the Digital Age 215
   I. Enabling environment for freedom of expression and media freedom 215
   II. Media environment 216
   III. Pluralism and diversity 217
   IV. Media, information technologies and conflict prevention 220

4 European Union   223
Section 1 223
Charter of Fundamental Rights of the European Union 223

Chapter III 223
Equality 223
    Non-discrimination 223
    Cultural, religious and linguistic diversity 223
    Treaty on the European Union (arts 2 and 49); Treaty on the Functioning of The European Union (arts 10, 17 and 19) 224
A. Non-discrimination 225
    A.1. European Parliament's Committee on Civil Liberties, Justice and Home Affairs, Towards a comprehensive EU protection system for minorities, *August 2017*. 225
        Non-discrimination is the first and traditional EU approach to minority protection 228
        The second approach is that of minority rights 229
        Religious minorities 233
B. Right to profess and practise religion or belief 233
    B.1. Council of the European Union, EU Guidelines on the promotion and protection of freedom of religion or belief, 24 June 2013. 233
        I. Introduction 233
            A. Reason for action 233
            B. Purpose and scope 234
            C. Definitions 235
                Right to have a religion, to hold a belief, or not to believe 235
                Right to manifest one's religion or belief 235
        II. Operational guidelines 236
    B. Priority areas of action 237
Section II 239
Charter of Fundamental Rights of the European Union 239
    Right to asylum 239
        Treaty on the functioning of the European Union 240
Title V 240
Area of freedom, security and justice 240
    Chapter 1 240
        General provisions 240
    Chapter 2 240
        Policies on border checks, asylum and immigration 240
    Chapter I 243
        General provisions 243
        Definitions 243
        Reasons for persecution 243

A. Right to Asylum 244
  A.1. European Asylum Support Office (EASO), country
    guidance Afghanistan, *June 2019.* 244
      Common analysis 244
      COI summary 245
      Risk analysis 245
      Nexus to a reason for persecution 245
      Common analysis 246
      COI summary 246
      Risk analysis 246
      Nexus to a reason for persecution 246

Chronological index of institutional documents and judgements	247
Chronological index of legal sources	251
Index of rights and principles	253
Principle of non-discrimination 253	
Right to access to media 254	
Right to access to justice 254	
Right to association 254	
Right to asylum 254	
Right to culture 255	
Right to education 255	
Right to existence 255	
Right to free self-identification 256	
Right to legal personality 256	
Right to maintain religion or belief 256	
Right to participation 256	
Right to profess and practise religion or belief 257	
Bibliography	258
Name index	260
Subject index	262

Introduction

Daniele Ferrari

I The genealogy of the notion of religious minority in international and European law: Introductory remarks

Under international and European law, the conceptual definition of 'religious minority' began shifting after World War II. Such changes have mirrored different phases of development linked to innovative approaches to human rights. In this regard, despite the absence of a clear definition of 'religious minority' under the 1948 Universal Declaration of Human Rights, international institutions have re-evaluated minority rights against the backdrop of effective protection of human rights. Formulating a definition of religious minorities requires reinforcing institutional specialisation in the United Nations' (UN's) approach to minority rights.[1] Moreover, a shared notion of religious minority would necessarily have to develop progressively through the UN's external relations with the Council of Europe (CoE), the European Union (EU), and the Organization for Security and Cooperation in Europe (OSCE).[2] The growing interest in minority rights in the international and European arenas is due to several interconnected factors, including a) convergent and divergent elaborations of the concept of religious minority by various international and European institutions; b) new interpretations of freedom of conscience and religion (freedom to belong or not belong to a religious minority); c) equality between believers and non-believers;[3] d) the development of non-discrimination principles (multiple discrimination and intersectional discrimination);[4] e) implementation of human rights on the basis of

---

1 Nazila Ghanea and Alexandra Xanthaki *(eds), Minorities, Peoples and Self-Determination: Essays in Honour of Patrick Thornberry* (Martinus Nijhoff Publishers 2005); Natan Lerner, 'The Evolution of Minority Rights in International Law' in Catherine Brölmann *et al. (eds), Peoples and Minorities in International Law* (Martinus Nijhoff Publishers 1993) 44; Heiner Bielefeldt, Nazila Ghanea, and Michael Wiener (eds*), Freedom of Religion or Belief. An International Law Commentary* (Oxford University Press 2016).
2 Timofey Agarin and Malte Brosig (eds), *Trajectories of Minority Rights Issues in Europe* (Routledge 2015).
3 Kerry O'Halloran, *Human Rights, Religion and International Law* (Routledge 2019).
4 About the concept of multiple and intersectional discrimination, see Shreya Atrey, *Intersectional Discrimination* (Oxford University Press 2019).

sexual orientation or gender identity (LGBT people);[5] f) the recognition of new minorities; g) increased protection of foreigners (migrants, refugees);[6] h) new judicial interpretations of the concept of religious minority; i) the facilitation and acceleration of international synergies in human rights policies rendering cultural and religious relations more competitive and dynamic; and j) religious actors' growing ambitions in the field of religious diplomacy.

Based on these insights, the aim of this chapter is to reconstruct the legal concept of 'religious minority'. This will be done in three phases: Origin, implementation, and synergy.

II Origin

At the UN level, the theoretical discussion on the legal status of religious minorities peaked between 1947 and 1966, regardless of the possibility of founding the legal notion of religious minority in international sources.[7]

In 1996, the UN provided a first legal definition of 'minority' in Article 27 of the International Covenant on Civil and Political Rights (hereinafter ICCPR).[8] This definition also includes religious minorities. Article 27 guarantees members of religious minorities the right to profess and practise their religion. Thus, after World War II, Article 27 of the ICCPR became the main legal source of protection for religious minority rights. It provided a new element to the discussion around the concept of religious minority among UN institutions.[9] More precisely, it not only defined religious minorities but also required that adhering States acknowledge and respect their status.[10] It is worth noting that the reconstruction of the legal definition of 'religious minority' must necessarily be traced back to the 1966 institutional acts of the UN on the interpretation of Article 27.

---

5 About the relation between LGBT rights and religion, see William N. Eskridge Jr and Robin Fretwell Wilson *(eds), Religious Freedom, LGBT Rights, and the Prospects of Common Ground* (Cambridge University Press 2018).
6 Rüdiger Wolfrum, 'The Emergence of "New Minorities" as a Result of "Migration"', in Catherine Brölmann, René Lefeber, and Marjoleine Zieck *(eds), Peoples and Minorities in International Law* (Martinus Nijhoff Publishers 1993) 153–166.
7 See, among which, Secretary General, *Suggested Studies of the Problem of Minorities* (E/CN.4/Sub.2/89 1949); Secretary General, *Definition and Classification of Minorities: Memorandum Submitted by the Secretary General* (E/CN.4/Sub.2/85 1949).
8 In particular, Article 27 provides that: 'In those States in which ethnic, religious or linguistic minorities exist, persons belonging to such minorities shall not be denied the right, in community with the other members of their group, to enjoy their own culture, to profess and practise their own religion, or to use their own language'.
9 Francesco Capotorti, 'Les développements possibles de la protection internationale des minorités' [1986] Le Cahiers de droit 239.
10 Ulrike Barten, 'Article 27 ICCPR. A First Point of Reference' in Ugo Caruso and Rainer Hofmann (eds), *The United Declarations on Minorities* (Brill 2015) 46.

Such acts offered an official definition of the term that the UN had thus far failed to provide.¹¹

Subsequent international developments in the field of minority rights can be traced back to the work of the Sub-Commission on Prevention of Discrimination and Protection of Minorities (since 1999 the Sub-Commission on the Promotion and Protection of Human Rights) and the Human Rights Committee.

In 1967, the Sub-Commission on Prevention of Discrimination and Protection of Minorities adopted Resolution n. 9 (XX) on the protection of minorities. In this document, the Sub-Commission proposed to the Social and Economic Council the commission of a specific study on Article 27 given 'the difficulty of establishing a general definition of minorities owing to the great differences in the situation and structure of ethnic, religious and linguistic groups throughout the world'. After granting the Sub-Commission approval for the study in question in 1969,¹² the Social and Economic Council appointed Francesco Capotorti as an expert. Capotorti was the first to examine the issues in question, producing in 1979 an extensive report entitled *Study on the Rights of Persons Belonging to Ethnic, Religious and Linguistic Minorities*.¹³ Capotorti dedicated the first chapter of his study to the notion of *minority*. Starting from the premise that 'a generally accepted definition of the term minority' does not exist,¹⁴ Capotorti offered a first and provisional definition of the term. Overall, in Capotorti's definition, religious minority 'is a group numerically smaller than the rest of the population of the State to which it belongs and possessing cultural, physical or historical characteristics, a religion ... different from those of the rest of the population'.¹⁵

In light of this definition, Capotorti moved on to frame the rights of the members of religious minorities in terms of a) the legal status of religious minorities at a national level; b) freedom to worship; c) protection of minority groups from attempts of conversion; d) right of religious minorities to administrate their internal religious affairs; and e) freedom of education through the establishment of religious institutions and schools. In describing each of these categories, Capotorti carved out the specific qualities of religious freedom for members of minorities. However, he also clarified that religious groups could benefit from such liberties upon condition that they hold citizenship status. This is because foreigners generally fall outside the scope of Article 27. Capotorti concluded that a homogeneous application of Article 27 across countries might be difficult due to the different linguistic formulations of the term.¹⁶ To address this imple-

---

11 Borhan Uddin Khan and Muhammad Mahbubur Rahman, *Protection of Minorities: Regimes, Norms and Issues in South Asia* (Newcastle upon Tyne 2012) 1 ss.
12 Conseil économique et social, *Protection des minorités* (Résolution 1418 (LVI) 1969).
13 Francesco Capotorti, *Study on the Rights of Persons Belonging to Ethnic, Religious and Linguistic Minorities* (ST/HR(05)/H852/no.5 1979).
14 *Ivi, Chapter I, The concept of a minority*, para 20, 5.
15 *Ivi*, para 28, 7.
16 *Ivi, Chapter V, Conclusions et recommandations*, para 610 ss., 101 ss.

4 *Introduction*

mentation gap, Capotorti asked the Sub-Commission to draft a new Convention of Minority Rights. He recommended that the new Convention encompass all forms of protection deriving from Article 27, with the principal goal being that of putting an obligation on States to protect minorities. In 1992, drawing on Article 27, the UN General Assembly codified the Declaration on the Rights of Persons Belonging to National or Ethnic, Religious and Linguistic Minorities.

In 1985,[17] the Sub-Commission on Prevention of Discrimination and Protection of Minorities entrusted a new study about the definition of minorities to Jules Deschênes, who adopted a substantially different methodological approach from Capotorti's. Starting from the observation that 'the United Nations itself has, after 40 years of trying, been forced to concede its inability to provide a satisfactory answer'[18] to the definitional issue of 'religious minority', his analysis relied on the following theoretical underpinnings: Exclusion of specific issues[19] and identification of internal variables and constants in the concept of religious minority. Deschênes's first step was to identify the limits of the concept, highlighting which groups cannot be qualified as religious minorities. The second step was to assess whether individual criteria represent variables or constants in the elaboration of a general definition. In particular, in Deschênes's point of view, 'one of the main difficulties which has so far prevented the adoption of a universally acceptable definition of minorities is the great diversity of the situations of minorities – and frequently even their radical opposition – from one country to another'.[20] He attempted to overcome this problem by comparing and triangulating different sources, including judgements, doctrinal opinions, and observations by governments. Based on this analysis, the expert defined a minority as:

> a group of citizens numbering less than half the population of a State and in a non-dominant position in the State, endowed with ethnic, religious or linguistic characteristics which differ from those of the majority of the population, having a sense of solidarity with one another, motivated, if only implicitly, by a collective will to survive and whose aim is to achieve equality with the majority in fact and in law.[21]

In 1994 in General Comment n. 23, the Human Rights Committee defined the notion of religious minority as follows: 'The terms used in Article 27 indicate that the persons designed to be protected are those who belong to a group and who share in common ... a religion'.[22] The Committee clarified that citizenship is not a

---

17 Jules Deschênes, *Proposal Concerning a Definition of the Term 'Minority'* (E/CN.4/Sub.2 1985) para 5.1.
18 *Ivi, Introduction*, para 3, 3.
19 *Ivi, Chapter I. Elimination of non-problems*, para 23 ss., 5 ss.
20 *Ivi, Chapter II. Isolation of the variables of the minority concept*, para 58, 10.
21 *Ivi, Chapter IV. Conclusion: A Definition of Minority*, para 181, 30.
22 UN Human Rights Committee (HRC), *CCPR General Comment No. 23: Article 27 (Rights of Minorities)* (CCPR/C/21/Rev.1/Add.5 1994) para 5.2.

prerequisite for the identification of a religious minority. Rather, it observed that groups of migrant workers might also benefit from this qualification, provided that they share common religious practices.[23] Overall, this amounted to an extensive interpretation that refused citizenship as the sole ground for the protection of religious groups. Besides, the emphasis that this definition puts on the word 'existence' hints to a general factual requirement as the main justification for protection. Hence, in the Human Rights Committee's view, the citizenship requirement would result in unwarranted exclusion. In this perspective, the Committee concluded that

> article 27 confers rights on persons belonging to minorities which exist in a State party. Given the nature and scope of the rights envisaged under that article, it is not relevant to determine the degree of permanence that the term 'exist' connotes.[24]

Moreover, if the existence qualifies as a *de facto* condition to exercise minority rights, 'the existence of an ethnic, religious or linguistic minority in a given State party does not depend upon a decision by that State party but requires to be established by objective criteria'.[25] The Committee confirmed Capotorti's opinion, describing minority rights as 'individual rights' in connection with the capacity of a 'minority group to maintain its culture, language or religion'.[26]

In conclusion, by comparing the three definitions, it is possible to note points of both convergence and divergence. In terms of convergence, all three definitions identify religious minorities on the basis of an objective criterion (religion as an element to qualify a group as a minority; numerical inferiority with regard to the professed religion) and a subjective criterion (relationship between majorities and minorities given by the non-dominant position; group's desire to preserve religious identity). Whilst as regards the aspects of divergence, in Capotorti's and Deschênes's studies, the possession of nationality or citizenship is an objective condition to exercise minority rights, whereas in the Committee's new interpretation, citizenship is replaced by existence of minority as a *de facto* condition to apply Article 27 to all minority groups.

III Implementation

The absence of an official definition of religious minority in the UN system is symptomatic of the influence of several factors: National/international law competition; non-discrimination as the new international approach to religious freedom issues; and the intersection between the protection of a minority and that of other groups. Furthermore, this definitional gap makes the concept of 'religious

23 Ibid.
24 Ibid.
25 Ibid.
26 *Ivi*, para 6.2.

minority' a dynamic one. International law implements its categories in relation to major developments at the national level – this guarantees effective protection. Following this trend, 'religious minority' has become a variable-geometry concept, which can be calibrated to different religious groups. The implementation of religious minority rights is meaningful in relation to the UN's standing concerning human rights. In particular, the idea of indivisibility, interdependence, and interrelatedness of human rights reshapes the meaning, interpretation, and application of 'minority' in international legal sources. In the traditional definition of minority rights as a part of human rights,[27] indivisibility, interdependence, and interrelatedness[28] produce a new range of legal understanding. Within it, human rights and minority rights are not isolated but express, at the same time, a different aspect of human identity. In this vein, there might be continuous intersections and connections between human rights, insomuch as religious minority rights might be claimed, for instance, in conjunction with asylum or LGBT rights.[29] The possibility to recompose people's different qualities and specificities in an integrated approach, for a more comprehensive protection of human rights is the core of holistic theory.[30] Such an approach to human rights might be defined as 'holistic' in that all rights contribute to guaranteeing human dignity and social justice.[31]

The new holistic conception of minority rights emerges from the development of new legal sources inspired by Article 27 of the Covenant, the recognition of the overlaps between religious minorities and other social groups protected by international law (indigenous peoples, particular social groups), the disappearance of the link between citizenship and minority, and the development of the principle of non-discrimination. The legal implementation of religious minority

---

27 See, Commission on Human Rights, *Study of the Legal Validity of the Undertaking Concerning Minorities* (E/CN.4/367 1950). In particular, in this document the Commission clarifies that: 'The protection of human rights is a substantial element in the protection of minorities', 19. In the same sense, Francesco Capotorti in his study in 1979 affirms that 'the rights provided to members of ethnic, religious and linguistic minorities under article 27 should be regarded as forming an integral part of the system of protection of human rights and fundamental freedoms established after the Second World War by the United Nations'; Francesco Capotorti, *Study on the Rights of Persons Belonging to Ethnic, Religious and Linguistic Minorities*, cit., Chapter IV, 57.
28 In fact, as the UN underlines: 'All human rights are universal, indivisible and interrelated and interdependent'; see Vienna Declaration and Programme of Action, Part I, chapter III, section I, para 5 (A/CONF.157/24, 1993).
29 Pasquale Annicchino, 'The Persecution of Religious and LGBTI Minorities and Asylum Law: Recent Trends in the Adjudication of European Supranational Courts' [2015] European Public Law 571.
30 A. Belden Fields, 'Human Rights as a Holistic Concept' [1992] Human Rights Quarterly 1; A. Belden Fields, *Rethinking Human Rights for the New Millennium* (New York University Press 2003) 73 ss.
31 Gillian MacNaughton, 'Decent Work for All: A Holistic Human Rights Approach' [2011] American University International Law Review 441.

rights can therefore be investigated in four different areas of development regarding new legal sources, social groups, foreigners, and non-discrimination.

a) New legal sources

In relation to new legal sources, UN institutions produced two pivotal legal documents to strengthen minority rights: The Convention on the Rights of the Child in 1989 and the Declaration on the Rights of Persons Belonging to National or Ethnic, Religious and Linguistic Minorities in 1992.

The Convention on the Rights of the Child contains a specific provision, absent from the 1959 Declaration on the Rights of the Child, to protect minors belonging to ethnic, religious, or linguistic minorities. Particularly, Article 30 of the Convention provides that:

> In those States in which ethnic, religious or linguistic minorities or persons of indigenous origin exist, a child belonging to such a minority or who is indigenous shall not be denied the right, in community with other members of his or her group, to enjoy his or her own culture, to profess and practice his or her own religion, or to use his or her own language.

This provision (with the only difference represented by the reference to indigenous children) uses the same language of Article 27. Besides, as far as religious minorities are concerned, it establishes the right of the child to practice and profess his/her own religion.

The Declaration on the Rights of Persons Belonging to National or Ethnic, Religious and Linguistic Minorities of 1992, although not legally binding, represented the first detailed international catalogue of the rights of national or ethnic, religious, and linguistic minorities. Turning to the rights of religious minorities, these were broken down into: a) Freedom to demonstrate and profess one's doctrine, in private or in public, without interference and discrimination (Art. 2, para 1); b) the right to participate in social, cultural, religious, economic, and public life (Art. 2, para 2); c) the right to take part in the decision-making procedures concerning their legal status (Art. 2, para 2.3.); d) freedom of association (Art. 2, para 2.4); and e) freedom to maintain relations between members of the same minority or other minorities at national and transnational levels. The duties of States towards religious minorities, however, were detailed as: a) The protection of the existence and identity of religious minorities, including through the adoption of suitable legislative measures (Art. 1, para 1–2); b) the adoption of effective measures so that these groups can exercise their rights, express their specificities, and develop their traditions (Art. 4, para 1–2); c) the provision of tools for the knowledge of minority traditions and culture in the public education sector (Art. 4, para 4); d) measures capable of ensuring the participation of minorities in the country's economic progress and development (Art. 4, para 5); e) the development of national or supranational policies and programs that include the legitimate interests of minorities (Art. 5); f) forms of collaboration between States on

8 Introduction

the issue of minorities (Art. 6); and g) forms of cooperation between States to promote respect of the rights provided for in the Declaration (Art. 7).

The interpretation of these provisions has been the focus of specific commentary edited by the Working Group on Minorities in 2005[32] and more recently of several recommendations adopted at the end of the Forum on Minority Issues in 2013.[33] With regard to these documents, it is useful to focus on the recipients of religious minority rights, so as to evaluate how these rights are implemented. Indeed, the Commentary of the Working Group on Minorities to the United Nations Declaration on the Rights of Persons Belonging to National or Ethnic, Religious and Linguistic Minorities notes that by comparison with Article 27, 'The Declaration on Minorities adds the term "national minorities" '.[34] The Working Group highlights that it is not possible to affirm a rigid separation between four different categories of minorities. In fact, 'the Declaration does not, in its substantive provisions, make such distinctions'[35] and in practice there are a lot of possibilities for an intersection between ethnic, linguistic, religious, and national minorities. Following this suggestion, we can argue that religious minority rights are applicable also to ethnic, linguistic, or national minorities, when the group coincides with a multi-minority group as in the case of Jews (religion and language) or Armenians (religion and ethnicity). According to the last example, the Working Group observes that 'in some cases religion and ethnicity coincide'.[36] In 2013, the Forum on Minority Issues relied on the criterion of religion professed by groups for a new interpretation of religious freedom that is not limited to traditional religious confessions. This orientation was developed in the final recommendations of the meeting:

> The term 'religious minorities' as used in the present document therefore encompasses a broad range of religious or belief communities, traditional and non-traditional, whether recognized by the State or not, including more recently established faith or belief groups, and large and small communities, that seek protection of their rights under minority rights standards.

---

32 Commission on Human Rights, Sub-Commission on the Promotion and Protection of Human Rights, Fifty-seventh session, Working Group on Minorities, *Commentary of the Working Group on Minorities to the United Nations Declaration on the Rights of Persons Belonging to National or Ethnic, Religious and Linguistic Minorities* (E/CN.4/Sub.2/AC.5/2005/2 2005).
33 Human Rights Council, *Recommendations of the Forum on Minority Issues at its Sixth Session: Guaranteeing the Rights of Religious Minorities* (26 and 27 November 2013) (A/HRC/25/66 2014).
34 Commission on Human Rights, Sub-Commission on the Promotion and Protection of Human Rights, Fifty-seventh session, Working Group on Minorities, *Commentary of the Working Group on Minorities*..., cit., 3.
35 Ibid.
36 *Ivi*, 10.

Non-believers, atheists or agnostics may also face challenges and discrimination and require protection of their rights.[37]

b) Social groups

With reference to social groups, in the UN setting, the connection between such groups and religious minorities coincides with indigenous populations, religious group, national minorities, groups, racial groups, and particular social groups.

As to the indigenous people, the UN institutions have progressively highlighted specific cases in which religious minorities and indigenous population overlap.[38] Since 1994, the UN Committee has recognised that indigenous representatives have a right to claim the guarantees of religious, ethnic, and linguistic minorities protected under Article 27 of the International Covenant on Civil and Political Rights. The Committee clarifies:

> The enjoyment of the rights to which article 27 relates does not prejudice the sovereignty and territorial integrity of a State party. At the same time, one or other aspects of the rights of individuals protected under that article – for example, to enjoy a specific culture – may consist in a way of life which is closely associated with territory and use of its resources. 2. This may be particularly true regarding members of indigenous communities constituting a minority.[39]

Indigenous people, therefore, can enjoy the rights recognized to religious minorities. This freedom was stressed by the Office of the United Nations High Commissioner for Human Rights (OHCHR). As such, the OHCHR claims:

> In practical terms, a number of connections and commonalities exist between indigenous peoples and national, ethnic, linguistic and religious minorities. Both groups are usually in a non-dominant position in the society in which they live and their cultures, languages or religious beliefs may be different from the majority or the dominant groups.[40]

---

37 Human Rights Council, *Recommendations of the Forum on Minority Issues at Its Sixth Session: Guaranteeing the Rights of Religious Minorities*, cit., 4. In this perspective of definition, see also Office of the United Nations High Commissioner for Human Rights, *Minority Rights: International Standards and Guidance for Implementation*, (HR/PUB/10/3 2010) 4.
38 ILO, Indigenous and Tribal Peoples Convention 1989; UN Declaration on the Rights of Indigenous Peoples 2007.
39 Office of the United Nations High Commissioner for Human Rights, *General Comment 23, Article 27: Compilation of General Comments and General Recommendations Adopted by Human Rights Treaty Bodies* (U.N. Doc. HRI\GEN\1\Rev.1 1994) para 3.2.
40 Office of the United Nations High Commissioner for Human Rights, *Minority Rights: International Standards and Guidance for Implementation*, cit., 2011, 3.

10 *Introduction*

From this perspective, 'Minorities and indigenous peoples have similar rights under international law'.[41] Following these trends, it was considered how the scope of protection of indigenous people can also be framed in terms of 'religious minority rights'. And this, in turn, provides strong evidence of how indigenous peoples often manifest their religious identity through a combination of several elements, spanning religious belief, cultural traditions and territory.[42] With reference to the connection between religion and indigenous culture, as highlighted by the UN, the recognition of religious freedom of indigenous minority groups emerges in the concept of 'indigenous spirituality'.[43]

Turning to the formula religious group, the connection between religious minorities and religious groups comes to the fore in the protection of the right of existence of a minority within the Convention on the Prevention and Punishment of the Crime of Genocide. Although the Convention lacks a notion of 'religious minority', it makes general references to religious groups. Hence, the Working Group recognises the Convention as the most relevant tool to protect the physical existence of a minority. In fact: 'The right to existence in its physical sense is sustained by the Convention on the Prevention and Punishment of the Crime of Genocide, which codified customary law in 1948'.[44]

In a different perspective, it should be noted that the concept of nationality has expanded definitional criteria with regard to possible overlaps between religious minorities and national minorities. The definition elaborated by UN institutions describes the national minority, depending on the specific case, as coinciding or not with ethnic, religious, or linguistic minorities. The Working Group on Minorities has supported the view, in its Commentary on the Declaration on the Rights of Persons Belonging to National or Ethnic, Religious and Linguistic Minorities, that there are no national minorities that are not also ethnic, linguistic, or religious minorities. Put differently, as highlighted in the Capotorti Report of 1977,[45] the overlap between national and religious minorities depends on the origin of the minority: Only historical religious minorities can also qualify as national minorities, while new religious minorities resulting, for example, from migratory processes, cannot be considered as national minorities. A religious group's belonging to one category or the other affects the rights accorded to it at international and national levels. In accordance with these principles, the UN expert group clarifies that 'persons belonging to groups defined solely as religious

---

41 Office of the United Nations High Commissioner for Human Rights, *Indigenous Peoples and the United Nations Human Rights System* (2013) 3.
42 *Rights of indigenous peoples*, Final report of the Sofia Conference 2012 (Conclusions and Recommendations).
43 Asia Pacific Forum of National Human Rights, *The United Nations Declaration on the Rights of Indigenous Peoples: A Manual for National Human Rights Institutions* (2013) 14.
44 *Ivi*, 6.
45 Francesco Capotorti, *Study on the Rights of Persons Belonging to Ethnic, Religious and Linguistic Minorities by Francesco Capotorti, Special Rapporteur of the Sub-Commission on Prevention of Discrimination and Protection of Minorities* (New York University Press 1979), Chapter I. The Concept of a Minority, para 57, 12.

minorities might be held to have only those special minority rights which relate to the profession and practice of their religion', unlike national religious minorities that shall be recipients of 'stronger rights relating not only to their culture but to the preservation and development of their national identity'.[46] In this sense, the criterion of nationality distinguishes an old religious minority from a new religious minority.

Following the different trajectory of a linguistic expressions group, a racial group, or a particular social group, a religious minority can be qualified as a group, a racial group, or a particular social group when the members of the minority are victims of segregation or persecution. First, the interdiction of segregation for a religious minority, as a consequence of the right to participate granted by Article 2 of the Declaration on the Rights of Persons Belonging to National or Ethnic, Religious and Linguistic Minorities, is protected under the Convention on the Suppression and Punishment of the Crime of Apartheid. The utility of the definition of the crime of apartheid in the context of minority rights is stressed by the Working Group on Minorities. In fact, despite the fact that the text of the Convention sheds light on the more general notions of group and racial group as possible victims of apartheid, this crime, with reference to Article 2 of the Declaration, represents 'the extreme version of exclusion of different groups from equal participation in the national society as a whole'.[47] Refugee status on grounds of religious persecution is accorded by the Geneva Convention (Art. 1, para. 2) to members of particular social groups persecuted because they share the same spiritual identity. In light of this definition, religious minorities and persecuted religious groups may or may not coincide, since refugee status can be accorded to subjects belonging 'to a religious minority or majority'.[48] In this context, the United Nations High Commissioner on Refugees (UNHCR) published an analytical report about the condition of religious minorities in Pakistan.

c) Foreigners

Despite the traditional exclusion of foreigners from minority rights, international institutions have gradually included migrants and stateless people in the legal notion of minority. In 1982, the United Nations Educational, Scientific

---

46 Commission on Human Rights, Sub-Commission on the Promotion and Protection of Human Rights, Fifty-third session, Working Group on Minorities, *Final Text of the Commentary to the Declaration on the Rights of Persons Belonging to National or Ethnic, Religious and Linguistic Minorities* (E/CN.4/Sub.2/AC.5/2001/2 2001) 3 ss.
47 Commission on Human Rights, Sub-Commission on the Promotion and Protection of Human Rights, Fifty-seventh session, Working Group on Minorities, *Commentary of the Working Group on Minorities to the United Nations Declaration on the Rights of Persons Belonging to National or Ethnic, Religious and Linguistic Minorities* (E/CN.4/Sub.2/AC.5/2005/2 2005) 7.
48 UNHCR, *Guidelines on International Protection: Religion-Based Refugee Claims under Article 1A(2) of the 1951 Convention and/or the 1967 Protocol relating to the Status of Refugees* (UNHCR 2004) 5.

and Cultural Organization (UNESCO), at the end of the World Conference on cultural politics, developed the innovative notion of 'foreign minorities from migrations',[49] which encapsulated the disconnect between minorities and citizenship, stressed by the Office of the High Commissioner for Human Rights in 2010. In the publication 'Minority Rights: International Standards and Guidance for Implementation', the OHCHR clarified that migrations and statelessness can be linked to affiliation to a minority. The connection between these categories is rooted in the violation of minority rights and finds, in different ways, its legal term of reference in the principle of non-discrimination. The principle of non-discrimination, guaranteed to migrants in international legal sources, can also be applied to minorities, if the victim of discrimination is a migrant belonging to a minority group. Empowerment and protection of minority rights is bolstered by

> The International Convention on the Protection of the Rights of All Migrant Workers and Members of Their Families, the Convention relating to the Status of Stateless Persons, the Convention relating to the Status of Refugees, and the Declaration on the Human Rights of Individuals Who are not Nationals of the Country in which They Live.[50]

With reference to statelessness, the intersection with minority rights can be produced, when 'discrimination against minorities may be a cause of statelessness'.[51]

d) *The principle of non-discrimination*

The principle of non-discrimination expresses a new general framework in the international approach to freedom of religion or belief (FoRB). Acknowledging that 'all human rights are universal, indivisible and interrelated and interdependent',[52] international institutions underline 'the positive interrelatedness of civil and political rights on the one hand, and economic, social and cultural rights, on the other'.[53] In this field, non-discrimination is an extremely useful tool to define an innovative understanding of FoRB under the umbrella of other human rights. This relationship can produce a clash, when freedom of religion or belief comes into conflict with other human rights and produces discrimination.

---

49 V. UNESCO, Conférence mondiale sur les politiques culturelles, Rapport Final, Recomandation n. 18, Mexico 26 juillet-6 août 1982, 72.
50 UN Office of the High Commissioner for Human Rights (OHCHR), *Minority Rights: International Standards and Guidance for Implementation* (HR/PUB/10/3 2010) 5.
51 *Ivi*, 6.
52 Vienna Declaration and Programme of Action, s 1(5), (A/CONF.157/24 1993).
53 UN Special Rapporteur on Freedom of Religion or Belief (ed), 'Introductory Remarks' in *Special Rapporteur's Compilation of Articles on Freedom of Religion or Belief and Sexuality* (2017) 3 <>www.ohchr.org/Documents/Issues/Religion/ArticlesCompilationForbAndSexuality.pdf>.

In particular, with regard to the religious element, international institutions have examined the links between religion, sexual orientation, and gender in terms of the qualification of religion against sexual orientation and gender identity[54] and of the qualification of religion as part of LGBT or gender identity.[55] Following this approach and with specific reference to religious minority, the intersection between the access to human rights for LGBT people and minority rights is developed by UN institutions through the notion of multiple or intersectional discrimination. For instance, LGBT people or women could undergo multiple or intersectional discrimination. when they are also members of a religious minority. Accordingly, the High Commissioner for Human Rights brought to the fore in the UN's human rights agenda that:

> The Minorities Declaration identifies only national or ethnic, religious and linguistic minorities as falling within its scope. However, the Independent Expert can consider issues with regard to people belonging to other marginalized groups, such as those with disabilities, or issues relating to sexual orientation where they intersect with the issues and rights of persons belonging to national or ethnic, religious and linguistic minorities.[56]

Similarly, the Secretary General observed:

> While this Guidance Note and the Declaration on Minority Rights focus on the rights of persons belonging to 'national or ethnic, religious and linguistic' minorities, there are persons belonging to other groups that are regularly in a non-dominant position and merit specific UN attention from the perspective of non-discrimination and other human rights standards, including, for example, stateless persons, migrants, victims of forced displacement, persons with disabilities, people living with HIV and lesbian, gay, bisexual, or transgender (LGBT) persons. Their concerns also frequently involve multiple discrimination, including where a person belonging to a national, ethnic, religious or linguistic minority is also discriminated against on other grounds such as disability or sexual orientation.[57]

---

54 UNHCR, *Guidelines on International Protection no. 9: Applications for Recognition of Refugee Status Based on Sexual Orientation and/or Gender Identity in the Context of Article 1A (2) of the 1951 Convention and/or its 1967 Protocol Relating to the Status of Refugees*, 23 October 2012; Special Rapporteur on freedom of religion or belief, *Report of the Special Rapporteur on Freedom of Religion or Belief – Freedom of Religion or Belief* (A/HRC/43/48 2020).
55 V. Secretary General, *Guidance Note of the Secretary General on Racial Discrimination and Protection of Minorities* (2013) 9.
56 V. High Commissioner for Human Rights, *Promoting and Protecting Minority Rights. A Guide for Advocates* (HR/PUB/12/7 2012) 35.
57 V. Secretary General, *Guidance Note of the Secretary General on Racial Discrimination and Protection of Minorities*, cit., 9.

In terms of implementation, therefore, members of religious minorities are entitled to the application of provisions contained in different legal sources not specifically dedicated to minority rights.

IV Synergy

The implementation of religious minority rights not only concerns the internal dimension of the UN, but also its external dimension within the collaboration between the United Nations, Council of Europe, OSCE, and European Union. Specifically, this collaboration highlights the global institutional and political approach of international and European bodies to minority rights through constant dialogue aimed at interpreting and applying legal sources around the world. Considering these international and European trajectories, Kristin Henrard developed the notion of synergy as a driving factor to describe the circulation of linguistic expressions, working methods, interpretive approaches, and the creation of specific forms of collaboration between bodies belonging to different organisations.[58] The dynamics of synergy can be analysed, with reference to religious minorities, according to the criterion of the object of synergy. The object of synergy describes the different linguistic formulations of religious minorities, which express the relationship between global and regional organisations.

The object of synergy shows two trajectories regarding, on the one hand, the use of the notion of religious minority and, on the other, the mobilisation of different legal expressions coinciding, based on the different institutional framework, with national minority or minorities. These two distinct dynamics can be qualified as explicit synergy and implicit synergy. Explicit synergy is directly related to Article 27 by the European institutions. Implicit synergy

---

58 About the notion of synergy, K. Henrard clarifies that: 'There are several different types of possible synergies, of which the following three are of particular relevance: 1. express cross-referencing; 2. substantive convergences; and 3. emergence of similar working methods. By express cross-referencing we mean the explicit and specific referencing of the standards of one or more monitoring bodies or organisations in the standard-setting of another organisation or the work of another monitoring bodies ... Another synergy which is less explicit but which undoubtedly underlies such synergies is the emergence in the work of monitoring bodies and international organisations of common understandings of particular issues, common approaches towards how particular themes are addressed, similarities in how particular issues are resolved, and similarities in the recognition of particular themes and in how such themes are dealt with, all of which might be described as substantive synergies ... A final type of synergy is what may be described as synergies in working methods, which would include similarities in the way in which treaty monitoring bodies and international organisations involved in minority issues carry out their monitoring activities'; see Kristin Henrard and Robert Dunbar, 'Introduction' in Kristin Henrard and Robert Dunbar (eds), *Synergies in Minority Protection. European and International Law Perspectives* (Cambridge University Press 2009) 8 ss.

indirectly references Article 27 through the different concepts of national minority or minorities.

a) *The explicit synergy*

From a chronological point of view, explicit synergy emerged for the first time ever in the Council of Europe as well as in different institutions at distinct points in time. In 1990, the Parliamentary Assembly, observed that 'there are many kinds of minorities in Europe. They have certain characteristics which may be ethnic, linguistic, religious or other which distinguish them from the majority in a given area or country', to then recommend that member States commit to respecting the obligations arising from Article 27 of the ICCPR. In this sense, the implementation of this article requires attention 'to the obligations contained in the international instruments relating to national, ethnic, religious and linguistic minorities'.[59] One year later, during the drafting of the European Convention for the Protection of Minorities, the European Commission for Democracy through legislation made many references to the notion of religious minority. More precisely, Article 10 states: 'Any person belonging to a religious minority shall have the right to manifest his religion or belief, either alone or in community with others and in public or private, in worship, teaching, practice or observance'.[60]

More recently, the European Court of Human Rights (ECtHR) applied the notion of religious minority[61] in two different cases regarding the Muslim minority in Greece.[62] In particular, the ECtHR referred to Article 27 of the International Covenant on Civil and Political Rights with an innovative evaluation of the intersections between belonging to a religious minority, freedom of religion, right to the property, and non-discrimination.[63] This interpretation of the European Convention on Human Rights (ECHR) emerged in the use of religious minority and Muslim minority as new linguistic categories. In the judgement

---

59 Parliamentary Assembly, Recommendation 1134 (1990).
60 Commission for Democracy through law, *The Protection of Minorities – Science and technique of democracy No. 9* (CDL-STD(1994)009, 1994) s c(2).
61 More in general, the expression 'religious minority' is used in several decisions of the European Court of Human Rights (ECtHR). In these terms, see, for example, *İzzettin Doğan and others v. Turkey* App. No. 62649/10 (ECtHR, 26 April 2016); *Jehovah's Witnesses of Moscow v. Russia* App. No. 302/02 (ECtHR, 18 August 2010); *Otto-Preminger-Institut v. Austria* App. No. 13470/87 (ECHR, 20 September 1994).
62 *Serif v. Greece* App. No. 38178/97 (ECtHR, 14 December 1999); *Molla Sali v. Greece* App. no. 20452/14 (ECtHR, GC, 19 December 2018).
63 Kristin Henrard, 'The European Court of Human Rights, Ethnic and Religious Minorities and the Two Dimensions of the Right to Equal Treatment: Jurisprudence at Different Speeds?' [2016] Nordic Journal of Human Rights 157; Effie Fokas, 'The Legal Status of Religious Minorities: Exploring the Impact of the European Court of Human Rights' [2018] Social Compass 25.

Molla Sali v. Greece, the Grand Chamber used the notion of Muslim minority and reframed the meaning of Article 14 – with reference 'to the right to choose not to be treated as a member of a minority'[64] – through the new notion of discrimination by association. As Judge Mits clarified in his concurring opinion:

> This is the first time the Grand Chamber has examined and found discrimination by association. In other words, the violation of Article 14 in conjunction with Article 1 of Protocol No.1 was established not because of the applicant's, but her husband's Muslim faith.[65]

Turning to the European Union, the notion of religious minority with reference to the UN's legal provisions is stressed by European institutions in different legal documents. First, in 2013 the Foreign Affairs Council approved the 'EU Guidelines on the promotion and protection of freedom of religion or belief'. In these Guidelines, the Council, recalling the conclusions of the Council of European Union,[66] argued that the protection of religious minorities also implies their inclusion within the category of freedom of thought, conscience, and religion or belief. The legal status of a religious minority, as emerged in the text of the document, is rooted in Article 27 of the International Covenant on Civil and Political Rights.

Furthermore, in 2017 the European Parliament Committee on Civil Liberties, Justice and Home Affairs entrusted a group of experts with a study concerning European law on minorities.[67] The study 'covers three different thematic areas of direct relevance to the state of minority protection in the EU: i) ethnic, ii) linguistic and iii) religious minorities'[68] and proposes a useful mapping of different international and European actors and legal standards. Regarding religious minorities, in a specific section dedicated to the topic, experts clarify that:

> At UN level, the key documents are the ICCPR[69] and ICERD.[70] The ICCPR sets the international standard for any person belonging to a religion or belief to practice his/her religion. The clause applies to citizens as well as migrants and refugees. However, it does not prevent the State from making special arrangements for the dominant or recognised religious institutions, as for example in tax law.[71]

---

64 *Molla Sali v. Greece*, para 157.
65 *Ivi*, Concurring opinion of Judge Mits.
66 Council of European Union, *Council Conclusions on Freedom of Religion or Belief* (2973rd ed, General Affairs Council meeting Brussels 2009).
67 Sergio Carrera and others, *Towards a Comprehensive EU Protection System for Minorities* (2017) <available at >www.ceps.eu/system/files/ProtectionSystemForMinorities.pdf>.
68 *Ivi*, 17.
69 This acronym stands for International Covenant on Civil and Political Rights.
70 This acronym stands for International Convention on the Elimination of All Forms of Racial Discrimination.
71 *Ivi*, 50.

With regard to the UN's legal model, the group of experts of the European Union developed an innovative interpretation to overcome the distinction between ethnic, linguistic, religion, and national minorities, rooted in a 'cross-minority approach' that develops a synergy between ethnic, linguistic, religious, and national factors.[72] The overlap between minorities in the social sphere is stressed by experts in light of the principle of non-discrimination, viewed as a useful tool to 'capture synergetic or cross-group manifestations of structural discrimination against minorities, but also to capture cases where special public policy measures covering group or theme-specific protection may indirectly lead to discrimination for other vulnerable minorities'.[73] The intersectional criterion, as an instrument to interpret the non-discrimination principle, is, in the group of experts' vision, the key element to shift from the traditional tripartite definition of minorities to a new intersectional model. The intersectional model is defined in the document with specific reference to religious minorities. In particular:

> The cross-country comparative review in the area of religious minorities highlights the intersectionality of minority protection grounds. In many of the countries under assessment it is difficult in practice to distinguish between discrimination based on grounds of race, ethnicity or national minority origin and discrimination based on religion, as anti-Semitism and Islamophobia often include aspects of both. In addition, the laws have traditionally favored the 'majority religion'.[74]

b) *The implicit synergy*

The implicit synergy emerges in two different ways concerning the different legal notion of national minority and minorities. It appears, first, as a legal category within the frameworks of the CoE, the OSCE and the EU generally; and, second, as a specificity of EU legal sources in particular. More specifically, implicit synergy can be defined as the description of the European legal approach to the use of the concept of religious minority and UN standards for the interpretation of national minority and minorities. In fact, despite the use of different legal categories, European institutions do not exclude reference to the UN model but reposition the concept of religious minority in the new field of national minority and minorities. This institutional twist has many theoretical and practical implications and is relevant in understanding how the relationship between religious minority, national minority, and minorities re-conceptualises the UN's legal framework under implicit synergy.

Starting from the Council of Europe, European institutions have elaborated the notion of national minorities not only around Article 14 of the ECHR, but

---

72 *Ivi*, 17.
73 *Ivi*, 23.
74 *Ivi*, 76.

also through Article 27. The latter has become a blueprint for the inclusion of ethnic, religious, and linguistic minorities. Since 1973, this process has given rise to several attempts to codify an additional protocol about national minority rights to the ECHR.[75] In particular, recalling Article 27 as a criterion to define a national minority the 1973 Committee of Experts on Human Rights observed that 'while article 14 of the European Convention on Human Rights referred to national minorities, article 27 of the Covenant referred to ethnic, religious or linguistic minorities. The first question, therefore, was whether these two terms covered the same thing'.[76] The Committee proposed a possible answer to this issue, noting that 'in most cases a national minority would also constitute an ethnic, linguistic or religious minority. On the other hand, there are clearly certain ethnic, linguistic or religious minorities which do not constitute "national minorities"'.[77] The process of construction of the concept of religious minority culminated in the elaboration of the Framework Convention for the Protection of National Minorities, adopted by the Council of Europe Committee of Ministers on 8 November 1994.[78] Turning to the legal contents of the Convention, which entered into force in 1998, religion emerges in conjunction with national minorities in five different perspectives regarding the identity of the group; discrimination; freedom of conscience and religion; cultural and educational dynamics; and relations between national minorities.[79] In light of these provisions, the national identity of the group reveals numerous intersections with the religious dimension and confirms, as the Committee of Experts had already clarified in 1973, the possibility of an overlap between national minorities and religious minorities. This overlap has been developed by the Advisory Committee on the Framework Convention for the Protection of National Minorities via thematic commentary and opinions. For example, in 2016, the Advisory Committee observed that

> in a variety of State parties, the understanding of the term 'national minority' is linked to specific characteristics that are often considered as emblematic for identity and to differentiate the minority from the majority, including language, religion, culture, ethnic background, specific traditions or visible features.[80]

---

75 Claudia Tavani, *Collective Rights and the Cultural Identity of the Roma. A Case Study of Italy* (Martinus Nijhoff Publishers 2012) 52 ss.
76 V. Council of Europe, *Report of the Committee of Experts on Human Rights to the Committee of Ministers* (DH/EXO73 1973) 47.
77 Ibid.
78 Asbjørn Eide, 'The Council of Europe's Framework Convention for the Protection of National Minorities' in Kristin Henrard and Robert Dunbar *(eds)*, *Synergies in Minority Protection* (Cambridge University Press 2009) 119 ss.
79 See articles 5, para 1 and 6, para 2, 7, 8, 12, para 1, of the Framework Convention for the Protection of National Minorities.
80 Advisory Committee on the Framework Convention for the Protection of National Minorities, *The Framework Convention: A Key Tool to Managing Diversity Through Minority Rights* (ACFC/56DOC(2016)001), g) Specific identity markers and ascribed categories, para 37 (2016), 15.

The protection of freedom of religion or belief for the members of national minority covers also the right to register 'religious organisations in order to manifest their beliefs in community with others'.[81]

The OSCE has been more prone to agree with the UN's view regarding minority groups as falling under ethnic, linguistic, religious, and national groups, but it has also developed a specific understanding of national minority. In fact, the 1994 Budapest decisions,[82] which converted the then Conference on Security and Co-operation in Europe (CSCE) into the OSCE, evoked the notion of national minority to highlight the necessity of protecting minority rights and the importance of 'continuation of the activities of the High Commissioner on National Minorities'.[83] The OSCE shares with the UN the same approach to interpreting and promoting minority rights: On one hand by understanding these rights as a part of human rights; on the other, through reliance on a specialised body to protect national minorities. The High Commissioner on National Minorities, despite the lack of provisions about religious minorities, framed the notion of national minority as an open category useful to protect freedom of religion or belief. This trajectory emerges clearly in the 2006 'Recommendations on Policing in Multi-Ethnic Societies'. In this document, the High Commissioner underlines the meaning of national minority as a concept that 'encompasses a wide range of minority groups, including religious, linguistic and cultural as well as ethnic minorities'.[84]

Furthermore, in the field of protection of freedom of religion or belief, the OSCE published the 2014 'Guidelines on the Legal Personality of Religious or Belief Communities'.[85] The document is relevant both because of its reliance on the innovative category of '(minority) communities' concerning the protection of freedom of religion or belief in the procedure to obtain the legal personality[86] and because of the explicit mention of the notion of national minorities as a relevant tool to protect religious communities.[87]

Finally, the concept of religious minority has been re-conceptualized at the EU level through different categories of national minority and minorities. These concepts were introduced under EU law in different historical phases and with distinct purposes, including the codification of non-discrimination (national minority); the procedure for States to become members of the European Union (minorities); and the affirmation of minority rights as an added value for the European Union (minorities). Article 21, para 1 of the Charter of Fundamental Rights of the European Union evokes the status of members of a national minority as

---

81 *Ivi*, 3. Association and religion – Articles 7 and 8, para 68, 26.
82 CSCE, *Budapest Document. Towards a Genuine Partnership in a New Era* (CSCE 1994).
83 *Ivi*, *Budapest Decisions*, I. Strengthening the CSCE, para 21, 3.
84 Office of the OSCE High Commissioner on National Minorities, *Recommendations on Policing in Multi-Ethnic Societies* (2006) 3.
85 OSCE, *Guidelines on the Legal Personality of Religious or Belief Communities* (2014).
86 *Ivi*, Part IV. Privileges of religious or belief communities or organisations, para 42, 39.
87 *Ivi*, Annex, 41 ss.

part of the prohibition of discrimination.[88] Starting from the 1993 Copenhagen European Council,[89] the respect of minority rights qualifies as a criterion for the enlargement of the Union to new States, expressed in Article 2 of the Treaty on European Union as one of the founding values of the European Union.[90]

The two references to the concept of minorities found in Article 49 of the Treaty on European Union are an important model of joint application. This article qualifies the respect of EU values, as defined in Article 2, as a condition for European States to apply to become members of the Union. Thus, the respect of minorities as a value isn't only cosmetic but a specific prerequisite for the admission of new candidate countries.

European institutions have fostered the protection of minorities in two different directions concerning the internal and external dimensions of European Union.[91] The internal dimension regards the work on a new directive to foster the respect of minority rights by member States. In particular, in 2018 the Committee on Civil Liberties, Justice and Home Affairs of the European Commission developed a specific 'Motion on minimum standards for minorities in the EU' for the European Parliament.[92] In the document, the Committee observed:

> There is no common EU standard for minority rights in the EU, nor a common understanding of who can be considered a person belonging to a minority ... there is no definition of minorities in the United Nations Declaration on the Rights of Persons Belonging to National or Ethnic, Religious and Linguistic Minorities, nor in the Framework Convention for the Protection of National Minorities (FCNM).[93]

Parliament adopted the Commission's proposal with the Resolution of November 2018.[94] The resolution appears relevant with respect to the legal scope of

---

88 Article 21. Non-discrimination. 1. Any discrimination based on any ground such as sex, race, colour, ethnic or social origin, genetic features, language, religion or belief, political or any other opinion, membership of a national minority, property, birth, disability, age or sexual orientation shall be prohibited.
89 See European Council, *Copenhagen criteria*, para. 7 '*Relations with the Countries of Central and Eastern Europe*', l. A) '*The Associated Countries*', para. iii (1993); Art. 49, Consolidated version of the Treaty on European Union (C 362/13) 26 October 2012.
90 Treaty on European Union, Article 2. The Union is founded on the values of respect for human dignity, freedom, democracy, equality, the rule of law, and respect for human rights, including the rights of persons belonging to minorities. These values are common to the Member States in a society in which pluralism, non-discrimination, tolerance, justice, solidarity, and equality between women and men prevail.
91 Marco Ventura, 'Non discriminazione e tutela delle diversità e delle minoranze' in *Europa. Un'utopia in costruzione* (Istituto della Enciclopedia Italiana 2018) 140.
92 V. Committee on Civil Liberties, *Justice and Home Affairs, Report on Minimum Standards for Minorities in the EU* (2018/2036(INI) 2018).
93 *Ivi*, para 7.
94 European Parliament, *European Parliament Resolution of 13 November 2018 on Minimum Standards for Minorities in the EU* (2018/2036(INI) 2018).

Article 2 (TEU), in relation to the project of a new directive about minority rights. In fact, the European Parliament asks the European Commission for 'a legislative proposal for a directive ... on minimum standards for minorities in the EU, including clear benchmarks and sanctions'.

The external dimension describes the enlargement of the Union to new States. For instance, during the negotiation for the admission of Turkey, the European Parliament underlined the lack of protection for religious minorities.[95] Similarly, in 2016, the European Commission noted specific issues about the legal status of religious minorities in Turkey. In particular:

> Outstanding issues concerning the Alevi community need to be tackled, including the implementation of several ECtHR judgments. The Ecumenical Patriarchate received no indication from the authorities that it may use the 'ecumenical' title freely. Venice Commission recommendations on this issue are yet to be implemented. No steps were taken to open the Halki (Heybeliada) Greek Orthodox Seminary. There were reactions triggered by the controversial use of the Hagia Sophia, which is a museum situated within a listed UNESCO world heritage site, for marking religious celebrations. The Armenian Patriarchate's proposal to open a university department for Armenian language and clergy has been pending for several years. Similar demands have been made by different Christian communities who sought to train clergy. Similar problems exist over the construction of places of worship. Hate speech and hate crimes against Christians and Jews continued to be repeatedly reported.[96]

V Conclusion

The transformation of the legal concept of religious minority, at the international and European levels, stems from the inclusion of minority rights within human rights. Under Article 27 ICCPR, FoRB is protected as a matter of belonging to a group. The individual and non-collective dimension of rights granted to religious minorities represents a key factor in the evolution of the concept. In fact, religious freedom, as a criterion of relationship between the individual and the group, becomes increasingly relevant as a dimension to integrate different

---

95 V., for example, European Parliament, *European Parliament Resolution of 10 February 2010 on Turkey's Progress Report 2009* (2010).
96 V. European Commission, Commission Staff Working Document, *Turkey 2016 Report. Accompanying the Document Communication from the Commission to the European Parliament, the Council, the European Economic and Social Committee and the Committee of the Regions* (COM(2016) 715 final) 71–72. Commission Staff Working Document, *Turkey 2018 Report Accompanying the document Communication from the Commission to the European Parliament, the Council, the European Economic and Social Committee and the Committee of the Regions 2018 Communication on EU Enlargement Policy* (Commission Staff Working Document 2018).

aspects of human identity. The idea that minority rights can protect different intersections between religious freedom and other human rights can be described through the well-known notion of holistic approach to human rights. The holistic approach develops the principle, affirmed by the United Nations, that 'all human rights are universal, indivisible and interrelated and interdependent'.[97] The application of this principle, through the holistic approach, reshapes the rights of religious minorities in two perspectives regarding the interpretation of the legal sources and the working methods of international and European institutions.

From the first point of view, the holistic approach to religious freedom is articulated in a pluralistic and intersectional interpretation of freedom. This process concerns the content of religious freedom, the instruments of guarantee and their limits, as well as the intersections with other human rights. In terms of content, international and European institutions define a new holistic meaning of religion, as an inclusive dimension for believers, non-believers, atheists, and agnostics. Overall, this approach interprets the concept of religious minority in a pluralistic and democratic key. Compared to historical or traditional religious minorities,[98] in fact, international instruments become accessible to groups of non-believers or to new religious minorities.[99] In this context, if religious freedom is expressed through diversity, the first holistic effect of religious freedom is the inclusion of new groups within the concept of religious minority. In terms of instruments of guarantee and intersection with other human rights, the necessary connection between the religious freedom of members of minorities and other human rights produces, at the same time, a strengthening of protections, but also new limits to religious freedom. The intersectional guarantee of religious freedom represents both the link between religious freedom and other human rights and the boundaries of the conflict between religious freedom and human rights. In these terms, if the intersection between LGBT rights and religious minority rights highlights the existence of sexual or gender minorities within religious minorities, more in general the manifestation of religious freedom cannot justify discrimination against homosexuals or transgender people. This double dynamic produces two different meanings of the holistic approach to religious freedom of minorities: The first is the strengthening of the guarantee of this freedom, as a new dimension of expression and promotion of new human rights; the second is the limit that the relationship between rights can place on the exercise of religious freedom.

Moving from the working methods of international and European institutions, the holistic approach is evident in the collaboration between international

---

97 *Vienna Declaration and Programme of Action* (A/CONF.157/24), Part I, chapter III, section I (5).
98 Daniele Ferrari, *Il concetto di minoranza religiosa dal diritto internazionale al diritto europeo. Genesi, sviluppo e circolazione* (Il Mulino 2019) 25 ss.
99 Fabienne Bretscher, *Protecting the Religious Freedom of New Minorities in International Law* (Routledge 2020).

institutions, as a model for developing a sound agenda for the implementation of various legal sources of minority rights and human rights, and the involvement of different social actors in the work of international and European institutions.[100] In this context, the indivisibility of human rights emerges in the relationship between the UN, the CoE, the OSCE, and the EU through a coordinated and multilevel approach to human and minority rights. The dialogue among international institutions and European bodies is evident in the cooperation of the Delegation of the European Union to the UN with the United Nations.[101] This European body actively participates in the activities of the Council for Human Rights. This was stressed by the Forum on Minority Issues:

> Protection of the rights of persons belonging to national or ethnic, religious and linguistic minorities is also integrated into the EU's external action through the EU Human Rights Action plan 2015–2019, which contributes to cultivating an environment of non-discrimination inter alia through supporting the UN, regional organisations, partner countries', and civil society's efforts aimed at protecting and promoting the rights of persons belonging to minorities.[102]

Moreover, the holistic approach to human rights is a useful tool to foster the relationship among social actors, who claim interconnected rights. This dynamic has been emphasised by international and European institutions through the inclusion of religious actors in the reflection about human rights. This new dimension of reflection, in addition to defining an innovative laboratory of religious diplomacy,[103] has highlighted, beyond traditional litigation strategies, the usefulness of dialogue to apply the holistic model to possible conflicts between human rights. In these terms, for example, during a conference, organised by the UN's Special Rapporteur on Freedom of Religion or Belief and Muslims for Progressive Values,[104] speakers observed that the 'misunderstanding of freedom of religion or belief and sexuality' can be resolved, thanks to the awareness that 'when negotiating differences and resolving apparent clashes, reciprocity, mutual respect, compromise, and mediation are essential'.[105] In particular, if 'human rights and respect for diversity are inextricably linked',[106] the 'dialogue between conflicting groups

---

100 Ioana Cismas, *Religious Actors and International Law* (Oxford University Press 2014).
101 V. https://eeas.europa.eu/delegations/un-geneva/659/about-eu-delegation-geneva_en.
102 Permanent Delegation to the United Nations Office and other international organisations in Geneva, Forum on Minority Issues, *Minorities in Situations of Humanitarian Crises, Item2 - Legal Framework and Key Concepts EU Intervention* (9th session 2016).
103 Scott Thomas, *Diplomacy and Religion* (Oxford University Press 2017).
104 Shafferan Sonneveld, *Conference Summary: Freedom of Religion and Belief and Sexuality* (Ani Zonneveld 2016).
105 *Ivi*, p. 7.
106 *Ivi*, p. 5.

should be encouraged and facilitated' to promote alliances and reconciliations between religion and LGBT people.[107]

Diversity in the name of human rights sheds light on a novel challenge: That of recognising the multidimensional meaning that religion has for human identity in the endless debate within and without minorities.

---

107 *Ivi*, p. 14.

Law reading guides

This code proposes a systematic collection of the various international and European sources that define the rights of religious minorities. The goal is to collect all the relevant material to describe and qualify the legal concept of religious minorities. For this purpose, this code includes material that spans from the UN to the EU, the CoE and, ultimately, the OSCE. The analysis of this material proceeds according to the following criteria: Legal system of belonging, interpretation, relation, and use of the concept.

First, the sources are grouped and sorted in relation to the legal systems from which they originated. As a result, they are organised in four chapters touching on the UN, the CoE, the OSCE and the EU, respectively. Each chapter corresponds to a different international or European organisation and is split into sections. Each section collects one or more legal sources. The sections are then structured into subsections corresponding to the rights guaranteed to religious minorities by the source of the corresponding section. The content of the guaranteed rights is defined in subsections through the acts and the sentences of the international institution of reference, which have interpreted and applied the legal provisions indicated in that section. To highlight the criteria that qualify a group as a religious minority, the first sections of the first and the third chapters set forth the legal definition of the topic elaborated by UN's and OSCE's institutions. In this sense, despite the fact that there is no official definition of religious minority, different definitional attempts are useful to underline the genesis and the evolution of the concept in the international and European framework.

Second, the code does not limit itself to listing the different legal sources but also proposes a mapping of the acts, drawn up by international and European institutions, which have contributed to interpreting and developing the rights of religious minority. In this sense, the legal provisions included in the various chapters are always followed by the acts that have interpreted or applied them. Interpretation is very important, especially in those systems that protect the rights of religious minorities through the exegesis of different legal categories (for example, national minority).

Third, the code, through a system of internal references, highlights the relationships between the sources of the different chapters, to underscore, for example, when the European Union uses the concept of religious minority elaborated by the United Nations.

Fourth, the sources gathered concern international law at global and European levels, without considering other international regional sources, as only the United Nations, the OSCE, the Council of Europe, and the European Union have extensively used the concept of religious minority.

Moreover, in all sections the legal sources are in chronological order from oldest to most recent. This criterion changes only in chapter one, section two, because despite the Convention relating to the Status of Refugees preceding the International Covenant on Civil and Political Rights, the interpretation of international protection, as a useful tool also for religious minority, is linked to the entry into force of Article 27 in 1966. The code, through an organic collection of international and European law of religious minorities, wants to reconstruct the genesis of this concept, its development, and the current developments that are affecting guarantees and standards in international and European law.

Moving to the description of chapters, the first chapter concerns the protection of the rights of religious minorities since the approval of the Covenant on Civil and Political Rights in 1966. The chapter is divided into five sections concerning the Covenant on Civil and Political Rights (section 1); the Convention relating to the Status of Refugees (section 2); the Convention on the Elimination of All Forms of Discrimination against Women (section 3); the Covenant on Civil and Political Rights and the Convention on the Rights of the Child (section 4); and the Declaration on the Rights of Persons Belonging to National or Ethnic, Religious and Linguistic Minorities (section 5). The Pact is included in the first section, as it represents the first international source containing an anticipation of the rights of linguistic, ethnic, and religious minorities (Art. 27).

The second chapter reconstructs the protection of the rights of religious minorities within the European Convention on Human Rights (section 1) and the Framework Convention for the Protection of National Minorities (section 2) adopted by the Committee of Ministers of the Council of Europe on 8 November 1994. These sources are commented on through the judgements of the European Court of Human Rights that have protected the rights of religious minorities and the various institutional acts that have reduced the rights of religious minorities to the guarantees provided for national minorities.

The third chapter, dedicated to the OSCE, defines the rights of religious minorities in relation to the definition of national minority within the 1993 Helsinki Declaration. With respect to this source, the documents collected within the subsections highlight the terms in which the High Commissioner on National Minorities has interpreted the link between religious minority and national minority and discussed whether these guidelines have had a concrete impact on the application of the category.

The last chapter, devoted to the European Union, gathers in the first section the contents of the Treaty of Lisbon and the Charter of Fundamental Rights of the European Union. Moving from the general linguistic formula 'minorities', the concept of religious minority is explored through its implementation via the principle of non-discrimination and the right to manifest a religion or belief. The second section concerns the legal sources, which protect the right to asylum for members of persecuted religious minorities.

I United Nations

Section 1

International Covenant on Civil and Political Rights

> *[Adopted and opened for signature, ratification and accession by General Assembly resolution 2200A (XXI) of 16 December 1966 – entry into force 23 March 1976, in accordance with Article 49]*

Article 4

1 In time of public emergency which threatens the life of the nation and the existence of which is officially proclaimed, the States Parties to the present Covenant may take measures derogating from their obligations under the present Covenant to the extent strictly required by the exigencies of the situation, provided that such measures are not inconsistent with their other obligations under international law and do not involve discrimination solely on the ground of race, colour, sex, language, religion or social origin.
2 No derogation from articles 6, 7, 8 (paragraphs I and II), 11, 15, 16 and 18 may be made under this provision.
3 Any State Party to the present Covenant availing itself of the right of derogation shall immediately inform the other States Parties to the present Covenant, through the intermediary of the Secretary-General of the United Nations, of the provisions from which it has derogated and of the reasons by which it was actuated. A further communication shall be made, through the same intermediary, on the date on which it terminates such derogation.

Article 18

1 Everyone shall have the right to freedom of thought, conscience and religion. This right shall include freedom to have or to adopt a religion or belief of his choice, and freedom, either individually or in community with others

and in public or private, to manifest his religion or belief in worship, observance, practice and teaching.
2. No one shall be subject to coercion which would impair his freedom to have or to adopt a religion or belief of his choice.
3. Freedom to manifest one's religion or beliefs may be subject only to such limitations as are prescribed by law and are necessary to protect public safety, order, health, or morals or the fundamental rights and freedoms of others.
4. The States Parties to the present Covenant undertake to have respect for the liberty of parents and, when applicable, legal guardians to ensure the religious and moral education of their children in conformity with their own convictions.

Article 20

1. Any propaganda for war shall be prohibited by law.
2. Any advocacy of national, racial or religious hatred that constitutes incitement to discrimination, hostility or violence shall be prohibited by law.

Article 24

1. Every child shall have, without any discrimination as to race, colour, sex, language, religion, national or social origin, property or birth, the right to such measures of protection as are required by his status as a minor, on the part of his family, society and the State.
2. Every child shall be registered immediately after birth and shall have a name.
3. Every child has the right to acquire a nationality.

Article 26

All persons are equal before the law and are entitled without any discrimination to the equal protection of the law. In this respect, the law shall prohibit any discrimination and guarantee to all persons equal and effective protection against discrimination on any ground such as race, colour, sex, language, religion, political or other opinion, national or social origin, property, birth or other status.

Article 27

In those States in which ethnic, religious or linguistic minorities exist, persons belonging to such minorities shall not be denied the right, in community with the other members of their group, to enjoy their own culture, to profess and practise their own religion, or to use their own language.

Optional Protocol to the International Covenant on Civil and Political Rights

[Adopted and opened for signature, ratification and accession by General Assembly resolution 2200A (XXI) of 16 December 1966 – entry into force 23 March 1976, in accordance with Article 9]

Article 1

A State Party to the Covenant that becomes a Party to the present Protocol recognizes the competence of the Committee to receive and consider communications from individuals subject to its jurisdiction who claim to be victims of a violation by that State Party of any of the rights set forth in the Covenant. No communication shall be received by the Committee if it concerns a State Party to the Covenant which is not a Party to the present Protocol.

Article 2

Subject to the provisions of article 1, individuals who claim that any of their rights enumerated in the Covenant have been violated and who have exhausted all available domestic remedies may submit a written communication to the Committee for consideration.

Article 3

The Committee shall consider inadmissible any communication under the present Protocol which is anonymous, or which it considers to be an abuse of the right of submission of such communications or to be incompatible with the provisions of the Covenant.

Article 4

1 Subject to the provisions of article 3, the Committee shall bring any communications submitted to it under the present Protocol to the attention of the State Party to the present Protocol alleged to be violating any provision of the Covenant.
2 Within six months, the receiving State shall submit to the Committee written explanations or statements clarifying the matter and the remedy, if any, that may have been taken by that State.

Article 5

1. The Committee shall consider communications received under the present Protocol in the light of all written information made available to it by the individual and by the State Party concerned.
2. The Committee shall not consider any communication from an individual unless it has ascertained that:
   (a) The same matter is not being examined under another procedure of international investigation or settlement;
   (b) The individual has exhausted all available domestic remedies. This shall not be the rule where the application of the remedies is unreasonably prolonged.
3. The Committee shall hold closed meetings when examining communications under the present Protocol.
4. The Committee shall forward its views to the State Party concerned and to the individual.

Article 6

The Committee shall include in its annual report under article 45 of the Covenant a summary of its activities under the present Protocol.

Article 7

Pending the achievement of the objectives of resolution 1514(XV) adopted by the General Assembly of the United Nations on 14 December 1960 concerning the Declaration on the Granting of Independence to Colonial Countries and Peoples, the provisions of the present Protocol shall in no way limit the right of petition granted to these peoples by the Charter of the United Nations and other international conventions and instruments under the United Nations and its specialized agencies.

Article 8

1. The present Protocol is open for signature by any State which has signed the Covenant.
2. The present Protocol is subject to ratification by any State which has ratified or acceded to the Covenant. Instruments of ratification shall be deposited with the Secretary-General of the United Nations.
3. The present Protocol shall be open to accession by any State which has ratified or acceded to the Covenant.
4. Accession shall be effected by the deposit of an instrument of accession with the Secretary-General of the United Nations.
5. The Secretary-General of the United Nations shall inform all States which have signed the present Protocol or acceded to it of the deposit of each instrument of ratification or accession.

Article 9

1   Subject to the entry into force of the Covenant, the present Protocol shall enter into force three months after the date of the deposit with the Secretary-General of the United Nations of the tenth instrument of ratification or instrument of accession.
2   For each State ratifying the present Protocol or acceding to it after the deposit of the tenth instrument of ratification or instrument of accession, the present Protocol shall enter into force three months after the date of the deposit of its own instrument of ratification or instrument of accession.

Article 10

The provisions of the present Protocol shall extend to all parts of federal States without any limitations or exceptions.

Article 11

1   Any State Party to the present Protocol may propose an amendment and file it with the Secretary-General of the United Nations. The Secretary-General shall thereupon communicate any proposed amendments to the States Parties to the present Protocol with a request that they notify him whether they favour a conference of States Parties for the purpose of considering and voting upon the proposal. In the event that at least one third of the States Parties favours such a conference, the Secretary-General shall convene the conference under the auspices of the United Nations. Any amendment adopted by a majority of the States Parties present and voting at the conference shall be submitted to the General Assembly of the United Nations for approval.
2   Amendments shall come into force when they have been approved by the General Assembly of the United Nations and accepted by a two-thirds majority of the States Parties to the present Protocol in accordance with their respective constitutional processes.
3   When amendments come into force, they shall be binding on those States Parties which have accepted them, other States Parties still being bound by the provisions of the present Protocol and any earlier amendment which they have accepted.

Article 12

1   Any State Party may denounce the present Protocol at any time by written notification addressed to the Secretary-General of the United Nations. Denunciation shall take effect three months after the date of receipt of the notification by the Secretary-General.

2. Denunciation shall be without prejudice to the continued application of the provisions of the present Protocol to any communication submitted under article 2 before the effective date of denunciation.

Article 13

Irrespective of the notifications made under article 8, paragraph 5, of the present Protocol, the Secretary-General of the United Nations shall inform all States referred to in article 48, paragraph I, of the Covenant of the following particulars:

(a) Signatures, ratifications and accessions under article 8;
(b) The date of the entry into force of the present Protocol under article 9 and the date of the entry into force of any amendments under article 11;
(c) Denunciations under article 12.

Article 14

1. The present Protocol, of which the Chinese, English, French, Russian and Spanish texts are equally authentic, shall be deposited in the archives of the United Nations.
2. The Secretary-General of the United Nations shall transmit certified copies of the present Protocol to all States referred to in article 48 of the Covenant.

A Legal definition

A.1. FRANCESCO CAPOTORTI *(Special Rapporteur of the Sub-Commission on Prevention of Discrimination and Protection of Minorities)*, **Study on the Rights of Persons Belonging to Ethnic, Religious and Linguistic Minorities *(ST/HR(05)/H852/no.5), 1979.*** *

Chapter I. The concept of a minority

A ANALYSIS OF THE CONCEPT OF A MINORITY

20. Despite the many references to minorities to be found in international legal instruments of all kinds (multilateral conventions, bilateral treaties and resolutions of international organizations), there is no generally accepted definition of the term "minority". The preparation of a definition capable of being universally accepted has always proved a task of such difficulty and complexity that neither

---

* From *Study on the Rights of Persons Belonging to Ethnic, Religious and Linguistic Minorities*, by Francesco Capotorti, © (1979) United Nations. Reprinted with the permission of the United Nations.

the experts in this field nor the organs of the international agencies have been able to accomplish it to date. The reason for this is the number of different aspects to be considered. Should the concept of a minority be based on the numerical ratio of the "minority" group to the population as a whole or is this quantitative aspect secondary or even unimportant? Is it necessary to limit the concept by introducing the idea of a minimum size? Should only objective criteria be taken into account or should it be assumed that "subjective" factors also have a part to play? Does the origin of the minorities matter for the purposes of a definition? Should we understand by minorities groups of nationals only, excluding groups of foreigners? These – the major issues that arise – must now be analysed.

(...)

2   *Definition proposed by the Sub-Commission on Prevention of Discrimination and Protection of Minorities at its third, fourth and fifth sessions.*

22. Three times – at its third, fourth and fifth sessions[1] – the Sub-Commission has recommended that the Commission on Human Rights adopt a draft resolution defining minorities for purposes of protection by the United Nations.[2] The draft resolution adopted by the Sub-Commission at the third session and amended at the fourth session indicated, as follows, the factors which it felt should be taken into account in establishing a definition of "minorities":

(a) The existence among the nationals of many States of separate population groups habitually known as minorities and having ethnic, religious or linguistic traditions or characteristics which differ from those of the rest of the population and which should be protected by special measures at the national and international levels so that they may preserve and develop such traditions or characteristics;
(b) The existence of a special factor, namely, that certain minority groups do not need protection. Such groups include, above all, those which, while numerically smaller than the rest of the population, constitute the dominant element in it and those who seek to be treated in exactly the same way as the rest of the population;
(c) The undesirability of interfering with the spontaneous developments which take place in a society when impacts such as that of a new environment, or that of modern means of communication, produce a state of rapid racial, social, cultural, or linguistic evolution;
(d) The risk of taking measures that might lend themselves to misuse amongst a minority whose members' spontaneous desires might be disturbed by parties interested in fomenting amongst them a disloyalty to the State in which they live;

1   E/CN.4/Sub.2/119, para. 32; E/CN.4/Sub. 2/140, annex I, draft resolution II; E/CN.4/Sub. 2/149, para. 26.
2   On each of the occasions, the Commission, after considering the draft resolution, referred it back to the Sub-Commission for further study.

(e) The undesirability of affording protection to practices which are inconsistent with the rights proclaimed in the Universal Declaration of Human Rights;
(f) The difficulties raised by claims to the status of minorities by groups so small that special treatment could, for instance, place a disproportionate burden upon the resources of the State.

23. Taking account of the above-mentioned factors, the Sub-Commission at its fifth session recommended that the Commission adopt a draft resolution concerning the definition of the term "minority", according to which the definition would be based on the following elements: (i) the term minority includes only those non-dominant groups in a population which possess and wish to preserve stable ethnic, religious or linguistic traditions or characteristics markedly different from those of the rest of the population; (ii) such minorities should properly include a number of persons sufficient by themselves to preserve such traditions or characteristics; (iii) such minorities must be loyal to the State of which they are nationals.

24. At its sixth session, the Sub-Commission resolved, in its resolution F, to initiate a study of the position as regards minorities throughout the world and to apply for the purposes of that study a modified version of the definition contained in the draft resolution referred to in the preceding paragraph. However, that decision was not implemented since, at its ninth session, the Commission on Human Rights, having noted resolution F[3] of the Sub-Commission, invited the latter to give further study to the whole question, including the definition of the term "minority".[4] During the debates in the Commission on the question, several members criticized[5] the definition of "minorities" contained in resolution F of the Sub-Commission. Some felt that it contained provisions that might result in eliminating from the definition certain national groups which should be given special protection. They stated that the inclusion of only such groups as might wish to "preserve ethnic, religious or linguistic traditions or characteristics" was subjective, since dominant groups which did not wish to extend equal rights to certain minorities could justify their action by claiming that those minorities did not wish to maintain their individual character. Others considered that the definition recommended by the Sub-Commission did not make it sufficiently clear that minorities did not include foreigners residing in the territory of the State or groups which had come into existence as the result of immigration. It was also pointed out that it was hard to see how such a study, dealing with every minority in need of special measures of protection, could be made, particularly in the absence of any criterion by which to judge which minorities needed special protection and which did not need it.

---

3 See E/CN.4/703, para. 200.
4 See E/CN.4/705, para. 438.
5 See E/CN.4/705, paras. 422–437.

25. At its seventh session, in 1954, the Sub-Commission decided to concentrate its attention on the various aspects of the problem of discrimination and to defer work on a further study of the whole problem of the special protection of minorities, including the definition of the term "minority", pending the issue by the Commission on Human Rights of a specific directive on the subject.[6]

26. A memorandum prepared by the Secretary-General in 1950, entitled *Definition and Classification of Minorities* and submitted to the third session of the Sub-Commission, contains the following statement:

> It follows from the analysis [of the concept of the community, the nation and the State] ... that the term "minority" cannot for practical purposes be defined simply by interpreting the word in its literal sense. If this were the case, nearly all the communities existing within a State would be styled minorities, including families, social classes, cultural groups, speakers of dialects, etc. Such a definition would be useless. As a matter of fact, the term "minority" is frequently used at present in a more restricted sense; it has come to refer mainly to a particular kind of community, and especially to a national or similar community, which differs from the predominant group in the State. Such a minority may have originated in any of the following ways:
>
> (a) It may formerly have constituted an independent nation with its own State (or a more or less independent tribal organization);
> (b) It may formerly have been part of a nation living under its own State, which was later segregated from this jurisdiction and annexed to another State; or
> (c) It may have been, or may still be, a regional or scattered group which, although bound to the predominant group by certain feeling of solidarity, has not reached even a minimum degree of real assimilation with the predominant group[7];

27. Both in the Sub-Commission and in the Commission on Human Rights it was generally recognized, therefore, that it was difficult, if not impossible, to group together under a generally satisfactory definition every minority group in need of special measures of protection. In an attempt to describe the reasons for that difficulty, an author writes:

> When the General Assembly of the United Nations expressed the consideration that "the United Nations cannot remain indifferent to the fate of minorities", it thrust itself directly into one of the most complex and perplexing problems in the entire realm of international relations. The "problem of minorities", with all its manifold implications, has troubled world peace and

---

6 See E/CN.4/Sub. 2/170, para. 171, resolution F.
7 United Nations publication, Sales No. 1950.XIV.3, paras. 37–38.

international goodwill for centuries. It has constituted a constant irritating friction between states, an instrument of political design and aggression, a means of toppling state structures and a direct and indirect cause of local and general wars. Its vast international significance has been matched by its awing perplexity. "The" problem of minorities is in reality a multitude of particular problems, each one hinging on a whole network of complex economic, social, historical, ethnic and political factors.

Never before has an international organization concerned itself with the fate of minorities us such. The United Nations, without reference to any specific manifestations of a "minority problem" took upon itself the task of "protection of minorities", thereby establishing "minorities" as a general universal conception whose primary characteristics are its imprecision and vagueness and breadth of scope. When the League of Nations referred to the minority problem, it was not concerning itself with a general concept: its "minority problem" consisted of the particular problems of certain minorities in a few specified states in a given region, problems which arose from the territorial settlements at the Peace Conference of Paris. The justification for international minority protection and the minorities for which it was devised being sharply outlined and delimited, there was no necessity to make the concepts involved more precise, nor to define them beyond certain broad outlines.[8]

3 *Provisional interpretation by the Special Rapporteur of the term "minority" for the purposes of this study and the observations made thereon*

(a) *Provisional interpretation by the Special Rapporteur*

28. In the plan for the collection of information relating to the study (see annex II) the Special Rapporteur stated that he envisaged for the study the following interpretation of the term "minority": for the purposes of the study, an ethnic, religious or linguistic minority is a group numerically smaller than the rest of the population of the State to which it belongs and possessing cultural, physical or historical characteristics, a religion or a language different from those of the rest of the population.

(...)

6 *Observations of the Special Rapporteur*

52. The Special Rapporteur wishes in the first place to recall that the present study has been carried out pursuant to Sub-Commission resolution 9 (XX) under which the study is to analyse the concept of minority taking into account the

---

8 T. H. Bagley, *General Principles and Problems in the International Protection of Minorities* (Imprimeries Populaires 1950) 9.

ethnic, religious and linguistic factors and considering also the position of ethnic, religious or linguistic groups in "multinational" societies.

53. Examination of the available documentation reveals the existence of different ethnic, religious or linguistic groups in almost all the countries studied. The numerical importance of these various groups varies, however, from country to country and, in general, three types of situations can be distinguished. In some countries these groups are roughly equal in size. In others, besides an ethnic, religious or linguistic group, constituting a numerical majority, there are one or more other groups forming, in some cases, a small and, in others, an appreciable percentage of the total population of the country. Elsewhere, there may be a group which is numerically large, but not a majority, together with a number of other groups which individually constitute communities smaller in size but in conjunction form a majority of the population.

54. The examination of the documentation also confirms the observations concerning the classification of numerically non-majority groups contained in a memorandum submitted by the Secretary-General to the Sub-Commission in 1950:[9]

(a) Measured by the criterion of contiguity, the following types of minorities may be distinguished:

  (i) Groups which constitute nearly the only population of a section of the country;
  (ii) Groups which constitute the largest part of a section of the country;
  (iii) Groups, settled in a section of the country, which constitute only a small part of the population of that section;
  (iv) A group, the members of which live partly in a section of the country and partly scattered throughout the remainder of the territory;
  (v) Groups which are scattered throughout the whole country;
  (vi) Groups which live partly within the country and partly in one or more other countries.

(b) Measured against the criterion of the origin of groups and their situation in relation to the State, the following types of minorities can be distinguished:

  (i) Groups which existed in the country before the establishment of the State;
  (ii) Groups which formerly belonged to another State, but which afterwards came under the jurisdiction of the State through annexation or transfer of territory;
  (iii) Groups formed by persons having a common origin, religion, language etc. who have become nationals of the State.

---

9 *Definition and Classification of Minorities* (United Nations Publication, Sales No. 1950. XIV.3).

55. It is on the basis of these considerations and bearing in mind the observations of Governments and the suggestions made by members of the Sub-Commission that the Special Rapporteur has prepared this study and has indicated in the chapter containing his conclusions and recommendations the elements which, in his view, should be included in a definition of the term "minority". The groups whose situation has been examined with a view to determining to what extent the principles enunciated in article 27 of the Covenant have been applied in respect of their members are those which constitute communities possessing, from an ethnic, religious or linguistic standpoint, their own characteristics which differ from those of the rest of the population. This objectively recognizable fact is obviously the starting-point for any definition. It should be emphasized, however, that as soon as one speaks of communities having their own identity, the objective differences are clearly linked with the "subjective" factor (desire to preserve the characteristics of the group). A group as such cannot have an identity throughout history if its members have no wish to help in preserving it. On the other hand, the numerical factor (numerical inferiority as compared with the rest of the population of the State) is of an undeniable importance in view of the fact that the need to protect minorities derives essentially from the weakness of their position even within the context of a democratic State, i.e. one conforming to the model which emerges from the human rights instruments of the United Nations. In such a State, it is the will of the majority which makes the laws and determines the country's general attitude. The object of every international system for the protection of minorities has always been to ensure that the majority does not ignore the special requirements of minority groups. As for the situation caused by dominant minority groups which establish (as in southern Africa) a hateful regime of oppression and racial discrimination in disregard of the elementary principles of respect for the dignity of human beings, it is the application of the principle of the right of peoples to self-determination which is challenged in this case. It is obvious that the dominant minority groups do not need protective measures, while the oppressed majorities have rights which far exceed the very limited contents of article 27 of the Covenant.

56. There are, of course, countries in which groups of almost equal numerical size coexist. In such cases, the situation of all the groups has been taken into account since each of them is numerically in a minority position in respect of the population as a whole. As for the minimum size that a minority should have in order to be recognized as such, the problem is a practical one rather than a theoretical one. In principle, even quite a small group has the right to claim the protection provided for in article 27, to the extent to which it seems reasonable to expect the State to introduce special measures of protection.

57. The interpretation adopted excludes foreigners residing in a country. The Special Rapporteur is not unaware of the problems encountered nowadays as a result of phenomena such as the migration of workers and the establishment of sometimes quite substantial groups of foreign workers in certain industrialized countries. The case of foreigners is different, however, from that of persons who

possess the nationality of the country in which they live. As long as a person retains his status as a foreigner, he has the right to benefit from the protection granted by customary international law to persons who are in countries other than their own, as well as from any other special rights which may be conferred upon him by treaties or other special agreements. Article 27 of the Covenant should thus be interpreted as relating solely to nationals of the State.

58. Lastly, with regard to the undoubted influence exercised by the factor of the origin of a minority, the Special Rapporteur is of the opinion that this influence manifests itself in connexion with the group's reefing of identity (which largely depends on its origin) but that the concept of minority is, in itself, independent of this factor. Persons of the same origin who have their own particular characteristics which differ from those of the remainder of the population of a State (e.g. immigrants) are not automatically bound to form a minority group. There can be no doubt regarding the freedom of each individual to help to form a minority group or to integrate himself into the remainder of the population.

B THE QUESTION OF OFFICIAL RECOGNITION BY STATES OF ETHNIC, RELIGIOUS OR LINGUISTIC MINORITIES WITHIN THEIR POPULATION

59. The official attitude of States towards minority groups forming part of their population can and does vary considerably. It might be said that the two extremes are represented by the case of recognition in the Constitution of the existence of a minority and the absence of any recognition at all. Between these two extremes, however, there are some middle positions: recognition of the basis of special legislation or administrative measures or the simple recognition of private institutions representing the interests of minority groups.

60. The word "recognition" itself does not by any means always have the same meaning. It could mean that the State grants to one or more minorities the status of legal persons, subjects of law, but this is very rarely encountered. It may mean that a coherent set of rights – connected with the principle of protecting the identity of minorities – is granted to members of such minorities. Sometimes, however, the only measure is the granting of some specific rights to the minorities without there being any over-all plan. In this last case, the recognition of the minority benefiting from the rights is usually implicit and partial.

61. In any case, what must be emphasized – before the attitudes of a number of States are examined more closely – is the fact that international protection of minorities does depend on official recognition of their existence. In the preceding pages, reference has been made to the difficulties of finding a definition of the term "minority". Nevertheless, the presence of sufficient elements to indicate that a minority exists is sufficient to make applicable the pertinent international rules, and particularly article 27 of the International Covenant on Civil and Political Rights.

62. It is, of course, acknowledged that, in practice, the recognition of a minority by the State in which it lives improves this situation, facilitates the application

of the principles enunciated in article 27 of the Covenant and gives the members of the minority a solid basis for effective protection of the rights guaranteed them at the international level.

63. The problem involved can be examined from two angles. In the first place, the precise legal meaning of the official recognition of certain population groups as minorities must be determined. In the second place, we must examine the procedure by which the fact that an individual belongs to a group is established, with a view to applying a particular status to the individual concerned.

64. The question of the recognition of religious minorities as such has lost much of its urgency as a result of the almost universal acceptance of the principle of freedom of conscience and religion which is now incorporated into the domestic law of almost all States. The situation with regard to recognition of ethnic and linguistic minorities is not the same, however. The approach adopted by States to this question differs not only from country to country but also, very frequently, within countries according to the groups involved. In some cases, certain ethnic and linguistic groups have been officially recognized as distinct groups entitled to special rights, while others have not been so recognized. Moreover, the terminology used to designate the groups which are officially recognized is not the same everywhere.

65. As for the question of implicit recognition, it should be pointed out that general constitutional provisions forbidding discrimination based on race, national or ethnic origin, religion or language cannot be interpreted as constituting a recognition of ethnic, religious or linguistic minorities. The same applies to official statistics concerning the composition of the population of various countries. Official statistics frequently classify the population by ethnic, religious or linguistic groups and it may be asked whether this presentation has any legal significance. Although such statistics prove the existence of such groups, it does not appear that, in themselves, they enable one to conclude that the State has granted such groups a recognition with legal significance.

2   *The question of an individual's membership of a given group*

78. A question closely linked with the official recognition of ethnic, religious or linguistic minorities concerns the procedure followed for determining whether an individual is a member of a given group. The available documentation provides little information on this point. It is not always easy in practice to decide whether or not an individual belongs to a minority. When such a determination must be made in order to apply a particular status to the individual concerned, it can, in theory, be done on the basis of a definition provided by the law, of the categorically expressed desire of the individual, or of objective criteria. Problems arise whatever the criterion applied. In the opinion of some, to rely wholly on the subjective criterion is not without danger, inasmuch as an individual who declares that he belongs to a minority may be acting under the influence of external pressure or solely for political reasons. The objective criterion requires membership

of a minority to be determined by the presence of certain traits or characteristics which can be evaluated without reference to a statement by the individual concerned. One of the most important traits is undoubtedly the language generally used by the individual. Other such traits or characteristics include the individual's name and origin. But, as has frequently been pointed out, the use of objective criteria does not always lead to satisfactory results. It has been observed that the criterion of the name is, to say the least, questionable and that the value of the criterion of origin is very limited. As for the criterion of language, it has been pointed out in many cases that members of a linguistic minority generally use not only their own language but also the language of the majority. It has been said, for example, that in the Soviet Union ethnographers and demographers consider it incorrect to assign national ethnic affiliation on the basis of mother tongue, since the people inhabiting the Soviet Union have drawn so much together socially that there are frequent cases of individuals making their basic everyday tongue the language not of their own people but of the people among whom they live, though at the same time preserving awareness of their own national identity. Accordingly, in Soviet censuses nationality and mother tongue are separate indicators.

A.2. JULES DESCHÊNES *(Special Rapporteur of the Sub-Commission on Prevention of Discrimination and Protection of Minorities),* **Proposal concerning a definition of the term "minority"** *(E/CN.4/Sub.2/1985/31), 1985.* *

Introduction

18. (...) It is important to establish a point of reference. Our research must be carried out within the framework of article 27 of the International Covenant on Civil and Political Rights, of 1966. There is no question of attempting to encompass all possible and imaginable minorities within a single definition. Article 27 of the Covenant is concerned with "ethnic, religious or linguistic minorities", and it is with these alone that we shall deal.

21. I suggest that we proceed in three stages:

Firstly, we shall eliminate what I would call the "non-problems";
Secondly, we shall isolate the variables of the concept of minority;
Thirdly, we shall attempt to identify the constants of this same concept.

22. In conclusion, we shall endeavour to construct a definition which is both sufficiently general and sufficiently specific.

---

* From Proposal concerning a definition of the term "minority", by Jules Deschênes, ©(1985) United Nations. Reprinted with the permission of the United Nations.

I ELIMINATION OF NON-PROBLEMS

23. By "non-problems" I mean a matter with could raise difficulties but which, for our purposes, should be considered as resolved. There are three such issues: the question of indigenous populations, the question of resident aliens, and the question of the relationship between groups and their members. I propose to deal with them in that order.

A. *The question of indigenous populations* 24. The problem, let me recall, is as follows: should a definition of minorities cover indigenous populations?
(…)
36. All the above illustrate quite clearly the reluctance to include indigenous populations in a definition of minorities. It is conceivable that, in its final report, the Working Group on Indigenous Populations will suggest a definition coinciding with the more general definition which the Commission on Human Rights requested the Sub-Commission to submit. However, it would seem premature to attempt to do so and the question should, for the time-being, be considered a non-problem.
(…)
38. The unavoidable conclusion is that the definition which we seek should not attempt to deal with the question of indigenous populations.

B. *The question of resident aliens* 39. Migrations of workers create minorities of various sizes, the members of which retain the nationality of their country of origin. Although resident for an indefinite period in their country of choice, they nevertheless owe no allegiance to it. Should a definition be fashioned to take account of this special phenomenon of minorities composed of aliens?
(…)
43. Clearly then citizenship was a prerequisite for the accession by members of minorities to such elementary rights. Moreover, in order to enjoy such rights, the members of a minority group had to be citizens of the country concerned, and it was on that condition that they could claim the protection provided for in the minority's treaties.
44. This conception of things has not changed. Not that a country can avail itself of it in order to persecute aliens residing in its territory; but, when it comes to defining the rights of minorities, the first duty of a State is towards its own citizens. To the others, it owes only courtesy, which does not give rise to any rights.
(…)
46. On 22 October 1984, a different opinion was expressed by a Working Group of the Human Rights Committee with regard to the two matters considered above. The Working Group prepared draft general comments on article 27 (CCPR/C/23/CRP.1) in paragraph 4 of which it asserted:

> "The quality of a community as a minority under article 27 does not necessarily depend on a formal bond of citizenship of its members with the host

State. The text employs the word 'persons' and does not speak of noted that the Committee has always considered indigenous communities to come within the purview of article 27".

(...)
49. For the time being, in carrying out the mandate entrusted to me by the Sub-Commission, I prefer to proceed on the basis of the decision already taken with regard to non-citizens and of the cautious approach dictated by circumstances with regard to indigenous populations.

C. Relationship between groups and their members (...) 51. In the same tradition, after referring to "ethnic, religious or linguistic minorities", the authors of article 27 of the 1966 Covenant took care to protect "persons belonging to such minorities". The distinction is significant. The intention was probably to avoid the risk of setting one group against another or to giving one segment of the population of a country an advantage over the remainder of its citizens. Affording protection to a minority as a group suggests the possibility of privilege, perhaps even secession, and endangers a country's unity. Such was of course not the aim of the United Nations in adopting article 27 of the Covenant.

(...)
56. We should therefore adhere to the decision which has already been taken elsewhere: for our purposes, the debate between minorities and their members is closed. Every minority undoubtedly constitutes a group, but where it is a question of determining its rights, it is on the individual as a member of the minority that the emphasis should be placed.

57. That then disposes of the three non-problems to which I referred at the outset namely, the question of indigenous population, which our draft definition will not deal with; the question of resident aliens which our draft will not consider either; and the question of the relationship between groups and their members, where the emphasis will be placed upon the latter.

II ISOLATION OF THE VARIABLES OF THE MINORITY CONCEPT

58. One of the main difficulties which has so far prevented the adoption of a universally acceptable definition of minorities is the great diversity of the situations of minorities – and frequently even their radical opposition – from one country to another.

59. It is therefore important to make an inventory of these variables, since to have any hope of defeating an adversary, it is first necessary to try to know both his strengths and his weaknesses. In a country of minorities, however, weakness is reflected in the phenomenon of discrimination. This adversary must be known in order to be overcome and sometimes it is necessary to know how to recognize it in oneself. Therefore, let us not point to the mote in our neighbour's eye, but let us note two examples of the beam that is obstructing our own vision.

(...)

A. The will of the minority to survive 70. The first variable contains a significant element of subjectivity in that it relates to the determination of the minority to survive. This variable may lead in turn to a great number of diverse situations.

71. If the minority group wishes to preserve its cultural or religious independence, for example, it will tend to choose a political approach leading either to a sort of federal association in mutual tolerance – a well-known example being Switzerland – or to autonomy, then to secession; the history of our own country is a clear illustration of this type of constant and continually recurring tension.

72. On the other hand, if the minority group does not wish to preserve its independence, it may wish to melt into the surrounding society. Then it is a social approach which will prevail, and non-discriminatory measures will help to bring about the blending of the various elements of society. It may happen, however, that the majority, imbued with its prejudices, will refuse to accept the integration sought by the minority and wish to keep it apart. I shall refrain here from giving examples, for fear of offending national susceptibilities.

73. Lastly, the Jewish minority provides a mixed example in many countries, since its members wish to be integrated into the local economic system but isolate themselves in their own family and religious system. How is it possible to achieve the former while at the same time preserving the latter?

74. This chameleon-like quality therefore creates considerable difficulties for the definition of minorities. But these difficulties can be alleviated by reverting to the main object of the exercise, which is to ensure the protection of minorities. Therefore, for the purposes of a definition, the only minorities of interest are those who wish to continue to exist and to be recognized as such, with their own ethnic, linguistic or religious characteristics. The others, those who wish to merge into the dominant mass, do not require protection. At the very most, they may perhaps have to combat insidious discrimination designed to perpetuate, against the will of the minority, an exceptional situation rejected by that minority. But that is an entirely different matter which strikes at the very foundation of the theory of protection of the rights of minorities.

75. For the purposes of defining minorities, it will therefore be necessary to retain the positive aspect of this first variable, namely, the collective will to survive. Failure to demonstrate such a will excludes the minority from the definition.

B. The number of members of the minority 76. The second variables relates to the number of members of the minority. Here, too, two problems arise.

1   *Minimum number*

77. It must be first asked whether, to be recognized, a minority group has to consist of a minimum number of members. Clearly, there can be no mathematical answer to this question. At best, the number should be of no importance whatever. But it was said long ago that politics is the art of the possible,

and this question concerns the organization of the State. In the distribution of public resources, account must be taken, as Mr. Capotorti stressed in his study of minorities,[10] "of a reasonable proportionality between the effort involved and the benefit to be derived from it". To justify official recognition, a minority should therefore not be so small as to tap a percentage of public resources entirely out of proportion with the benefit which society should derive from the expenditure. That, it should be added, is purely a question of fact which a definition cannot attempt to decide.

2 Oppressed majority

78. The other problem raised by the second variable falls squarely, however, within the purview of our definition, namely, does a minority necessarily have to be in the minority? This somewhat paradoxical question reflects a serious problem of our time. No one has expressed it more strikingly than the poet Rabindranath Tagore in describing a world in which "the few are more than the many".[11]

79. Etymologically, the question can have only one answer: to be a minority, a group has to be able to claim that it is in a minority situation, in other words that it is less numerous than the total of its neighbours. For some, however, that is a false premise. In their opinion, it is not a question of etymology, but of sociology, since the number of members of a group is of little importance; if it is dominated, it comes within the social category of minorities. It is therefore necessary to have an over-all view of a particular society, including the various social, economic and especially political aspects. For, if the society is heterogenous and one group has to live under the domination of another, its numerical size is of little significance. The group must be considered to be subjugated as a minority. The classical example always given to support this thesis is the case of the black majority subjugated by the white minority in South Africa.

(...)

82. Moreover, that is how things inevitably happen in all large organizations: a small group of determined persons finally takes the initiative and directs the activities of the majority. The same is true of political parties, trade-union organizations and the councils of the Catholic Church.

(...)

86. On the one hand, the active and dominating minority has no more need of protection than the minority which wishes to blend with the majority does. Within the framework of a regime of protection of the rights of minorities, the minority in a domination situation has to be excluded from the definition which we are formulating.

10 United Nations Publication, sales no.: E.78.XIV.1, para. 566.
11 Quoted by S. Ramphal, 'Human Rights Today: Must the Few be More than the Many?' in B. Whitaker (ed), *Minorities – A Question of Human Rights?* (Pergamon Press Ltd 1984) 107.

87. On the other hand, it would be an insult to the dominated majority to consider it to be similar to a minority and, while claiming to protect it, to appear to restrict its rights to those set forth in article 27 of the Covenant, namely culture, language and religion. The oppressed majority requires, not protection, but liberation; it is not its rights as a "minority" which are being flouted, but its fundamental right to self-determination recognized by the Charter of the United and the law of nations.

88. Consequently, there is no need to stretch the traditional meaning of the word "minority" to make it encompass a reality which is essentially alien to it and to make it play a role doomed in advance to failure. The second question raised with regard to the second variable should therefore receive an affirmative reply: to qualify as a minority, a group has to be smaller in number than the rest of the population of the country of which it is a part and to be in a non-dominant situation. To return to the paradox mentioned above, the definition we are seeking should cover only minorities that are truly in a minority situation in the strict sense of the term.

III IDENTIFICATION OF THE CONSTANTS IN THE CONCEPT OF MINORITY

89. After eliminating some non-problems and making a selection from among several variables, it remains for us to identify, as a third phase, the last ingredients, namely, the constants which will give the definition of minority its particular flavour.

A. National minorities 90. An important preliminary question arises. The terms of reference of the competent bodies of the United Nations are based on article 27 of the International Covenant on Civil and Political Rights. The declaration which is being prepared, in particular its basic definition, will therefore cover, in principle, the minorities mentioned in article 27, i.e. ethnic, religious and linguistic minorities. However, the Working Group of the Commission on Human Rights decided to give its draft a title encompassing "(national or) ethnic, religious or linguistic minorities". Therefore, exactly which are the minorities concerned – national minorities, other minorities, or all minorities taken together? The difficulty arises from the fact that the terms have not been defined. We know almost instinctively the meaning of "religious minority" or "linguistic minority", but the distinction between "ethnic minority" and "national minority" is not so evident.

(...)

100. Four years later, Mr. Capotorti interpreted article 27 of the International Covenant as follows[12]:

> "In the context of article 27 of the Covenant, the substitution of the term 'ethnic minorities' for the term 'racial minorities' and the omission of any reference to 'national' minorities would seem to reflect a wish to use the

---

12 United Nations Publication, sales no. E.78.XIV.1, para. 51.

broadest expression and to imply that racial and national minorities should therefore be regarded as included in the category of ethnic minorities".

101. What does this mean? Quite simply, Mr. Capotorti includes national in ethnic, while the Council of Europe includes ethnic in national. I do not say that one is right or that the other is wrong; but all these examples amply demonstrate the importance of avoiding any possible source of ambiguity by eliminating the use of expressions on whose meanings there may not be unanimous agreement.

102. Therefore, it would be appropriate to delete the reference to "national minorities" and to define the rights of ethnic, religious or linguistic minorities only, in accordance with the terms of article 27 of the Covenant.

B Judicial opinions

1 The Permanent Court of International Justice

(...)
109. From this decision by the Permanent Court of International Justice some elements may therefore be drawn for incorporation in a definition of minorities:

a Distinct groups;
b Real minorities;
c Race, religion or language different from those of the majority;
d Sentiment of solidarity;
e Desire to preserve its distinctive characteristics;
f Peaceful co-existence and equality in law and in fact with the majority.

2 The International Court of Justice

110. In the nearly 40 years of its existence, the International Court of Justice has not been called upon to consider the question of concern to use here.

3 The European Court of Human Rights

111. In general, the same is true with regard to the European Court of Human Rights. It must be understood that the Convention for the Protection of Human Rights and Fundamental Freedoms, signed at Rome on 4 November 1950, contains no provision concerning the rights of minorities. Therefore, in 1965, within the framework of a debate in the Belgian State, the Minister for Foreign Affairs, Mr. Spaak, stated[13]:

> "It is essential for the Court to make, as the Convention instructs it to do, a clear distinction between the defence of individual rights and the defence of minorities which is excluded from its competence".

---

13 Minority schools in Albania, Advisory Opinion of July 31st 1930, Publications of the Permanent Court of International Justice, series A/B, no. 64.

(...)

113. Therefore, the decisions of the European Court of Human Rights do not shed any light on the problem.

4 Indian Courts

115. The courts in India have, for their part, acquired great experience in the field of the rights of minorities, particularly religious or linguistic minorities. The pertinent paragraphs of article 29 and 30 of the Indian Constitution of 1949 as follows:

29 *Protection of interests of minorities*

1   Any section of the citizens residing in the territory of India or any part there of having a distinct language, script or culture of its own shall have the right to conserve the same.
2   No citizen shall be denied admission into any educational institution maintained by the State or receiving aid out of State funds on grounds only of religion, race, caste, language or any of them.

30 *Right of minorities to establish and administer educational institutions*

1   All minorities, whether based on religion or language, shall have the right to establish and administer educational institutions of their choice.
(...)
2   The State shall not, in granting aid to educational institutions, discriminate against any educational institution on the ground that it is under the management of a minority, whether based on religion or language,
(...)

117. In Kerala Education Bill (1957),[14] the Supreme Court dwelled specifically on the question: "What is a minority?" (p. 976) It considered it self-evident that a minority should be a group numerically less than 50 per cent of the total population but, it asked, of what population: of India as a whole, of the State concerned, or of one region only? In the event, the Bill under attack related to the entire State of Kerala, and the Supreme Court appeared to consider with sympathy the proposition that it was therefore necessary to think of the Christian, Muslim and Anglo-Indian groups in terms of the entire population of the State. Nevertheless, the Court ended its lengthy of the question by stating (p. 977):

> "... strictly speaking (...) we need not enquire as to what a minority community means or how it is to be ascertained".

(...)

---

14 1958, A. SC. 956.

120. In Patroni vs. Kasavan,[15] the issue was the power of appointment of the Superior of a Jesuit College. All the judges on the High Court of Kerala recognized that such a right belonged to the religious minority under article 30 of the Constitution and prohibited governmental intervention. With regard to the subject of concern to us, the Court made the following statement:

> "The word 'minority' is not defined in the Constitution; and in the absence of any special definition we must hold that any community, religious or linguistic, which is numerically less than 50 per cent of the population of the State is entitled to the fundamental right guaranteed by the article.
> The Christians, at the 1961 census, amounted only to 21.26 per cent of the population of the State. The Roman Catholics with whom we are concerned form a section of that community".

(...)

124. What is shown by this brief survey of Indian constitutional jurisprudence? Two main criteria emerge:

a The concept of minority should be applied in relation to the territory of the State whose legislation is in question;
b The concept of minority implies a group numerically less than half the total of the population of the State concerned;

5 Canadian courts

125. Canadian legislation also refers to minorities but without providing a guide that is genuinely useful to the courts.
(...)
130. In Mather v. Town of Portland,[16] the Catholics of New Brunswick complained about the method of distribution of tax revenues. In 1873, the Court of Appeals spoke of "large majority" (p. 350) and, the following year, the Privy Council referred to a "great majority" (p. 367).

131. Twenty years later, the Privy Council studied the school situation in Manitoba in Brophy v. Attorney-General of Manitoba.[17] It noted that, at one time Catholics and Protestants had been equal in number; then it added, referring to 1871:

> "But the future was uncertain. Either Roman Catholics or Protestants might become the preponderating power in the Legislature, and it might under such conditions be impossible for the minority to prevent the creation at

---

15 1965, A. Ker. 75.
16 1986 Wheeler's Confederation Law of Canada, 338.
17 1895 A.C. 202.

the public cost of schools, which, though acceptable to the majority, could only be taken advantage of by the minority on the terms of sacrificing their cherished convictions".

133. Lastly, the Privy Council handed down a decision in 1928 in the case of Hirsch v. Protestant Board of School Commissioners of Montreal.[18] The case concerned a referral by the Government of Quebec concerning the place of Jews in the Protestant system of education. On the subject of dissenting schools outside Montreal and Quebec, the Privy Council pointed out that they could be set up at the request of "any number of inhabitants professing a religious faith different from that of the majority". Here, too, would it not be possible to draw the same conclusion as in the Brophy case?

134. Canadian judicial decisions with regard to minorities do not make it possible to go further; however, they do not contradict the proposition that a minority is a group numerically less than half the total of the population of the political entity concerned.

C Quasi-judicial opinions

HUMAN RIGHTS COMMITTEE 135. The United Nations Human Rights Committee does not hand down judgements strictly speaking. As modestly called upon to do in article 5, paragraph 4, of the Optional Protocol to the International Covenant on Civil and Political Rights, the Committee puts forward "views". While the subtle difference in meaning may be important elsewhere, such is not the case in this context.

(...)

D. Doctrinal opinions 141. Let us now proceed from court decisions to doctrine. I shall concentrate on six authors who, over a period of about 40 years, have tried to resolve this problem of the definition of minority.

(...)

147. In 1973, Mr. Sampat-Mehta published in Ottawa an important dissertation entitled, Minority Rights and Obligations.[19] He raised directly the question: "What constitutes a minority group?" Unfortunately, he provided no direct reply to his own question. It is nevertheless interesting to read the following observation: "Since they (the minorities) are numerically less in numbers they must generally abide by the majority decisions in the State". I gather from this that the author would support a definition in which a number less than 50 per cent of the population constitutes one of the criteria of differentiation.

148. A new effort was made in 1974 during the Seminar on the promotion and protection of the human rights of national, ethnic and other minorities, held at

---

18 1928 A.C. 200.
19 R. Sampat-Mehta, *Minority Rights and Obligations* (Herpell's Press 1973).

Ohrid, Yugoslavia. One of the participants proposed the following definition of the "term" minority[20]:

> "A group of citizens, sufficient in number to pursue the aims of the group, but numerically smaller than the rest of the people, linked together by historical, ethnic, cultural, and religious or linguistic bonds and wishing to preserve such bonds, which are different from those of the rest of the people".

(...)

E. Observations by Governments 156. Our task would of course be made much easier by the acceptance of the argument put forward by the French Government on 16 September 1976, when the Permanent Representative of France wrote to the Director of the Division of Human Rights to the effect that the French people recognized no distinction based on ethnic characteristics and thus ruled out any concept of minority.

157. Referring to the study assigned to Mr. Capotorti, he said that the French Government was compelled, under the terms of the Constitution of the French Republic, to oppose the very principle of such a study.

158. While the domestic situation in France may enable the Government to adopt such a detached attitude with regard to the question of minorities – although recent developments would seem to cast some doubt on the official position – it is nevertheless true that the international community has recognized the existence of the problem of minorities and has for some years been seeking the most effective means of affording them protection. We cannot, therefore, turn our backs on the issue or claim complete ignorance of it. Let us continue on our course.

(...)

IV CONCLUSION: A DEFINITION OF MINORITY

169. This brings us to the end of our long journey. We must now assess the results of our research – on the debit side, the elements discarded, and on the credit side those retained. The definition of minority should then become quite clear of itself.

170. On the debit side, our definition will not take account of the following factors:

National minorities;
Indigenous populations;
Resident aliens;
Groups in preference to individuals;

20 See ST/TAO/HR/49, para. 36.

Minimum number of members;
Dominant minorities;
Oppressed majorities;

Relationship with geographical area.

171. On the credit side, the following elements should be included:

Distinguishable groups;
Ethnic, religious or linguistic characteristics;
Number less than half the population of the State;
Non-dominant situation;
Citizenship;
Solidarity;
Collective will to survive;
De jure and de facto equality with the majority.

(...)

181. However, after further reflection, I have come to the conclusion that this definition could be tightened and would benefit from a more logical ordering of its various elements. Consequently, I propose the following definition of minority:

> "A group of citizens of a State, constituting a numerical minority and in a non-dominant position in that State, endowed with ethnic, religious or linguistic characteristics which differ from those of the majority of the population, having a sense of solidarity with one another, motivated, if only implicitly, by a collective will to survive and whose aim is to achieve equality with the majority in fact and in law".

A.3. UN HUMAN RIGHTS COMMITTEE (HRC), CCPR General Comment No. 23: Article 27 (Rights of Minorities) *(CCPR/C/21/Rev.1/Add.5), 8 April 1994.*

(...)

5.1. The terms used in article 27 indicate that the persons designed to be protected are those who belong to a group and who share in common a culture, a religion and/or a language. Those terms also indicate that the individuals designed to be protected need not be citizens of the State party. In this regard, the obligations deriving from article 2.1 are also relevant, since a State party is required under that article to ensure that the rights protected under the Covenant are available to all individuals within its territory and subject to its jurisdiction, except rights which are expressly made to apply to citizens, for example, political rights under article 25. A State party may not, therefore, restrict the rights under article 27 to its citizens alone.

A.4. OFFICE OF THE HIGH COMMISSIONER FOR HUMAN RIGHTS *(OHCHR)*, **Minority Rights: International Standards and Guidance for Implementation *(HR/PUB/10/3), 2010.*** *

I Definitions

A WHO ARE MINORITIES UNDER INTERNATIONAL LAW?

Adopted by consensus in 1992, the United Nations Minorities Declaration in its article 1 refers to minorities as based on national or ethnic, cultural, religious and linguistic identity, and provides that States should protect their existence. There is no internationally agreed definition as to which groups constitute minorities. It is often stressed that the existence of a minority is a question of fact and that any definition must include both objective factors (such as the existence of a shared ethnicity, language or religion) and subjective factors (including that individuals must identify themselves as members of a minority).

The difficulty in arriving at a widely acceptable definition lies in the variety of situations in which minorities live. Some live together in well-defined areas, separated from the dominant part of the population. Others are scattered throughout the country. Some minorities have a strong sense of collective identity and recorded history; others retain only a fragmented notion of their common heritage.

The term minority as used in the United Nations human rights system usually refers to national or ethnic, religious and linguistic minorities, pursuant to the United Nations Minorities Declaration. All States have one or more minority groups within their national territories, characterized by their own national, ethnic, linguistic or religious identity, which differs from that of the majority population.

According to a definition offered in 1977 by Francesco Capotorti, Special Rapporteur of the United Nations Sub-Commission on Prevention of Discrimination and Protection of Minorities, a minority is:

> A group numerically inferior to the rest of the population of a State, in a non-dominant position, whose members – being nationals of the State – possess ethnic, religious or linguistic characteristics differing from those of the rest of the population and show, if only implicitly, a sense of solidarity, directed towards preserving their culture, traditions, religion or language.[21]

While the nationality criterion included in the above definition has often been challenged, the requirement to be in a non-dominant position remains important.

---

* From Minority Rights: International Standards and Guidance for Implementation, by UN Office of the High Commissioner for Human Rights (OHCHR), ©(2010) United Nations. Reprinted with the permission of the United Nations.
21 E/CN.4/Sub.2/384/Rev.1, para. 568.

In most instances a minority group will be a numerical minority, but in others a numerical majority may also find itself in a minority-like or non-dominant position, such as Blacks under the apartheid regime in South 1 E/CN.4/Sub.2/384/ Rev.1, para. 568.3 Africa. In some situations, a group which constitutes a majority in a State as a whole may be in a non-dominant position within a particular region of the State in question.

In addition, it has been argued that the use of subjective criteria, such as the will on the part of the members of the groups in question to preserve their own characteristics and the wish of the individuals concerned to be considered part of that group, combined with certain specific objective requirements, such as those listed in the Capotorti definition, should be taken into account. It is now commonly accepted that recognition of minority status is not solely for the State to decide but should be based on both objective and subjective criteria.

The question often arises as to whether, for example, persons with disabilities, persons belonging to certain political groups or persons with a particular sexual orientation or identity (lesbian, gay, bisexual, transgender or intersexual persons) constitute minorities. While the United Nations Minorities Declaration is devoted to national, ethnic, religious and linguistic minorities, it is also important to combat multiple discrimination and to address situations where a person belonging to a national or ethnic, religious and linguistic minority is also discriminated against on other grounds such as gender, disability or sexual orientation. Similarly, it is important to keep in mind that, in many countries, minorities are often found to be among the most marginalized groups in society and severely affected by, for example, pandemic diseases, such as HIV/AIDS, and in general have limited access to health services.

B ARE INDIGENOUS PEOPLES CONSIDERED TO BE MINORITIES?

Similarly, to minorities, there is no universally accepted international definition of indigenous peoples. Guidance in this regard can be obtained, for instance, from the work of the Working Group on Indigenous Populations, the provisions of Convention No. 169 of the International Labour Organization (ILO) and the contents of the United Nations Declaration on the Rights of Indigenous Peoples. Various sources cite the following characteristics, either alone or in combination: indigenous peoples are descendants of the peoples who inhabited the land or territory prior to colonization or the establishment of State borders; they possess distinct social, economic and political systems, languages, cultures and beliefs, and are determined to maintain and develop this distinct identity; they exhibit strong attachment to their ancestral lands and the natural resources contained therein; and/or they belong to the non-dominant groups of a society and identify themselves as indigenous peoples.

While indigenous peoples can claim minority rights under international law, there are United Nations mandates and mechanisms dedicated specifically to protecting their rights. In its work, the United Nations has applied the principle of self-identification with regard to indigenous peoples and minorities. In practical terms, a number of connections and commonalities exist between indigenous peoples and national, ethnic, linguistic and religious minorities. Both groups are usually in a non-dominant position in the society in which they live and their cultures, languages or religious beliefs may be different from the majority or the dominant groups.

Both indigenous peoples and minorities commonly wish to retain and promote their identity. Situations can be found on the ground where an indigenous group could find itself in a minority-like situation and, equally, some minorities have strong and long-standing attachments to their lands and territories as do indigenous peoples. Minorities, however, do not necessarily have the long ancestral, traditional and spiritual attachment and connections to their lands and territories that are usually associated with self-identification as indigenous peoples.

In terms of rights, minorities have traditionally highlighted their rights to have their existence as a group protected, their identity recognized and their effective participation in public life and respect for their cultural, religious and linguistic pluralism safeguarded. Indigenous peoples, while also highlighting such rights, have also traditionally advocated recognition of their rights over land and resources, self-determination and being part of decision-making in matters that affect them. The United Nations Declaration on the Rights of Indigenous Peoples requires States to consult and cooperate with indigenous peoples to obtain their free, prior and informed consent before undertaking development activities that might have an impact on them, whereas the United Nations Minorities Declaration contains a more general right to participate in decision-making and requires that the legitimate interests of persons belonging to minorities should be taken into account in national planning and programming.

This publication does not address the specificities of indigenous peoples, as its main focus is on non-indigenous national, ethnic, linguistic and religious minorities.

C DO MINORITY RIGHTS APPLY TO NON-CITIZENS?

Under the provisions of human rights instruments, States have an obligation to protect the rights of all persons subject to or under their jurisdictions. Express exceptions to this principle relate, inter alia, to political rights.

The Commentary on the United Nations Minorities Declaration by the Working Group on Minorities is important as it clarifies the interpretation of the substantive provisions of the document. Regarding citizenship for instance, it considers that "while citizenship as such should not be a distinguishing criterion that excludes some persons or groups from enjoying minority rights under the Declaration, other factors can be relevant in distinguishing between the rights that can be demanded by different minorities".

For example, "those who have been established for a long time on the territory may have stronger rights than those who have recently arrived." It suggests that "the best approach appears to be to avoid making an absolute distinction between 'new' and 'old' minorities by excluding the former and including the latter, but to recognize that in the application of the Declaration the 'old' minorities have stronger entitlements than the 'new' ".[22]

In practice, under international law, certain minority rights have been made applicable to recently arrived migrants who share an ethnic, religious or linguistic identity. Their treatment is to be rooted in the customary international law principle of non-discrimination, which is fundamental in international law and is reflected in all human rights instruments and documents. Indeed, the right not to be discriminated against is guaranteed under several instruments of direct relevance to minorities. These include the International Convention on the Protection of the Rights of All Migrant Workers and Members of Their Families, the Convention relating to the Status of Stateless Persons, the Convention relating to the Status of Refugees, and the Declaration on the Human Rights of Individuals Who are not Nationals of the Country in which They Live.

D WHAT IS THE RELATIONSHIP BETWEEN MINORITIES, NON-CITIZENS AND STATELESS PERSONS?

A particular problem relating to minorities and citizenship is that all too often members of certain groups are denied or deprived of their citizenship because of their national or ethnic, religious and linguistic characteristics. This practice is contrary to international law, particularly in regard to article 9 of the 1961 Convention on the Reduction of Statelessness, which states that "a Contracting State may not deprive any person or group of persons of their nationality on racial, ethnic, religious or political grounds." It is thus important to note that discrimination against a person on one of the aforementioned grounds resulting in the arbitrary deprivation of nationality may contribute to meeting some of the requirements in the determination of refugee status.

Most of the world's estimated 15 million stateless persons also belong to ethnic, religious or linguistic minorities. Discrimination against minorities has frequently led to their exclusion from citizenship. Such exclusion is often experienced in newly independent States that define citizenship in a manner that excludes persons belonging to certain minority groups who are considered as "outsiders" despite long-standing ties to the territory of the new State. Just as discrimination against minorities may be a cause of statelessness, the very fact that members of a group are stateless can undermine their exercise of a broad range of human rights. Although in principle most human rights are guaranteed to everyone under the jurisdiction of the State, in practice non-citizens, including stateless persons, face obstacles in exercising these rights. These obstacles may be greater still if the stateless person also belongs to a minority group. Statelessness can be addressed by applying the norms set out in the major universal and regional human rights instruments, including those pertaining to birth registration, the right to acquire a nationality, non-discrimination in the acquisition, change and

---

22 E/CN.4/Sub.2/AC.5/2005/2, paras. 10–11.

retention of nationality by men and women, and the conferral of nationality on children. The Convention on the Reduction of Statelessness provides detailed guidance in this respect.

A.5. FORUM ON MINORITY ISSUES, Recommendations of the Forum on Minority Issues at its Sixth Session: Guaranteeing the Rights of Religious Minorities *(A/HRC/25/66), 26 and 27 November 2013.*

(…)

8   The term "religious minorities" as used in the present document therefore encompasses a broad range of religious or belief communities, traditional and non-traditional, whether recognized by the State or not, including more recently established faith or belief groups, and large and small communities, that seek protection of their rights under minority rights standards. Non-believers, atheists or agnostics may also face challenges and discrimination and require protection of their rights. Attention should likewise be given to the situation of religious minorities where they form the minority in a particular region or locality, but not in the country as a whole.

A.6. UN OFFICE OF THE HIGH COMMISSIONER FOR HUMAN RIGHTS (OHCHR), The inclusion of religious minorities in consultative and decision-making bodies, *2014.*

Who are religious minorities?

The term "religious minorities" encompasses a broad range of religious communities, traditional and non-traditional, recognized by the State or not, large and small, which seek protection of their rights under minority rights standards. The diversity that exists within minority religious groups must be recognized. Religious minorities may also be national, ethnic or linguistic minorities.

A.7. FERNAND DE VARENNES *(Special Rapporteur on Minority Issues)*, Report of the Special Rapporteur on Minority Issues *(A/74/160), 15 July 2019.*

IV Conclusions and recommendations

(…)
59. The Special Rapporteur invites United Nations entities to take note of the following working definition on the concept of a minority under article 27 of the International Covenant on Civil and Political Rights and of the Human Rights Committee's jurisprudence and comment on who is a member of a minority in

order to adopt and apply more consistently a common approach and understanding and therefore more effectively ensure the full and effective realization of the rights of persons belonging to minorities:

> An ethnic, religious or linguistic minority is any group of persons which constitutes less than half of the population in the entire territory of a State whose members share common characteristics of culture, religion or language, or a combination of any of these. A person can freely belong to an ethnic, religious or linguistic minority without any requirement of citizenship, residence, official recognition or any other status.

A.8. FERNAND DE VARENNES *(Special rapporteur on minority issues)*, Report of the Special Rapporteur on Minority Issues, Effective Promotion of the Declaration on the Rights of Persons Belonging to National or Ethnic, Religious and Linguistic Minorities *(A/75/211), 21 July 2020.*

3 *Religious or belief minorities*

(...)

(a) The category of "religious minority" includes non-religious or non-theistic and other beliefs. This category should be understood broadly to include unrecognized and non-traditional religions or beliefs, including animists, atheists, agnostics, humanists, "new religions", etc.;
(b) As in the case of the category of linguistic minorities, a religion can be a minority religion even if it is official or recognized;
(c) Refusal by authorities to acknowledge the existence of a particular religion or belief, or an official categorization of a religion or belief as a sect, a prohibited cult, an aberration or even a threat, and therefore not a "real religion or belief", is not determinative. Whether a religious or belief minority exists is a factual, objective matter of whether there are in a State a minority of individuals who freely ascribe to a particular religion or belief;
(d) Religious or belief minorities, such as atheists, Scientologists, Baha'is, Ahmadis, Mormons, agnostics and others, however they are described or recognized in a State, are entitled to the full protection of their human rights in international law, including as persons who belong to a religious or belief minority and against acts of violence or persecution;
(e) Large religious groupings can be made up of different sets of beliefs or traditions. Christianity, Hinduism, Islam and Judaism include a number of religious or belief divisions and therefore potentially minorities. Catholics are a religious or belief minority in the United Kingdom of Great Britain and Northern Ireland, as are Shi'a in Yemen. Shaktism in India and Haredi Judaism are also minority religions or beliefs;

(f) Followers of non-hierarchical or non-formalized religions or beliefs, including shamanism and new religions, can also constitute a religious or belief minority. The presence of a religious or belief minority, such as the Falun Gong in China, of brujería followers in the United States of America and Latin American countries, or Rastafarians in Ethiopia, or of böö mörgöl shamanism in Mongolia, all objectively constitute religious or beliefs minorities, regardless of their traditional link or degree of presence in a State.

B Right to profess and practise religion or belief

B.1. FRANCESCO CAPOTORTI (Special Rapporteur of the Sub-Commission on Prevention of Discrimination and Protection of Minorities), **Study on the Rights of Persons Belonging to Ethnic, Religious and Linguistic Minorities *(ST/HR(05)/ H852/no.5), 1979.* **

IV Application of the principles set forth in Article 27 of the International Covenant on Civil and Political Rights

(...)

B. THE RIGHT OF PERSONS BELONGING TO RELIGIOUS MINORITIES TO PROFESS AND PRACTISE THEIR OWN RELIGION

386. The question of the rights of persons belonging to religious minorities can be looked at, first, from the standpoint of non-discrimination – which involves consideration of the problems presented by the enjoyment and exercise of freedom of thought, conscience and religion, a freedom which should, of course, be recognized for all individuals without discrimination of any kind – and also from the point of view of special measures of protection. By the very nature of religions and religious communities, the exercise of freedom of religion has many implications not only at the individual level but also at the collective level, as witness the extremely complex nature of the relations between States and the various religions. From the standpoint of special measures of protection, it would be more appropriate to concentrate on measures by which the State can promote the material equality of religious communities. Through a policy of subsidies, for instance, the State can give assistance to the activities of minority communities. This aspect of the question tends to be overlooked, and more attention is generally given to the multiple implications of freedom of thought, conscience and religion at the collective level. In the opinion of the Special Rapporteur, both the

---

* From *Study on the Rights of Persons Belonging to Ethnic, Religious and Linguistic Minorities*, by Francesco Capotorti, © (1979) United Nations. Reprinted with the permission of the United Nations.

subject itself and the practical attitude of Governments, as revealed in the available information, are such that the two aspects mentioned above cannot be clearly separated, even though from the logical point of view they appear distinct. In the paragraphs that follow, problems concerning freedom of thought, conscience and religion and problems relating to special measures in favour of members of religious minorities, where such measures are conceivable or have been adopted, will be examined together.[23]

387. The following topics will be covered: (i) the question of the status granted to a religious minority: the analysis of this question will be concerned with examining the practice of formal recognition followed in some countries, as well as the problem of financing by the State of the activities of religious communities, and with determining whether religious laws and customs in certain field are recognized as valid within the State; (ii) the free participation by members of the religious minority in the worship and rites of their religion; (iii) the right of members of religious communities not to be compelled to participate in the activities of other religions; (iv) the right of persons belonging to religious minorities to administer the affairs of their communities; (v) the question of the establishment and maintenance of religious institutions and denominational schools and the granting of financial assistance to such institutions and schools.

1 *Juridical status of a religion professed by a minority*

(a) *The question of recognition*

388. From the point of view of the juridical relationship between the State and minority religions, the countries surveyed fall into two broad categories: those in which a religious community must be formally recognized in order to have a juridical status, and those in which no religion is accorded a juridical status, religion being considered a purely private affair.

389. It cannot be assumed that the mere fact of separation of State and religion ensures non-discrimination and that the existence of a State religion or the need for formal recognition necessarily gives rise to discrimination. In this connexion the observations made by Mr. Arcot Krishnaswami, Special Rapporteur of the Sub-Commission for the question of religious rights and practices, are worth recalling:

> There is no doubt that historically the principle of separation of State and religion emerged as a reaction against the privileged position of the

---

23 As indicated in paras. 225–227, a comprehensive study on the question of discrimination in the matter of religious rights and practices was prepared by Mr. Arcot Krishnaswami, Special Rapporteur of the Sub-Commission. Furthermore, the question of the elimination of all forms of religious intolerance is under active consideration by various organs of the United Nations. At the request of the General Assembly, the Commission on Human Rights is elaborating a draft declaration on the subject. In the light of these developments and in order to avoid unnecessary duplication, this chapter will be limited in scope.

Established Church or the State religion, and that its purpose was to assure a large measure of equality to the members of various religions. Within the framework of this principle of separation, however, de facto pre-eminence is sometimes achieved by a particular religion and the law of the country – although equally applicable to everyone –reflects in certain important matters the concepts of the predominant group. Thus rules regulating marriage and its dissolution are often taken over from the religious law of the predominant group. Similarly, official holidays and days of rest in many countries correspond to a large extent to the religious holidays and days of rest of the predominant group.

The State, even when applying the principle of separation, may accord a special status to religious organizations, distinct from that accorded to other kinds of associations. But such a status may be granted only on condition that the religious group satisfies certain specified conditions – a possibility for some but not for others.

Even if a State maintains strict neutrality as between various faiths, inequality of treatment is not necessarily excluded. The demands of various religions are different, and a law prohibiting certain acts, or enjoining the performance of others, may prevent one religious group from performing an essential rite or from following a basic observance, but be of no importance at all to another group.[24]

(...)

(b) *Financing by the State of the activities of religious communities*

393. Financing by the State of religious activities is one of the factors which may place members of minority religions at a disadvantage if the organizations of the religious majority receive subsidies from the State while the others do not, or when individuals are compelled, through taxation, to support a religion to which they do not belong. In this connexion, mention should be made of a provision contained in the draft declaration on the elimination of all forms of religious intolerance prepared by the Sub-Commission on Prevention of Discrimination and Protection of Minorities'[25] according to which "No State shall discriminate in the granting of subsidies, in taxation or in exemptions From taxation, between different religions or beliefs or their adherents".

(c) *Validity of the laws and customs of the religion professed by a minority in the field of private law and in some other matters*

---

24 *Study of Discrimination in the Matter of Religious Rights and Practices* (United Nations Publication, Sales No. 60, XIV.2) 41–48.
25 See A/8330, annex I.

Celebration of marriage   398. The Sub-Commission recommended in the draft declaration on the elimination of all forms of religious intolerance that "everyone shall have the right to have marriage rites performed in accordance with the prescriptions of his religion or belief and no one shall be compelled to undergo a religious marriage ceremony not in conformity with his convictions". Once the freedom to celebrate a religious marriage is recognized, it remains to be ascertained whether the State recognizes such a marriage as producing effects at civil law. In some countries it does so; and wherever this possibility is open, the marriage ceremonies of minority religions should have the same effects as those of the majority religion.

399. In a number of the countries surveyed, the available information indicates that, in varying ways, marriages performed according to the rites of a minority religion are regarded as legally valid. Thus, in Sweden, the marriage code provides that a marriage may be concluded in a civil or religious ceremony and that a religious marriage may be solemnized "according to the usages of any religious society if so authorised by the Crown and if one or both of the prospective spouses is a member of that society. Marriages solemnized according to the usages of religious societies other than the Established Swedish Church shall be solemnized by the person authorized to do so."

400. Under the terms of the Marriage Act of Finland, marriage may be concluded in a church ceremony. But after stating that a church ceremony can take place according to the rites of any religious community other than the Evangelical Lutheran Church or the Orthodox Church, to which the Government has granted the right to celebrate marriages, the law adds, however, that, if either of the partners or both belong to a non-recognized religious community, marriage must be concluded in a civil ceremony. The law further declares that the same rule applies if one of the partners belongs to a Christian religious community and the other to a non-Christian community, or if both belong to a non-Christian religious community. The Governments of Denmark and Norway report that the fact that a religious community is recognized has the consequence that ministers of this religion have the right to perform acts such as weddings with civil validity. No such right is granted to non-recognized religious communities. In Italy, under a law adopted in 1929, a person who wishes his marriage to be performed by a minister of a religion other than the Catholic religion must apply to the registrar who would be competent to perform the marriage. Having ascertained that there is no obstacle to the marriage under civil law, the registrar issues a written authorization stating the name of the minister who is to perform the marriage and the date of the measure which sanctioned his appointment. The Government of Canada reports that:

> In general, religious laws and customs do not receive any recognition except insofar as they are embodied in a statute. In Ontario, recognition is given to religious marriages by conferring civil authority upon clergymen of any denomination which has been in existence for a continuous period. This allows the performance of legally valid marriages by the religions officials

of many minority religions. In addition, where the religion does not have a clergy as such, an exemption may be made in their favour so as to allow marriages to be solemnized according to their customs, This now exists in favour of the Society of Friends (Quakers), ...

401. In India, Muslim, Christian and Parsee marriage customs are protected by special laws. In Trinidad and Tobago legally valid marriages may be performed according to Hindu and Moslem rights. Sudanese law also provides that a legally valid marriage may be performed according to the customs of any religious group.[26] There are, however, instances where the validity of the marriages performed according to the rites of religious minorities is subject to some restrictions. In the Philippines, for example, the Civil Code stipulates that marriages between members of the Moslem minority may be performed according to their own rites only if they live in the non-Christian provinces.

Other matters of personal status 402. In several countries the validity of the laws and customs of the religion professed by a minority is recognized in other matters of personal status. In India, for example, family life continues to be governed in many instances by the laws of the various religious communities. Although local governments are empowered to legislate in the field of private law, efforts undertaken to modify or eliminate certain customs which are regarded by the central Government as obsolete in a modern State are reported to have met limited success.

403. In Malaysia, members of all religious minorities are granted the right to follow their religious laws and customs in all matters of personal status, whereas in some countries only certain specified minorities have been granted that right. Thus, in Ethiopia a law was adopted in 1942 with a view to allowing Moslems of that country to apply the law of their religion in civil and religious matters which are governed by the Koran. The law allows members of the Moslem minority to set up their own courts in matters affecting their family life. No such right appears to have been granted to other religious minorities. In Greece, members of the Moslem community are governed by the Koran in all matters relating to family law. Israel has recognized the right of the Druzes to jurisdiction in matters of personal status. Christian religious courts have also sole jurisdiction in matters of marriage, divorce, maintenance and the executing of wills. In Singapore and in Thailand, religious courts are empowered to hear cases relating to the personal status of the members of the Moslem religious group. The Government of Iraq observes that under the constitution special religious courts have been set up for the Christian and Jewish communities.

404. The Egyptian Government reports that, although the State recognizes the identity of religious faiths and communities, the religious courts have been abolished and only the national courts are competent to rule on matters of personal

---

26 As in Bangladesh, Malaysia, Pakistan, Singapore and Thailand.

status. However, since the unification of the courts has not been accompanied by unification of the legislation, the law provides that decisions taken with regard to personal status among non-Moslem Egyptians of the same faith should nevertheless be in accordance with their religious law. There are, however, matters in which the laws of religious minorities are not taken into account in Egypt. Questions of succession in particular are subject, for all Egyptians of different religions, to an Act of 1943 which unified the provisions on the devolution of estates and made Moslem law applicable in all cases of succession.

Observance of religious holidays 405. Every faith attaches great importance to the observance of its religious holidays. The question that arises is whether the State takes into account the faith of persons belonging to religious minorities in this respect and allows them to observe their religious holidays as official holidays. It may be mentioned that the draft declaration on the elimination of all forms of religious intolerance proposed by the Sub-Commission contains a provision stating that "due account shall be taken of the prescriptions of each religion or belief relating to days of rest and all discrimination in this regard between persons of different religions or beliefs shall be prohibited". Measures of that nature have been taken in some countries.

406. It has been reported that in Egypt the State recognizes the religious festivals of Christian minorities, permits employers to suspend work in order to celebrate their holidays and allows Christian employees of government institutions paid leave on religious feast days. In Malaysia, the schedule to the Holiday Ordinance lists public holidays, which include the religious celebrations of the main ethnic and religious groups of the country. In Poland, where the principle of separation of Church and State is applied, the law recognizes the most important Christian feasts as holidays. With regard to the members of religious groups which celebrate other religious holidays, a principle of tolerance is practised whereby employees and employers are authorized to make mutually satisfactory arrangements. In such cases, however, employees must subsequently make up for the days of leave granted to them. In Sri Lanka, the religious festivals of the four major religions professed in the country are celebrated as national holidays. In Israel the non-Jews have the right to observe their own weekly religious holidays and festivals as rest days. The Government of Iraq reports that the Official Holiday Act of 1972 provides that "religious festivals are additional public holidays for the following communities: Christian, Jewish, Samaean and Yazidi". Eighteen holidays are officially observed in Pakistan, of which four are national, eight Moslem, four Hindu and two Christian. In addition, provision is made for 16 "optional holidays", of which two are national, four Moslem, three Hindu, two Christian, two Parsee and three Sikh.

407. The observance as days of rest of the holidays of all the religious groups may give rise to some difficulties. In this connexion the Government of Austria reports that the Holiday Rest Act of 1957 provides that to the extent justifiable in a modern State with a modern economic system, no work is to be done on the days prescribed as holidays or days of rest by the religious communities

most widespread in the country. To the extent that exceptions to the general rule of rest on Sundays and holidays are permissible, the law also provides that persons working on those days must be granted the free time necessary to attend religious services. Nevertheless, it would be out of the question to take account of all the holidays or days of rest of all the religious communities which now exist in the country without the most serious consequences for the general public. However, as regards attendance at schools, pupils belonging to religious minorities are exempted from classes in order to observe the holidays of their religions.

Conscientious objection to military service 408. In countries where the principle of conscientious objection is recognized, members of religious minorities would find themselves at a disadvantage if their religion was excluded from the application of such principle. The available information tends to indicate that all authorized religions are taken into account when conscientious objection is a right recognized in legislation.

Taking of an oath 409. In some circumstances, in particular when testifying before courts, individuals are required in many countries to take an oath and that oath is usually based on the religion professed by the majority of the population. It can be affirmed that the right of persons belonging to religious minorities is violated if they are compelled under the law to take an oath in disregard of the prescriptions of their faith. That situation was taken into account by the Sub-Commission when it recommended in the draft declaration on the elimination of all forms of religious intolerance that "no one shall be compelled to take an oath of a religious nature contrary to his convictions".

410. In the countries for which information is available, the rule is that no one should be compelled to take an oath contrary to the prescriptions of his religion, at least when such religion is legally recognized.

2 Freedom of persons belonging to religious minorities to participate in the worship and rites of their religion

411. The right of everyone, including persons belonging to minority groups, to freedom of thought and conscience and to participate in the worship and rites of his religion is now a principle universally recognized. It is embodied in article 18 of the Universal Declaration of Human Rights and in article 18 of the International Covenant on Civil and Political Rights.

412. The draft articles for an international convention on the elimination of all forms of religious intolerance prepared by the Commission on Human Rights[27] contain the following provisions:

---

27 See A/8330, annex III.

Article III

1. States Parties undertake to ensure to everyone within their jurisdiction the right to freedom of thought, conscience, religion or belief. This right shall include:

    (a) Freedom to adhere or not to adhere to any religion or belief and to change his religion or belief in accordance with the dictates of his conscience without being subjected either to any of the limitations referred to in article XII or to any coercion likely to impair his freedom of choice or decision in the matter, provided that this subparagraph shall not be interpreted as extending to manifestations of religion or belief;

    (b) Freedom to manifest his religion or belief either alone or in community with others, and in public or in private, without being subjected to any discrimination on the ground of religion or belief;

    (c) Freedom to express opinions on questions concerning a religion or belief.

2. States Parties shall in particular ensure to everyone within their jurisdiction:

    (a) Freedom to worship, to hold assemblies related to religion or belief and to establish and maintain places of worship or assembly for these purposes;

    (b) Freedom to teach, to disseminate and to learn his religion or belief and its sacred languages or traditions, to write, print and publish religious books and texts, and to train personnel intending to devote themselves to its practices or observances;

    (c) Freedom to practise his religion or belief by establishing and maintaining charitable and educational institutions and by expressing in public life the implications of religion or belief;

    (d) Freedom to observe the rituals and the dietary and other practices of his religion or belief and to produce or if necessary, import the objects, foods and other articles and facilities customarily used in its observances and practices;

    (e) Freedom to make pilgrimages and other journeys in connexon with his religion or belief, whether inside or outside country;

    (f) Equal legal protection for the places of worship or assembly the rites, ceremonies and activities, and the places of disposal of the dead associated with his religion or belief;

    (g) Freedom to organize and maintain local, regional, national and international associations in connexion with his religion belief, to participate in their activities, and to communicate with his co- religionists and believers;

    (h) Freedom from compulsion to take an oath of a religious nature

413. In all the countries surveyed, including those in which a religion has been declared the State religion, the constitution or the law proclaims the principle of

freedom of religion and generally guarantees to everyone the freedom to change his religion or belief and in particular the freedom, either alone or in community with others, and both in public and in private, to manifest his religion or belief in worship, teaching and observance. In some countries, this right is also guaranteed on the basis of treaties concluded with other countries.

414. Undoubtedly, there are still cases where this principle has not been fully applied, and the United Nation has undertaken within recent years efforts with a view to ensuring greater respect for the right to freedom of religion. It must be further pointed out that while this right is now universally accepted, it is also generally agreed that it may be subject to some limitations. It may be recalled in this connexion that the above-quoted article 18 of the International Covenant on Civil and Political Rights confirms the admissibility of certain limitations, when it states in paragraph 3 that "freedom to manifest one's religion or beliefs may be subject only to such limitations as are prescribed by law and are necessary to protect public safety order, health or morals or the fundamental rights and freedoms of others".

415. In nearly all the countries studied, limitations of this kind have been introduced. Thus, in Sweden, the law dealing with freedom of conscience and religion specifies that everyone is entitled to practise his religion so long as he does not thereby disturb the peace or cause a public nuisance. With respect to the Philippines, the Government reports that the State does not interfere in religious affairs when they do not contravene the laws of the country. As regards Austria, the constitution provides that "all inhabitants of Austria shall be entitled to the free exercise whether public or private of any creed, religion or belief, whose practices are not inconsistent with public order or public morals". The constitution of Ethiopia stresses that religious rites should not be utilized for political purposes and should not be prejudicial to public order or morality, whereas the constitution of Switzerland stipulates that the exercise of religious freedom is confined "within the limits compatible with law and order". According to the constitution of Egypt, "the State shall protect the freedom of worship provided that law and order and morality are not affected". The constitution of Tonga puts as a condition for the exercise of the right of citizens to practise their religion that they do not commit "evil and licentious acts".

3   *The right of persons belonging to religious minorities not to be compelled to participate in the activities of other religions*

416. A corollary of the freedom of persons belonging to religious minorities to profess and practise their own religion is the right not to be compelled to participate in the activities of other religions. In several of the countries studied,[28] measures have been taken to that effect either by the constitution or by law.

---

28 Bulgaria; Bangladesh; Germany; Federal Republic of Guyana; Hungary; India; Iraq; Italy; Japan; Malaysia; New Zealand; Pakistan; United Kingdom; Ukrainian SSR; United States of America; USSR.

417. The provisions contained in the constitutions of Sweden and Switzerland may be cited as examples of the type of action taken. In Sweden, the law provides that "no one shall be compelled to belong to a religious denomination. Any agreement contrary to this provision shall be null and void." In Switzerland, the constitution stresses that "no one may be forced to belong to any religious association". In connexion with the application of that right, two questions appear to require special attention: the payment of special taxes for the support of a religion, and compulsory religious education in public schools.

(a) *The right of persons belonging to religious minorities not to be compelled to contribute financially to the activities of a religious denomination other than their own*

418. The constitutions of some countries contain provisions according to which no person should be compelled to pay any tax, the proceeds of which are allocated in whole or in part for the support of a religion other than his own.[29] In some other countries, in particular in the countries in which a religion has been declared the State religion, a special tax collected by State authorities is levied upon all citizens, irrespective of their faith, to support a particular church. Measures to remedy the discriminatory situation thus created have been adopted in some of these countries. In Sweden, for example, individuals who are not members of the Swedish Established Church pay a church tax reduced by 70 per cent. The reduced amount for non-members, it has been stated, has to be paid because the Established Church is in charge of the civil registration of the population. The Government of Norway reports that, while the law exempts non-members of the State Church from personal contributions to the Church, a certain portion of the municipal taxes paid covers the expenses of the State Church. Only taxpayers who are registered members of an organized dissenter congregation are exempted from this municipal tax. Otherwise, it is up to the municipal council to decide whether an exemption should be granted.

(...)

4 *The right of persons belonging to religious minorities to administer the affairs of their own religious communities*

420. The available information indicates that the State generally refrains from interference in questions relating to internal discipline in religious communities, except in cases where the practices of a religion may conflict with requirements of public order, good morals or national security. It also usually accords the same kind of freedom as regards the administration of a church's financial affairs, although in some instances the power of religious communities to undertake financial transactions is subject to a number of restrictions. The Government of Sweden has reported that general legislation regarding the finances of

---

29 India, Italy, Malaysia, Switzerland, United States of America.

associations also applies to organizations of a religious character outside the Established Swedish Church and that such legislation does not prevent a religious community from itself appointing its representatives or from making decisions relating to the property and assets of the community. In some countries, the right of members of religious minorities to administer their own affairs is contained in specific provisions of the constitution or the law. In Romania, under the terms of the constitution, religious denominations have their own administration and manage their own property. Every religious denomination is free to draw up its own organizational and operational statutes, to lay down the principles of eligibility to its governing bodies, to determine the functions and powers thereof and to lay down rules for their operation. The leaders of religious denominations, without distinction as to nationality, are elected by the statutory authorities of their denomination and recognized by decrees of the State Council. The constitution of Malaysia provides that every religious group has the right to manage its own religious affairs, to acquire and own property and hold and administer it in accordance with the law. The Government of Iran has reported that religious minorities decide for themselves on the choice of their leaders and on the conditions for appointment to a governing post in their religious communities, and that there is no restriction on the financial management of, or the acquisition and administration of property by, religious communities. In Austria, the right of religious minorities to administer their own affairs is guaranteed by law. Thus under the terms of article 26 of the Basic Law of 1867, every recognized religious society has the right to administer its internal affairs autonomously and retains possession of its institutions, endowments and funds devoted to worship, instruction and welfare, but is, like every society, subject to the general law of the land. In various other countries the right of persons belonging to religious minorities to administer their own affairs is provided by law.

B.2. UN HUMAN RIGHTS COMMITTEE (HRC), CCPR General Comment No. 22: Article 18 (Freedom of Thought, Conscience or Religion) *(CCPR/C/21/Rev.1/Add.4)*, 30 July 1993.

(...)

9   The fact that a religion is recognized as a State religion or that it is established as official or traditional or that its followers comprise the majority of the population, shall not result in any impairment of the enjoyment of any of the rights under the Covenant, including articles 18 and 27, nor in any discrimination against adherents to other religions or non-believers. In particular, certain measures discriminating against the latter, such as measures restricting eligibility for government service to members of the predominant religion or giving economic privileges to them or imposing special restrictions on the practice of other faiths, are not in accordance with the prohibition of discrimination based on religion or belief and the guarantee of equal

protection under article 26. The measures contemplated by article 20, paragraph 2 of the Covenant constitute important safeguards against infringement of the rights of religious minorities and of other religious groups to exercise the rights guaranteed by articles 18 and 27, and against acts of violence or persecution directed towards those groups. The Committee wishes to be informed of measures taken by States parties concerned to protect the practices of all religions or beliefs from infringement and to protect their followers from discrimination. Similarly, information as to respect for the rights of religious minorities under article 27 is necessary for the Committee to assess the extent to which the right to freedom of thought, conscience, religion and belief has been implemented by States parties. States parties concerned should also include in their reports information relating to practices considered by their laws and jurisprudence to be punishable as blasphemous.

10 If a set of beliefs is treated as official ideology in constitutions, statutes, proclamations of ruling parties, etc., or in actual practice, this shall not result in any impairment of the freedoms under article 18 or any other rights recognized under the Covenant nor in any discrimination against persons who do not accept the official ideology or who oppose it.

B.3. UN HUMAN RIGHTS COMMITTEE (HRC), CCPR General Comment No. 23: Article 27 (Rights of Minorities) (CCPR/C/21/Rev.1/Add.5), 8 April 1994.

1 Article 27 of the Covenant provides that, in those States in which ethnic, religious or linguistic minorities exist, persons belonging to these minorities shall not be denied the right, in community with the other members of their group, to enjoy their own culture, to profess and practise their own religion, or to use their own language. The Committee observes that this article establishes and recognizes a right which is conferred on individuals belonging to minority groups and which is distinct from, and additional to, all the other rights which, as individuals in common with everyone else, they are already entitled to enjoy under the Covenant.

2 In some communications submitted to the Committee under the Optional Protocol, the right protected under article 27 has been confused with the right of peoples to self-determination proclaimed in article 1 of the Covenant. Further, in reports submitted by States parties under article 40 of the Covenant, the obligations placed upon States parties under article 27 have sometimes been confused with their duty under article 2.1 to ensure the enjoyment of the rights guaranteed under the Covenant without discrimination and also with equality before the law and equal protection of the law under article 26.

3.1 The Covenant draws a distinction between the right to self-determination and the rights protected under article 27. The former is expressed to be a right belonging to peoples and is dealt with in a separate part

(Part I) of the Covenant. Self-determination is not a right cognizable under the Optional Protocol. Article 27, on the other hand, relates to rights conferred on individuals as such and is included, like the articles relating to other personal rights conferred on individuals, in Part III of the Covenant and is cognizable under the Optional Protocol.[30]

3.2 The enjoyment of the rights to which article 27 relates does not prejudice the sovereignty and territorial integrity of a State party. At the same time, one or other aspect of the rights of individuals protected under that article – for example, to enjoy a particular culture – may consist in a way of life which is closely associated with territory and use of its resources.[31] This may particularly be true of members of indigenous communities constituting a minority.

4   The Covenant also distinguishes the rights protected under article 27 from the guarantees under articles 2.1 and 26. The entitlement, under article 2.1, to enjoy the rights under the Covenant without discrimination applies to all individuals within the territory or under the jurisdiction of the State whether or not those persons belong to a minority. In addition, there is a distinct right provided under article 26 for equality before the law, equal protection of the law, and non-discrimination in respect of rights granted and obligations imposed by the States. It governs the exercise of all rights, whether protected under the Covenant or not, which the State party confers by law on individuals within its territory or under its jurisdiction, irrespective of whether they belong to the minorities specified in article 27 or not.[32] Some States parties who claim that they do not discriminate on grounds of ethnicity, language or religion, wrongly contend, on that basis alone, that they have no minorities.

5.1 The terms used in article 27 indicate that the persons designed to be protected are those who belong to a group and who share in common a culture, a religion and/or a language. Those terms also indicate that the individuals designed to be protected need not be citizens of the State party. In this regard, the obligations deriving from article 2.1 are also relevant, since a State party is required under that article to ensure that

---

30 See Official Records of the General Assembly, Thirty-ninth Session, Supplement No. 40 (A/39/40), annex VI, General Comment No. 12 (21) (article 1), also issued in document CCPR/C/21/Rev.1; ibid., Forty-fifth Session, Supplement No. 40, (A/45/40), vol. II, annex IX, sect. A, Communication No. 167/1984, *Bernard Ominayak, Chief of the Lubicon Lake Band v. Canada*, views adopted on 26 March 1990.
31 See ibid., Forty-third Session, Supplement No. 40 (A/43/40), annex VII, sect. G, Communication No. 197/1985, *Kitok v. Sweden*, views adopted on 27 July 1988.
32 See ibid., Forty-second Session, Supplement No. 40 (A/42/40), annex VIII, sect. D, Communication No. 182/1984, *F.H. Zwaan-de Vries v. the Netherlands*, views adopted on 9 April 1987; ibid., sect. C, Communication No. 180/1984, *L.G. Danning v. the Netherlands*, views adopted on 9 April 1987.

the rights protected under the Covenant are available to all individuals within its territory and subject to its jurisdiction, except rights which are expressly made to apply to citizens, for example, political rights under article 25. A State party may not, therefore, restrict the rights under article 27 to its citizens alone.

5.2 Article 27 confers rights on persons belonging to minorities which "exist" in a State party. Given the nature and scope of the rights envisaged under that article, it is not relevant to determine the degree of permanence that the term "exist" connotes. Those rights simply are that individuals belonging to those minorities should not be denied the right, in community with members of their group, to enjoy their own culture, to practise their religion and speak their language. Just as they need not be nationals or citizens, they need not be permanent residents. Thus, migrant workers or even visitors in a State party constituting such minorities are entitled not to be denied the exercise of those rights. As any other individual in the territory of the State party, they would, also for this purpose, have the general rights, for example, to freedom of association, of assembly, and of expression. The existence of an ethnic, religious or linguistic minority in a given State party does not depend upon a decision by that State party but requires to be established by objective criteria.

5.3 The right of individuals belonging to a linguistic minority to use their language among themselves, in private or in public, is distinct from other language rights protected under the Covenant. In particular, it should be distinguished from the general right to freedom of expression protected under article 19. The latter right is available to all persons, irrespective of whether they belong to minorities or not. Further, the right protected under article 27 should be distinguished from the particular right which article 14.3 (f) of the Covenant confers on accused persons to interpretation where they cannot understand or speak the language used in the courts. Article 14.3 (f) does not, in any other circumstances, confer on accused persons the right to use or speak the language of their choice in court proceedings.[33]

(...)

6.1 Although article 27 is expressed in negative terms, that article, nevertheless, does recognize the existence of a "right" and requires that it shall not be denied. Consequently, a State party is under an obligation to ensure that the existence and the exercise of this right are protected against their denial or violation. Positive measures of protection are, therefore, required not only against the acts of the State party itself,

---

33 See ibid., Forty-fifth Session, Supplement No. 40, (A/45/40), vol. II, annex X, sect. A, Communication No. 220/1987, *T.K. v. France*, decision of 8 November 1989; ibid., sect. B, Communication No. 222/1987, *M.K. v. France*, decision of 8 November 1989.

whether through its legislative, judicial or administrative authorities, but also against the acts of other persons within the State party.

6.2 Although the rights protected under article 27 are individual rights, they depend in turn on the ability of the minority group to maintain its culture, language or religion. Accordingly, positive measures by States may also be necessary to protect the identity of a minority and the rights of its members to enjoy and develop their culture and language and to practise their religion, in community with the other members of the group. In this connection, it has to be observed that such positive measures must respect the provisions of articles 2.1 and 26 of the Covenant both as regards the treatment between different minorities and the treatment between the persons belonging to them and the remaining part of the population. However, as long as those measures are aimed at correcting conditions which prevent or impair the enjoyment of the rights guaranteed under article 27, they may constitute a legitimate differentiation under the Covenant, provided that they are based on reasonable and objective criteria.

(...)

7   With regard to the exercise of the cultural rights protected under article 27, the Committee observes that culture manifests itself in many forms, including a particular way of life associated with the use of land resources, especially in the case of indigenous peoples. That right may include such traditional activities as fishing or hunting and the right to live in reserves protected by law.[34] The enjoyment of those rights may require positive legal measures of protection and measures to ensure the effective participation of members of minority communities in decisions which affect them.

8   The Committee observes that none of the rights protected under article 27 of the Covenant may be legitimately exercised in a manner or to an extent inconsistent with the other provisions of the Covenant.

9   The Committee concludes that article 27 relates to rights whose protection imposes specific obligations on States parties. The protection of these rights is directed towards ensuring the survival and continued development of the cultural, religious and social identity of the minorities concerned, thus enriching the fabric of society as a whole. Accordingly, the Committee observes that these rights must be protected as such and should not be confused with other personal rights conferred on one and all under the Covenant. States parties, therefore, have an obligation to ensure that the exercise of these rights is fully protected and they should indicate in their reports the measures they have adopted to this end.

---

34 See notes 1 and 2 above, Communication No. 167/1984, *Bernard Ominayak, Chief of the Lubicon Lake Band v. Canada*, views adopted on 26 March 1990, and Communication No. 197/1985, *Kitok v. Sweden*, views adopted on 27 July 1988.

B.4. UN HUMAN RIGHTS COMMITTEE (HRC), Sister Immaculate Joseph and 80 Teaching Sisters of the Holy Cross of the Third Order of Saint Francis in Menzingen of Sri Lanka v. Sri Lanka (CCPR/C/85/D/1249/2004), communication no. 1249/2004, 4 April 2001.

1   The author of the communication, initially dated 14 February 2004, is Sister Immaculate Joseph, a Sri Lankan citizen and Roman Catholic nun presently serving as Provincial Superior of the Teaching Sisters of the Holy Cross of the Third Order of Saint Francis in Menzingen of Sri Lanka ('the Order'). She submits the communication on her own behalf and on behalf of 80 other sisters of the Order, who expressly authorize her to act on their behalf. They claim to be victims of violations by Sri Lanka of articles 2, paragraph (1); article 18, paragraph (1); article 19, paragraph (2), article 26 and article 27 of the Covenant. The Optional Protocol entered into force for Sri Lanka on 3 January 1998. The authors are not represented by counsel.

Factual background

2.1 The authors state that the Order, established in 1900, is engaged, among other things, in teaching and other charity and community work, which it provides to the community at large, irrespective of race or religion. In July 2003, the Order filed an application for incorporation, which in Sri Lanka occurs by way of statutory enactment. The Attorney-General, who the authors maintain is required by article 77 of the Constitution to examine every Bill for consistency with the Constitution, made no report to the President. After the Bill was published in the Government Gazette, an objection to the constitutionality of two clauses of the Bill, when read with the preamble,[35] apparently by a private

---

35 The contested clauses of the Bill were clauses 3 and 5, read with the preamble. These provided: Preamble. "Whereas the Teaching Sisters of [the Order] have established themselves as a Congregation for the propagation of Religion by establishing and maintaining catholic schools and other schools assisted or maintained by the State and engaged in educational and vocational training in several parts of Sri Lanka and in establishing and maintaining orphanages and homes for children and for the aged: and whereas it has become necessary for the aforesaid purposes to be more effectively prosecuted, pursued and attained to have the incorporation of the [the Order]: and whereas it has become expedient to have [the Order] duly incorporated". Clause 3. (a) The general objects for which the Corporation is constituted are hereby declared to be – (b) to spread knowledge of the Catholic religion; (c) to impart religious, educational and vocational training to youth; (d) to teach in Pre-Schools, Schools, Colleges and Educational Institutions; (e) to serve in Nursing Homes, Medical Clinics, Hospitals, Refugee Camps and like institutions; (f) to establish and maintain Creches, Day Care Centres, Homes for the elders, Orphanages, Nursing Homes and Mobile Clinics for the infants, aged, orphans, destitutes and sick; (g) to bring about society based on love and respect for one and all; and (h) to undertake and carry out all such works and services that will promote the aforesaid objects of the Corporation. Clause 5 gave the authority to the corporation to receive, hold and dispose of movable and immoveable property for the purposes set out in the Bill.

citizen ('the objector'), was filed on 14 July 2003 in the original jurisdiction of the Supreme Court.

2.2 Without advice of the objection or hearing to the Order, the Supreme Court heard the objector and the Attorney-General on the matter. The authors state that the Attorney-General, who was technically the respondent to the proceedings, supported the objector's arguments. On 1 August 2003, the Supreme Court handed down its Special Determination upholding the application, for inconsistency with articles 9 and 10 of the Constitution. The Court held that the challenged provisions of the Bill "create a situation which combines the observance and practice of a religion or belief with activities which would provide material and other benefits to the inexperience [sic], defenceless and vulnerable people to propagate a religion. The kind of [social and economic] activities projected in the Bill would necessarily result in imposing unnecessary and improper pressures on people, who are distressed and in need, with their free exercise of thought, conscience and religion with the freedom to have or to adopt a religion or belief of his choice as provided in article 10 of the Constitution." The Court thus considered that "the Constitution does not recognize a fundamental right to propagate a religion". In reaching its conclusions, the Court referred to article 18 of both the Universal Declaration of Human Rights and the Covenant, as well as two cases decided by the European Court of Human Rights.[36]

2.3 The Court went on to examine the application in the light of article 9 of the Constitution, which provides that: "The Republic of Sri Lanka shall give Buddhism the foremost place and accordingly it shall be the duty of the State to protect and foster the Buddha Sasana, while assuring all religions the rights granted by articles 10 and 14(1)(e)." The Court held, "the propagation and spreading Christianity as postulated in terms of clause 3 [of the Bill] would not be permissible as it would impair the very existence of Buddhism or the Buddha Sasana". In addition, subclauses 1(a) and (b) of clause 3 concerned spreading knowledge of a religion and were thus inconsistent with article 9 of the Constitution.

2.4 The authors point out that in reaching these conclusions the Court referred to decisions in two previous cases where similar bills for the incorporation of Christian associations had been found to be unconstitutional. The result of the decision, against which no appeal or review was possible, was that Parliament could not enact the Bill into law without a two-thirds special majority and approval by a popular referendum.

The complaint

3.1 The authors claim that the above facts disclose violations of article 2, paragraph 1, read with article 26, article 27, article 18, paragraph 1, and article 19, paragraph 2. As to article 2, paragraph 1, read with article 26, the authors

---

36 *Kokkinakis v Greece* Appl. n. 14307/88, judgment of 19 April 1993, and *Larissis v Greece* Appl. ns. 23372/94, 26377/94 and 26378/94, judgment of 24 February 1998.

argue that the Attorney-General's submissions in opposition to the Bill and the Supreme Court's determination violated these rights. The Attorney-General, not having recognized any constitutional infirmity under article 77, was obliged as a matter of equality of law to take the same position before the Court, doubly so given that the Order, although the affected entity, was neither notified nor heard. The determination that Clause 3 of the Bill was incompatible with article 9 of the Constitution was moreover so irrational and arbitrary as to breach fundamental norms of equality protected by article 26. With reference to the Committee's decision in Waldman v Canada,[37] the authors argue that to reject the Order's incorporation while many non-Christian religious bodies with similar object clauses have been incorporated violates article 26. In support, the author provides a (non-exhaustive) list of 28 religious bodies that have been incorporated and their statutory objects, of which most have Buddhist orientation, certain Islamic, and none Christian.

3.2 In terms of article 27, the authors invoke the Committee's General Comment 22 to the effect that the official establishment of a State religion should not impair the enjoyment of others' Covenant rights. The Court's reliance on the Buddhism primacy clause in article 9 to reject the Bill's constitutionality thus violated article 27. The authors emphasize that, like the lengthy list of other religious bodies receiving incorporation, the Order combined charitable and humanitarian activities (labeled social and economic activities by the Court) with religious ones, a practice common to all religions. To require a religious body's adherents to limit good works would be discriminatory, and contrary also to the objects of the other religious bodies that received incorporation. Propagation of belief, moreover, is an integral part of professing and practicing religion; indeed, all major religions in Sri Lanka (Buddhism, Hinduism, Islam and Christianity) were introduced by propagation. In any event, the authors state that in the seventy years of the Order's existence in Sri Lanka, there has neither been evidence nor allegation of inducements or allurements to conversion. This aspect of religious practice is thus protected by the rights of the Order's members under article 27 Covenant.

3.3 In terms of article 18, paragraph 2, and 19, paragraph 2, the authors argue that the Court's restrictions on social and economic activities of the Order breach its members' rights under these provisions. The right to propagate and disseminate information about a religion is similarly covered by these articles, and is not limited to a State's "foremost" religion. None of the Order's activities are coercive, and thus paragraph 2 of article 18 has no application to the Order's legitimate activities. Invoking article 6 of the Declaration on the Elimination of All Forms of Intolerance and of Discrimination Based on Religion and Belief as a guide to Covenant interpretation, the author goes on to argue that the inability to hold property in the name of the Order sharply limits its effective ability to establish places of worship and charitable and humanitarian institutions. The

---

37 Case No 694/1996, Views adopted on 3 November 1999.

Attorney-General's submissions and the Supreme Court's ascription to the Order of potentially coercive activities as a result of incorporation were wholly unsubstantiated and unfounded in fact.

The State party's submissions on admissibility and merits

4.1 By submissions of 15 April 2004 and 21 March 2005, the State party contested the admissibility and merits of the communication. At the outset, the State party described its understanding of the allegations as three-fold: a) that the author was not afforded an opportunity of being heard before the Supreme Court prior to the Court making its determination, b) that the Attorney-General supported the petitioner's submissions before the Supreme Court, and c) that the Supreme Court's determination itself violated the author's Covenant rights.

4.2 As to the allegation that the authors were not afforded an opportunity of being heard before the Supreme Court prior to the Court making its determination, the State party explains that under article 78 of the Constitution, any Bill shall be published in the Government gazette at least seven days before being placed on the Order paper of Parliament. The Constitution then lays down the procedure to be followed when a Bill is placed on the Order paper in Parliament. The Supreme Court is vested, under article 121 of the Constitution, with sole and exclusive jurisdiction to determine whether a Bill or any provision thereof is inconsistent with the Constitution. This jurisdiction may be invoked by the President by written reference to the Chief Justice, or by any citizen addressing the Court in writing. Either application must be filed within a week of the Bill being placed on the Order paper of Parliament.

4.3 When the Court's jurisdiction has thus been invoked, no Parliamentary proceedings may be held in relation to the Bill until three weeks have elapsed or the Court has determined the matter, whichever occurs first. The Court's proceedings take place in open court, and any person claiming to be interested in the determination of the question can make an application to the Court for intervenor status. The Court communicates its determination to the President or the Speaker within three weeks of the application. In the event that the Court finds an inconsistency, a special majority of two-thirds of all members of Parliament must pass the Bill, while if the Bill is in relation to articles 1 to 3 or 6 to 11, a people's referendum must also approve the Bill. The members of Parliament are aware when any Bill has been placed on the Order paper in Parliament.

4.4 The State party explains that the current Bill was presented as a Private Member's Bill. As such, it had not been examined by the Attorney-General under article 77 of the Constitution, and the Attorney-General expressed no view on it. If the authors had wished to intervene in the proceedings, they should have been vigilant to check with the Court's Registry if any application had been filed with the Registry within a week of the Bill being placed upon the Parliamentary Order paper. Had such due diligence been exercised and an intervenor application been made, there is no apparent reason why the Court would have refused the application, which would have been unprecedented. Rather than being a situation of denial of an opportunity to be heard therefore, it was a clear case of an author not taking proper steps to avail herself of the opportunity and the authors are now estopped from claiming otherwise.

4.5 As to the allegation that the Attorney-General supported the petitioner's submissions before the Supreme Court, the State party observes that when article 121 of the Constitution is invoked, the Constitution provides for the Attorney-General to be notified and to be heard. At that point, s/he is expected to consider the objections raised to the constitutionality of the item under reference and assist the Court in its determination. While the Attorney-General had not previously expressed a view on the Bill's constitutionality, the Bill being a private Bill, even if s/he had, it would be manifestly wrong and untenable to suggest s/he would be bound by that earlier determination when addressing the issue in article 121 proceedings.

4.6 As to the contention that the Supreme Court's determination itself violated the authors' Covenant rights, the State party argues that the Supreme Court is not empowered to change the Constitution but only to interpret it within the framework of its provisions. The Court considered the submissions made, took into consideration previous determinations and gave reasons for its conclusions. In any event, the authors, having failed to exercise due diligence to secure their right to be heard, are estopped from contesting the Court's determination in another forum. As a result, with respect to all three allegations, the State party argues that the authors have failed to exhaust domestic remedies.

4.7 The State party goes on to argue that the Supreme Court's determination does not prevent the authors from carrying on their previous activities in Sri Lanka. The State party argues that the Court's determinations in article 121 proceedings do not bind lower courts, and thus lower courts will not be compelled to restrict their right to engage in legitimate religious activity. Nor, for its part, does the Supreme Court's determination do so.

4.8 Moreover, the Court's determination does not prevent Parliament from passing the Bill, which, while inconsistent with articles 9 and 10 of the Constitution could still be passed by a special majority and referendum. Alternatively, the constitutionally impugned provisions of the Bill could be amended and the Bill resubmitted.

Authors' comments on the State party's submissions

5.1 By letter of 30 May 2005, the authors argue that the State party has confined itself to responding to three incidental allegations which do not form the core of the author's case. The authors argue that the issue is not whether the Court's determination prevents her from carrying on her activities, but rather whether there was a violation of Covenant rights, for the reasons detailed in the complaint. There is no remedy in domestic law against the Supreme Court's determination, which is final and thus the merits thereof are appropriately before the Committee.

5.2 As to the State party's response concerning the opportunity of being heard, the authors emphasize that only the Speaker and Attorney-general receive mandatory notice of an article 121 application, with there being no requirement to notify affected parties such as, in the present case, those involved in a Bill to incorporate a body. In some cases of Private member's Bills, the Supreme Court has adjourned the hearing and notified the concerned member of Parliament if s/he wishes to be heard.[38] In the present case, neither the relevant member of Parliament nor the authors were notified, amounting to a violation of article 2, paragraph 1, in connection with article 26 of the Covenant.

5.3 The authors argue that if the Attorney-General could deviate, in article 121 proceedings, from constitutional advice earlier provided, the whole purpose of the earlier advice would be rendered nugatory. The ability to change such opinions at will would leave room for gross abuse and undoubtedly affect the rights of individuals, contrary to article 21, in connection with article 26 of the Covenant. The authors go on to argue that the State party's response to the Covenant challenge to the Supreme Court's determination, to the effect that the Court made determination within the applicable legal framework, is insufficient answer to her complaint.

Issues and proceedings before the Committee

CONSIDERATION OF ADMISSIBILITY

6.1 Before considering any claim contained in a communication, the Human Rights Committee must, in accordance with rule 93 of its rules of procedure, decide whether or not the communication is admissible under the Optional Protocol to the Covenant.

6.2 With respect to the exhaustion of domestic remedies, the Committee notes the State party's argument that the authors did not exercise due diligence with respect to confirming through the Parliamentary order paper and then Supreme Court's registry whether an application under article 121 of the Constitution had been lodged, and accordingly filing a motion wishing to be heard. The Committee considers that, exceptional ex parte circumstances of urgency apart, when a Court hears an application directly affecting the rights of a person, elementary notions of fairness and due process contained in article 14, paragraph 1, of the Covenant require the affected party to be given notice of the proceeding, particularly when the adjudication of rights is final. In the present case, neither members of the Order nor the member of Parliament presenting the Bill were notified of the pending proceeding. Given not least that in previous proceedings the Court, on the information before the Committee, had notified members of Parliament in such proceedings, the authors thus cannot be faulted for failing to introduce an intervenor's motion before the Court. The Committee observes that there may

---

38 The authors cite the example of a Bill entitled "Nineteenth amendment to the Constitution" presented by a private member inter alia to make Buddhism the State's official religion as an example.

in any event be issues as to the effectiveness of this remedy, given the requirement that complex constitutional questions, including relevant oral argument, be resolved within three weeks of a challenge being filed, the challenge itself coming within a week of a Bill's publication in the Order paper. It follows that the communication is not inadmissible for failure to exhaust domestic remedies.

6.3 As to the claim that the authors' rights under articles 2 and 26 of the Covenant were violated by the Attorney-General contesting the constitutionality of the Bill before the Court in circumstances where s/he had previously expressed no view of constitutional infirmity, the State party has explained without rebuttal that the Attorney-General's duty to pass on the constitutionality of Bills at the initial stage does not apply to Private member's Bills such as the present. Accordingly, the Attorney-General's views expressed in the article 121 proceedings were his or her first formal views on the matter and were not precluded by a previously taken view. As a result, the Committee considers that this claim is insufficiently substantiated, for purposes of admissibility, and is accordingly inadmissible under article 2 of the Optional Protocol.

6.4 In the absence of any other objections to the admissibility of the communication, and recalling in particular that the Covenant guarantees in articles 18 and 27 freedom of religion exercised in community with others, the Committee considers the remaining claims as pleaded to be sufficiently substantiated, for purposes of admissibility, and proceeds to their consideration on the merits.

Consideration of the merits

7.1 The Human Rights Committee has considered the present communication in the light of all the information made available to it by the parties, as provided in article 5, paragraph 1 of the Optional Protocol.

7.2 As to the claim under article 18, the Committee observes that, for numerous religions, including according to the authors, their own, it is a central tenet to spread knowledge, to propagate their beliefs to others and to provide assistance to others. These aspects are part of an individual's manifestation of religion and free expression, and are thus protected by article 18, paragraph 1, to the extent not appropriately restricted by measures consistent with paragraph 3.[39] The authors have advanced, and the State party has not refuted, that incorporation of the Order would better enable them to realize the objects of their Order, religious as well as secular, including for example the construction of places of worship. Indeed, this was the purpose of the Bill and is reflected in its objects clause. It follows that the Supreme Court's determination of the Bill's

---

39 See *Malakhovsky et al. v Belarus*, Case No 1207/2003, Views adopted on 26 July 2005, and Article 6 of the Declaration on the Elimination of All Forms of Intolerance and of Discrimination Based on Religion or Belief, GA Resolution 36/55 of 25 November 1981, which provides: ".... the right to freedom of thought, conscience, religion or belief shall include, inter alia, the following freedoms: ... (b) the right to establish and maintain appropriate charitable or humanitarian institutions".

unconstitutionality restricted the authors' rights to freedom of religious practice and to freedom of expression, requiring limits to be justified, under paragraph 3 of the respective articles, by law and necessary for the protection of the rights and freedoms of others or for the protection of public safety, order, health or morals. While the Court's determination was undoubtedly a restriction imposed by law, it remains to be determined whether the restriction was necessary for one of the enumerated purposes. The Committee recalls that permissible restrictions on Covenant rights, being exceptions to the exercise of the right in question, must be interpreted narrowly and with careful scrutiny of the reasons advanced by way of justification.

7.3 In the present case, the State party has not sought to justify the infringement of rights other than by reliance on the reasons set out in the decision of the Supreme Court itself. The decision considered that the Order's activities would, through the provision of material and other benefits to vulnerable people, coercively or otherwise improperly propagate religion. The decision failed to provide any evidentiary or factual foundation for this assessment, or reconcile this assessment with the analogous benefits and services provided by other religious bodies that had been incorporated. Similarly, the decision provided no justification for the conclusion that the Bill, including through the spreading knowledge of a religion, would "impair the very existence of Buddhism or the Buddha Sasana". The Committee notes moreover that the international case law cited by the decision does not support its conclusions. In one case, criminal proceedings brought against a private party for proselytisation was found in breach of religious freedoms. In the other case, criminal proceedings were found permissible against military officers, as representatives of the State, who had proselytised certain subordinates, but not for proselytising private persons outside the military forces. In the Committee's view, the grounds advanced in the present case therefore were insufficient to demonstrate, from the perspective of the Covenant, that the restrictions in question were necessary for one or more of the enumerated purposes. It follows that there has been a breach of article 18, paragraph 1, of the Covenant.

7.4 As to the claim under article 26, the Committee refers to its long standing jurisprudence that there must be a reasonable and objective distinction to avoid a finding of discrimination, particularly on the enumerated grounds in article 26 which include religious belief. In the present case, the authors have supplied an extensive list of other religious bodies which have been provided incorporated status, with objects of the same kind as the authors' Order. The State party has provided no reasons why the authors' Order is differently situated, or otherwise why reasonable and objective grounds exist for distinguishing their claim. As the Committee has held in Waldman v Canada,[40] therefore, such a differential treatment in the conferral of a benefit by the State must be provided without discrimination on the basis of religious belief. The failure to do so in the present case thus

---

40 Ibid.

amounts to a violation of the right in article 26 to be free from discrimination on the basis of religious belief.

7.5 As to the remaining claim that the Supreme Court determined the application adversely to the authors' Order without either notification of the proceeding or offering an opportunity to be heard, the Committee refers to its considerations in the context of admissibility set out in paragraph 6.2. As the Committee observed in Kavanagh v Ireland,[41] the notion of equality before the law requires similarly situated individuals to be afforded the same process before the courts, unless objective and reasonable grounds are supplied to justify the differentiation. In the present case, the State party has not advanced justification for why, in other cases, proceedings were notified to affected parties, whilst in this case they were not. It follows that the Committee finds a violation of the first sentence of article 26, which guarantees equality before the law.

7.6 In the Committee's view, the claims under articles 19 and 27 do not add to the issues addressed above and do need to be separately considered.

8. The Human Rights Committee, acting under article 5, paragraph 4, of the Optional Protocol to the International Covenant on Civil and Political Rights, is of the view that the facts as found by the Committee reveal violations by Sri Lanka of articles 18, paragraph 1, and 26 of the Covenant.

9. In accordance with article 2, paragraph 3 (a), of the Covenant, the State party is under an obligation to provide the authors with an effective remedy giving full recognition to their rights under the Covenant. The State party is also under an obligation to prevent similar violations in the future.

10. Bearing in mind that, by becoming a party to the Optional Protocol, the State party has recognized the competence of the Committee to determine whether there has been a violation of the Covenant or not and that, pursuant to article 2 of the Covenant, the State party has undertaken to ensure to all individuals within its territory and subject to its jurisdiction the rights recognized in the Covenant, and to provide an effective and enforceable remedy in case a violation has been established, the Committee expects to receive from the State party, within 90 days, information about the measures taken to give effect to the Committee's Views. The State party is also requested to publish the Committee's Views.

B.5. *UN HUMAN RIGHTS COMMITTEE (HRC)*, **Gareth Anver Prince v. South Africa** *(CCPR/C/91/D/1474/2006), Communication No. 1474/2006, 14 November 2007.*

1   The author of the communication is Mr. Gareth Anver Prince, a South African national born on 6 December 1969. He claims to be the victim of violations by South Africa of his rights under article 18, paragraph 1; article 26; and article 27 of the International Covenant on Civil and Political Rights.

---

41 Case No 819/1998, Views adopted on 4 April 2001.

The Covenant and its Optional Protocol entered into force for South Africa respectively on 10 March 1999 and 28 November 2002. The author is represented by counsel, Prof. Frans Viljoen.

Facts as presented by the author

2.1 The author is a follower of the Rastafari religion, which originated in Jamaica and later in Ethiopia, as a black consciousness movement seeking to overthrow colonialism, oppression and domination. There are about 12 000 Rastafarians in South Africa. The use of cannabis sativa (cannabis) is central to the Rastafari religion. It is used at religious gatherings and in the privacy of one's home where it does not offend others. At religious ceremonies, it is smoked through a chalice (water-pipe) as part of Holy Communion and burnt as incense. In private, cannabis is also used as incense, to bathe in, for smoking, drinking and eating. Although not all Rastafarians in South Africa belong to formal organizations, there are four Rastafari houses and a Rastafari National Council.

2.2 The author fulfilled all academic requirements for becoming an attorney. Before being allowed to practice, prospective attorneys in South Africa must, in addition to these academic requirements, perform a period of community service, as required by the Attorneys Act.[42] The author applied to the relevant body (the Law Society of Cape of Good Hope) to register his contract of community service. In its determination of this issue, the Law Society must assess whether the candidate is a "fit and proper person". A criminal record, or a propensity to commit crime, will jeopardize such a finding.

2.3 Under the Drugs and Drugs Trafficking Act and the Medicines and Related Substances Control Act,[43] it is, among others, an offence to possess or use cannabis. These laws allow for exemptions under specified conditions for patients, medical practitioners, dentists, pharmacists, other professionals, or anyone that has "otherwise come into possession" of a prohibited substance in a lawful manner.[44]

2.4 When applying to the Law Society, the author disclosed that he had two previous convictions for possessing cannabis, and expressed his intention, in light of his religious dictates, to continue using cannabis. On this basis, his application for registration for community service was refused. He was thus placed in a position where he must choose between his faith and his legal career.

2.5 The author claimed before the South African courts that the failure of the relevant legislation to make provision for an exemption allowing bona fide Rastafarians to possess and use cannabis for religious purposes constitutes a violation of his constitutional rights under the South African Bill of Rights.[45] On 23 March 1998, the Cape High Court dismissed the author's application for review

---

42 Act 53 of 1979.
43 Act 108 of 1996.
44 See eg section 4(b) (i), (ii), (iii), (iv) and (v) of the Drugs and Drugs Trafficking Act.
45 See the Sections of the Constitution referred to in paragraph 4.11 below.

of the Law Society's decision.[46] On 25 May 2000, the Supreme Court dismissed his appeal.[47] The Constitutional Court delivered two judgements, on 12 December 2000 and 25 January 2002.[48] In the latter, it decided, by a majority of 5 to 4, that although the Drugs Act did limit the author's constitutional rights, such limitations were reasonable and justifiable under section 36[49] of the Constitution. The minority found unconstitutional the prohibition on the use and possession of cannabis in religious practices which does not pose an unacceptable risk to society and the individual and considered that the government should allow an exemption.

2.6 In 2002, the author applied to the African Commission on Human and Peoples' Rights. The issue was whether the failure to exempt bona fide Rastafarians from using and possessing cannabis for religious purposes violated the African Charter. In December 2004, the African Commission found no violation of the complainant's rights as alleged.

The complaint

3.1 The author claims a violation of article 18, paragraph 1, of the Covenant, and refers to General Comment No. 22, which states that the concept of worship "extends to ritual and ceremonial acts giving direct expression to belief". The author is a bona fide adherent to Rastafarianism. The use of cannabis is accepted to be an integral part of that religion and fundamental to its practice. The author claims that the State party has a positive obligation to take measures to ensure the de facto protection of his right to freedom of religion.

3.2 He argues that his case differs from the case of Bhinder v. Canada,[50] because the justification of the limitation in the present case is much less concrete,

---

46 *Prince v. President of the Law Society, Cape of Good Hope and Others* 1998 8 BCLR 976 (C), decided on 23 March 1998.
47 *Prince v. President, Cape Law Society and Others* 2000 3 SA 845 (SCA), decided on 25 May 2000.
48 *Prince v President, Cape Law Society and Others* 2001 2 SA 388 (CC), delivered on 12 December 2000 (Prince I) and *Prince v President, Cape Law Society and Others* 2002 2 SA 794 (CC), decided on 25 January 2002 (Prince II).
49 Section 36 of the Constitution: Limitations of rights

> "(1) The rights in the Bill of Rights may be limited only in terms of law of general application to the extent that the limitation is reasonable and justifiable in an open and democratic society based on human dignity, equality and freedom, taking into account all relevant factors, including:
> (a) the nature of the right;
> (b) the importance of the purpose of the limitation;
> (c) the nature and extent of the limitation;
> (d) the relation between the limitation and its purpose; and
> (e) less restrictive means to achieve the purpose.
> (2) Except as provided in subsection (1) or in any other provision of the Constitution, no law may limit any right entrenched in the Bill of Rights."

50 Communication 208/1986, Views adopted on 9 November 1989.

and the failure to exempt Rastafarians is based on pragmatic concerns such as the cost and difficulties to apply and enforce an exemption. The author is fully informed and prepared to accept any risk, if any, to him personally. He submits that the legitimate aim of preventing the harm associated with the use of dangerous dependence producing substances does not necessitate a blanket ban on the use and possession of cannabis for religious purposes. The limitation is excessive in that it affects all uses of cannabis by Rastafarians, no matter what the form of use, the amount involved, or the circumstances, while the use of cannabis for religious purposes takes many forms. A tailor-made exemption would not open the floodgates of illicit use; and there is no evidence that an exemption would pose substantial health or safety risks to society at large. The denial of his right to freedom of religion is greater than the necessary to achieve any legitimate aim.

3.3 The author claims to be the victim of a violation of article 26, as the failure to differentiate the Rastafari religion from other religions constitutes discrimination. He is coerced into a choice between adherence to his religion and respect for the laws of the land.

3.4 The author claims that the failure to explore and find an effective exemption for Rastafari constitutes a violation of article 27. Rastafarianism is essentially collective in nature, as it is a particular way of life, in community with others. This way of life has deep African roots.

3.5 The author contends that his complaint is admissible. His communication is not being examined under another procedure of international investigation or settlement, as the African Commission has already made a finding on the merits. He has exhausted domestic remedies, as his case was examined by the Supreme Court of Appeal and the Constitutional Court.

3.6 The author argues that his claim is admissible ratione temporis. Although the judgments of the national courts were issued before the entry into force of the Optional Protocol for the State party in 2002, the alleged violations constitute "continuous violations" with "continuing effects", which persist into the period after the entry into force and into the present. The Attorneys Act 53 of 1979 and the Drugs and Drug Trafficking Act 140 of 1992 remaining in force, the legislative framework still presents an obstacle to the author's free expression of his right to religion. He refers to the case of Lovelace v. Canada[51] and argues that his communication concerns the continuing effect of the Attorney's Act and the Drugs Traffic Act, as a result of which he cannot register for community service with the Law Society.

The State party's submission on admissibility and merits

4.1 On 24 July 2006, the State party commented on the admissibility of the communication. It argues that domestic remedies have not been exhausted, as the author did not, in his applications to the domestic courts, seek to have the

---

51 Communication No. 24/1977, Views adopted on 30 July 1981, paragraph 13.1.

prohibition of cannabis declared unconstitutional and invalid, and to have such prohibitions removed from the respective act for the benefit of the whole population, as is the usual way in challenging legislative provisions which are believed to be inconsistent with the Constitution. He only challenged the constitutionality of the laws prohibiting the use of cannabis in as far as they did not make an exception in the favour of a minority of 10,000 people, permitting the use of cannabis for religious purposes. The State party submits that the reason why the prohibition of possession and use of cannabis remains in force is the result of the author's misguided approach in the domestic courts.

4.2 The State party contends that the communication is inadmissible ratione temporis. The Optional Protocol entered into force for the State party on 28 November 2002. The facts and applications in domestic courts were completed before the entry into force of the Optional Protocol, with the Constitutional Court delivering its final judgment on 25 January 2002. On the author's argument that the violation has continuous effects because the laws still prohibit the possession and use of cannabis, the State party considers that it to be invalid, because the author did not seek to have the prohibition laws declared unconstitutional and invalid. He cannot therefore claim that the fact that these laws still apply amounts to a continuous violation. The State party refers to the Committee's jurisprudence[52] according to which continuous effects can be seen as an affirmation of previous alleged violations. It submits that it has not affirmed the concerned provisions of the relevant laws, as they remain unchanged.

4.3 The State party recalls that the same facts were already examined by the African Commission, which found no violation of the African Charter on Human and People's Rights. The State party suggests that the Committee should broaden its literal interpretation of the concept of "being examined" to address policy issues such as the phenomenon of "appeal" from one body to another, as the risk of "human rights forum shopping"[53] is considerable. It considers that the Committee, in dealing with the present case, has the opportunity to give clear guidance, in an innovative and creative manner, on how it intends to contribute to the maintenance of a credible and respected unified international human rights system.

4.4 On 24 November 2006, the State party commented on the merits. It argues that while its legislation indeed results in a limitation of the right to freedom of religion of Rastafarians, such limitation is reasonable and justifiable in terms of the limitation clause contained in article 18, paragraph 3. Furthermore, it is proportionate to and necessary for the achievement of the legitimate aims provided for in that article, namely the protection of public safety, order, health, morals

---

52 Communication No. 520/1992, *Könye and Könye v. Hungary*, Decision on Admissibility of 7 April 1994, paragraph 6.4; Communication No 422/1990, *Aduayoum et al v. Togo*, Views adopted on 12 July 1996, paragraph 6.2.
53 The State party refers to an article by J.S. Davidson, 'The Procedure and Practice of the Human Rights Committee under the First OP to the ICCPR' [1991] 4 Canterbury Law Review 337 at 342, which is annexed to its submissions.

or the fundamental rights and freedoms of others. The Cape High Court, the Supreme Court and the Constitutional Court all found that while the legislation the author complained about limited his constitutional rights, such limitation was reasonable and justifiable under Section 36 of the State party's Constitution.

4.5 For the State party, the essential question before the Committee is not whether a limitation on the rights of Rastafarians has taken place, but whether such limitation will be encompassed by the limitation clause contained in article 18, paragraph 3. It emphasises that at the national level, the author did not challenge the constitutionality of the prohibition on the possession and use of cannabis, accepting that it serves a legitimate purpose, but alleged that this prohibition is overbroad and that exemption should be made for the religious use by Rastafarians. In the case before the Cape High Court, it was requested that the possession and use of cannabis for religious purposes by Rastafarians be legalised. On appeal, it was requested that an exemption also be granted for transporting and cultivating cannabis, while the requested exemption became far wider before the Constitutional Court, where importation and transportation to centres of use and distribution to Rastafarians were requested. It follows that the practical relief sought by the author is an exemption to legalise a whole chain of cultivation, import, transport, supply and sale of cannabis to Rastafarians. In practice, the only workable solution would be the creation and implementation of a "legal" chain of supply of cannabis, as an exception and parallel to the illegal trade in cannabis. The majority in the 2002 Constitutional Court judgment found, after thoroughly considering the limitations clause in Section 36 of the Constitution and applicable foreign law, that the relief sought could not be implemented in practice.[54]

4.6 In finding that the "blanket" ban on the use of cannabis was proportional to the legitimate aim of protecting the public against the harm caused by the use of drugs, the Constitutional Court evaluated the importance of the limitation, the relationship between the limitation and its purpose, and the impact that an exemption for religious reasons would have on the overall purpose of the limitation, against the author's right to freedom of religion. It took into account the nature and importance of that right in a democratic society based on human

---

54 "There is no objective way in which a law enforcement official could distinguish between the use of cannabis for religious purpose and the use of cannabis for recreation purposes. It would be even more difficult, if not impossible, to distinguish objectively between the possession of cannabis for one or the other of the above purposes" (paragraph 130). There would be practical difficulties in enforcing a permit system .... They include the financial and administrative problems associated with setting up and implementing such a system, and the difficulties in policing that would follow if permits were issued sanctioning the possession and use of cannabis for religious purposes" (paragraph 134). "The use made of cannabis by Rastafari cannot in the circumstances be sanctioned without impairing the State's ability to enforce its legislation in the interests of the public at large and to honour its international obligation to do so. The failure to make provision for an exemption in respect of the possession and use of cannabis by Rastafari is thus reasonable and justifiable under our Constitution" (paragraph 139).

dignity, equality and freedom, the importance of the use of cannabis in the Rastafari religion and the impact of the limitation on the right to practice the religion.

4.7 On counsel's reference to the Bhinder case and his contention that allowing a permitted exemption for the benefit of Rastafarians would present little danger to public safety or health, the State party reiterates that implementing such a permit system would present practical difficulties, and that it is impossible to prevent a dangerous substance from escaping from the system and threatening the public at large. Medical evidence on the harmful effects of cannabis was considered and accepted by the Constitutional Court as such.[55]

4.8 The State party invokes the Committee's inadmissibility decision in M.A.B., W.A.T. and J.- A.Y.T. v Canada,[56] where it considered that the use of cannabis for religious purposes cannot be brought within the scope of article 18. The State party concludes that there was no violation of article 18.

4.9 With respect to the author's claim under article 26, the State party recalls that distinctions are justified, provided they are based on reasonable and objective criteria, which in turn depends on the specific circumstances and general situation in the country concerned. It refers to Views in Broeks,[57] where the Committee held that "the right to equality before the law and to equal protection of the law without any discrimination does not make all differences of treatment discriminatory. A differentiation based on reasonable and objective criteria does not amount to prohibited discrimination within the meaning of article 26".

4.10 The State party's legislation and the limitation relating to cannabis apply equally to all, Rastafarians and others. The limitation therefore does not violate the right to equal treatment and equality before the law. The author claims the right to see positive measures adopted, at great financial and administrative cost, in favour of Rastafarians to ensure equality for this group with any other religious groups. However, such special treatment in favour of Rastafarians may be interpreted as a form of discrimination against other groups in society who also feel that they have special needs and legitimate claims to be exempted from certain provisions of domestic legislation. The obligations contained in article 26 relate to equality, non-discrimination and equal protection before the law, norms also enshrined in and protected in terms of the State party's Constitution. Equal protection in this context does not include an obligation to make exemptions for certain classes of people.

4.11 On the author's claim under article 27, the State party points out that its Constitution contains the same right framed in almost identical language.[58] It

---

55 See paragraph 13 of the 2002 judgement.
56 Communication No. 570 / 1993, Admissibility decision of 8 April 1994.
57 Communication 172 / 1984, Views adopted on 9 April 1987, paragraph 13.
58 Section 31 of the South African Constitution: "(1) Persons belonging to a cultural, religious or linguistic community may not be denied the right, with other members of that community – (a) to enjoy their culture, practice their religion and use their language; and (b) to form, join and maintain cultural, religious and linguistic associations and other organs of civil society. (2) The rights in subsection (1) may not be exercised in a manner inconsistent with any provision of the Bill of Rights."

is common cause that the Rastafarians form a religious minority group in South African society. When it decided the issue, the Constitutional Court took into account the protection afforded to minority religious groups, like the Rastafarians, in terms of Section 15, paragraph 1,[59] and Section 31[60] of the Constitution, and the constitutional protection required by a small, vulnerable and marginalised group like the Rastafarians.[61] The Court concluded that the relief sought by the author was impractical and found that the legislation in question set reasonable and justifiable limitations to the right to freedom of religion, including within its association context provided for in Section 31 of the Constitution.

4.12 The State party emphasizes that the author did not act on behalf of Rastafarians as a group before domestic courts or the Committee. In addition, he failed to advance facts before the Committee on which to base his view that Rastafarians as a minority group are being singled out for discrimination. If a right to use cannabis during religious ceremonies does not accrue to a member of a minority group because of reasonable and justifiable limitations, such a right cannot be construed in a collective form, as the same limitations will apply.

(...)

Issues and proceedings before the Committee

CONSIDERATION OF ADMISSIBILITY

6.1 Before considering any claim contained in a communication, the Human Rights Committee must, in accordance with rule 93 of its rules of procedure, decide whether or not it is admissible under the Optional Protocol to the Covenant. The Committee has ascertained, as required under article 5, paragraph 2 (a), of the Optional Protocol, that the matter is not being examined under another procedure of international investigation or settlement.

6.2 The Committee notes the State party's contention that a similar claim filed by the author in the African Commission on Human and Peoples' Rights was dismissed on the merits in December 2004. However, article 5, paragraph 2 (a), of the Optional Protocol does not constitute an obstacle to the admissibility of the present communication, since the matter is no longer pending before another procedure of international investigation or settlement, and South Africa has not entered a reservation to article 5, paragraph 2, (a), of the Optional Protocol. The

---

59 Section 15, paragraph 1: "Everyone has the right to freedom of conscience, religion, thought, belief and opinion."
60 Section 31: "Cultural, religious and linguistic communities 1. Persons belonging to a cultural, religious or linguistic community may not be denied the right, with other members of that community a. to enjoy their culture, practise their religion and use their language; and b. to form, join and maintain cultural, religious and linguistic associations and other organs of civil society. 2. The rights in subsection (1) may not be exercised in a manner inconsistent with any provision of the Bill of Rights."
61 See para. 122 of the 2002 Constitutional Court decisions.

clear wording of the provisions of article 5, paragraph 2 (a) militates against the State party's interpretation in paragraph 4.3 above.

6.3 As to the State party's argument that the author has failed to exhaust domestic remedies because he has not brought a general challenge of the law before national courts, the Committee notes that the author brought the claim that Rastafarians should be granted a workable exemption from the general prohibition of the possession and use of cannabis up to the Constitutional Court, the highest court in the State party. As this is precisely the claim argued before the Committee, it concludes that the author has exhausted domestic remedies for the purpose of article 5, paragraph 2 (b), of the Optional Protocol.

6.4 The State party has challenged the admissibility ratione temporis of the communication, because the facts and applications in domestic courts were completed before the entry into force of the Optional Protocol on 28 November 2002, and because it has not affirmed the relevant provisions in the legislation in question. The Committee recalls that it is precluded from examining alleged violations of the Covenant which occurred before the entry into force of the Optional Protocol for the State party, unless these violations continue after that date or continue to have effects which in themselves constitute a violation of the Covenant.[62] While the author's complaint was finally decided by the domestic courts before the entry into force of the Optional Protocol, the Committee notes that the author's claims relate to the application of the Drugs and Drug Trafficking Act 140 of 1992 and the Attorneys Act 53 of 1979, which remain in force. The Committee considers that the issue of whether the effects of the challenged legislation, which continue after the entry into force of the Optional Protocol, constitute a violation is an issue closely interwoven with the merits of the case. It is therefore more appropriately examined at the same time as the substance of the author's claims under articles 18, 26 and 27.

6.5 Regarding the State party's reference to the Committee's inadmissibility decision in M.A.B., W.A.T. and J.A.Y.T. v. Canada,[63] the Committee considers that the factual and legal position in the present case can and should be distinguished from that in the Canadian case which, it understood, concerned the activities of a religious organization whose belief consisted primarily or exclusively in the worship and distribution of a narcotic drug. Rastafarianism as a religion within the meaning of article 18 is not an issue in the present case. The Committee concluded that such a belief could not be brought within the scope of article 18 of the Covenant.

6.6 For the above reasons, the Committee concludes that the communication is admissible.

---

62 See Communication No.24/1977, *Lovelace v. Canada*, Views adopted on 30 July 1981, para.7.3; Communication No. 1367/2005, *Anderson v. Australia*, Decision on Admissibility of 31 October 2006, para. 7.3; and Communication no. 1424/2005, *Anton v. Algeria*, Decision on Admissibility of 1 November 2006, para. 8.3.
63 See para. 4.8 above.

CONSIDERATION OF MERITS

7.1 The Human Rights Committee has considered the present communication in the light of all the information made available to it by the parties, as provided in article 5, paragraph 1, of the Optional Protocol.

7.2 The author has claimed a violation of his right to freedom of religion, because the impugned law does not make an exemption to allow him to use cannabis for religious purposes. The Committee recalls that the freedom to manifest religion or belief in worship, observance, practice and teaching encompasses a broad range of acts and that the concept of worship extends to ritual and ceremonial acts giving expression to belief, as well as various acts integral to such acts.[64] The Committee notes that the material before it is to the effect that the use of cannabis is inherent to the manifestation of the Rastafari religion. In this regard, it recalls that the freedom to manifest one's religion or beliefs is not absolute and may be subject to limitations, which are prescribed by law and are necessary to protect public safety, order, health, or morals, or the fundamental rights and freedoms of others.

7.3 The Committee observes that the prohibition of the possession and use of cannabis, which constitutes the limitation on the author's freedom to manifest his religion, is prescribed by the law (the Drugs and Drug Trafficking Act 140 of 1992). It further notes the State party's conclusion that the law in question was designed to protect public safety, order, health, morals or the fundamental rights and freedoms of others, based on the harmful effects of cannabis, and that an exemption allowing a system of importation, transportation and distribution to Rastafarians may constitute a threat to the public at large, were any of the cannabis enter into general circulation. Under these circumstances the Committee cannot conclude that the prohibition of the possession and use of drugs, without any exemption for specific religious groups, is not proportionate and necessary to achieve this purpose. The Committee finds that the failure of the State party to grant Rastafarians an exemption to its general prohibition of possession and use of cannabis is, in the circumstances of the present case, justified under article 18, paragraph 3, and accordingly finds that the facts of the case do not disclose a violation of article 18, paragraph 1.

7.4 On the author's claim that the failure to provide an exemption for Rastafarians violates his rights under article 27, the Committee notes that it is undisputed that the author is a member of a religious minority and that the use of cannabis is an essential part of the practice of his religion. The State party's legislation therefore constitutes interference with the author's right, as a member of a religious minority, to practice his own religion, in community with the other members of his group. However, the Committee recalls that not every interference can be regarded as a denial of rights within the meaning of article 27.[65] Certain limitations on the right

---

64 See Communication No. 721/1996, *Clement Boodoo v. Trinidad and Tobago*, Views adopted on 2 April 2002, para. 6.6.
65 See Communication No.24/1977, *Lovelace v. Canada*, Views adopted on 30 July 1981, para. 15.

to practice one's religion through the use of drugs are compatible with the exercise of the right under article 27 of the Covenant. The Committee cannot conclude that a general prohibition of possession and use of cannabis constitutes an unreasonable justification for the interference with the author's rights under this article and concludes that the facts do not disclose a violation of article 27.

7.5 The author argues that he is the victim of a de facto discrimination because unlike others, he has to choose between adherence to his religion and respect for the laws of the land. The Committee recalls that a violation of article 26 may result from the discriminatory effect of a rule or measure that is neutral at face value or without intent to discriminate. However, such indirect discrimination can only be said to be based on the grounds set out in article 26 of the Covenant if the detrimental effects of a rule or decision exclusively or disproportionably affect persons having a particular race, colour, sex, language, religion, political or other opinion, national or social origin, property, birth or other status. Furthermore, rules or decisions with such an impact do not amount to discrimination if they are based on objective and reasonable grounds.[66] In the circumstances of the present case, the Committee notes that the prohibition of the possession and use of cannabis affects all individuals equally, including members of other religious movements who may also believe in the beneficial nature of drugs. Accordingly, it considers that the prohibition is based on objective and reasonable grounds. It concludes that the failure of the State party to provide an exemption for Rastafarians does not constitute differential treatment contrary to article 26.

8. The Human Rights Committee, acting under article 5, paragraph 4, of the Optional Protocol to the International Covenant on Civil and Political Rights, is of the view that the facts before it do not reveal a breach of any articles of the Covenant.

C Non-discrimination

C.1. FRANCESCO CAPOTORTI *(Special Rapporteur of the Sub-Commission on Prevention of Discrimination and Protection of Minorities),* **Study on the Rights of Persons Belonging to Ethnic, Religious and Linguistic Minorities *(ST/HR(05)/H852/no.5), 1979.* ***

III *The position of persons belonging to ethnic, religious and linguistic minorities in the society in which they live*

(...)

d *Non-discrimination as a pre-condition of special measures in favour of persons belonging to ethnic, religious and linguistic minorities*

---

66 See the Committee's General Comment No. 18 on non-discrimination and Communication No. 998/2001, *Rupert Althammer et al. v. Austria*, Views adopted on 8 August 2003, para. 10.2.

* From *Study on the Rights of Persons Belonging to Ethnic, Religious and Linguistic Minorities*, by Francesco Capotorti, © (1979) United Nations. Reprinted with the permission of the United Nations.

316. As has been stressed earlier in this study, the effective implementation of the right of persons belonging to ethnic, religious and linguistic minorities to enjoy their own culture, to profess and practise their own religion and to use their own language requires, as an absolute precondition, that the principles of equality and non-discrimination be firmly established in the society in which those persons live.

317. At the seminar on the multinational society held in Ljubljana, Yugoslavia, in 1965, the question of equality and non-discrimination with respect to minorities was discussed in the following terms:

> Certain speakers recalled the many historical instances in which inequitable treatment of ethnic, religious or linguistic groups within a State had provoked internal and international unrest. In this connexion, many of those taking part in the discussion supported the view that certain principles had to be accepted as mandatory: first, the majority must not practise against the minority any form of discrimination whatever, but must extend to it every cultural freedom and an absolute equality of opportunity; secondly, the minority must have the right and facilities to play an active role in the social life of its country of residence;
>
> (...)
>
> In the opinion of many participants, the essential aim was the attainment of equality of treatment in every sphere. It was elementary that every human being had the right to grow to his full stature, enjoying economic security, cultural equality and the freedom of thought and expression; and from that principle of equality flowed the almost universally expressed determination to prohibit discrimination in any form. The State's preventive function in the matter of discrimination, in its turn, called for protective action to safeguard the rights of minority groupings. Some speakers who supported this view also felt that there had been too great a tendency to look on minority problems as merely an issue of liberty. Differences in cultural levels and in living standards often complicated matters; and the primary requirement was not so much liberty in the abstract as equality of opportunity in everyday life.[67]

318. On the reason why non-discrimination is an essential aspect of the international status of minorities, an author wrote:

> The concern frequently expressed by the United Nations Commission on Human Rights, as well as by many Member States, for the protection of minorities and the harmonious development of the multinational or multi-ethnic society appears to owe its origin to two major considerations, In the first place, the goal of abolishing discrimination against individuals, as embodied in the Universal Declaration of Human Rights, is seen to be inseparable from the problem of discrimination against ethnic groups. Many of the desires, needs and values

---

67 ST/TAO/HR/23, paras 26 and 30.

of an individual arise from and are identified with a way of life characteristic of a group, and can be realized only through group activity. An undertaking to abolish discrimination against an individual if he becomes similar to the majority is obviously unsatisfactory in the case of those who do not seek to become completely like the majority. In the second place, it seems highly probable that one of the motives operating here is the growing belief in the value of diversity, the enrichment of community life through the maintenance of cultural variations, the fruitfulness of continuing contrast between different ways of life. Both of these objectives may be said to have been accepted in high places (at United Nations and, in theory at least, by most governments).[68]

319. This attitude implies respect for minorities and for the uniqueness and individuality of persons with different cultures, religions and linguistic backgrounds. It also means that the numerical strength of a group may not be the decisive element in formulating a policy in that matter. The important guiding principle is that no individual should be placed at a disadvantage merely because he is a member of a particular ethnic, religious or linguistic group. Above all, because inter-ethnic differences are in most instances deep-rooted, the display of a spirit of tolerance and the strict application of the principles of equality and non-discrimination are indispensable requirements for maintaining the political and spiritual unity of the States concerned and achieving understanding and harmonious relations between the various components of society, in any multi-ethnic, multi-religious and multilinguistic country.

320. The constitutions or the laws of all the countries surveyed contain provisions which proclaim the principles of equality and non-discrimination and provide that all persons are entitled to the fundamental rights and freedoms of the individual regardless of their race, place of origin, colour or creed. In some constitutions, reference is also made to language,[69] while in some others it is specified that the principle of equality is to be applied to all aspects of the economic, political, juridical, social and cultural life of the country.[70]

C.2. UN HUMAN RIGHTS COMMITTEE (HRC), General Comment No. 22: The Right to Freedom of Thought, Conscience and Religion: Art. 18 *(CCPR/C/21/Rev.1/Add.4), 30 July 1993.*

(...)

9   The fact that a religion is recognized as a State religion or that it is established as official or traditional or that its followers comprise the majority of the population, shall not result in any impairment of the enjoyment of any of the rights under the Covenant, including articles 18 and 27, nor in any

---

68   Otto Klineberg, Background paper C, prepared for the seminar on the multinational society held in Ljubljana, Yugoslavia, in 1965.
69   Denmark; Egypt; Federal Republic of Germany; Greece; India; Israel; Italy; Kuwait.
70   Bulgaria, Czechoslovakia, Romania, Ukrainian SSR, USSR, Yugoslavia.

discrimination against adherents to other religions or non-believers. In particular, certain measures discriminating against the latter, such as measures restricting eligibility for government service to members of the predominant religion or giving economic privileges to them or imposing special restrictions on the practice of other faiths, are not in accordance with the prohibition of discrimination based on religion or belief and the guarantee of equal protection under article 26. The measures contemplated by article 20, paragraph 2, of the Covenant constitute important safeguards against infringement of the rights of religious minorities and of other religious groups to exercise the rights guaranteed by articles 18 and 27, and against acts of violence or persecution directed towards those groups. The Committee wishes to be informed of measures taken by States parties concerned to protect the practices of all religions or beliefs from infringement and to protect their followers from discrimination. Similarly, information as to respect for the rights of religious minorities under article 27 is necessary for the Committee to assess the extent to which the right to freedom of thought, conscience, religion and belief has been implemented by States parties. States parties concerned should also include in their reports information relating to practices considered by their laws and jurisprudence to be punishable as blasphemous.

10 If a set of beliefs is treated as official ideology in constitutions, statutes, proclamations of ruling parties, etc., or in actual practice, this shall not result in any impairment of the freedoms under article 18 or any other rights recognized under the Covenant nor in any discrimination against persons who do not accept the official ideology or who oppose it.

C.3. UN HUMAN RIGHTS COMMITTEE (HRC), CCPR General Comment No. 23: Article 27 (Rights of Minorities) (CCPR/C/21/Rev.1/Add.5), 8 April 1994.

(...)

4 The Covenant also distinguishes the rights protected under article 27 from the guarantees under articles 2.1 and 26. The entitlement, under article 2.1, to enjoy the rights under the Covenant without discrimination applies to all individuals within the territory or under the jurisdiction of the State whether or not those persons belong to a minority. In addition, there is a distinct right provided under article 26 for equality before the law, equal protection of the law, and non-discrimination in respect of rights granted and obligations imposed by the States. It governs the exercise of all rights, whether protected under the Covenant or not, which the State party confers by law on individuals within its territory or under its jurisdiction, irrespective of whether they belong to the minorities specified in article 27 or not.[71] Some

---

71 Official Records of the General Assembly, Thirty-ninth Session, Supplement No. 40 (A/39/40), annex VI, general comment No. 12 (21) (art. 1), also issued in document

States parties who claim that they do not discriminate on grounds of ethnicity, language or religion, wrongly contend, on that basis alone, that they have no minorities.

C.4. UN HUMAN RIGHTS COMMITTEE (HRC), Fatima Anderson v. Denmark (CCPR/C/99/D/1868/2009), Communication No. 1868/2009, 7 September 2010.

Decision on admissibility

1 The author of the communication is Ms. Fatima Andersen, a Danish citizen, born in Denmark on 2 September 1960. She claims to be a victim by Denmark of her rights under articles 2; 20, paragraph 2; and 27 of the Covenant. She is represented by Mr. Niels-Erik Hansen of the Documentation and Advisory Centre on Racial Discrimination (DACoRD). The Optional Protocol entered into force for the State Party on 6 April 1972.

The facts as presented by the author

2.1 On 29 April 2007, the leader of the Danish People's Party (DPP), Member of Parliament Ms. Pia Kjærsgaard, made a statement on the National Danish Television comparing the Muslim headscarves with the Nazi symbol of the swastika. Another member of the Danish People's Party, Member of Parliament Mr. Søren Krarup, had recently made a similar comparison. The author adheres to the Muslim faith and wears a headscarf for religious reasons. She considers that this statement comparing the use of headscarf with the Nazi swastika is a personal insult to her. Moreover, it creates a hostile environment and concrete discrimination against her. For example, it is difficult for her to find a job because of a double discrimination based on her gender and the fact that she wears a headscarf.

2.2 On 30 April 2007, the author's counsel reported the statement to the Copenhagen Metropolitan police, alleging a violation of section 266 (b) of the Danish Criminal Code. On 20 September 2007, the Copenhagen Metropolitan police notified the counsel that on 7 September 2007 the Public Prosecutor for Copenhagen and Bornholm decided, under section 749, paragraph 2, of the Administration of Justice Act, not to prosecute Ms. Kjærsgaard. The letter also advised about the possibility to appeal this decision to the Public Prosecutor General. On 16 October 2007, the author's counsel appealed the decision to the Public Prosecutor General who, on 28 August 2008, upheld the decision of

---

CCPR/C/21/Rev.1, Forty-second Session, Supplement No. 40 (A/42/40), annex VIII, section D, Communication No. 182/1984 (F.H. Zwaan-de Vries v. the Netherlands), views adopted on 9 April 1987; ibid., section C, Communication No. 180/1984, *L.G. Danning v. the Netherlands*, views adopted on 9 April 1987.

the Public Prosecutor for Copenhagen and Bornholm, stating that neither the author nor her counsel could be considered legitimate complainants in the case. He added that statements covered by 266 (b) of the Criminal Code are usually of such a general nature that there would be no individuals who are legitimate complainants. There did not seem to be any information that would prove that Fatima Andersen, the author, could be regarded as an injured person under section 749, paragraph 3, of the Administration of Justice Act, because she could not be said to have such a substantial, direct, personal and legal interest in the outcome of the case. As a result, the counsel, as the author's representative, could not be considered as a legitimate complainant either.

2.3 Under section 99, paragraph 3, subsection 2, of the Administration of Justice Act, this decision is final and can not be appealed. According to the author, there are no other administrative remedies available as the public prosecuting authority has a monopoly to bring cases to the courts in relation to section 266 (b) of the Criminal Code.

The complaint

3.1 The author claims that the State party violated articles 2; 20, paragraph 2; and 27 of the Covenant. The author contends that her case is based on a clear pattern of Islamophobic statements amounting to hate propaganda against Muslims in Denmark carried out by a number of leading members of the DPP. The statements made by Kjærsgaard are only an illustration of a long lasting pattern of crimes committed against Muslims in Denmark. As violations of section 266 (b) of the Criminal Code can be raised only by public prosecutors and because freedom of speech is always favoured over the right not to be subject to hate speech, none of the accusations based on article 20, paragraph 2 of the Covenant make it to court.

3.2 The types of statements such as those of some members of the DPP form part of the overall ongoing campaign stirring up hatred against Danish Muslims. In the author's opinion, those politicians influence the public opinion, and some of them then take action in the form of hate crimes against innocent Muslims living in Denmark. According to section 266 (b) (2) of the Criminal Code, hate speech, which is part of a systematic propaganda by political parties against racial, ethnic or religious groups, is an aggravated factor. The author compares such campaigns to the ones which led to the Holocaust or the genocide in Rwanda. By authorizing such speeches, the Danish authorities allegedly failed to acknowledge the need to protect Muslims against hate speech and thus prevent future hate crimes against members of this religious group. The State party has therefore allegedly violated both articles 20, paragraph 2; and 27 of the Covenant.

3.3 With regard to the exhaustion of domestic remedies, the author refers to the Opinion of the Committee on the Elimination Racial Discrimination in its communication No. 34/2004, Gelle v. Denmark, stressing that in matters related to violations of section 266 (b) of the Criminal Code, the prosecution in Denmark has the final word and can obstruct any attempt of exhaustion of domestic remedies against racist propaganda. By denying the author the right to appeal the case, the State party has further denied her the possibility to exhaust domestic remedies. The author claims, therefore, that all available domestic remedies have been exhausted.

3.4 With regard to her status as a victim, the author quotes the Committee on the Elimination of Racial Discrimination's communication No. 30/2003, The Jewish community of Oslo et al. v. Norway, whereby the State party argued that the authors (including the Jewish community) did not have a victim status. The Committee on the Elimination of Racial Discrimination adopted an approach to the concept of "victim" status similar to the one taken by the Human Rights Committee in the case of Toonen v. Australia and by the European Court of Human Rights in Open Door and Dublin Well Women v. Ireland. In the latter, the Court found certain authors to be "victims" because they belonged to a class/group of persons which might in the future be adversely affected by the acts complained of. The author argues, therefore, that as a member of such a group, she is also a victim. As a Muslim, the ongoing statements against her community directly affect her daily life in Denmark. These statements not only hurt her but put her at risk of attacks by some Danes who believe that Muslims are responsible for crimes they have in fact not committed. Finally, those statements directly reduce her chances to find employment because of the stereotypes related to Muslims.

3.5 Contrary to the prosecutor general's opinion, DACoRD has a right, as the author's legal representative, to file a petition against hate speech on her behalf. By trying to undermine the protection guaranteed by the Covenant, leaving victims of Islamophobic hate speech without effective remedy, the State party has also allegedly violated article 2 of the Covenant.

The state party's observations on the admissibility and merits of the communication

(...)

4.9 The State party strongly rejects the author's claim that, by not prosecuting Ms. Kjærsgaard for her statement, the Danish authorities have given the Danish People's Party a carte blanche to conduct a "systematic Islamophobic and racist campaign against Muslims and other minority groups living in Denmark" and thereby failed its positive obligations under the Covenant. There have been several prosecutions for violation of section 266 (b) of the Criminal Code in connection with politicians' statements relating to Muslims and/or Islam, including for propaganda activities under section 266 (b) (2) of the Criminal Code. The author's evidence proving the risk of attacks consists solely in a reference to a study from 1999 from which it appears that people from Turkey, Lebanon and Somalia living in Denmark suffer from racist attacks in the streets. In the State party's view, such study cannot be considered sufficient evidence to prove that the author has a real reason to fear attacks or assaults, and in fact she has not stated anything about any actual attacks – whether verbal or physical – to which she has been subjected due to Ms. Kjærsgaard's statement even though almost two years had passed after the television broadcast containing the statement when the communication was filed with the Committee.

4.10 The State party therefore requests the Committee to declare the communication inadmissible for failing to establish a prima facie case under article 20, paragraph 2, of the Covenant and for failing to exhaust domestic remedies. Should the Committee declare the communication admissible, it is requested to conclude that no violation of the Covenant has occurred.

(…)

Issues and proceedings before the Committee

CONSIDERATION OF ADMISSIBILITY

6.1 Before considering any claim contained in a communication, the Human Rights Committee must, in accordance with rule 93 of its rules of procedure, decide whether or not the communication is admissible under the Optional Protocol to the Covenant.

6.2 The Committee notes, as required by article 5, paragraph 2 (a), of the Optional Protocol, that the same matter is not being examined under any other international procedure of investigation or settlement.

6.3 The Committee notes the State party's argument that the author did not exhaust domestic remedies, by failing to institute proceedings for defamatory statements, which are applicable to racist statements (sections 267 and 275(1) of the Criminal Code). The Committee also notes that according to the author, both provisions (section 266 (b) on the one hand and sections 267 and 268 on the other) do not protect the same interests (collective interest vs. private interest) and that contrary to the requirement of section 267, an insulting or degrading statement under section 266 needs not to be false to fall within the scope of that provision. It takes note of the author's argument that private litigation is not by definition a remedy to secure the implementation by the State party of its international obligations. The Committee considers that it would be unreasonable to expect the author to initiate separate proceedings under the general provisions of section 267, after having unsuccessfully invoked section 266 (b) of the Criminal Code in respect of circumstances directly implicating the language and object of that provision.[72] Accordingly, the Committee concludes that domestic remedies have been exhausted.

6.4 With regard to the author's allegations under articles 20, paragraph 2, and 27 of the Covenant, the Committee observes that no person may, in theoretical terms and by actio popularis, object to a law or practice which he holds to be at variance with the Covenant. Any person claiming to be a victim of a violation of a right protected by the Covenant must demonstrate either that a State

---

[72] Communication No. 34/2004, *Gelle v. Denmark*, Opinion adopted on 6 March 2006, para. 6.5.14; Committee on the Elimination of Racial Discrimination, communication No. 41/2008, *Jama v. Denmark*, Opinion adopted on 21 August 2009, para. 6.5.

party has by an act or omission already impaired the exercise of his right or that such impairment is imminent, basing his argument for example on legislation in force or on a judicial or administrative decision or practice.[73] In the Committee's decision regarding Toonen v. Australia, the Committee had considered that the author had made reasonable efforts to demonstrate that the threat of enforcement and the pervasive impact of the continued existence of the incriminated facts on administrative practices and public opinion had affected him and continued to affect him personally.[74] In the present case, the Committee considers that the author has failed to establish that the statement made by Ms. Kjærsgaard had specific consequence for her or that the specific consequences of the statements were imminent and would personally affect the author. The Committee therefore considers that the author has failed to demonstrate that she was a victim for purposes of the Covenant. This part of the communication is therefore inadmissible under article 1 of the Optional Protocol.

6.5 The Committee points out that article 2 may be invoked by individuals only in relation to other provisions of the Covenant.[75] A State party cannot reasonably be required, on the basis of article 2, paragraph 3 (b), to make such procedures available in respect of complaints which are insufficiently founded and where the author has not been able to prove that she was a direct victim of such violations. Since the author has failed to demonstrate that she was a victim for purposes of admissibility in relation to articles 20, paragraph 2, and 27 of the Covenant, her allegation of a violation of article 2 of the Covenant is also inadmissible under article 2 of the Optional Protocol.

7 The Committee therefore decides that: (a) The communication is inadmissible pursuant to articles 1 and 2 of the Optional Protocol; (b) This decision will be transmitted to the author and, for information, to the State party.

C.5. UN OFFICE OF THE HIGH COMMISSIONER FOR HUMAN RIGHTS (OHCHR), Minority Rights: International Standards and Guidance for Implementation (HR/PUB/10/3), 2010.*

(...)

---

73 Communications No. 1400/2005, *Beydon et al. v. France*, decision on inadmissibility adopted on 31 October 2005, para. 4.3; No. 1440/005, *Aalbersberg et al. v. The Netherlands*, decision on inadmissibility adopted on 12 July 2006, para. 6.3; and *Brun v. France* (note 15 above), para. 6.3.
74 *Toonen v. Australia* (note 11 above), para. 5.1.
75 Communications No. 972/2001, *Kazantzis v. Cyprus*, decision on inadmissibility adopted on 7 August 2003, para. 6.6; No. 1036/2001, *Faure v. Australia*, Views adopted on 31 October 2005, para. 7.2; and *S.E. v. Argentina* (note 1 above), para. 5.3.
* From Minority Rights: International Standards and Guidance for Implementation, by UN Office of the High Commissioner for Human Rights (OHCHR), ©(2010) United Nations. Reprinted with the permission of the United Nations.

C Equality and non-discrimination

The right not to be discriminated against is paramount in protecting the rights of persons belonging to minorities in all regions of the world. Minorities everywhere experience direct and indirect, de jure and de facto discrimination in their daily lives.

Non-discrimination and equality before the law are two of the basic principles of international human rights law. The principle of non-discrimination prohibits any distinction, exclusion, restriction or preference which has the purpose or effect of impairing or nullifying the recognition, enjoyment or exercise by all persons, on an equal footing, of all rights and freedoms.[76] There is no requirement to demonstrate discriminatory intent. The phrase "purpose or effect" refers to legislation and/or policies which may be textually neutral but are interpreted in a manner that results in discrimination. International human rights law prohibits both direct and indirect discrimination.

Indirect discrimination is more subtle and, therefore, harder to recognize and eliminate. It occurs when a practice, rule or requirement is neutral on its face but has a disproportionate impact on particular groups, unless the practice, rule or requirement is necessary and appropriate to achieve a legitimate objective. Focusing on the unequal impact of a measure on an individual as a member of a group helps to better identify the root causes of discrimination and inequality.

Differential treatment may be permissible if its objective is to overcome past discrimination or address persisting inequalities. In fact, international human rights law provides for the adoption of special measures in favour of certain persons or groups for the purpose of eliminating discrimination and achieving full equality, not only in law but also in practice. Several legal instruments envisage this. The International Convention on the Elimination of All Forms of Racial Discrimination permits the implementation of special measures "for the sole purpose of securing adequate advancement of certain racial or ethnic groups or individuals requiring such protection as may be necessary in order to ensure such groups or individuals equal enjoyment or exercise of human rights and fundamental freedoms".[77]

The Convention on the Elimination of All Forms of Discrimination against Women allows for "temporary special measures" which accelerate de facto equality between men and women.[78] The Human Rights Committee, in its general comment No. 18 (1989) on non-discrimination, held that States parties are sometimes required to "take affirmative action in order to diminish or eliminate conditions which cause or help to perpetuate discrimination prohibited by the Covenant" and that "such action may involve granting for a time to the part of the population concerned certain preferential treatment in specific matters as

---

76 See International Convention on the Elimination of All Forms of Racial Discrimination, art. 1 (1).
77 Art. 1, para. 4. See also art. 2, para. 2.
78 Art. 4, para. 1.

compared with the rest of the population... as long as such action is needed to correct discrimination in fact".

In its general recommendation No. 32 (2009), the Committee on the Elimination of Racial Discrimination provided further guidance on the scope of the principle of non-discrimination under article 1 (1) of the Convention and, more importantly, the meaning of "special measures". The Committee specified that "the list of human rights to which the principle applies under the Convention is not closed and extends to any field of human rights regulated by the public authorities in the State party [...] to address racial discrimination 'by any persons, group or organization' ".[79]

Regarding "special measures" to advance equality, the Committee asserted that the term also includes measures that in some countries may be described as "affirmative measures", "affirmative action" or "positive action", whereas the term "positive discrimination" is, in the context of international human rights standards, a *contradictio in terminis* and should be avoided. "Measures" includes the full span of legislative, executive, administrative, budgetary and regulatory instruments, at every level in the State apparatus, as well as plans, policies, programmes and preferential regimes in areas such as employment, housing, education, culture, and participation in public life for disfavoured groups, devised and implemented on the basis of such instruments. The obligation to take special measures is distinct from the general positive obligation of States parties to the Convention to secure human rights and fundamental freedoms on a non-discriminatory basis to persons and groups subject to their jurisdiction; this is a general obligation flowing from the provisions of the Convention as a whole and integral to all parts of the Convention. Special measures should be appropriate to the situation to be remedied, be legitimate, be necessary in a democratic society, respect the principles of fairness and proportionality, and be temporary.

It is important to note that the Committee, in its general recommendation, also specified that "special measures should not be confused with specific rights pertaining to certain categories of person or community, such as, for example the rights of persons belonging to minorities to enjoy their own culture, profess and practise their own religion and use their own language [...]. Such rights are permanent rights, recognized as such in human rights instruments, including those adopted in the context of the United Nations and its agencies. States parties should carefully observe distinctions between special measures and permanent human rights in their law and practice. The distinction between special measures and permanent rights implies that those entitled to permanent rights may also enjoy the benefits of special measures".[80]

---

79 See also art. 2 (1) (d) and (b).
80 See also Committee on the Elimination of Discrimination against Women, general recommendation No. 25 (2004), para. 19, and "Recommendations of the Forum on Minority Issues" (A/HRC/10/11/ Add.1, para. 12).

While the implementation of the International Convention on the Elimination of All Forms of Racial Discrimination can contribute to successful integration in societies, it is extremely important to ensure that integration is not understood to mean, and does not lead to, forced assimilation into the dominant culture. The implementation of the rights of persons belonging to minorities has highlighted the need not only to understand and redress inequality but also to accommodate difference and diversity. Special measures to protect the existence and identity of minorities and encourage conditions for the promotion of that identity, including through minority language education, are to be distinguished from temporary special measures. Special measures to protect minorities can be permanent. The open-ended engagement of a State to ensure effective participation by adopting special procedures resulting in the creation of institutions, and making arrangements through which members of minorities are able to make decisions, exercise legislative and administrative powers, and develop their culture, constitutes the best approach to preventing conflicts. In this regard, the Committee on Economic, Social and Cultural Rights adopted general comment No. 21 (2009) on the right of everyone to take part in cultural life, which entails an obligation on States parties to recognize, respect and protect minority cultures as an essential component of the identity of the States themselves.

To further the protection of minorities in accordance with the principle of non-discrimination, they should have equal access to social services, and to employment in the public and private sectors, including through positive action. In many instances, the root causes of human rights violations are found in the inequalities between groups in their enjoyment of economic, social and cultural rights. Due regard must, therefore, be paid to the implementation of the International Convention on the Elimination of All Forms of Racial Discrimination and the International Covenant on Economic, Social and Cultural Rights. It is particularly important to pay attention to the situation of persons belonging to minorities when developing, implementing and evaluating poverty reduction programmes, and working towards achieving the Millennium Development Goals (MDGs). Moreover, measures for minorities to effectively participate in and be consulted on development and economic projects should be adopted and the impact of such projects on persons belonging to minorities assessed.

Individuals must not be subjected to discrimination for manifesting their group identity. The importance of this principle is captured in the Commentary of the Working Group on Minorities as follows: "Governments or persons belonging to majorities are often tolerant of persons of other national or ethnic origins until such time as the latter assert their own identity, language and traditions. It is often only when they assert their rights as persons belonging to a group that discrimination or persecution starts".[81]

More recently, the Committee on Economic, Social and Cultural Rights adopted general comment No. 20 (2009), which provides guidance on the

---

81 E/CN.4/Sub.2/AC.5/2005/2, para. 53.

obligation of States parties to guarantee non-discrimination in the exercise of each of the economic, social and cultural rights enshrined in the Covenant. It spells out various distinctions in the manifestation of discrimination. It clarifies how formal and substantive discrimination, direct and indirect forms of differential treatment, and discrimination in the private and public spheres can amount to a violation of article 2 (2) of the Covenant. As an example of indirect discrimination, it notes that requiring a birth registration certificate for school enrolment may discriminate against ethnic minorities or non-nationals who do not possess, or have been denied, such certificates.

The 2001 Durban Declaration and Programme of Action of the World Conference against Racism, Racial Discrimination, Xenophobia and Related Intolerance provides an innovative anti-discrimination agenda with specific reference to Africans and people of African descent, Asians and persons of Asian descent, indigenous peoples, migrants, refugees, minorities, the Roma and others. Regarding people of African descent in particular, the World Conference, in its Programme of Action, specifically "requests the Commission on Human Rights to consider establishing a working group or other mechanism of the United Nations to study the problems of racial discrimination faced by people of African descent". To this end, the Working Group of Experts on People of African Descent was established by Commission on Human Rights resolution 2002/68 of 25 April 2002. Its mandate is, inter alia, to make proposals on the elimination of racial discrimination against Africans and people of African descent in all parts of the world.

The need to ensure that minorities are treated equally and enjoy human rights and fundamental freedoms without discrimination of any kind was reiterated by the Durban Review Conference, which in its Outcome Document "urges States to bolster measures to eliminate the barriers and to broaden access to opportunities for greater and more meaningful participation by [...] persons belonging to national or ethnic, religious and linguistic minorities in the political, economic, social and cultural spheres of society".

D Right to culture

D.1. UN HUMAN RIGHTS COMMITTEE (HRC), **CCPR General Comment No. 23: Article 27 (Rights of Minorities) (CCPR/C/21/Rev.1/Add.5), 8 April 1994.**

(...)

7   With regard to the exercise of the cultural rights protected under article 27, the Committee observes that culture manifests itself in many forms, including a particular way of life associated with the use of land resources, especially in the case of indigenous peoples. That right may include such traditional activities as fishing or hunting and the right to live in reserves protected by law. The enjoyment of those rights may require positive legal measures of

protection and measures to ensure the effective participation of members of minority communities in decisions which affect them.[82]

(...)

9   The Committee concludes that article 27 relates to rights whose protection imposes specific obligations on States parties. The protection of these rights is directed towards ensuring the survival and continued development of the cultural, religious and social identity of the minorities concerned, thus enriching the fabric of society as a whole. Accordingly, the Committee observes that these rights must be protected as such and should not be confused with other personal rights conferred on one and all under the Covenant. States parties, therefore, have an obligation to ensure that the exercise of these rights is fully protected and they should indicate in their reports the measures they have adopted to this end.

E   Right to education

E.1. FRANCESCO CAPOTORTI (Special Rapporteur of the Sub-Commission on Prevention of Discrimination and Protection of Minorities), **Study on the Rights of Persons Belonging to Ethnic, Religious and Linguistic Minorities *(ST/HR(05)/H852/no.5), 1979.*** [*]

(...)

(b)   The right of persons belonging to religious minorities not to be compelled to follow instruction in a religion other than their own

419. The principle according to which "no one shall be compelled to receive instruction in a religion or belief contrary to his convictions or, in the case of children, contrary to the wishes of their parents or legal guardians" has been included among those proposed by the Sub-Commission in the draft declaration on the elimination of all forms of religious intolerance. In most of the countries surveyed, including those having a State religion, such a right has been affirmed in the constitution or in the law. Thus, in Malaysia the Constitution provides that no person shall be required to receive instruction in a religion other than his own and "for the purpose of this clause, the religion of a person under the age

---

82   See notes 1 and 2 above, Communication No. 167/1984, *Bernard Ominayak, Chief of the Lubicon Lake Band v. Canada*, views adopted on 26 March 1990, and Communication No. 197/1985, *Kitok v. Sweden*, views adopted on 27 July 1988.
*   From *Study on the Rights of Persons Belonging to Ethnic, Religious and Linguistic Minorities*, by Francesco Capotorti, © (1979) United Nations. Reprinted with the permission of the United Nations.

of eighteen shall be decided by his parents or guardian". Under the terms of article 49 of the Swiss constitution, "no one may be forced to receive any religious instruction, it being understood that the right to decide on the religious education of children up to the age of 16 years vests in their parents or guardians". According to the laws of Finland, no one may be compelled to receive instruction in a religion to which he does not adhere. The Nigerian constitution provides that "no person attending any place of education shall be required to receive religious instruction or take part in or attend any religious ceremony or observances if such instruction, ceremony and observances relate to a religion other than his own". Regarding Ethiopia, it has been said that, while religious instruction given in public schools is based upon the teaching of the National Church, every parent enjoys full freedom to withdraw his child from religious classes. In Austria, the School Organisation Act provides that a child cannot be forced against his parents' will to take part in the religious rites or to follow instruction in a religion other than his own.

(...)

5   The right of persons belonging to religious minorities to establish educational institutions

421. It is a widely held view that the right of members of religious groups to establish denominational schools, and to maintain institutions to train the personnel required for the practices prescribed by their religion, is also a corollary of everyone's freedom to manifest his own religion.

(a) Establishment of denominational schools

422. In several countries, the establishment of schools is considered to be the exclusive responsibility of States, and religious communities are not therefore permitted to establish separate schools.[83] However, in a great number of the countries studied, various religious groups are reported to have established their own schools at the primary and secondary level, often with financial assistance from the State. Thus, in Malaysia, the constitution accords to every religious group the right to establish and maintain institutions for the education of children and to provide therein instruction in its own religion. It further provides that there shall be no discrimination on the ground only of religion in any law relating to such institutions or in the administration of any such law. The constitution of Nigeria provides "that no religious community or denomination shall be prevented from providing religious instruction for persons of that community or denomination in any educational institution maintained wholly by that community or denomination".

---

83   Bulgaria, Czechoslovakia, German Democratic Republic, Hungary, Poland, USSR, Yugoslavia.

423. There may be, however, instances where the question of the establishment of denominational schools has been a subject of friction between various population groups. Thus it has been said, regarding Sri Lanka, that after independence that question created controversy because, as a result of the patronage extended to Christian missionary schools during the colonial period, schools managed by the Christian minority occupied a pre-eminent position. Liberal State aid was available to these schools, while the funds allocated to public schools were said to be grossly inadequate for their barest needs. A further cause of bitterness against Christian denominational schools was that the large numbers of non-Christian children who attended them were denied education in their religion. It is in these circumstances that during the post-colonial period, popular agitation led to the taking over by the State of a number of denominational schools. Also in Sudan, action is reported to have been taken to curb the expansion of schools operated by Christian missionaries. Under a law adopted after independence, non-Mohammedan religious schools are to be regulated by the Council of Ministers. No religious school can be opened without the consent of the Regulatory Ministry, which may grant such consent unconditionally or subject to such conditions as it sees fit.

424. A question of great importance for the operation and development of schools run by members of religious minorities is whether these schools are subsidized by the State. The way this problem is dealt with varies from one country to another, and often from one group to another within a country. In some cases, such schools or some of them receive financial assistance, while in others the principle of strict neutrality between the State and religion is applied and consequently no public funds are provided to denominational schools. Thus the Government of Sweden reports that it does not financially support the Catholic schools established in the country, but provides funds for one Jewish school. The official attitude is that in principle the general Swedish compulsory school is responsible for the education of all children and, consequently, except in special circumstances, religious schools founded on private initiative do not receive State subsidies.

425. Under the terms of the constitution of Ethiopia, financial aid may be provided for the establishment and maintenance of Moslem institutions or the instruction in the Moslem religion of persons professing that religion. Four exclusively Moslem schools are maintained by the Ministry of Education. It is further noted that scholarships or other forms of aid to students, such as free or subsidized housing, meals, transportation and clothing are provided without discrimination. In Switzerland the federal court has ruled that subsidies for denominational schools are compatible with the federal constitution but that the manner of granting such subsidies is a matter for the jurisdiction of each canton. In Finland, subject to requirements laid down by the law, schools established by religious communities may be subsidized by the State. The constitution of Fiji provides that "every religious community shall be entitled, at its own expense, to establish and maintain places of education and to manage any place of education

which it wholly maintains".[84] Notwithstanding, it has been reported that the Government of Fiji trains teachers for primary schools run by members of the Christian minorities and pays a substantial part of their salaries. In Austria, according to the Act on Private Schools, total staff expenses for teachers employed by authorized denominational schools are now paid by the State. Furthermore, pupils attending denominational schools enjoy the same advantages as do the pupils of public schools, such as allowances, free transportation and free supply of educational material. This is also the case in a number of communities in the United States of America.

426. Since the public schools in all countries are educational institutions open to every child, the question may be asked whether pupils belonging to religious minorities are given in such schools the opportunity to receive instruction in their religion. In some instances, no such opportunities are offered, while in others religious instruction is given on a voluntary basis. In still other countries, the State is under obligation to provide at its own expense facilities for religious instruction in public schools. The Government of Sweden states that special religious instruction is not provided in the Swedish compulsory schools. In the Philippines lay schools offer religious instruction outside the normal curricula and school hours. Furthermore, these classes of religious instruction are voluntary on the part of teachers and students and are undertaken only upon the petition of parents or guardians. The constitution of Switzerland provides that "the public schools shall be open to the adherents of all faiths, who shall not be made to suffer in any way in their freedom of conscience or belief". Consequently, religious instruction in public schools can only be optional. Most municipalities in Switzerland, however, facilitate the provision of such instruction by making school premises available to ministers and priests. Moreover, school prayers are still the rule in many places.

427. The Government of Poland reports that the right to give religious instruction is granted to each religious denomination. When secular education was introduced, the State not only allowed religious instruction to be organized in special centres outside the schools but also took measures to ensure that members of religious communities would not be liable to additional expenditures by providing a special remuneration to religious instructors and by placing them on an equal footing with public service officials. In Finland, according to the Act on Elementary Schools and the Act on the Principles of the School System, when five or more pupils belong to the same religious denomination, instruction in their own religion shall be given to them, if so required by their parents or guardians. In Austria, the School Organization Act provides that the public schools have, inter alia, the task of fostering the talents and potential abilities of young persons, in accordance with religious values, and schools are therefore required to draw up syllabuses accordingly. Under the Act on Religious Instruction, the preparation of manuals and educational material for the purposes of religious

---

84 The constitution of Nigeria contains a similar clause.

instruction is the responsibility of the legally recognized churches. The Act further provides that the staff expenses for religious instructors at public schools are borne by the State. A minimum number of five pupils is however required for the application of this provision.

(b) Establishment of educational institutions for the training of clergy

428. In many of the countries surveyed, the State provides facilities to religious minority groups to train their personnel, whereas in some others, each religious group has to provide the facilities for training its personnel at its own expense. While the available information does not reveal any case where the State hinders or prevents a religion from training its clergy, it shows, however, that in a number of cases minority religions are given a treatment different from that accorded to the State religion, which very often enjoys considerable financial assistance from public authorities for that purpose.

Section 2

Convention relating to the Status of Refugees

[Adopted by the United Nations Conference of Plenipotentiaries on the Status of Refugees and Stateless Persons, held at Geneva from 2 to 25 July 1951]

Article 1

Definition of the term "refugee"

A   For the purposes of the present Convention, the term "refugee" shall apply to any person who: Has been considered a refugee under the Arrangements of 12 May 1926 and 30 June 1928 or under the Conventions of 28 October 1933 and 10 February 1938, the Protocol of 14 September 1939 or the Constitution of the International Refugee Organization;

Decisions of non-eligibility taken by the International Refugee Organization during the period of its activities shall not prevent the status of refugee being accorded to persons who fulfil the conditions of paragraph 2 of this section;

(2) As a result of events occurring before 1 January 1951 and owing to well-founded fear of being persecuted for reasons of race, religion, nationality, membership of a particular social group or political opinion, is outside the country of his nationality and is unable or, owing to such fear, is unwilling to avail himself of the protection of that country; or who, not having a nationality and being

Protocol relating to the status of refugees

[*Protocol was taken note of with approval by the Economic and Social Council in resolution 1186 (XLI) of 18 November 1966 and was taken note of by the General Assembly in resolution 2198 (XXI) of 16 December 1966. In the same resolution the General Assembly requested the Secretary-General to transmit the text of the Protocol to the States mentioned in article V thereof, with a view to enabling them to accede to the Protocol. Entry into force 4 October 1967, in accordance with article VIII*]

Article 1

General provision

1 The States Parties to the present Protocol undertake to apply articles 2 to 34 inclusive of the Convention to refugees as hereinafter defined.
2 For the purpose of the present Protocol, the term "refugee" shall, except as regards the application of paragraph 3 of this article, mean any person within the definition of article I of the Convention as if the words "As a result of events occurring before 1 January 1951 and ..." and the words "... as a result of such events", in article 1 A (2) were omitted.
3 The present Protocol shall be applied by the States Parties hereto without any geographic limitation, save that existing declarations made by States already Parties to the Convention in accordance with article I B (I) (a) of the Convention, shall, unless extended under article I B (2) thereof, apply also under the present Protocol.

Article 2

Co-operation of the national authorities with the United Nations

1 The States Parties to the present Protocol undertake to co-operate with the Office of the United Nations High Commissioner for Refugees, or any other agency of the United Nations which may succeed it, in the exercise of its functions, and shall in particular facilitate its duty of supervising the application of the provisions of the present Protocol.
2 In order to enable the Office of the High Commissioner or any other agency of the United Nations which may succeed it, to make reports to the competent organs of the United Nations, the States Parties to the present Protocol undertake to provide them with the information and statistical data requested, in the appropriate form, concerning:

   (a) The condition of refugees;
   (b) The implementation of the present Protocol;
   (c) Laws, regulations and decrees which are, or may hereafter be, in force relating to refugees.

Article 3

Information on national legislation

The States Parties to the present Protocol shall communicate to the Secretary-General of the United Nations the laws and regulations which they may adopt to ensure the application of the present Protocol.

Article 4

Settlement of disputes

Any dispute between States Parties to the present Protocol which relates to its interpretation or application and which cannot be settled by other means shall be referred to the International Court of Justice at the request of any one of the parties to the dispute.

Article 5

Accession

The present Protocol shall be open for accession on behalf of all States Parties to the Convention and of any other State Member of the United Nations or member of any of the specialized agencies or to which an invitation to accede may have been addressed by the General Assembly of the United Nations. Accession shall be effected by the deposit of an instrument of accession with the Secretary-General of the United Nations.

Article 6

Federal clause

In the case of a Federal or non-unitary State, the following provisions shall apply:

(a) With respect to those articles of the Convention to be applied in accordance with article I, paragraph 1, of the present Protocol that come within the legislative jurisdiction of the federal legislative authority, the obligations of the Federal Government shall to this extent be the same as those of States Parties which are not Federal States;

(b) With respect to those articles of the Convention to be applied in accordance with article I, paragraph 1, of the present Protocol that come within the legislative jurisdiction of constituent States, provinces or cantons which are not, under the constitutional system of the Federation, bound to take legislative action, the Federal Government shall bring such articles with a favourable

recommendation to the notice of the appropriate authorities of States, provinces or cantons at the earliest possible moment;
(c) A Federal State Party to the present Protocol shall, at the request of any other State Party hereto transmitted through the Secretary-General of the United Nations, supply a statement of the law and practice of the Federation and its constituent units in regard to any particular provision of the Convention to be applied in accordance with article I, paragraph 1, of the present Protocol, showing the extent to which effect has been given to that provision by legislative or other action.

Article 7

Reservations and declarations

1 At the time of accession, any State may make reservations in respect of article IV of the present Protocol and in respect of the application in accordance with article I of the present Protocol of any provisions of the Convention other than those contained in articles 1, 3, 4, 16(1) and 33 thereof, provided that in the case of a State Party to the Convention reservations made under this article shall not extend to refugees in respect of whom the Convention applies.
2 Reservations made by States Parties to the Convention in accordance with article 42 thereof shall, unless withdrawn, be applicable in relation to their obligations under the present Protocol.
3 Any State making a reservation in accordance with paragraph I of this article may at any time withdraw such reservation by a communication to that effect addressed to the Secretary-General of the United Nations.
4 Declarations made under article 40, paragraphs I and 2, of the Convention by a State Party thereto which accedes to the present Protocol shall be deemed to apply in respect of the present Protocol, unless upon accession a notification to the contrary is addressed by the State Party concerned to the Secretary-General of the United Nations. The provisions of article 40, paragraphs 2 and 3, and of article 44, paragraph 3, of the Convention shall be deemed to apply mutatis mutandis to the present Protocol.

Article 8

Entry into protocol

1 The present Protocol shall come into force on the day of deposit of the sixth instrument of accession.
2 For each State acceding to the Protocol after the deposit of the sixth instrument of accession, the Protocol shall come into force on the date of deposit by such State of its instrument of accession.

Article 9

Denunciation

1   Any State Party hereto may denounce this Protocol at any time by a notification addressed to the Secretary-General of the United Nations.
2   Such denunciation shall take effect for the State Party concerned one year from the date on which it is received by the Secretary-General of the United Nations.

Article 10

Notifications by the Secretary-General of the United Nations

The Secretary-General of the United Nations shall inform the States referred to in article V above of the date of entry into force, accessions, reservations and withdrawals of reservations to and denunciations of the present Protocol, and of declarations and notifications relating hereto.

Article 11

Deposit in the Archives of the Secretariat of the United Nations

A copy of the present Protocol, of which the Chinese, English, French, Russian and Spanish texts are equally authentic, signed by the President of the General Assembly and by the Secretary-General of the United Nations, shall be deposited in the archives of the Secretariat of the United Nations. The Secretary-General will transmit certified copies thereof to all States Members of the United Nations and to the other States referred to in article 5 above.

A Right to asylum

A.1. UN REFUGEE AGENCY (UNHCR), **Guidelines on International Protection: "Membership of a particular social group" within the context of Article 1A(2) of the 1951 Convention and/or its 1967 Protocol relating to the Status of Refugees** *(HCR/GIP/02/02), 7 May 2002.*

(…)

B UNHCR's definition

10. Given the varying approaches, and the protection gaps which can result, UNHCR believes that the two approaches ought to be reconciled.

11 The protected characteristics approach may be understood to identify a set of groups that constitute the core of the social perception analysis. Accordingly, it is appropriate to adopt a single standard that incorporates both dominant approaches:

a particular social group is a group of persons who share a common characteristic other than their risk of being persecuted, or who are perceived as a group by society. The characteristic will often be one which is innate, unchangeable, or which is otherwise fundamental to identity, conscience or the exercise of one's human rights.

12 This definition includes characteristics which are historical and therefore cannot be changed, and those which, though it is possible to change them, ought not to be required to be changed because they are so closely linked to the identity of the person or are an expression of fundamental human rights. It follows that sex can properly be within the ambit of the social group category, with women being a clear example of a social subset defined by innate and immutable characteristics, and who are frequently treated differently to men.[85]

(...)

Relevance of size

18 The size of the purported social group is not a relevant criterion in determining whether a particular social group exists within the meaning of Article 1A(2). This is true as well for cases arising under the other Convention grounds. For example, States may seek to suppress religious or political ideologies that are widely shared among members of a particular society – perhaps even by a majority of the population; the fact that large numbers of persons risk persecution cannot be a ground for refusing to extend international protection where it is otherwise appropriate.

19 Cases in a number of jurisdictions have recognized "women" as a particular social group. This does not mean that all women in the society qualify for refugee status. A claimant must still demonstrate a well-founded fear of being persecuted based on her membership in the particular social group, not be within one of the exclusion grounds, and meet other relevant criteria.

---

85 For more information on gender-related claims, see UNHCR's Guidelines on International Protection: Gender-Related Persecution within the Context of Article 1A(2) of the 1951 Convention and/or its 1967. Protocol relating to the Status of Refugees (HCR/GIP/02/01, 10 May 2002), as well as Summary Conclusions of the Expert Roundtable on Gender-Related Persecution, San Remo, 6-8 September 2001, no.5.

A.2. UN REFUGEE AGENCY (UNHCR), Guidelines on International Protection: Religion-Based Refugee Claims under Article 1A(2) of the 1951 Convention and/or the 1967 Protocol relating to the Status of Refugees *(HCR/GIP/04/06), 28 April 2004.*

I. Introduction

1   Claims to refugee status based on religion can be among the most complex. Decision-makers have not always taken a consistent approach, especially when applying the term "religion" contained in the refugee definition of the 1951 Convention relating to the Status of Refugees and when determining what constitutes "persecution" in this context. Religion-based refugee claims may overlap with one or more of the other grounds in the refugee definition or, as can often happen, they may involve post-departure conversions, that is, sur place claims. While these Guidelines do not purport to offer a definitive definition of "religion", they provide decisionmakers with guiding parameters to facilitate refugee status determination in such cases.

2   The right to freedom of thought, conscience and religion is one of the fundamental rights and freedoms in international human rights law. In determining religion-based claims, it is therefore useful, inter alia, to draw on Article 18 of the 1948 Universal Declaration of Human Rights (the "Universal Declaration") and Articles 18 and 27 of the 1966 International Covenant on Civil and Political Rights (the "International Covenant"). Also relevant are the General Comments issued by the Human Rights Committee,[86] the 1981 Declaration on the Elimination of All Forms of Intolerance and Discrimination based on Religion or Belief, the 1992 Declaration on the Rights of Persons belonging to National or Ethnic, Religious and Linguistic Minorities and the body of reports of the Special Rapporteur on Religious Intolerance.[87] These international human rights standards provide guidance in defining the term "religion" also in the context of international refugee law, against which action taken by States to restrict or prohibit certain practices can be examined.

---

86   See, in particular, Human Rights Committee, General Comment No. 22, adopted 20 July 1993, UN doc. CCPR/C/21/Rev.1/ADD.4, 27 September 1993.

87   The latter can be found at http://www.unhchr.ch/huridocda/huridoca.nsf/FramePage/intolerance+En?OpenDocument. Relevant regional instruments include Article 9 of the 1950 European Convention on Human Rights; Article 12 of the 1969 American Convention on Human Rights; Article 8 of the 1981 African Charter on Human and Peoples' Rights.

II. Substantive analysis

A. DEFINING "RELIGION"

3   The refugee definition contained in Article 1A(2) of the 1951 Convention states: A. For the purposes of the present Convention, the term "refugee" shall apply to any person who: ... (2) ... owing to well-founded fear of being persecuted for reasons of race, religion, nationality, membership of a particular social group or political opinion, is outside the country of his nationality and is unable or, owing to such fear, is unwilling to avail himself of the protection of that country; or who, not having a nationality and being outside the country of his former habitual residence as a result of such events, is unable or, owing to such fear, is unwilling to return to it.

4   The travaux préparatoires of the 1951 Convention show that religion-based persecution formed an integral and accepted part of the refugee definition throughout the drafting process. There was, however, no attempt to define the term as such.[88] No universally accepted definition of "religion" exists, but the instruments mentioned in paragraph 2 above certainly inform the interpretation of the term "religion" in the international refugee law context. Its use in the 1951 Convention can therefore be taken to encompass freedom of thought, conscience or belief.[89] As the Human Rights Committee notes, "religion" is "not limited ... to traditional religions or to religions and beliefs with institutional characteristics or practices analogous to those of traditional religions".[90] It also broadly covers acts of failing or refusing to observe a religion or to hold any particular religious belief. The term is not, however, without limits and international human rights law foresees a number of legitimate boundaries on the exercise of religious freedom as outlined in greater detail in paragraphs 15–16 below.

5   Claims based on "religion" may involve one or more of the following elements: a) religion as belief (including non-belief); b) religion as identity; c) religion as a way of life.

6.   "Belief", in this context, should be interpreted so as to include theistic, non-theistic and atheistic beliefs. Beliefs may take the form of convictions or values about the divine or ultimate reality or the spiritual destiny of humankind. Claimants may also be considered heretics, apostates, schismatic, pagans or superstitious, even by other adherents of their religious tradition and be persecuted for that reason.

---

88 A key source in States' deliberations was the refugee definition set out in the 1946 Constitution of the International Refugee Organisation (IRO). This included those expressing valid objections to return because of a fear of persecution on grounds of "race, religion, nationality or political opinions". (A fifth ground, membership of a particular social group, was approved later in the negotiating process for the 1951 Convention.).
89 See, also, UNHCR, Handbook on Procedures and Criteria for Determining Refugee Status 1979, Geneva, re-edited 1992 (hereafter "UNHCR Handbook"), paragraph 71.
90 Human Rights Committee, General Comment No. 22, above note 1, paragraph 2.

7 "Identity" is less a matter of theological beliefs than membership of a community that observes or is bound together by common beliefs, rituals, traditions, ethnicity, nationality, or ancestry. A claimant may identify with, or have a sense of belonging to, or be identified by others as belonging to, a particular group or community. In many cases, persecutors are likely to target religious groups that are different from their own because they see that religious identity as part of a threat to their own identity or legitimacy.

8 For some individuals, "religion" is a vital aspect of their "way of life" and how they relate, either completely or partially, to the world. Their religion may manifest itself in such activities as the wearing of distinctive clothing or observance of particular religious practices, including observing religious holidays or dietary requirements. Such practices may seem trivial to non-adherents, but may be at the core of the religion for the adherent concerned.

9 Establishing sincerity of belief, identity and/or a certain way of life may not necessarily be relevant in every case.[91] It may not be necessary, for instance, for an individual (or a group) to declare that he or she belongs to a religion, is of a particular religious faith, or adheres to religious practices, where the persecutor imputes or attributes this religion, faith or practice to the individual or group. As is discussed further below in paragraph 31, it may also not be necessary for the claimant to know or understand anything about the religion, if he or she has been identified by others as belonging to that group and fears persecution as a result. An individual (or group) may be persecuted on the basis of religion, even if the individual or other members of the group adamantly deny that their belief, identity and/or way of life constitute a "religion".

10 Similarly, birth into a particular religious community, or a close correlation between race and/or ethnicity on the one hand and religion on the other could preclude the need to enquire into the adherence of an individual to a particular faith or the bona fides of a claim to membership of that community, if adherence to that religion is attributed to the individual.

B WELL-FOUNDED FEAR OF PERSECUTION

a) General

11 The right to freedom of religion includes the freedom to manifest one's religion or belief, either individually or in community with others and in public or private in worship, observance, practice and teaching.[92] The only circumstances under which this freedom may be restricted are set out in Article 18(3) of the International Covenant, as described in paragraphs 15–16 below.

---

91 For further analysis of credibility issues, see paragraphs 28–33 below.
92 See Universal Declaration, Article 18 and International Covenant, Article 18(1).

12 Persecution for reasons of religion may therefore take various forms. Depending on the particular circumstances of the case, including the effect on the individual concerned, examples could include prohibition of membership of a religious community, of worship in community with others in public or in private, of religious instruction, or serious measures of discrimination imposed on individuals because they practise their religion, belong to or are identified with a particular religious community, or have changed their faith.[93] Equally, in communities in which a dominant religion exists or where there is a close correlation between the State and religious institutions, discrimination on account of one's failure to adopt the dominant religion or to adhere to its practices, could amount to persecution in a particular case.[94] Persecution may be inter-religious (directed against adherents or communities of different faiths), intra-religious (within the same religion, but between different sects, or among members of the same sect), or a combination of both.[95] The claimant may belong to a religious minority or majority. Religion-based claims may also be made by individuals in marriages of mixed religions.

13 Applying the same standard as for other Convention grounds, religious belief, identity, or way of life can be seen as so fundamental to human identity that one should not be compelled to hide, change or renounce this in order to avoid persecution.[96] Indeed, the Convention would give no protection from persecution for reasons of religion if it was a condition that the person affected must take steps – reasonable or otherwise – to avoid offending the wishes of the persecutors. Bearing witness in words and deeds is often bound up with the existence of religious convictions.

14 Each claim requires examination on its merits on the basis of the individual's situation. Relevant areas of enquiry include the individual profile and

---

93 UNHCR Handbook, above note 4, paragraph 72.
94 In this context, Article 27 of the International Covenant reads: "In those States in which ethnic, religious or linguistic minorities exist, persons belonging to such minorities shall not be denied the right, in community with the other members of their group, to enjoy their own culture, to profess and practise their own religion, or to use their own language."
95 Interim Report of the Special Rapporteur on Religious Intolerance, "Implementation of the Declaration on the Elimination of All Forms of Intolerance and of Discrimination based on Religion or Belief", UN doc. A/53/279, 24 August 1998, paragraph 129.
96 See also, UNHCR, "Guidelines on International Protection: 'Membership of a particular social group' within the Context of Article 1A(2) of the 1951 Convention and/or 1967 Protocol relating to the Status of Refugees", HCR/GIP/02/02, 7 May 2002, paragraph 6. Similarly, in internal flight or relocation cases, the claimant should not be expected or required to suppress his or her religious views to avoid persecution in the internal flight or relocation area. See UNHCR, "Guidelines on International Protection: 'Internal Flight or Relocation Alternative' within the Context of Article 1A(2) of the 1951 Convention and/or 1967 Protocol relating to the Status of Refugees", HCR/GIP/03/04, 23 July 2003, paragraphs 19, 25.

personal experiences of the claimant, his or her religious belief, identity and/ or way of life, how important this is for the claimant, what effect the restrictions have on the individual, the nature of his or her role and activities within the religion, whether these activities have been or could be brought to the attention of the persecutor and whether they could result in treatment rising to the level of persecution. In this context, the well-founded fear "need not necessarily be based on the applicant's own personal experience". What, for example, happened to the claimant's friends and relatives, other members of the same religious group, that is to say to other similarly situated individuals, "may well show that his [or her] fear that sooner or later he [or she] also will become a victim of persecution is well-founded".[97] Mere membership of a particular religious community will normally not be enough to substantiate a claim to refugee status. As the UNHCR Handbook notes, there may, however, be special circumstances where mere membership suffices, particularly when taking account of the overall political and religious situation in the country of origin, which may indicate a climate of genuine insecurity for the members of the religious community concerned.[98]

Section 3

Convention on the elimination of all forms of discrimination against women

[*Adopted by United Nations General Assembly in 18 December 1979*]

(...)

Part I
Article 1

For the purposes of the present Convention, the term "discrimination against women" shall mean any distinction, exclusion or restriction made on the basis of sex which has the effect or purpose of impairing or nullifying the recognition, enjoyment or exercise by women, irrespective of their marital status, on a basis of equality of men and women, of human rights and fundamental freedoms in the political, economic, social, cultural, civil or any other field.

---

97 UNHCR Handbook, above note 4, paragraph 43.
98 UNHCR Handbook, above note 4, paragraph 73.

Article 2

States Parties condemn discrimination against women in all its forms, agree to pursue by all appropriate means and without delay a policy of eliminating discrimination against women and, to this end, undertake:

(a) To embody the principle of the equality of men and women in their national constitutions or other appropriate legislation if not yet incorporated therein and to ensure, through law and other appropriate means, the practical realization of this principle;
(b) To adopt appropriate legislative and other measures, including sanctions where appropriate, prohibiting all discrimination against women;
(c) To establish legal protection of the rights of women on an equal basis with men and to ensure through competent national tribunals and other public institutions the effective protection of women against any act of discrimination;
(d) To refrain from engaging in any act or practice of discrimination against women and to ensure that public authorities and institutions shall act in conformity with this obligation;
(e) To take all appropriate measures to eliminate discrimination against women by any person, organization or enterprise;
(f) To take all appropriate measures, including legislation, to modify or abolish existing laws, regulations, customs and practices which constitute discrimination against women;
(g) To repeal all national penal provisions which constitute discrimination against women.

Article 3

States Parties shall take in all fields, in particular in the political, social, economic and cultural fields, all appropriate measures, including legislation, to ensure the full development and advancement of women, for the purpose of guaranteeing them the exercise and enjoyment of human rights and fundamental freedoms on a basis of equality with men.

A Discrimination against minority women

A.1. COMMITTEE ON THE ELIMINATION OF DISCRIMINATION AGAINST WOMEN (CEDAW), **Concluding Comments of the Committee on the Elimination of Discrimination Against Women: Greece (CEDAW/C/GRC/CO/6), 2007.**

(...)

16 The Committee requests that the State party remove impediments women may face in gaining access to justice. The Committee urges the State party

to provide legal aid services and sensitization about how to utilize available legal recourses against discrimination, as well as to monitor the results of such efforts.

17 While noting the measures taken by the State party to enhance the integration of minority women into Greek society, such as the Integrated Action Plan for the Social Integration of Roma Women, the Committee remains concerned that women from ethnic minority groups, in particular Roma and Muslim women, continue to face multiple forms of discrimination with respect to access to education, employment and health care. The Committee regrets the lack of information and data in the report about those groups of women.

18 The Committee calls on the State party to implement effective measures to eliminate discrimination against ethnic minority women, in particular Roma and Muslim women, and to enhance their enjoyment of human rights. The Committee requests the State party to provide, in its next report, information on the situation of women from ethnic minority groups, including with regard to access to education, employment and health care, and on the impact of measures taken to enhance such access and results achieved, as well as trends over time.

(…)

26. The Committee recommends that the State party implement programmes and policies aimed at providing effective access for women, including minority women and adolescent girls, to health-care information and contraceptives, and CEDAW/C/GRC/CO/6 07–24374 5 to family planning services, thus avoiding the need for women to resort to abortion as a method of birth control. The Committee urges the State party to implement programmes of sexual and reproductive health education for men, women and adolescents in order to foster responsible sexual behaviour. The Committee further calls on the State party to implement initiatives, in close consultation with the medical profession, aimed at reducing the number of caesarean sections performed.

A.2. UN HUMAN RIGHTS COUNCIL (HRC), Freedom of religion or belief. Report of the Special Rapporteur on freedom of religion or belief (A/HRC/43/48), 27 February 2020.

(…)

19. Participants at the Special Rapporteur's consultation on South and Southeast Asia reported that in many countries governments have advanced efforts to combat gender-based violence and discrimination, such as by criminalizing marital rape, mandating written consent for marriage from all parties and by specifying a minimum age for marriage. Some States, however, delegate legal authority to minority religious communities to respect pluralism and multiculturalism; but do so in ways that dilute gender equality norms. For example, Sri Lanka's Muslim Marriage and Divorce Act which, unlike national legal provisions for non-Muslim women, does not identify a minimum age requirement or require a woman to consent to

marriage; leaving Muslim women and girls unprotected by national provisions.[99] Such arrangements, they emphasized, mean that people are accorded different degrees of protection, depending on their religious identity, and many women and girls are left at risk of sexual and gender-based violence within their religious communities without any legal remedy. The Special Rapporteur and his predecessors have repeatedly called on States to eliminate in law and practice, including in plural legal systems, all forms of marriage that restrict and/or deny women and girls' rights, well-being, and dignity, including early and forced marriage.[100]

(…)

4   Discrimination on the basis of gender and religious identity

26. Participants in consultations focused on the South and Southeast Asian region reported that women and girls from religious minority communities are often at particular risk of violence, including violence associated with forced conversions and forced marriage, and that 'counter-extremism' measures adopted by States have targeted women from Muslim minority communities with rape, forced sterilization, and forced abortion.[101]

27. The Special Rapporteur and other Special Procedures mandate-holders have also expressed concern about the imposition of restrictive garments or "modest" dress codes by law inspired by religious beliefs and the impact of such measures on women's and girl's ability to enjoy their human rights. In a 2019 communication to the government of the Islamic Republic of Iran, the Special Rapporteur raised concern about the Government's compulsory veil legislation and the reported arrest, enforced disappearance, and arbitrary detention of women's human rights defenders who protested against it.[102] In that communication, the Special Procedure mandate-holders recalled a recent recommendation to the government to reject any cultural or religious practice that violates human rights and the principle of equality or prevents the establishment of an egalitarian society free of gender-based discrimination.

28. In other instances, consultation participants noted, that some States have opted to limit religious practices such as publicly wearing headscarves or full-face veils – attire predominantly worn by Muslim women – in their efforts to combat gender-based discrimination, but without sufficient attention to the self-understanding and agency of women.[103] Critics of such policies have noted the danger that such policies pose to the right to freedom of religion or belief, along with myriad other rights, noting that efforts to combat gender-based discrimination often fail to incorporate freedom of religion or belief and force individuals to choose between their faith and national protections for human rights.

---

99   http://connectblog.com/2019/09/challenging-divine-law-protecting-gender-rights-in-sri-lanka-and-beynd/.
100 See JUA SDN 3/2018.
101 See, www.icj-cij.org/files/case-related/178/178-20200123-PRE-01-00-EN.pdf.
102 JUA IRN 5/2019.
103 See, www.ohchr.org/Documents/Issues/Women/WRGS/VeilinEuropereport.pdf.

Section 4

Convention on the rights of the child

> [Adopted and opened for signature, ratification and accession by General Assembly resolution 44/25 of 20 November 1989 entry into force 2 September 1990, in accordance with article 49]

Article 30

In those States in which ethnic, religious or linguistic minorities or persons of indigenous origin exist, a child belonging to such a minority or who is indigenous shall not be denied the right, in community with other members of his or her group, to enjoy his or her own culture, to profess and practise his or her own religion, or to use his or her own language.

Article 32

1   States Parties recognize the right of the child to be protected from economic exploitation and from performing any work that is likely to be hazardous or to interfere with the child's education, or to be harmful to the child's health or physical, mental, spiritual, moral or social development.
2   States Parties shall take legislative, administrative, social and educational measures to ensure the implementation of the present article. To this end, and having regard to the relevant provisions of other international instruments, States Parties shall in particular:
    (a) Provide for a minimum age or minimum ages for admission to employment;
    (b) Provide for appropriate regulation of the hours and conditions of employment;
    (c) Provide for appropriate penalties or other sanctions to ensure the effective enforcement of the present article.

Article 34

States Parties undertake to protect the child from all forms of sexual exploitation and sexual abuse. For these purposes, States Parties shall in particular take all appropriate national, bilateral and multilateral measures to prevent:

(a) The inducement or coercion of a child to engage in any unlawful sexual activity;
(b) The exploitative use of children in prostitution or other unlawful sexual practices;
(c) The exploitative use of children in pornographic performances and materials.

A Right to education

A.1. OFFICE OF THE HIGH COMMISSIONER FOR HUMAN RIGHTS, **Promoting and Protecting Minority Rights. A Guide for Advocates (HR/PUB/12/7), 2012.***

(...)

Minority children

Article 30 of the Convention on the Rights of the Child guarantees that the same rights set forth in article 27 of the International Covenant on Civil and Political Rights also apply to children. The Independent Expert seeks to collaborate closely with the Committee on the Rights of the Child and share expertise with that body, particularly in regard to issues such as education, health, adequate housing and trafficking. In the course of country visits, the Independent Expert also seeks to hear the views and perspectives of children and young people, by visiting schools, universities and youth facilities.

In the field of education, the Independent Expert has been concerned that minority children often lack equal access to quality education. They may also face obstacles and challenges even where they do have access, such as lack of instruction in their own minority language, which puts them at a disadvantage in relation to other children. Minorities also commonly report that school curricula, text, books and approaches to teaching frequently neglect minority culture and history, and the contributions of minorities to wider society. In 2008, the first session of the Forum on Minority Issues was devoted to the issue of minorities and the right to education and produced comprehensive recommendations on this subject.

(...)

Basic education and gender equality

Within this focus area UNICEF seeks to implement the right to education of every boy and girl, as stipulated under the Convention (arts. 28 and 29). It also contributes to the achievement of two of the Millennium Development Goals, the achievement of universal primary education, and the promotion of gender equality and the empowerment of women. Most commonly, working for minorities in this area involves improving educational quality and increasing school retention, completion and achievement rates, and improving children's developmental readiness to start primary school on time. Particular focus has been given

---

* From Promoting and Protecting Minority Rights. A Guide for Advocates, by Office of the High Commissioner for Human Rights, ©(2012) United Nations. Reprinted with the permission of the United Nations.

to marginalized children in Thailand, where Muslim minority children affected by conflict benefited from the training of Islamic teachers through the Child-Friendly School quality standards approach. In the conflict-affected Northern Province of Sri Lanka, the primary home of the Tamil minority, education officers were trained in emergency preparedness and response planning. They carried out rapid assessments and reopened schools near areas with internally displaced children to ensure minimal disruption to education. In addition, 1,260 teachers and principals from more than 300 schools were trained in developing school-level plans.

B Right to maintain religion or belief

B.1. Special Rapporteur on freedom of religion or belief – Independent Expert on minority issues – Special Rapporteur on the sale of children, child prostitution and child pornography – Special Rapporteur on trafficking in persons, especially women and children – Chair-Rapporteur of the Working Group on the issue of discrimination against women in law and in practice – Special Rapporteur on violence against women, its causes and consequences, **Special procedures of the Human Rights Council, Communication 29 May 2013 – Iraq** *(IRQ 2/2013).*

13 February 2013
  Excellency,

> We have the honour to address you in our capacity as Special Rapporteur on freedom of religion or belief; Independent Expert on minority issues; Special Rapporteur on the sale of children, child prostitution and child pornography; Special Rapporteur on trafficking in persons, especially women and children; Chair-Rapporteur of the Working Group on the issue of discrimination against women in law and in practice; and Special Rapporteur on violence against women, its causes and consequences pursuant to Human Rights Council resolutions 14/11, 16/6, 16/12, 17/1, 15/23 and 16/7.

In this connection, we would like to draw the attention of your Excellency's Government to information we have received concerning the abduction of Simon Dawod Ismael, an 11-year old girl from the Yazidi town of Sheikha, in the sub-district of Alqoush, District of Tel-Kef, Ninewa Governorate in northern Iraq. We would like to appeal to your Excellency's Government to attach, in the best interest of the child, utmost importance to preserving the confidentiality of the identity the child victim due to her age, due to the possibility of reprisal attacks and the stigma attached to the case. The name of the victim shall not be disclosed in any public UN document.

According to the information received:

> On 9 January 2013, Simon Dawod Ismael was allegedly forcefully abducted by Mr. Hassan Nasrullah of the Goran tribe, from Kalakchi village. Mr. Nasrullah is a 20-year old vegetable vendor who has been selling his produce at the market of Sheikha. The kidnapping was reportedly witnessed by one of the members of Simon's family, who informed that Simon Dawod Ismael was forced into a car and taken away by Mr. Nasrullah. The alleged intention of Mr. Nasrullah was to marry the girl, and it is feared that she may have been raped. It is reported that the two individuals have since married without parental consent.

The father of the abducted girl reported the incident to police authorities, including to the Alqush Police Station which forwarded the file to the Telkaif Court. Additionally, the father filed a case at the Shekhan Court, which belongs to the Kurdistan Regional Government, but no investigation or prosecution has taken place yet.

KNN television, a Kurdish channel owned by the Gorran Party in Sulaimaniyah, reportedly conducted an interview with Simon in Mosul, and alleged in the interview that the girl was 15 years old, wanted to convert to Islam and marry Mr. Hassan Nasrullah, who is of Muslim religion. In the interview Simon reportedly talks about her dreams of becoming Muslim, although, according to her family, she has a very limited understanding both of her own Yazidi religion, (the Yazidi are an ethno-religious group with Indo-Iranian roots living in the northern part of Iraq) and Islam. Additionally, Simon's family is of the opinion that the interview with the TV channel was forced on her and the views expressed in it by Simon are not actually hers.

Simon's family and the leader of the Yazidi community, Prince Mir Tahseen Beq, reportedly gave assurances that they only want Simon back and that she would not be harmed.

According to the information received, there have allegedly been other similar incidents of kidnapping of Yazidi girls by men from the Goran tribe. Due to such incidents, a number of individuals from the Yazidi community were reportedly compelled to leave the areas where they lived.

Concern is expressed about the physical and psychological integrity of Simon Dawod Ismael. Further serious concerns are expressed at the apparent lack of swift action, including prosecution, on the part of the relevant police, judicial and government authorities.

Without in any way implying any determination on the facts of the case, we would like to draw your attention to the Protocol to Prevent, Suppress and Punish Trafficking in Persons, Especially Women and Children, supplementing the United Nations Convention against Transnational Organized Crime. The Protocol defines trafficking in persons as the recruitment, transportation, transfer, harbouring or receipt of persons, by means of the threat or use of force or other forms of coercion, of abduction, of fraud, of deception, of the abuse of power or of a position of vulnerability or of the giving or receiving of payments or benefits to achieve the consent of a person having control over another person, for the purpose of exploitation.

We also deem it appropriate to make reference to article 34 of the International Convention on the Rights of the Child (CRC), which your Excellency's Government ratified on 15 June 1994, which provides that States Parties undertake to protect the child from all forms of sexual exploitation and sexual abuse. We note in this regard that the victim falls within the definition of the child under article 1 of the CRC. For these purposes, States Parties shall in particular take all appropriate national, bilateral and multilateral measures to prevent:

(a) The inducement or coercion of a child to engage in any unlawful sexual activity;
(b) The exploitative use of children in prostitution or other unlawful sexual practices;
(c) The exploitative use of children in pornographic performances and materials.

Moreover, article 35 provides that States Parties shall take all appropriate national, bilateral and multilateral measures to prevent the abduction of, the sale of or traffic in children for any purpose or in any form.

We would also like to bring to the attention of your Excellency's Government article 4 (c & d) of the United Nations Declaration on the Elimination of Violence against Women, which notes the responsibility of States to exercise due diligence to prevent, investigate and, in accordance with national legislation, punish acts of violence against women, whether those acts are perpetrated by the State or by private persons. In this context, we recall that the Committee on the Elimination of Discrimination against Women (CEDAW) in its General Recommendation No. 19 (1992), defines gender-based violence against women as impairing or nullifying the enjoyment by women of human rights and fundamental freedoms, and constitutes discrimination within the meaning of article 1 of the Convention on the Elimination of All forms of Discrimination Against Women (acceded to by your Excellency's Government on 13 August 1986), whether perpetrated by a State official or a private citizen, in public or private life. Thus, the Committee considers that States parties are under an obligation to act with due diligence to investigate all crimes, including that of sexual violence perpetrated against women and girls, to punish perpetrators and to provide adequate compensation without delay. In General Recommendation No. 19, the Committee sets out specific punitive, rehabilitative, preventive and protective measures States should introduce to fulfil this obligation; in paragraph 9, it makes clear that "under general international law and specific human rights covenants, States may also be responsible for private acts if they fail to act with due diligence to prevent violations of rights or to investigate and punish acts of violence, and for providing compensation".

Furthermore, we would like to bring to the attention of your Excellency's Government article 4 of the United Nations Declaration on the Elimination of

Violence against Women which underlines the responsibility of States to condemn violence against women and which calls on States not to invoke any custom, tradition or religious consideration to avoid their obligations with respect to its elimination. States should pursue by all appropriate means and without delay a policy of eliminating violence against women and, to this end, should adopt all appropriate measures, especially in the field of education, to modify the social and cultural patterns of conduct of men and women and to eliminate prejudices, customary practices and all other practices based on the idea of the inferiority or superiority of either of the sexes and on stereotyped roles for men and women. In paragraph 11 of General Recommendation No. 19 (1992), the Committee states that "Traditional attitudes by which women are regarded as subordinate to men or as having stereotyped roles perpetuate widespread practices involving violence or coercion, such as family violence and abuse, forced marriage, dowry deaths, acid attacks and female circumcision" and that "such prejudices and practices may justify gender-based violence as a form of protection or control of women. The effect of such violence on the physical and mental integrity of women is to deprive them the equal enjoyment, exercise and knowledge of human rights and fundamental freedoms."

We would also like to recall that the right to marry only with one's free and full consent is recognized in the Universal Declaration of Human Rights (article 16(2)) and in a number of subsequent international human rights treaties such as the 1956 Supplementary Slavery Convention, Convention on Consent to Marriage, Minimum Age for Marriage and Registration of Marriages. Furthermore, we would like to draw the attention of your Excellency's Government to article 16 of the Convention on the Elimination of All Forms of Discrimination Against Women, on the right of women and men to freely choose a spouse, to enter into marriage only with their free and full consent and to have the same rights and responsibilities during the marriage and at its dissolution.

We would also like to refer to a the right to freedom of religion or belief set forth in the Declaration on the Elimination of All Forms of Intolerance and of Discrimination based on Religion or Belief and article 18 of the Universal Declaration on Human Rights as well as of the International Covenant on Civil and Political Rights. Article 18 (2) of ICCPR and Article 1(2) of the 1981 Declaration prescribe that "No one shall be subject to coercion which would impair his freedom to have a religion or belief of his choice."

The Human Rights Committee General Comment 22, Para. 5 states that "Article 18 (2) bars coercion that would impair the right to have or adopt a religion or belief, including the use of threat of physical force or penal sanctions to compel believers or non-believers to adhere to their religious beliefs and congregations, to recant their religion or belief or to convert."

In view of the urgency of the matter, we would appreciate a response on the initial steps taken by your Excellency's Government to safeguard the rights of Simon Dawod Ismael in compliance with the above international instruments. Moreover, as it is our responsibility under the mandates provided to us by the Human Rights Council, to seek to clarify all cases brought to our attention, we would be grateful for your observations on the following matters, when relevant to the case under consideration:

1 Are the facts alleged in the summary of the case accurate?
2 Please provide information on the current whereabouts of Simon Dawod Ismael.
3 Please provide the details, and where available the results, of any judicial investigation, prosecution or any criminal charges, medical examinations, and other inquiries carried out in relation to this case. If no inquiries or prosecutions have taken place, please explain why.

We undertake to ensure that your Excellency's Government's response to each of these questions is accurately reflected in the report we will submit to the Human Rights Council for its consideration.

While waiting for your response, we urge your Excellency's Government to take all necessary measures to guarantee that the rights and freedoms of Simon Dawod Ismael are respected, especially her right to privacy and, in the event that your investigations support or suggest the allegations to be correct, the accountability of any person responsible of the alleged violations should be ensured. We also request that your Excellency's Government adopt effective measures to prevent the recurrence of these acts.

Section 5

Declaration on the Rights of Persons Belonging to National or Ethnic, Religious and Linguistic Minorities

[*Adopted by General Assembly resolution 47/135 of 18 December 1992*]

Article 1

1 States shall protect the existence and the national or ethnic, cultural, religious and linguistic identity of minorities within their respective territories and shall encourage conditions for the promotion of that identity.
2 States shall adopt appropriate legislative and other measures to achieve those ends.

Article 2

1 Persons belonging to national or ethnic, religious and linguistic minorities (hereinafter referred to as persons belonging to minorities) have the right to enjoy their own culture, to profess and practise their own religion, and to use their own language, in private and in public, freely and without interference or any form of discrimination.

2   Persons belonging to minorities have the right to participate effectively in cultural, religious, social, economic and public life.
3   Persons belonging to minorities have the right to participate effectively in decisions on the national and, where appropriate, regional level concerning the minority to which they belong or the regions in which they live, in a manner not incompatible with national legislation.
4   Persons belonging to minorities have the right to establish and maintain their own associations.
5   Persons belonging to minorities have the right to establish and maintain, without any discrimination, free and peaceful contacts with other members of their group and with persons belonging to other minorities, as well as contacts across frontiers with citizens of other States to whom they are related by national or ethnic, religious or linguistic ties.

Article 3

1   Persons belonging to minorities may exercise their rights, including those set forth in the present Declaration, individually as well as in community with other members of their group, without any discrimination.
2   No disadvantage shall result for any person belonging to a minority as the consequence of the exercise or non-exercise of the rights set forth in the present Declaration.

Article 4

1   States shall take measures where required to ensure that persons belonging to minorities may exercise fully and effectively all their human rights and fundamental freedoms without any discrimination and in full equality before the law.
2   States shall take measures to create favourable conditions to enable persons belonging to minorities to express their characteristics and to develop their culture, language, religion, traditions and customs, except where specific practices are in violation of national law and contrary to international standards.
3   States should take appropriate measures so that, wherever possible, persons belonging to minorities may have adequate opportunities to learn their mother tongue or to have instruction in their mother tongue.
4   States should, where appropriate, take measures in the field of education, in order to encourage knowledge of the history, traditions, language and culture of the minorities existing within their territory. Persons belonging to minorities should have adequate opportunities to gain knowledge of the society as a whole.
5   States should consider appropriate measures so that persons belonging to minorities may participate fully in the economic progress and development in their country.

Article 5

1. National policies and programmes shall be planned and implemented with due regard for the legitimate interests of persons belonging to minorities.
2. Programmes of cooperation and assistance among States should be planned and implemented with due regard for the legitimate interests of persons belonging to minorities.

Article 6

States should cooperate on questions relating to persons belonging to minorities, inter alia, exchanging information and experiences, in order to promote mutual understanding and confidence.

Article 7

States should cooperate in order to promote respect for the rights set forth in the present Declaration.

Article 8

1. Nothing in the present Declaration shall prevent the fulfilment of international obligations of States in relation to persons belonging to minorities. In particular, States shall fulfil in good faith the obligations and commitments they have assumed under international treaties and agreements to which they are parties.
2. The exercise of the rights set forth in the present Declaration shall not prejudice the enjoyment by all persons of universally recognized human rights and fundamental freedoms.
3. Measures taken by States to ensure the effective enjoyment of the rights set forth in the present Declaration shall not prima facie be considered contrary to the principle of equality contained in the Universal Declaration of Human Rights.
4. Nothing in the present Declaration may be construed as permitting any activity contrary to the purposes and principles of the United Nations, including sovereign equality, territorial integrity and political independence of States.

Article 9

The specialized agencies and other organizations of the United Nations system shall contribute to the full realization of the rights and principles set forth in the present Declaration, within their respective fields of competence.

A Right to existence

A.1. UN COMMISSION ON HUMAN RIGHTS, SUB-COMMISSION ON THE PROMOTION AND PROTECTION OF HUMAN RIGHTS,* Commentary of the Working Group on Minorities to the United Nations Declaration on the Rights of Persons Belonging to National or Ethnic, Religious and Linguistic Minorities *(E/CN.4/Sub.2/ AC.5/2005/2), 4 April 2005.

(...)

21. The relationship between the State and its minorities has in the past taken five different forms: elimination, assimilation, toleration, protection and promotion. Under present international law, elimination is clearly illegal. The Declaration is based on the consideration that forced assimilation is unacceptable. While a degree of integration is required in every national society in order to make it possible for the State to respect and ensure human rights to every person within its territory without discrimination, the protection of minorities is intended to ensure that integration does not become unwanted assimilation or undermine the group identity of persons living on the territory of the State.

22. Integration differs from assimilation in that while it develops and maintains a common domain where equal treatment and a common rule of law prevail, it also allows for pluralism. The areas of pluralism covered by the Declaration are culture, language and religion.

23. Minority protection is based on four requirements: protection of the existence, non-exclusion, non-discrimination and non-assimilation of the groups concerned.

24. The protection of the existence of minorities includes their physical existence, their continued existence on the territories on which they live and their continued access to the material resources required to continue their existence on those territories. The minorities shall neither be physically excluded from the territory nor be excluded from access to the resources required for their livelihood. The right to existence in its physical sense is sustained by the Convention on the Prevention and Punishment of the Crime of Genocide, which codified customary law in 1948. Forced population transfers intended to move persons belonging to minorities away from the territory on which they live, or with that effect, would constitute serious breaches of contemporary international standards, including the Rome Statute of the International Criminal Court. But protection of their existence goes beyond the duty not to destroy or deliberately weaken minority groups. It also requires respect for and protection of their religious and cultural heritage, essential to their group identity, including buildings and sites such as libraries, churches, mosques, temples and synagogues.

25. The second requirement is that minorities shall not be excluded from the national society. Apartheid was the extreme version of exclusion of different groups from equal participation in the national society as a whole. The

Declaration on Minorities repeatedly underlines the rights of all groups, small as well as large, to participate effectively in society (arts. 2.2 and 2.3).

26. The third requirement is non-discrimination, which is a general principle of human rights law and elaborated by, inter alia, the International Convention on the Elimination of All Forms of Racial Discrimination, which also covers discrimination on ethnic grounds. The Declaration on Minorities elaborates the principle of non-discrimination in its provision that the exercise of their rights as persons belonging to minorities shall not justify any discrimination in any other field, and that no disadvantage shall result from the exercise or non-exercise of these rights (art. 3).

27. The fourth requirement is non-assimilation and its corollary, which is to protect and promote conditions for the group identity of minorities. Many recent international instruments use the term "identity", which expresses a clear trend towards the protection and promotion of cultural diversity, both internationally and internally within States. Relevant provisions are articles 29 and 30 of the Convention on the Rights of the Child, article 31 of the International Convention on the Protection of the Rights of All Migrant Workers and Members of Their Families, article 2.2 (b) of ILO Convention No. 169, which refers to respect for the social and cultural identity, customs and traditions and institutions of indigenous peoples, as well as provisions of regional instruments such as those of the Organization on Security and Cooperation in Europe, including its 1990 Copenhagen Conference on the Human Dimension and its 1991 Geneva Meeting of Experts on National Minorities. Another recent instrument in the same direction is the European Framework Convention for the Protection of National Minorities.

28. Minority group identity requires not only tolerance but a positive attitude towards cultural pluralism on the part of the State and the larger society. Not only acceptance but also respect for the distinctive characteristics and contribution of minorities to the life of the national society as a whole are required. Protection of their identity means not only that the State should abstain from policies which have the purpose or effect of assimilating minorities into the dominant culture, but also that it should protect them against activities by third parties which have an assimilatory effect. The language and educational policies of the State concerned are crucial in this regard. Denying minorities the possibility of learning their own language and of receiving instruction in their own language, or excluding from their education the transmission of knowledge about their own culture, history, tradition and language, would be a violation of the obligation to protect their identity.

29. Promotion of the identity of minorities requires special measures to facilitate the maintenance, reproduction and further development of their culture. Cultures are not static; minorities should be given the opportunity to develop their own culture in the context of an ongoing process. That process should be an interaction between the persons belonging to the minority themselves, between the minority and the State, and between the minority and the wider national society. The measures required to achieve this purpose are set out in greater detail in article 4 of the Declaration.

A.2. UN OFFICE OF THE HIGH COMMISSIONER FOR HUMAN RIGHTS (OHCHR), Minority Rights: International Standards and Guidance for Implementation *(HR/PUB/10/3)*, 2010.*

(...)

B. Promotion and protection of the identity of minorities

Central to the rights of minorities are the promotion and protection of their identity. Promoting and protecting their identity prevent forced assimilation and the loss of cultures, religions and languages – the basis of the richness of the world and therefore part of its heritage. Non-assimilation requires diversity and plural identities to be not only tolerated but protected and respected. Minority rights are about ensuring respect for distinctive identities while ensuring that any differential treatment towards groups or persons belonging to such groups does not mask discriminatory practices and policies. Therefore, positive action is required to respect cultural, religious and linguistic diversity, and acknowledge that minorities enrich society through this diversity.

A.3. FORUM ON MINORITY ISSUES, Note by the Independent Expert on minority issues, Rita Izsák, on guaranteeing the rights of religious minorities *(A/HRC/FMI/2013/2)*, 3 October 2013.

(...)

III. Legal framework

5. Article 27 of the International Covenant on Civil and Political Rights provides the following: "In those States in which ethnic, religious or linguistic minorities exist, persons belonging to such minorities shall not be denied the right, in community with the other members of their group, to enjoy their own culture, to profess and practise their own religion, or to use their own language." The Declaration on the Rights of Persons Belonging to National or Ethnic, Religious and Linguistic Minorities builds on article 27 and establishes the responsibility of States to ensure the protection of religious identity. It establishes in article 1, paragraph 1, that States "shall protect the existence and the national or ethnic, cultural, religious and linguistic identity of minorities within their respective territories and shall encourage conditions for the promotion of that identity".

(...)

---

* From Minority Rights: International Standards and Guidance for Implementation, by Office of the High Commissioner for Human Rights (OHCHR), ©(2010) United Nations. Reprinted with the permission of the United Nations.

A PROTECTION OF THE EXISTENCE OF AND PREVENTION OF VIOLENCE
AGAINST RELIGIOUS MINORITIES

12. The Forum will identify steps taken by States and other actors to prevent tensions and any acts of violence against persons belonging to religious minorities or their places of worship, associations and offices. It will consider practical measures, policies and practices that States can adopt to respond more effectively to problems faced by religious minorities, including violence against them. Further, the Forum will identify effective measures to eradicate incitement to religious hatred, including national laws, constructive dialogue, education and training, and the establishment of effective media monitoring bodies. While one emphasis of this session of the Forum is on prevention, the situation of religious minorities in conflict and post-conflict situations will also be addressed.

B PROMOTION AND PROTECTION OF THE IDENTITY OF RELIGIOUS
MINORITIES

13. Religious identity is not only about the right to worship freely but also the right to express and enjoy aspects of one's identity in all spheres of life and society, including in educational settings, in the workplace, in private and in public, as an individual or in community with others. The Forum will seek to identify effective practices to ensure the promotion and protection of the identity of religious minorities so that they can freely maintain and develop their unique religious and cultural practices and traditions. Full enjoyment of the right to religious identity requires first and foremost the recognition by States of the religious diversity within society, along with the fostering of an enabling environment on the part of governments, local authorities, public and private bodies, and the wider society.

B Right to culture

***B.1. UN COMMISSION ON HUMAN RIGHTS, SUB-COMMISSION ON THE
PROMOTION AND PROTECTION OF HUMAN RIGHTS,*** **Commentary
of the Working Group on Minorities to the United Nations
Declaration on the Rights of Persons Belonging to National
or Ethnic, Religious and Linguistic Minorities** *(E/CN.4/Sub.2/
AC.5/2005/2), 4 April 2005.*

(…)
65. Experience has shown that in societies where different national, ethnic, religious or linguistic groups coexist, the culture, history and traditions of minority groups have often been neglected and the majorities are frequently ignorant of those traditions and cultures. Where there has been conflict, the minority groups' culture, history and traditions have often been subject to distorted representations, resulting in low self-esteem within the groups and negative stereotypes towards members of the group on the part of the wider community. Racial hatred, xenophobia and intolerance sometimes take root.

66. To avoid such circumstances, there is a need for both multicultural and intercultural education. Multicultural education involves educational policies and practices which meet the separate educational needs of groups in society belonging to different cultural traditions, while intercultural education involves educational policies and practices whereby persons belonging to different cultures, whether in a majority or minority position, learn to interact constructively with each other.

67. Article 4.4 calls for intercultural education, by encouraging knowledge in the society as a whole of the history, tradition and culture of the minorities living there. Cultures and languages of minorities should be made accessible to the majorities as a means of encouraging interaction and conflict prevention in pluri-ethnic societies. Such knowledge should be presented in a positive way in order to encourage tolerance and respect. History textbooks are particularly important in this regard. Bias in the presentation of the history and neglect of the contributions of the minority are significant causes of ethnic tension. The United Nations Educational, Scientific and Cultural Organization has concerned itself with the need to eliminate such prejudices and misrepresentations in history textbooks, but much remains to be done.

68. This paragraph of article 4 also emphasizes the complementary duty to ensure that persons belonging to minorities gain knowledge of the society as a whole. This provision should counteract tendencies towards fundamentalist or closed religious or ethnic groups, which can be as much affected by xenophobia and intolerance as the majorities.

69. The overall purpose of article 4.4 is to ensure egalitarian integration based on non-discrimination and respect for each of the cultural, linguistic or religious groups which together form the national society. The formation of more or less involuntary ghettos where the different groups live in their own world without knowledge of, or tolerance for, persons belonging to the other parts of the national society would be a violation of the purpose and spirit of the Declaration.

70. A concern similar to that of article 4.4 is expressed in the International Convention on the Elimination of All Forms of Racial Discrimination (art. 7) and in the Convention on the Rights of the Child (art. 29).

C Right to profess and practise religion or belief

C.1. UN COMMISSION ON HUMAN RIGHTS, SUB-COMMISSION ON THE PROMOTION AND PROTECTION OF HUMAN RIGHTS, **Commentary of the Working Group on Minorities to the United Nations Declaration on the Rights of Persons Belonging to National or Ethnic, Religious and Linguistic Minorities** *(E/CN.4/Sub.2/ AC.5/2005/2), 4 April 2005.*

(…)

III Interpretation of and comments on the title and the individual articles

The title and scope of the Declaration

6. The beneficiaries of the rights under article 27 of the International Covenant on Civil and Political Rights, which has inspired the Declaration, are persons belonging to "ethnic, religious or linguistic minorities". The Declaration on Minorities adds the term "national minorities". That addition does not extend the overall scope of application beyond the groups already covered by article 27. There is hardly any national minority, however defined, that is not also an ethnic or linguistic minority. A relevant question, however, would be whether the title indicates that the Declaration covers four different categories of minorities, whose rights have somewhat different content and strength. Persons belonging to groups defined solely as religious minorities might be held to have only those special minority rights which relate to the profession and practice of their religion. Persons belonging to groups solely defined as linguistic minorities might similarly be held to have only those special minority rights which are related to education and use of their language. Persons who belong to groups defined as ethnic would have more extensive rights relating to the preservation and development of other aspects of their culture also, since ethnicity is generally defined by a broad conception of culture, including a way of life. The category of national minority would then have still stronger rights relating not only to their culture but to the preservation and development of their national identity.

(...)

IV FRAMING QUESTIONS FOR ACTION

A. Does the situation of persons belonging to religious minorities require particular attention?

There are several issues of particular concern to religious minorities which should be considered when monitoring the situation on the ground and devising strategies. These can be identified by raising the following questions:

- Have there been cases before the courts or complaints brought to the attention of United Nations human rights treaty bodies or special procedures, in particular the Special Rapporteur on freedom of religion or belief, with respect to the rights of persons belonging to religious minorities?
- Is there recognition and respect for the right to profess and practise religion without discrimination and interference from the State or others? Do guarantees exist for this?
- Are there limitations or restrictions placed on the right to manifest one's religion or belief?

- Is there freedom to adopt, change or renounce a religion or belief? How is freedom to adopt, change or renounce a religion or belief recognized and respected in law and in practice?
- What measures are in place to ensure freedom of worship or assembly in connection with a religion or belief?
- Is social pressure or forced conversion an issue affecting minorities? If so, how is the Government addressing this?
- Is there recognition of religious minorities' holy days by the State? Are they recognized as public holidays?
- Is there recognition and protection of the right to hold religious ceremonies?
- What is the procedure for the appointment of religious leaders, priests and teachers, for those belonging to religious minorities?

D Right to participation

D.1. UN COMMISSION ON HUMAN RIGHTS, SUB-COMMISSION ON THE PROMOTION AND PROTECTION OF HUMAN RIGHTS,* Commentary of the Working Group on Minorities to the United Nations Declaration on the Rights of Persons Belonging to National or Ethnic, Religious and Linguistic Minorities *(E/CN.4/Sub.2/ AC.5/2005/2), 4 April 2005.

(...)

35. The right to participate in all aspects of the life of the larger national society is essential, both in order for persons belonging to minorities to promote their interests and values and to create an integrated but pluralist society based on tolerance and dialogue. By their participation in all forms of public life in their country, they are able both to shape their own destinies and to contribute to political change in the larger society.

36. The words "public life" must be understood in the same broad sense as in article 1 of the International Convention on the Elimination of All Forms of Racial Discrimination, though much is covered already by the preceding words "cultural, religious, social and economic". Included in "public life" are, among other rights, rights relating to election and to being elected, the holding of public office, and other political and administrative domains.

37. Participation can be ensured in many ways, including the use of minority associations (see also article 2.4), membership in other associations, and through their free contacts both inside the State and across borders (see article 2.5).

2.3 Persons belonging to minorities have the right to participate effectively in decisions on the national, and where appropriate, regional level concerning the minority to which they belong or the regions in which they live, in a manner not incompatible with national legislation.

38. While article 2.2 deals generally with the right to participation in all aspects of the public life of a society, article 2.3 deals specifically with the right of persons belonging to minorities to effective participation "in decisions ... concerning the

minority to which they belong or the regions in which they live". As such decisions have a particular impact on persons belonging to minorities, the emphasis on effective participation is here of particular importance. Representatives of persons belonging to minorities should be involved beginning at the initial stages of decision-making. Experience has shown that it is of little use to involve them only at the final stages where there is very little room for compromise. Minorities should be involved at the local, national and international levels in the formulation, adoption, implementation and monitoring of standards and policies affecting them.

39. In 1991, the Conference on Security and Cooperation in Europe held a Meeting of Experts on National Minorities in Geneva. The States there assembled noted approaches used with positive results in some of the participating States. These included advisory and decision-making bodies – in particular with regard to education, culture and religion – on which minorities were represented. Also mentioned were assemblies for national minority affairs, local and autonomous administration, as well as autonomy on a territorial basis, including the existence of consultative, legislative and executive bodies chosen through free and periodic elections. Reference was further made to forms of self-administration by a national minority of aspects concerning its identity in situations where autonomy on a territorial basis did not apply, and decentralized or local forms of government.[104]

40. In early May 1999, a group of independent experts met in Lund, Sweden, to draw up a set of recommendations on the effective participation of national minorities in public life. The recommendations are built upon fundamental principles and rules of international law, such as respect for human dignity, equal rights and non-discrimination, as they affect the rights of national minorities to participate in public life and to enjoy other political rights.[105] At its fifth session, at the end of May 1999, the Working Group on Minorities adopted a set of recommendations on the same topic.[106]

41. The following commentary draws extensively on these recommendations. The purpose is not to set out only the minimum rights under article 2.3 of persons belonging to minorities, but also to provide a list of good practices which may be of use to Governments and minorities in finding appropriate solutions to issues confronting them.

42. Effective participation provides channels for consultation between and among minorities and Governments. It can serve as a means of dispute resolution

---

104 Report of the CSCE Meeting of Experts on National Minorities, Geneva, 19 July 1991, Part IV. See also the second progress report of Special Rapporteur A. Eide on possible ways and means of facilitating the peaceful and constructive solution of problems involving minorities (E/CN.4/Sub.2/1992/37), paragraphs 122–155.
105 The Lund recommendations can be found on the web site of the OSCE High Commissioner on National Minorities, www.osce.org/hcnm/documents/lund.htm.
106 Report of the Working Group on Minorities on its fifth session (E/CN.4/Sub.2/1999/21), paragraphs 81–88.

and sustain diversity as a condition for the dynamic stability of a society. The number of persons belonging to minorities is by definition too small for them to determine the outcome of decisions in majoritarian democracy. They must as a minimum have the right to have their opinions heard and fully taken into account before decisions which concern them are adopted. A wide range of constitutional and political measures are used around the world to provide access for minorities to decision-making.

43. The variety in the composition, needs and aspirations of different types of minority groups requires identification and adoption of the most appropriate ways to create conditions for effective participation in each case. The mechanisms chosen have to take into account whether the persons belonging to the minority in question live dispersed or in compactly settled groups, whether the minority is small or large, or an old or a new minority. Religious minorities may also require different types or contexts of participation than ethnic or national minorities. It should be noted, however, that in some cases religion and ethnicity coincide.

44. Effective participation requires representation in legislative, administrative and advisory bodies and more generally in public life. Persons belonging to minorities, like all others, are entitled to assemble and to form their associations and thereby to aggregate their interests and values to make the greatest possible impact on national and regional decision-making. They are entitled not only to set up and make use of ethnic, cultural and religious associations and societies (see commentary to article 2.4 below), but also to establish political parties, should they so wish. In a well-integrated society, however, many persons belonging to minorities often prefer to be members of or vote for parties which are not organized on ethnic lines but are sensitive to the concerns of the minorities.

45. Where minorities are concentrated territorially, single-member districts may provide sufficient minority representation. Proportional representation systems, where a political party's share in the national vote is reflected in its share of the legislative seats, may assist in the representation of minorities. Some forms of preference voting, where voters rank candidates in order of choice, may also facilitate minority representation and promote inter-communal cooperation.

46. Decentralization of powers based on the principle of subsidiarity, whether called self-government or devolved power, and whether the arrangements are symmetrical or asymmetrical, would increase the chances of minorities to participate in the exercise of authority over matters affecting themselves and the entire society in which they live.

47. Public institutions should not, however, be based on ethnic or religious criteria. Governments at local, regional and national levels should recognize the role of multiple identities in contributing to open communities and in establishing useful distinctions between public institutional structures and cultural identities.

48. States should also establish advisory or consultative bodies involving minorities within appropriate institutional frameworks. Such bodies or round tables should be attributed political weight and effectively consulted on issues affecting the minority population.

49. There should be equal access to public sector employment across the various ethnic, linguistic and religious communities.

50. Citizenship remains an important condition for full and effective participation. Barriers to the acquisition of citizenship for members of minorities should be reduced. Forms of participation by resident non-citizens should also be developed, including local voting rights after a certain period of residence and inclusion of elected non-citizen observers in municipal, regional and national legislative and decision-making assemblies.

D.2. UN HUMAN RIGHTS COUNCIL (HRC), Recommendations of the second session of the Forum on Minority Issues on minorities and effective political participation (A/HRC/13/25), 12 and 13 November 2009.

I. Introduction

(...)

9   The implementation of the right to effective political participation of minorities is fundamental to the effective realization of full minority participation in political life. It is also a necessary condition to ensure the enjoyment of other fundamental human rights by persons belonging to minorities. Effective participation may be manifested in a wide range of forms, such as dissemination of information, civic advocacy and activism, as well as direct involvement in electoral politics. It can be ensured through many different means, ranging from consultative mechanisms to special parliamentary arrangements and, where appropriate, may even include forms of territorial or personal autonomy.

II Recommendations

A GOVERNMENTS (NATIONAL, REGIONAL, LOCAL) AND PARLIAMENTS

10 Governments should take effective measures to end discrimination. They should consider, for instance, instituting independent monitoring and complaints mechanisms designed to prevent discrimination in voting, vote fraud, intimidation and similar acts that inhibit the effective participation of all, especially members of minorities, in electoral activities. Such mechanisms might include, inter alia, ombudspersons, independent electoral commissions and/or free legal services. These mechanisms should be made available in the geographic regions and languages of minority communities and should be adequately resourced.
11 Governments should adopt a policy statement that recognizes the diversity within their respective societies with respect to race, ethnicity, religion and

language, and that highlights the importance of ensuring that this diversity is indeed reflected as widely as practicable in public institutions and bodies, including national parliaments, the civil service, the police and the judiciary.

12   The policy statement should be followed by measures to ensure effective and sustainable minority political participation, including the development of a national plan of action. The plan of action should include, inter alia, the development of educational programmes and campaigns that promote political participation, ensure diversity and interculturalism among public administration staff, the adoption of positive measures to increase political participation of minorities and the allocation of sufficient resources to realize identified objectives. Minorities must be involved effectively in every step leading to the development and adoption of such a plan of action.

13   A specific mechanism or institutional procedure should be created to conduct a baseline survey and to monitor, on a regular basis, the progress achieved towards increasing effective minority participation. These data should be published regularly in an easily accessible format and discussed in public meetings with civil society.

14   Governments should regularly collect up-to-date data on the situation of persons belonging to minorities in order to monitor their effective and meaningful participation. Such data-gathering exercises should take place in a sensitive manner, proceeding through statistical or other operations on a voluntary basis, with full respect for the privacy and anonymity of the individuals concerned, in accordance with international standards of personal data protection, as well as on the basis of their self-identification as members of groups concerned. States should design methods of collection of such data in close cooperation with minorities. Wherever possible, representatives of the minorities concerned should be involved throughout the process of data collection.

15   At the national level, a proportional representation system or some other electoral design should be put in place, where practicable, to increase opportunities for minorities to participate effectively in State-wide political life. Conversely, Governments should not change the electoral system or electoral boundaries in a way that would be likely to weaken minority representation.

16   Where minorities are concentrated geographically, consideration should be given in appropriate circumstances to devolving power, creating autonomous or other sub-State divisions, or adopting other means to enable minorities to have a significant and direct impact on matters that directly affect them. Such solutions need not detract from overall State responsibilities, but might be based on the concept of "subsidiarity", namely that decision-making should generally occur at the lowest level of government consistent with the goals to be attained.

17   Mechanisms for the effective political participation of minorities at the local and State levels should not result in the entrenchment of political power based on ethnicity, religion, language or similar factors, which may only heighten divisions within society. While it is essential to ensure minority

participation at all levels, the representation of all relevant interests should not result in governmental gridlock or the over-politicization of ethnic or other minority identity. Access to meaningful political power should not be dependent on one's status as a member of a minority.

18 Literacy, language, religious or other requirements that exclude minorities from the right to vote or to stand for elected office at the national, regional or local level should be removed, as they may breach the prohibition of discrimination and result in minorities not being able to participate effectively in political life.

19 There should be no prohibition or unreasonable restriction placed on the use of any minority language during election campaigns, although language use should naturally be determined by assessing how the broadest constituencies possible may be reached. As far as possible, electoral authorities should provide voting information in both the official language and those minority languages used by voters in the areas where they are concentrated.

20 Civic education programmes specifically directed at informing minorities about how they can have access to the electoral system should be developed and tailored, as far as possible, to every minority group present in the State. Civic education should be a central component of all public education curricula, describing citizens' roles and responsibilities and encouraging broad-based political participation for all. Governments should sponsor projects to boost political participation, enhance civic activism and education and promote issue-based advocacy, particularly within minority communities. Efforts should be made to ensure that qualified minorities are hired to develop, manage and/or implement government programmes targeted towards minorities.

21 Positive measures should be taken to overcome specific difficulties, such as illiteracy, language barriers, poverty or impediments to freedom of movement, which prevent people entitled to vote from exercising their rights effectively.

22 Governments and parliaments should ensure the effective functioning and funding of national agencies, institutions and/or mechanisms with responsibility for promoting minority political participation. Effective coordination between ministries and with all governmental institutions dealing with issues related to effective participation of minorities should be ensured.

23 States should ensure that all mechanisms, procedures and institutions established to promote and increase the political participation of persons belonging to minorities take into account the specific needs of minority women, as well as those of other groups within minority communities potentially subjected to intersectional discrimination, such as minorities with disabilities.

24 States should consider what special arrangements are necessary to secure the right of minorities to political participation at different stages of a country's transition, from situations of gross human rights violations and armed conflict, particularly with regard to refugees and internally displaced persons.

25 States should also consider what special arrangements are necessary to guarantee the right to effective political participation for persons belonging to nomadic communities who are least likely to have traditional documentation or proof of long-term residency in electoral districts.

26 Where citizenship is a requirement for voting, election to political office or appointment to a position in the public service, there should be a reasonable process for attaining such citizenship that is clearly defined, widely communicated and non-discriminatory with regard to race, ethnicity or religion. The process should not be prohibitive or present deterrents, such as being unduly lengthy, costly or otherwise burdensome for persons who meet the requirements.

27 Efforts should be made to accommodate the political participation of documented and regular migrant workers at the municipal level. This may include recognition of voting rights in municipal elections or the creation of special consultative bodies at the municipal level for enabling dialogue on issues of concern to migrants.

28 Respect for individual human rights must be the context within which measures to promote minority participation are taken; no one should suffer any detriment due to his or her membership or non-membership in a minority, including in systems of regional autonomy.

29 Parliaments are encouraged to establish special parliamentary committees to address issues of particular importance to minorities, and to enhance legislative attention to these issues.

B POLITICAL PARTIES

30 Political parties should be aware of the diversity of the society and/or communities that they represent and make active efforts to take concrete steps to reflect such diversity. They should adopt policies that recognize the importance of reflecting diversity in their work and develop plans to increase the level of minority participation within their ranks.

31 Political parties should adopt codes of conduct to prohibit inflammatory racist rhetoric and racist political platforms, not only during campaign periods but also between elections. Furthermore, there should be internal party mechanisms with the capacity to impose strong sanctions against party candidates who violate such codes of conduct.

32 Political parties with a national or broadly based constituency should develop strategies for more effective outreach to potential supporters and constituents within both majority and minority communities. They should allocate resources to determining the specific needs of members of minorities to facilitate their full participation in political, economic, social and cultural life. Parties should actively seek to ensure that all groups in society are aware of minority concerns and should provide opportunities for meaningful consultation among all groups within society.

33 Political parties based primarily on minority or regional affiliation should not be prohibited solely for this reason. Nevertheless, narrowly drawn restrictions may be placed on the advocacy of violence to achieve political goals or on political platforms that incite hatred or discrimination.
34 In electoral systems of proportional representation using a party list, political parties should ensure that the names of persons belonging to minorities are placed high enough on the party list to ensure that they gain seats in the legislative body.
35 Political parties should consider establishing mentoring programmes through which successful minority politicians could act as role models, encouraging others to run for office, raising awareness of minority political participation and reaching out to the majority population to ensure continuous dialogue between all groups.

C NATIONAL HUMAN RIGHTS INSTITUTIONS

36 National human rights institutions should ensure that they are representative of the diversity of their respective societies, reflecting the full spectrum of views, issues and challenges. They should put in place a specific mechanism within their secretariat to address minority issues and develop outreach programmes and civic education aimed at increasing the effective political participation of persons belonging to minorities. They should ensure that persons belonging to minorities are both involved in and have access to all their programmes, including in complaint mechanisms, and ensure that human rights materials are available in the minority languages.

D CIVIL SOCIETY

37 Civil society should: (a) Continue to play its role in breaking down the barriers preventing effective political participation of minorities, including through capacity-building and training activities, to ensure that representatives of minorities may participate effectively; (b) Develop civic education projects targeted at minority communities, highlighting the citizen's rights, roles and responsibilities, and offer training to young persons belonging to minorities in the skills of negotiation, communication, advocacy, policy-making and governance; (c) Engage constructively with parliament, local councils and government agencies at all levels by clearly articulating policy options and utilizing citizen initiatives to promote a defined legislative agenda; (d) Coordinate and network more effectively, both among minority nongovernmental organizations and across ethnic lines, to share best practices and lessons learned, maximize resources, avoid duplication of projects and develop more effective issue-based coalitions; (e) Increase minority leaders' effectiveness in government through training, and the training of trainers for the organizations of minorities, on legislative processes, drafting, debate,

coalition-building, advocacy, strategic planning and public speaking; they should involve members of the majority in training to strengthen their support for the participation of minorities; (f) Cooperate with other stakeholders to advocate appropriate legal reforms to advance the role of minorities in government.

E UNITED NATIONS HUMAN RIGHTS MECHANISMS

38 Relevant treaty bodies and special procedures should continue to pay attention to the effective political participation of minorities and the obstacles to the effective realization of their rights during their dialogue with States parties on the implementation of their treaty obligations, as well as the measures taken to eliminate all forms of discrimination. They should encourage States parties to involve minorities in all stages of the monitoring and implementation process of international treaty obligations.

F THE INTERNATIONAL COMMUNITY AND UNITED NATIONS AGENCIES

39 The international community should allocate sufficient resources to projects aimed at ensuring political participation of minorities, enhancing civic engagement and education and promoting issue-based advocacy by minorities. A United Nations voluntary fund for minorities should be established with a mandate to channel support for such initiatives.

40 All intergovernmental structures that engage with civil society at the global and regional levels should take concrete steps to ensure that persons belonging to minority groups are able to participate in those processes.

41 United Nations agencies should support the implementation of recommendations of United Nations human rights mechanisms relating to the political participation of minorities by, inter alia, ensuring the translation of recommendations into minority languages and their broad dissemination and facilitating the use of the recommendations by all relevant actors at the national level, taking into account the observations and recommendations of United Nations human rights mechanisms and procedures when preparing United Nations planning instruments, such as the Common Country Assessment/ United Nations Development Assistance Frameworks and agencies' specific programmes.

42 The Office of the United Nations High Commissioner for Human Rights should: (a) Sponsor training workshops to support the implementation of the United Nations Declaration on the Rights of Persons Belonging to National or Ethnic, Religious and Linguistic Minorities, including reference to recommendations of the Forum on the effective political participation of minorities; (b) Develop regional workshops for minority political actors and other minority stakeholders; (c) Support activities for training/capacity-building and outreach, including for representatives of minorities; (d) Increase the proportion of the resources devoted to activities directly related

to the effective participation of minorities in political and economic life; (e) Encourage States to develop and/or enhance minority youth professional training initiatives, such as minority fellowships and internships in national, regional and international government agencies, such as those of the United Nations.

43   The United Nations country teams, should, where appropriate, establish country specific consultative structures for minorities on participation in political processes.
44   The Inter-Parliamentary Union should organize an international meeting of parliamentary representatives and their staff to discuss how the effective participation of minorities in political decision-making could best be promoted. It should also set up an online clearing house on the political participation of minorities to provide a single point of access to the large amount of information that is already available at the national, regional and international levels.
45   The Inter-Agency Group on Minority Issues should devote one of its upcoming meetings to the topic of effective participation by minorities to discuss the respective roles played by its members in promoting effective participation, within the broader framework of article 9 of the Declaration on the Rights of Persons Belonging to National or Ethnic, Religious and Linguistic Minorities.
46   In order to ensure the effective participation of minorities in the deliberations held at the level of the United Nations, Governments should consider providing funding for the participation of civil society minority representatives in future sessions of the Forum on Minority Issues and other relevant meetings.

G   THE MEDIA

47   In both the public and private sectors, the media should make efforts to inform the society at large of minority-related issues, including by broadcasting in minority languages and emphasizing the importance of political participation for minorities. Special programmes should be developed during elections with a view to raising awareness within minority communities of the issues at stake, the platforms of the various political parties, registration procedures and other relevant information related to the election process.
48   The media should strive for balanced coverage to ensure equitable media access to all candidates or, where appropriate, each political party in all elections.
49   The effective participation of persons belonging to minorities in various media related bodies, such as supervisory boards, independent regulatory bodies, public service broadcast committees, auditors' councils or production teams, should be encouraged. All mass media organizations should take positive steps to ensure that their workforces are diverse and representative of society as a whole while seeking access to multiple voices within communities.

50 The freedom of minorities to establish and maintain their own private and public media, both printed and electronic, must be ensured without restriction on the free choice of the language used therein.

51 States should promote equitable access to new information and communications technologies, including the Internet, as a vital aspect of the democratization of information and a vehicle for encouraging the effective participation of youth in public life.

D.3. OFFICE OF THE HIGH COMMISSIONER FOR HUMAN RIGHTS, Minority Rights: International Standards and Guidance for Implementation (HR/PUB/10/3), 2010.*

(...)

D Effective and meaningful participation

The participation of persons belonging to minorities in public affairs and in all aspects of the political, economic, social and cultural life of the country where they live is in fact essential to preserving their identity and combating social exclusion. Mechanisms are required to ensure that the diversity of society with regard to minority groups is reflected in public institutions, such as national parliaments, the civil service sector, including the police and the judiciary, and that persons belonging to minorities are adequately represented, consulted and have a voice in decisions which affect them or the territories and regions in which they live. Participation must be meaningful and not merely symbolic, and recognize, for instance, that minorities are commonly underrepresented and that their concerns may not be adequately addressed. The participation of women belonging to minorities is of particular concern.

Participation must be effective. During its second session, on 12 and 13 November 2009, the Forum on Minority Issues focused on minorities and effective political participation. A key reference for the session was article 2 (2) of the United Nations Minorities Declaration, which provides for the right of persons belonging to national or ethnic, religious and linguistic minorities "to participate effectively in cultural, religious, social, economic and public life". For the participation of persons belonging to minorities to be effective, it is not sufficient for States to ensure their formal participation; States must also ensure that the participation of representatives of minorities has a substantial influence on the decisions which are taken, so that there is, as far as possible, shared ownership of

---

* From Minority Rights: International Standards and Guidance for Implementation, by UN Office of the High Commissioner for Human Rights (OHCHR), ©(2010) United Nations. Reprinted with the permission of the United Nations.

these decisions.[107] The international community has recognized these challenges and has put at the disposal of minorities several instruments and mechanisms to ensure their international and national protection. However, as societies evolve, it is vital for these instruments and mechanisms to be continuously re-examined, evaluated and adjusted where necessary to ensure that they allow for effective participation.

D.4. UN OFFICE OF THE HIGH COMMISSIONER FOR HUMAN RIGHTS *(OHCHR)*, The inclusion of religious minorities in consultative and decision-making bodies, *2014*.

(…)

Why should religious minorities participate in decision-making?

Minority rights extend the protection of religious minorities and complement instruments concerned with freedom of religion or belief including as regards the effective participation of minorities in decisions affecting them. The minority rights standards emphasise the effective participation of religious minorities in decisions which affect them and their full participation in the progress and development of their country. The Declaration on the Rights of Persons Belonging to National or Ethnic, Religious and Linguistic Minorities, inspired by article 27 of the International Covenant on Civil and Political Rights, establishes the responsibility of States to protect religious identity of minorities and to encourage conditions for its promotion. The Minorities Declaration further calls for State cooperation with religious minorities on questions relating to them in order to "promote mutual understanding and confidence", as well as advancing respect for their rights. These rights complement, and go beyond, freedom of religion and religious identity. Participation of minorities in various areas of life is essential for the development of a truly inclusive society. It is through effective participation that a person belonging to a religious minority expresses and protects her or his identity. Measures required to improve participation of minorities in social, cultural and political life are to take into account the historical, cultural and religious contexts of a given country. Notwithstanding distinctions in circumstances, certain practices or initiatives that work in a given context may be drawn upon in another, and prove to be effective.

---

107 See A/HRC/13/23, para. 52, in which the independent expert on minority issues refers to: Council of Europe, Advisory Committee on the Framework Convention for the Protection of National Minorities, Commentary on the effective participation of persons belonging to national minorities in cultural, social and economic life and public affairs (ACFC/31DOC(2008)001, paras. 18 and 19).

How the participation of religious minorities facilitates conflict prevention?

Lack of participation of religious minorities can result in increased vulnerability to violence, discrimination, exclusion and other human rights violations. Tensions between communities or violations of the rights of persons belonging to religious minorities are at the root of a significant number of conflicts. The effective and meaningful participation of minorities in the political arena can be a pivotal element in avoiding violent conflict; however the reality is often quite different. Societies in which mechanisms are in place allowing minorities to practice their culture and religion, and participate in political and economic life on an equal footing with the rest of the population, are less likely to be societies in which tensions emerge and deteriorate into violent conflict. Minorities are underrepresented in the political processes and governing institutions in many countries because they are intentionally restricted from participation, inadvertently disadvantaged by facially-neutral laws or policies, or because there are structural barriers to their full and equal participation.

Participation in consultative and decision-making bodies: positive measures

States should facilitate the establishment of bodies and mechanisms aimed at creating a space for discussions and exchanges on issues relevant to religious minorities. They should promote the participation of religious communities in public dialogue and implement the general principles of equality and non-discrimination. They should, through participatory processes with religious minority groups, adopt measures to improve respect for all human rights of persons belonging to religious minorities. The participation of women and young people belonging to religious minorities should be particularly encouraged and ensured through active outreach.

There is a need to introduce specific measures to ensure consultation with and participation of all religious minorities at all levels of the society. States should promote equitable access for religious minorities to information and communications technologies, including the internet and online social media, as a vehicle for the dissemination of information and sharing of good practices.

Obstacles hindering religious minorities' participation in consultative structures

Specialized bodies can play a crucial role in advancing the protection of religious minorities. However, there are States that limit protection only to specific minorities or design consultative structures based exclusively on ethnic or linguistic criteria resulting in restrictions for religious minorities. Some countries have specialized bodies that operate with a mandate that covers ethnic but not religious minorities. In other cases, consultative mechanisms exist but are restricted to minorities belonging to those religions recognized by States.

E Right to association

E.1. UN COMMISSION ON HUMAN RIGHTS, SUB-COMMISSION ON THE PROMOTION AND PROTECTION OF HUMAN RIGHTS, Commentary of the Working Group on Minorities to the United Nations Declaration on the Rights of Persons Belonging to National or Ethnic, Religious and Linguistic Minorities *(E/CN.4/Sub.2/ AC.5/2005/2), 4 April 2005.*

(...)

51. Persons belonging to minorities are entitled, in the same way as other members of society, to set up any association they may want,[108] including educational or religious institutions, but their right to association is not limited to concerns related to their cultural, linguistic or religious identity. The right to associate of persons belonging to minorities extends both to national and to international associations. Their right to form or join associations can be limited only by law and the limitations can only be those which apply to associations of majorities: limitations must be those necessary in a democratic society in the interests of national security or public safety, public order, the protection of public health or morals, or the protection of rights and freedoms.

52. The right to contacts has three facets, permitting intra-minority contacts, inter-minority contacts, and transfrontier contacts. The right to intra-minority contacts is inherent in the right of association. Inter-minority contacts make it possible for persons belonging to minorities to share experience and information and to develop a common minority platform within the State. The right to transfrontier contacts constitutes the major innovation of the Declaration and serves in part to overcome some of the negative consequences of the often unavoidable division of ethnic groups by international frontiers. Such contacts must be "free", but also "peaceful". The latter limitation has two aspects: contacts must not involve the use of violent means or preparation of the use of such means; and the aims must be in conformity with the Declaration and generally with the purposes and principles of the Charter of the United Nations, as set out also in article 8.4 of the Declaration.

E.2. UN OFFICE OF THE HIGH COMMISSIONER FOR HUMAN RIGHTS, Minority Rights: International Standards and Guidance for Implementation *(HR/PUB/10/3), 2010.* *

(...)

---

108 Universal Declaration of Human Rights, article 20; International Covenant on Civil and Political Rights, article 22.

* From Minority Rights: International Standards and Guidance for Implementation, by UN Office of the High Commissioner for Human Rights (OHCHR), ©(2010) United Nations. Reprinted with the permission of the United Nations.

C Identifying priorities to address the situation of minorities

7   Promotion and protection of the right of minorities to maintain associations

- Is the right to form associations and trade unions ensured by national legislation and equally accessible to workers belonging to minorities?
- Is there any particular obstacle in the country to minorities fully enjoying these rights?
- Have efforts been made by minority civil society organizations to establish a network for the exchange of information and the coordination of action?

F Non-discrimination

F.1. HIGH COMMISSIONER FOR HUMAN RIGHTS (OHCHR), Promoting and Protecting Minority Rights. A Guide for Advocates (HR/PUB/12/7), 2012.*

(...)

Part one – minority rights focus in the United Nations

CHAPTER I – OVERVIEW: DEVELOPMENT OF MINORITY RIGHTS IN INTERNATIONAL LAW

The United Nations The Charter of the United Nations makes no mention of minority rights per se, but it does include several provisions on human rights, including Article 1 (3), which identifies as one of the purposes of the United Nations the achievement of international cooperation "in promoting and encouraging respect for human rights and for fundamental freedoms for all without distinction as to race, sex, language, or religion". In 1948, the General Assembly adopted the Universal Declaration of Human Rights, which articulated the content of human rights in much greater detail and remains one of the most important international human rights documents: its anti-discrimination provisions and other articles are of central importance also for persons belonging to minorities. While the General Assembly was unable to agree on any formulation in the Declaration concerning minority rights per se, it did note that the United Nations "cannot remain indifferent to the fate of minorities". It added, in the same resolution that proclaimed the Universal Declaration, that it was "difficult to adopt a uniform solution for this complex and delicate question [of minorities], which has special aspects in each State in which it arises".[109]

---

* From *Promoting and Protecting Minority Rights. A Guide for Advocates*, by Office of the High Commissioner for Human Rights, © (2012) United Nations. Reprinted with the permission of the United Nations.

109 Resolution 217 C(III).

While many argued that issues related to minorities would be best addressed through a combination of respect for individual human rights and the growing attention being paid to the right of colonial territories to self-determination, the United Nations did address minority issues in a number of specific cases. For example, the 1948 Convention on the Prevention and Punishment of the Crime of Genocide prohibits the destruction of "a national, ethnical, racial or religious group, as such". In 1947, the Sub-Commission on Prevention of Discrimination and Protection of Minorities was created as a sub-body of the Commission on Human Rights and an influential study on that issue prepared for the Sub-Commission by Special Rapporteur Francesco Capotorti was published in 1979.[110] In the 1960s, three important treaties were adopted that also addressed minority rights. In 1960, the United Nations Educational, Scientific and Cultural Organization (UNESCO) adopted the Convention against Discrimination in Education, which recognized the right of minority group members to carry out their own educational activities, including establishing their own schools and teaching their own language. In 1965, the United Nations adopted the International Convention on the Elimination of All Forms of Racial Discrimination, which prohibits any distinction "based on race, colour, descent, or national or ethnic origin". In 1966, the International Covenant on Civil and Political Rights included in article 27 a specific provision concerned with minorities, a principal legal tool to advance minority rights. The Convention and the Covenant are discussed more fully in chapter V.

While these developments were important, advancing the protection of minority rights received more attention as the cold war ended. The importance of minority rights and their contribution to the stability of States was increasingly recognized in the work of international institutions, including in Central and Eastern Europe and in the former Soviet Union.

CHAPTER II – THE OFFICE OF THE UNITED NATIONS HIGH COMMISSIONER
FOR HUMAN RIGHTS

The New York office of OHCHR represents the High Commissioner in New York.[111] It works for the effective integration of human rights norms and standards in the decision-making and operational activities of intergovernmental and inter-agency bodies based at United Nations headquarters. It also leads efforts to end discrimination based on sexual orientation and gender identity.[112]

---

110 Study on the Rights of Persons Belonging to Ethnic, Religious and Linguistic Minorities, reprinted as Human Rights Study Series No. 5 (United Nations publication, Sales No. E.91.XIV.2).
111 See www.ohchr.org/EN/NewYork/Pages/Overview.aspx (accessed 29 November 2012).
112 Since the Minorities Declaration is devoted to national or ethnic, linguistic and religious minorities, persons of particular sexual orientation or identity (e.g., lesbian, gay, bisexual, transgender or intersexual) fall under its scope when they are also members of a national or ethnic, linguistic and religious minority, in which case efforts aimed at guaranteeing their human rights require addressing multiple discrimination issues.

F.2. FORUM ON MINORITY ISSUES, Note by the Independent Expert on minority issues, Rita Izsák, on guaranteeing the rights of religious minorities *(A/HRC/FMI/2013/2), 3 October 2013.*

(...)

III Legal framework

6   The Declaration also recognizes a wider need for protection of the rights of minorities to include guarantees of equality, non-discrimination in all spheres of life, participation in public life and protection of existence. With a view to achieving such goals, the Declaration calls on States to implement positive measures, including the adoption of legislation and other measures, to ensure the promotion and protection of all minority rights. Pursuant to article 4, paragraph 2, of the Declaration, States should "take measures to create favourable conditions to enable persons belonging to minorities to express their characteristics and to develop their culture, language, religion, traditions and customs, except where specific practices are in violation of national laws and contrary to international standards".

7   The 1981 Declaration on the Elimination of All Forms of Intolerance and of Discrimination Based on Religion or Belief (1981 Declaration) does not explicitly mention religious minorities, however it establishes non-discrimination and equality as key principles and requirements of States in their treatment of religious groups. Article 2, paragraph 1, of the 1981 Declaration stresses that "no one shall be subject to discrimination by any State, institution, group of persons, or person on the grounds of religion or belief". Article 3 of the 1981 Declaration clearly establishes that "discrimination between human beings on the grounds of religion or belief constitutes an affront to human dignity and a disavowal of the principles of the Charter of the United Nations".

F.3. *UN SECRETARY GENERAL*, Guidance note of the Secretary General on racial discrimination and protection of minorities, *March 2013.*

(...)

II. Normative and conceptual foundations

4   The principles of equality and non-discrimination are embodied in the UN Charter, which underlines respect for human rights and for fundamental freedoms for all without distinction as to race, sex, language or religion. These principles have been further developed in the Universal Declaration of Human Rights and in all core international human rights treaties, such as the International Convention on the Elimination of All Forms of Racial Discrimination (ICERD), and in regional instruments.[113] Important additional guidance for the UN and other actors is provided in such key documents as the UN Declaration on the Rights of Persons belonging to National or Ethnic, Religious and Linguistic Minorities (1992) and the Durban Declaration and Programme of Action (2001) and in the Outcome Document of the Durban Review Conference (2009).
(...)

7   The UN can in many cases combine its efforts to combat and prevent racial discrimination and to advance minority protection, as these are frequently interlinked. On the one hand, standards and mechanisms devoted to combatting racial discrimination benefit minorities, who are often targets of racial discrimination. On the other hand, minority rights contribute to the efforts to combat racial discrimination, by directly reinforcing prohibition of racial discrimination and also through participatory rights and other rights that indirectly contribute to efforts to combat such discrimination. It is in recognition of these interlinkages that these two notions are addressed in one Guidance Note.

8   The UN pursues an inclusive approach to the concept of minorities, guided by the principle of self-identification and bearing in mind that there is no internationally agreed definition of the term. Using UN minority rights standards and mechanisms is not conditioned upon the use of the term minority in the domestic context, and the UN Human Rights Committee has stressed that the existence of an ethnic, religious or linguistic minority in a given State party does not depend upon a decision by that State party but requires to be established by objective criteria.[114] Standards to combat racial discrimination and minority rights can be also invoked by indigenous peoples, as a complement to the specific standards and initiatives that have been developed to address the particular concerns faced by them, including

---

113   See, e.g., International Convention on the Elimination of All Forms of Racial Discrimination; art. 26 and 27 of the International Covenant on Civil and Political Rights; and the ILO Discrimination (Employment and Occupation) Convention, 1958 (No. 111). For an overview of relevant international and regional standards and their monitoring mechanisms, see also Minority Rights: International Standards and Guidance for Implementation, OHCHR, 2010.

114   The UN Human Rights Committee, General Comment No. 23: The rights of minorities (Art. 27), 4 August 1994, CCPR/C/21/Rev.1/Add.5, General Comment No. 23.

the UN Declaration on the Rights of Indigenous Peoples and the ILO Indigenous and Tribal Peoples Convention, 1989 (No. 169).

9   While this Guidance Note and the Declaration on Minority Rights focus on the rights of persons belonging to "national or ethnic, religious and linguistic" minorities, there are persons belonging to other groups that are regularly in a non-dominant position and merit specific UN attention from the perspective of non-discrimination and other human rights standards, including, for example, stateless persons, migrants, victims of forced displacement, persons with disabilities, people living with HIV and lesbian, gay, bisexual, or transgender (LGBT) persons. Their concerns also frequently involve multiple discrimination, including where a person belonging to a national, ethnic, religious or linguistic minority is also discriminated against on other grounds such as disability or sexual orientation.

III Guiding principles for effective UN action

1 ENSURE COORDINATED ENGAGEMENT OF ALL THREE PILLARS

10   Combatting racial discrimination and protecting minorities need to be consistently integrated into the work of the UN at global, regional and country levels. The UN should proactively seize opportunities to support initiatives that pursue these goals, including with regional organizations, governments, civil society and the private sector. Given the relevance of these challenges to all three pillars of the UN, it is essential that UN action in this area engage the entire UN system and that coordination mechanisms between entities ranging from UNCTs and "Delivering as One" initiatives to a diverse range of related global-level mechanisms, such as the UN Development Group's Human Rights Mainstreaming Mechanism (UNDG HRM) and the UN Network on Racial Discrimination and Protection of Minorities, actively support coordination and cooperation in this sphere.

2 PURSUE A HUMAN RIGHTS-BASED APPROACH

11   The principles of equality and non-discrimination are cornerstones of the UN's human rights-based approach. All entities of the UN system are governed by the UN Charter, which embodies these principles. Therefore, UN action and policies in the spheres related to racial discrimination and minority protection must be guided by international standards and recommendations

of human rights mechanisms, including those devoted to racial discrimination and rights of persons belonging to minorities.[115]
12 A human rights-based approach is crucial in development programming as it analyses the underlying and structural causes of the violations of rights; assesses the capacities of both rights holders and duty bearers; and supports capacity development measures, including by examining the causes of non-realization of rights for persons belonging to minorities and building capacity to exercise and fulfil these rights.

3 ADDRESS MULTIPLE AND INTERSECTING FORMS OF DISCRIMINATION

13 The UN action and policies need to take into account the prevalence of multiple and intersecting forms of discrimination. They need to reflect particular experiences within minority communities of common targets of multiple and intersecting forms of discrimination, such as minority women, stateless persons, internally displaced persons, persons with disabilities, older persons, children, people living with HIV and LGBT persons. UN entities, together with other partners, should support measures to identify and address such discrimination, as part of States parties' obligations under human rights treaties and taking into account the relevant recommendations by treaty bodies, special procedures and other human rights mechanisms, including UPR. Dissemination of success stories should also be supported.
14 Addressing multiple and intersecting forms of discrimination requires a holistic look at the way societies are organized and at the differential impact of discrimination on the various groups within it. Such an approach has revealed, for example, that in many countries minorities face particular challenges with respect to the implementation of the right to health; they are disproportionately affected by poor-health, malnutrition and diseases, and HIV/AIDS prevalence among minority groups is far higher than within the majority population. This is due to a variety of legal, social and structural barriers and constructs as well as stigma, which in many cases amount to discrimination. Moreover, people living with HIV are often stigmatized and discriminated against because of their HIV status, thus further compounding multiple forms of discrimination. The UN must be sensitive to these realities and ensure that programmes and policies on health, education and other pertinent fields address the needs of persons belonging to minorities.

---

115 The term "international standards" refer to norms and standards contained and developed under the core international human rights treaties as well as relevant instruments of specialized agencies, and the term "human rights mechanisms" is meant to include the Charter- and Treaty-based bodies as well as monitoring and standard-setting mechanisms of relevant instruments of the specialized agencies, such as the ILO supervisory bodies.

4 APPLY A GENDER PERSPECTIVE

15 As the Durban Declaration and the Programme of Action states, "racism, racial discrimination, xenophobia and related intolerance reveal themselves in a differentiated manner for women and girls, and can be among the factors leading to a deterioration in their living conditions, poverty, violence, multiple forms of discrimination, and the limitation or denial of their human rights". Women and girls belonging to minorities often face unique challenges and multiple or intersecting forms of discrimination emanating from their gender and status as persons belonging to minorities.

16 A gender perspective that takes into account these women's and men's issues and different life experiences and multiple and intersecting forms of discrimination is critical in addressing racial discrimination, minority rights and the situation of minority women and girls. In line with the recommendations of the UN Forum on Minority Issues,[116] a gender perspective should apply to all analysis and actions. The UN system should ensure that its strategies and actions promote gender equality and the realization of human rights for women and men, girls and boys. The situation of minority women and girls requires special attention, intervention and protection in areas ranging from crime prevention and criminal justice responses to harmful traditional practices and violence against women. It is also a frequent concern in addressing nationality legislation, property rights and family and personal status laws as well as in ensuring equal access to health care, education, social security and income-generating opportunities.

17 In spite of being frequent victims of human rights violations, minority women are often excluded from decision-making when responses to human rights violations are being designed and implemented. Effective UN action requires continuous dialogue with a diverse representation of minority women, including with a view to ensuring their contributions to the design and implementation of UN action and enhancing their participation in decision-making, in areas ranging from land and property issues to peace processes and security sector reform in post-conflict situations, as well as their representation in elected and appointed positions both within their communities and in societies at large.

---

116 See recommendations from the fourth session of the Forum on Minority Issues in 2011 on guaranteeing the rights of minority women and girls. Established pursuant to the Human Rights Council resolution 6/15 of 28 September 2007, the Forum on Minority Issues provides a platform for promoting dialogue and cooperation on issues pertaining to national or ethnic, religious and linguistic minorities.

2 Council of Europe

Section 1

European Convention on Human Rights

[Signed at Rome on 4th November 1950]

Article 9

1 Everyone has the right to freedom of thought, conscience and religion; this right includes freedom to change his religion or belief, and freedom, either alone or in community with others and in public or private, to manifest his religion or belief, in worship, teaching, practice and observance.
2 Freedom to manifest one's religion or beliefs shall be subject only to such limitations as are prescribed by law and are necessary in a democratic society in the interests of public safety, for the protection of public order, health or morals, or the protection of the rights and freedoms of others.

Article 10

1 Everyone has the right to freedom of expression. This right shall include freedom to hold opinions and to receive and impart information and ideas without interference by public authority and regardless of frontiers. This article shall not prevent States from requiring the licensing of broadcasting, television or cinema enterprises.
2 The exercise of these freedoms, since it carries with it duties and responsibilities, may be subject to such formalities, conditions, restrictions or penalties as are prescribed by law and are necessary in a democratic society, in the interests of national security, territorial integrity or public safety, for the prevention of disorder or crime, for the protection of health or morals, for the protection of the reputation or the rights of others, for preventing the

disclosure of information received in confidence, or for maintaining the authority and impartiality of the judiciary.

Article 14

The enjoyment of the rights and freedoms set forth in this Convention shall be secured without discrimination on any ground such as sex, race, colour, language, religion, political or other opinion, national or social origin, association with a national minority, property, birth or other status.

Protocols 1 Enforcement of certain Rights and Freedoms not included in Section I of the Convention

[Paris 20th March 1952]

Article 1

Every natural or legal person is entitled to the peaceful enjoyment of his possessions. No one shall be deprived of his possessions except in the public interest and subject to the conditions provided for by law and by the general principles of international law.

The preceding provisions shall not, however, in any way impair the right of a State to enforce such laws as it deems necessary to control the use of property in accordance with the general interest or to secure the payment of taxes or other contributions or penalties.

A Right to profess and practise religion or belief

A.1. EUROPEAN COURTS OF HUMAN RIGHTS, Case of **Serif c. Greece** *(Application no. 38.178/97), 14 March 2000.*

(…)

The facts

I THE CIRCUMSTANCES OF THE CASE

7   The applicant is a Greek citizen, born in 1951. He is a theological school graduate and resides in Komotini.

A *The background of the case*

8   In 1985 one of the two Muslim religious leaders of Thrace, the Mufti of Rodopi, died. The State appointed a mufti ad interim. When he resigned,

a second mufti ad interim, Mr M.T., was appointed. On 6 April 1990 the President of the Republic confirmed M.T. in the post of Mufti of Rodopi.

9   In December 1990 the two independent Muslim Members of Parliament for Xanthi and Rodopi requested the State to organise elections for the post of Mufti of Rodopi, as the law then in force provided. They also requested that elections be organised by the State for the post of the other Muslim religious leader of Thrace, the Mufti of Xanthi. Having received no reply, the two independent MPs decided to organise elections themselves at the mosques on Friday 28 December 1990, after prayers.

10 On 24 December 1990 the President of the Republic, on the proposal of the Council of Ministers and under Article 44 § 1 of the Constitution, adopted a legislative decree by which the manner of selection of the muftis was changed.

11 On 28 December 1990 the applicant was elected Mufti of Rodopi by those attending Friday prayers at the mosques. Together with other Muslims, he challenged the lawfulness of M.T.'s appointment before the Supreme Administrative Court. These proceedings are still pending.

12 On 4 February 1991 Parliament enacted Law no. 1920, thereby retroactively validating the legislative decree of 24 December 1990.

B *The criminal proceedings against the applicant*

13 The Rodopi public prosecutor instituted criminal proceedings against the applicant under Articles 175 and 176 of the Criminal Code for having usurped the functions of a minister of a "known religion" and for having publicly worn the dress of such a minister without having the right to do so. On 8 November 1991 the Court of Cassation, considering that there might be disturbances in Rodopi, decided, under Articles 136 and 137 of the Code of Criminal Procedure, that the case should be heard in Salonika.

14 On 5 March 1993 the Salonika public prosecutor summoned the applicant to appear before the Salonika Criminal Court sitting at first instance and composed of a single judge to be tried for the offences provided for under Articles 175 and 176 of the Criminal Code.

15 The applicant was tried by the Salonika Criminal Court on 12 December 1994. He was represented by counsel. The court heard a number of prosecution and defence witnesses. Although one witness attested that the applicant had taken part in religious ceremonies, none of the witnesses stated that the applicant had purported to discharge the judicial functions with which muftis are entrusted in Greek law. Moreover, a number of witnesses attested that no official dress for muftis existed. However, one prosecution witness declared that, although in principle all Muslims were allowed to wear the black gown in which the applicant had been appearing, according to local custom this had become the privilege of muftis.

16 On 12 December 1994 the court found the applicant guilty of the offences provided for under Articles 175 and 176 of the Criminal Code. According to the court, these offences had been committed between 17 January and

28 February 1991, a period during which the applicant had discharged the entirety of the functions of the Mufti of Rodopi by officiating at weddings, "christening" children, preaching and engaging in administrative activities. In particular, the court found that on 17 January 1991 the applicant had issued a message to his fellow Muslims about the religious significance of the Regaib Kandil feast, thanking them at the same time for his election as mufti. On 15 February 1991, in the capacity of a mufti, he had attended the inauguration of the hall of the "Union of the Turkish Youth of Komotini" wearing clothes which, according to Muslim custom, only muftis were allowed to wear. On 27 February 1991 he had issued another message on the occasion of the Berat Kandil feast. Finally, on 28 February 1991 and in the same capacity, he had attended a religious gathering of 2,000 Muslims at Dokos, a village in Rodopi, and had delivered the keynote speech. Moreover, the court found that the applicant had repeatedly worn the official dress of a mufti in public. The court imposed on the applicant a commutable sentence of eight months' imprisonment.

17 The applicant appealed. The hearing before the Salonika Criminal Court sitting on appeal and composed of three judges was adjourned on 24 May 1995 and 30 April 1996 because, inter alia, M.T., the appointed mufti, who had been called by the prosecution, did not appear to testify. M.T. was fined. The appeal was heard on 21 October 1996. In a decision issued on the same date the court upheld the applicant's conviction and imposed on him a sentence of six months' imprisonment to be commuted to a fine.

18 The applicant paid the fine and appealed on points of law. He submitted, inter alia, that the appellate court had interpreted Article 175 of the Criminal Code erroneously when it considered that the offence was made out even where a person claimed to be a minister of a "known religion" without, however, discharging any of the functions of the minister's office. Moreover, the court had been wrong to disregard expert testimony that no official mufti dress existed. The applicant had the right under Article 10 of the Convention to make the statements for which he had been convicted. "The office of the mufti represented the free manifestation of the Muslim religion", the Muslim community had the right under the Treaty of Peace of Athens of 1913 to elect its muftis and, therefore, his conviction violated Articles 9 and 14 of the Convention.

19 On 2 April 1997 the Court of Cassation dismissed the applicant's appeal. It considered that the offence in Article 175 of the Criminal Code was made out "where somebody appeared in public as a minister of a 'known religion' and discharged the functions of the minister's office, including any of the administrative functions pertaining thereto". The court considered that the applicant had committed this offence because he had behaved and appeared in public as the Mufti of Rodopi, wearing the dress which, in people's minds, was that of a mufti. In particular, the court referred to the incidents of 17 January and 15, 27 and 28 February 1991. The Court of Cassation did not

specifically address the applicant's arguments under Articles 9, 10 and 14 of the Convention.

II RELEVANT LAW AND PRACTICE

A. International treaties 20. Article 11 of the Treaty of Peace of Athens between Greece and others, on the one hand, and the Ottoman Empire, on the other, which was concluded on 17 May 1913 and ratified by the Greek parliament by a law published in the Official Gazette on 14 November 1913, provides as follows:

> "The life, property, honour, religion and customs of the inhabitants of the districts ceded to Greece who will remain under Greek administration shall be scrupulously respected. They shall enjoy in full the same civil and political rights as the subjects of Greek origin. Muslims shall be entitled to freedom and to practise their religion openly. (...) There shall be no interference with the autonomy or hierarchical organisation of existing or future Muslim communities or in the management of their funds or property. (...) Each mufti shall be elected by Muslim voters in his own constituency. (...) In addition to their authority in purely religious matters and in the supervision of the management of vacouf property, the muftis shall have jurisdiction as between Muslims in the spheres of marriage, divorce, maintenance (nefaca), guardianship, administration, capacity of minors, Islamic wills and succession to the office of mutevelli (Tevliét). Judgments delivered by the muftis shall be enforced by the competent Greek authorities. As regards successions, any interested Muslim party may with prior agreement submit a dispute to the mufti as arbitrator. Unless the agreement expressly provides otherwise, all avenues of appeal to the Greek courts shall lie against an arbitral award."

21 On 10 August 1920 Greece concluded two treaties with the principal Allied Powers at Sèvres. By the first treaty the Allied Powers transferred to Greece all the rights and titles which they had acquired over Thrace by virtue of the peace treaty they had signed with Bulgaria at Neuilly-sur-Seine on 27 November 1919. The second treaty concerned the protection of minorities in Greece. Article 14 § 1 of the second treaty provides as follows:

> "Greece agrees to take all necessary measures in relation to the Muslims to enable questions of family law and personal status to be regulated in accordance with Muslim usage."

22 On 30 January 1923 Greece and Turkey signed a treaty for the exchange of populations. On 24 July 1923 Greece and others, on the one hand, and Turkey, on the other, signed the Treaty of Peace of Lausanne. Articles 42 and 45 of this treaty gave the Muslim minority of Greece the same protection as Article 14 § 1 of the Sèvres Treaty for the Protection of Minorities. On the

same day Greece signed a protocol with the principal Allied Powers bringing into force the two treaties concluded at Sèvres on 10 August 1920. The Greek parliament ratified the three above-mentioned treaties by a law published in the Official Gazette on 25 August 1923.

23 In its decision no. 1723/80 the Court of Cassation considered that it was obliged to apply Islamic law in certain disputes between Muslims by virtue of the Treaty of Peace of Athens of 1913, the Treaty for the Protection of Minorities of Sèvres of 1920 and the Treaty of Peace of Lausanne of 1923.

B. The legislation on the muftis

24 Law no. 2345/1920 provided that the muftis, in addition to their religious functions, had competence to adjudicate on family and inheritance disputes between Muslims to the extent that these disputes were governed by Islamic law. It also provided that the muftis were directly elected by the Muslims who had the right to vote in the national elections and who resided in the prefectoral district in which the muftis would serve. The elections were to be organised by the State and theological school graduates had the right to be candidates. Section 6(8) of the Law provided for the promulgation of a royal decree to make detailed arrangements for the elections of the muftis.

25 Such a decree was never promulgated. The State appointed a mufti in Rodopi in 1920 and another one in March 1935. In June 1935 a mufti ad interim was appointed by the State. In the course of the same year the State appointed a regular mufti. This mufti was replaced by another in 1941, when Bulgaria occupied Thrace. He was reappointed by the Greek State in 1944. In 1948 the Greek authorities appointed a mufti ad interim until 1949, when a regular mufti was appointed. The latter served until 1985, when he died.

26 Under the legislative decree of 24 December 1990 the functions and qualifications of the muftis remain largely unchanged. However, provision is made for the appointment of the muftis by presidential decree following a proposal by the Minister of Education who, in turn, must consult a committee composed of the local prefect and a number of Muslim dignitaries chosen by the State. The legislative decree expressly abrogates Law no. 2345/1920 and provides that it should be ratified by law in accordance with Article 44 § 1 of the Constitution.

27 Law no. 1920/1991 retroactively validated the legislative decree of 24 December 1990.

C. Legislative decrees under Article 44 § 1 of the Constitution

28 Article 44 § 1 of the Constitution provides as follows:

"In exceptional circumstances, when an extremely urgent and unforeseeable need arises, the President of the Republic may, on the proposal of the Council of Ministers, adopt legislative acts. These acts must be submitted to Parliament for approval ... within forty days ...".

D. *Articles 175 and 176 of the Criminal Code*
29. Article 175 of the Criminal Code provides as follows:

"1. A person who intentionally usurps the functions of a State or municipal official shall be liable to a term of imprisonment not exceeding one year or a fine.
2. This provision also applies where a person usurps the functions of a lawyer or a minister of the Greek Orthodox Church or another known religion."

30. The Court of Cassation considered that this provision applied in the case of a former priest of the Greek Orthodox Church who continued to wear the priests' robes (judgment no. 378/80). The priest in question had been defrocked after joining the Old Calendarists, a religious movement formed by Greek Orthodox priests who wanted the Church to maintain the Julian calendar. In judgment no. 454/66 the Court of Cassation considered that the offence in Article 175 of the Criminal Code was also committed by a person who purported to discharge the administrative functions of a priest. In judgments nos. 140/64 and 476/71 the Court of Cassation applied Article 175 of the Code to cases of persons who had purported to exercise the religious functions of an Orthodox priest by conducting services, "christening" children, etc.

31. Article 176 of the Criminal Code provides as follows:

"A person who publicly wears the dress or the insignia of a State or municipal official or of a minister of a religion referred to in Article 175 § 2 without having the right to do so ... shall be liable to a term of imprisonment not exceeding six months or a fine."

E. *The legislation on ministers of "known religions"* 32. Ministers of the Greek Orthodox Church and other "known religions" enjoy a number of privileges under domestic law. Inter alia, the religious weddings they celebrate produce the same legal effects as civil weddings and they are exempt from military service.

The Law

I ALLEGED VIOLATION OF ARTICLE 9 OF THE CONVENTION

33. The applicant complained that his conviction amounted to a violation of Article 9 of the Convention, which provides as follows:

"1 Everyone has the right to freedom of thought, conscience and religion; this right includes freedom to change his religion or belief and freedom, either alone or in community with others and in public or private, to manifest his religion or belief, in worship, teaching, practice and observance.
2 Freedom to manifest one's religion or beliefs shall be subject only to such limitations as are prescribed by law and are necessary in a democratic society

in the interests of public safety, for the protection of public order, health or morals, or for the protection of the rights and freedoms of others."

34. The Government denied that there had been any such breach. In their view, there had been no interference with the applicant's right to freedom of religion. Even if there had been an interference, the Government argued that it would have been justified under the second paragraph of Article 9 of the Convention.

35. The Court must consider whether the applicant's Article 9 rights were interfered with and, if so, whether such interference was "prescribed by law", pursued a legitimate aim and was "necessary in a democratic society" within the meaning of Article 9 § 2 of the Convention.

A. *Existence of an interference* 36. The applicant argued that his conviction amounted to an interference with his right to be free to exercise his religion together with all those who turned to him for spiritual guidance.

37. The Government submitted that there had been no interference with the applicant's right to freedom of religion because Article 9 of the Convention did not guarantee for the applicant the right to impose on others his understanding as to Greece's obligations under the Treaty of Peace of Athens.

38. The Court recalls that, while religious freedom is primarily a matter of individual conscience, it also includes, inter alia, freedom, in community with others and in public, to manifest one's religion in worship and teaching (see, mutatis mutandis, the Kokkinakis v. Greece judgment of 25 May 1993, Series A no. 260-A, p. 17, § 31).

39. The Court further recalls that the applicant was convicted for having usurped the functions of a minister of a "known religion" and for having publicly worn the dress of such a minister without having the right to do so. The facts underlying the applicant's conviction, as they transpire from the relevant domestic court decisions, were issuing a message about the religious significance of a feast, delivering a speech at a religious gathering, issuing another message on the occasion of a religious holiday and appearing in public wearing the dress of a religious leader. In these circumstances, the Court considers that the applicant's conviction amounts to an interference with his right under Article 9 § 1 of the Convention, "in community with others and in public ..., to manifest his religion ... in worship [and] teaching".

B. *"Prescribed by law"* 40. The Government submitted that the applicant's conviction was provided by law, namely Articles 175 and 176 of the Criminal Code. Given the manner in which these provisions had been interpreted by the courts, the outcome of the proceedings against the applicant was foreseeable. In the Government's view, the issue of whether the applicant's conviction was prescribed by law was not related to Law no. 2345 on the election of the muftis or the Treaty of Peace of Athens. In any event, the Government argued that Law no. 2345 had fallen into disuse. Moreover, the provisions of the Treaty of Peace of Athens, which had been concluded when Thrace was not part of Greece, became devoid of purpose after the compulsory exchange of populations in 1923. This was when Greece exchanged all the Muslims who were living on the territories in its possession when the Treaty of Peace of Athens had been concluded. In the alternative, the Government argued that the provisions of the Treaty of Peace of Athens had been superseded by the provisions of the Treaty of Sèvres for the Protection of Minorities in Greece and the Treaty of Peace of Lausanne, and these treaties made no provision for the election of the muftis.

41. The applicant disagreed. He considered that the Treaty of Peace of Athens remained in force. The Greek Prime Minister had accepted that at the Diplomatic Conference leading to the 1923 Treaty of Peace of Lausanne. Moreover, the Court of Cassation had confirmed the continued validity of the Treaty of Peace of Athens and legal scholars held the same view. The Muslims had never accepted the abrogation of Law no. 2345.

42. The Court does not consider it necessary to rule on the question whether the interference in issue was "prescribed by law" because, in any event, it is incompatible with Article 9 on other grounds (see the Manoussakis and Others v. Greece judgment of 26 September 1996, Reports of Judgments and Decisions 1996-IV, p. 1362, § 38).

C. *Legitimate aim*   43. The Government argued that the interference served a legitimate purpose. By protecting the authority of the lawful mufti the domestic courts sought to preserve order in the particular religious community and in society at large. They also sought to protect the international relations of the country, an area over which States exercise unlimited discretion.

44. The applicant disagreed.

45. The Court accepts that the interference in question pursued a legitimate aim under Article 9 § 2 of the Convention, namely "to protect public order". It notes in this connection that the applicant was not the only person claiming to be the religious leader of the local Muslim community. On 6 April 1990 the authorities had appointed another person as Mufti of Rodopi and the relevant decision had been challenged before the Supreme Administrative Court.

D. *"Necessary in a democratic society"*   46. The Government submitted that the interference was necessary in a democratic society. In many countries, the muftis were appointed by the State. Moreover, muftis exercised important judicial functions in Greece and judges could not be elected by the people. As a result, the appointment of a mufti by the State could not in itself raise an issue under Article 9.

47. Moreover, the Government submitted that the Court of Cassation had not convicted the applicant simply because he had appeared in public as the mufti. The court considered that the offence in Article 175 was made out where somebody actually discharged the functions of a religious minister. The court also considered that the acts that the applicant engaged in fell within the administrative functions of a mufti in the broad sense of the term. Given that there were two muftis in Rodopi at the time, the courts had to convict the spurious one in order to avoid the creation of tension among the Muslims, between the Muslims

and Christians and between Turkey and Greece. The applicant had questioned the legality of the acts of the lawful mufti. In any event, the State had to protect the office of the mufti and, even if there had not existed a lawfully appointed mufti, the applicant would have had to be punished. Finally, the "election" of the applicant had been flawed because it had not been the result of a democratic procedure and the applicant had been used by the local Muslim MP for party political purposes.

48. The applicant considered that his conviction was not necessary in a democratic society. He pointed out that the Christians and Jews in Greece had the right to elect their religious leaders. Depriving the Muslims of this possibility amounted to discriminatory treatment. The applicant further contended that the vast majority of Muslims in Thrace wanted him to be their mufti. Such an interference could not be justified in a democratic society, where the State should not interfere with individual choices in the field of personal conscience. His conviction was just one aspect of the policy of repression applied by the Greek State vis-à-vis the Turkish-Muslim minority of western Thrace.

49. The Court recalls that freedom of thought, conscience and religion is one of the foundations of a "democratic society" within the meaning of the Convention. The pluralism indissociable from a democratic society, which has been dearly won over the centuries, depends on it. It is true that in a democratic society it may be necessary to place restrictions on freedom of religion to reconcile the interests of the various religious groups (see the Kokkinakis judgment cited above, pp. 17 and 18, §§ 31 and 33). However, any such restriction must correspond to a "pressing social need" and must be "proportionate to the legitimate aim pursued" (see, among others, the Wingrove v. the United Kingdom judgment of 25 November 1996, Reports 1996-V, p. 1956, § 53).

50. The Court also recalls that the applicant was convicted under Articles 175 and 176 of the Criminal Code, which render criminal offences certain acts against ministers of "known religions". The Court notes in this connection that, although Article 9 of the Convention does not require States to give legal effect to religious weddings and religious courts' decisions, under Greek law weddings celebrated by ministers of "known religions" are assimilated to civil ones and the muftis have competence to adjudicate on certain family and inheritance disputes between Muslims. In such circumstances, it could be argued that it is in the public interest for the State to take special measures to protect from deceit those whose legal relationships can be affected by the acts of religious ministers. However, the Court does not consider it necessary to decide this issue, which does not arise in the applicant's case.

51. The Court notes in this connection that, despite a vague assertion that the applicant had officiated at wedding ceremonies and engaged in administrative activities, the domestic courts that convicted him did not mention in their decisions any specific acts by the applicant with a view to producing legal effects. The domestic courts convicted the applicant on the following established facts:

issuing a message about the religious significance of a feast, delivering a speech at a religious gathering, issuing another message on the occasion of a religious holiday and appearing in public in the dress of a religious leader. Moreover, it has not been disputed that the applicant had the support of at least part of the Muslim community in Rodopi. However, in the Court's view, punishing a person for merely acting as the religious leader of a group that willingly followed him can hardly be considered compatible with the demands of religious pluralism in a democratic society.

52. The Court is not oblivious of the fact that in Rodopi there existed, in addition to the applicant, an officially appointed mufti. Moreover, the Government argued that the applicant's conviction was necessary in a democratic society because his actions undermined the system put in place by the State for the organisation of the religious life of the Muslim community in the region. However, the Court recalls that there is no indication that the applicant attempted at any time to exercise the judicial and administrative functions for which the legislation on the muftis and other ministers of "known religions" makes provision. As for the rest, the Court does not consider that, in democratic societies, the State needs to take measures to ensure that religious communities remain or are brought under a unified leadership.

53. It is true that the Government argued that, in the particular circumstances of the case, the authorities had to intervene in order to avoid the creation of tension among the Muslims in Rodopi and between the Muslims and the Christians of the area as well as Greece and Turkey. Although the Court recognises that it is possible that tension is created in situations where a religious or any other community becomes divided, it considers that this is one of the unavoidable consequences of pluralism. The role of the authorities in such circumstances is not to remove the cause of tension by eliminating pluralism, but to ensure that the competing groups tolerate each other (see, mutatis mutandis, the Plattform "Ärzte für das Leben" v. Austria judgment of 21 June 1988, Series A no. 139, p. 12, § 32). In this connection, the Court notes that, apart from a general reference to the creation of tension, the Government did not make any allusion to disturbances among the Muslims in Rodopi that had actually been or could have been caused by the existence of two religious leaders. Moreover, the Court considers that nothing was adduced that could warrant qualifying the risk of tension between the Muslims and Christians or between Greece and Turkey as anything more than a very remote possibility.

54. In the light of all the above, the Court considers that it has not been shown that the applicant's conviction under Articles 175 and 176 of the Criminal Code was justified in the circumstances of the case by "a pressing social need". As a result, the interference with the applicant's right, in community with others and in public, to manifest his religion in worship and teaching was not "necessary in a democratic society ..., for the protection of public order" under Article 9 § 2 of the Convention. There has, therefore, been a violation of Article 9 of the Convention.

II. ALLEGED VIOLATION OF ARTICLE 10 OF THE CONVENTION

55. The applicant complained that, since he had been convicted for certain statements he had made and for wearing certain clothes in public, there had also been a violation of Article 10 of the Convention, which provides as follows:

"1 Everyone has the right to freedom of expression. This right shall include freedom to hold opinions and to receive and impart information and ideas without interference by public authority and regardless of frontiers ...
2 The exercise of these freedoms, since it carries with it duties and responsibilities, may be subject to such formalities, conditions, restrictions or penalties as are prescribed by law and are necessary in a democratic society, in the interests of national security, territorial integrity or public safety, for the prevention of disorder or crime, for the protection of health or morals, for the protection of the reputation or rights of others, for preventing the disclosure of information received in confidence, or for maintaining the authority and impartiality of the judiciary."

56. The Government argued that there had been no violation because the applicant had not been punished for expressing certain views but for usurping the functions of a mufti.

57. Given its finding that there has been a violation of Article 9 of the Convention, the Court does not consider it necessary to examine whether Article 10 was also violated, because no separate issue arises under the latter provision.

III. APPLICATION OF ARTICLE 41 OF THE CONVENTION

58. Article 41 of the Convention provides:

"If the Court finds that there has been a violation of the Convention or the Protocols thereto, and if the internal law of the High Contracting Party concerned allows only partial reparation to be made, the Court shall, if necessary, afford just satisfaction to the injured party."

A. Damage 59. The applicant claimed repayment of the fine he had paid as a result of his conviction, which was approximately 700,000 drachmas (GRD). He also claimed GRD 10,000,000 for non-pecuniary damage.

60. The Government did not accept these claims.

61. The Court recalls its finding that the applicant's conviction amounted to a violation of Article 9 of the Convention. It therefore awards the applicant as compensation for pecuniary damage the equivalent of the fine he had to pay, namely GRD 700,000. The Court further considers that, as a result of the above violation, the applicant has suffered non-pecuniary damage for which the finding in this judgment does not afford sufficient satisfaction. Making its assessment on an equitable basis, the Court awards the applicant GRD 2,000,000 in this respect.

B. *Costs and expenses* 62. The applicant did not make any claim in respect of costs and expenses.

63. The Court, having regard to the above and to the fact that the applicant had the benefit of legal aid in the proceedings before it, does not consider it appropriate to make an award in this connection.

C. *Default interest* 64. According to the information available to the Court, the statutory rate of interest applicable in Greece at the date of adoption of the present judgment is 6% per annum.

FOR THESE REASONS, THE COURT UNANIMOUSLY

1   Holds that there has been a violation of Article 9 of the Convention;
2   Holds that no separate issue arises under Article 10 of the Convention;
3   Holds that the respondent State is to pay the applicant, within three months from the date on which the judgment becomes final according to Article 44 § 2 of the Convention, 2,700,000 (two million seven hundred thousand) drachmas for damage, and that simple interest at an annual rate of 6% shall be payable from the expiry of the above-mentioned three months until settlement;
4   Dismisses the remainder of the applicant's claim for just satisfaction.

B Right to free self-identification

B.1. EUROPEAN COURTS OF HUMAN RIGHTS, GC, *Case of* Molla Sali c. Greece *(Application no. 20.452/14), 19 December 2018.*

The facts

I THE CIRCUMSTANCES OF THE CASE

8   The applicant was born in 1950 and lives in Komotini.
9   The applicant's husband, Moustafa Molla Sali, a member of the Muslim community of Thrace, died on 21 March 2008. On 7 February 2003 he had drawn up a notarised public will in accordance with the relevant provisions of the Civil Code. He had bequeathed his whole estate to his wife, namely: one-third of a 2,000 sq. m plot of farmland near Komotini; one-half of a 127 sq. m apartment, a parking space and a basement in a block of flats in Komotini; one-quarter of a shop in Komotini with a surface area of 24 sq. m, and another shop measuring 31 sq. m in Komotini, which was subsequently expropriated in return for compensation that has already been paid to the applicant; and four properties in Istanbul.
10 By decision no. 12.785/2003 of 10 June 2008 the Komotini Court of First Instance, on the basis of a next-of-kin certificate submitted by the applicant, approved the will presented before it. On 6 April 2010 the applicant accepted her husband's estate by notarised deed. The Treasury was notified

and the applicant registered the property transferred to her with the Komotini Land Registry, paying the corresponding registration fees. It does not appear from the case file that the applicant had to pay any inheritance tax on the property transferred to her.

A Proceedings in the Rodopi Court of First Instance

11 On 12 December 2009, meanwhile, the deceased's two sisters had challenged the validity of the will before the Rodopi Court of First Instance. They asserted a claim to three-quarters of the property bequeathed. They submitted that they and the deceased belonged to the Thrace Muslim community and that therefore any questions relating to his estate were subject to Islamic religious law (Sharia law) and the jurisdiction of the mufti, rather than to the provisions of the Civil Code. They contended that the application of Muslim customs and Sharia law to Greek nationals of Muslim faith was laid down in the provisions of Article 14 § 1 of the 1920 Treaty of Sèvres (ratified by decree of 29 September/ 30 October 1923) and Articles 42 and 45 of the Treaty of Lausanne (ratified by decree of 25 August 1923) (see paragraphs 65–68 below). They argued that the law of succession applicable to Muslims was based on intestacy rather than testacy. Under Islamic law, where the deceased was survived by close relatives, the will only served to complement the intestate succession. Those provisions had continued to apply after the adoption of the Greek Civil Code, pursuant to section 6 of the Introductory Law to the Code, solely in respect of Greek nationals of Muslim faith living in Thrace.

12 By judgment no. 50/2010 of 1 June 2010, the Rodopi Court of First Instance dismissed the challenge brought by the deceased's sisters. It held that applying the Islamic law of succession to Greek Muslims in such a way as to prevent them from disposing of their property in anticipation of their death gave rise to unacceptable discrimination on grounds of religious beliefs. It found that the consequent inability of such persons to draw up a public will was in breach of Article 4 (principle of equality), Article 5 § 1 (free development of personality), Article 5 § 2 (principle of non-discrimination) and Article 13 § 1 (freedom of religious conscience) of the Constitution, as well as Article 14 of the Convention and Article 1 of Protocol No. 1. The court emphasised that even if it should be inferred from section 5(2) of Law no. 1920/1991 (ratifying the Legislative Act of 24 December 1990 on Muslim ministers of religion) that inheritance matters for Muslims were governed by Sharia law, such law should be applied in a manner compatible with the Constitution and the Convention. The incompatibility in the present case had stemmed from interpreting the Islamic law of succession in such a way as to deprive the persons concerned of some of their civil rights, against their wishes. The court added that although the application of Sharia law was based, inter alia, on international law, and in particular on the combined effect of Articles 42 and 45 of the Treaty of Lausanne, it should

not result in the Islamic law of succession being applied in such a way as to curtail the civil rights of Greek Muslims, because the aim of the treaty had not been to deprive the members of that minority of such rights, but to strengthen their protection.

13 The court pointed out that a Greek Muslim contacting a notary in order to draw up a public will was exercising his right to dispose of his property, in anticipation of his death, under the same conditions as other Greek citizens. It was consequently impossible to annul the will or to override any of its legal effects on the grounds that a will of that kind was prohibited by Sharia law. Upholding the claimants' arguments would thus amount to introducing an unacceptable difference in treatment among Greek nationals on the grounds of their religious beliefs.

B *Proceedings in the Thrace Court of Appeal*

14 On 16 June 2010 the deceased's sisters appealed against the aforementioned judgment.
15 On 28 September 2011 the Thrace Court of Appeal dismissed the appeal (judgment no. 392/2011). It emphasised, firstly, that the legislative provisions enacted pursuant to the Treaties of Sèvres and Lausanne had been intended to protect Greek nationals of Muslim faith and were in conformity with the Constitution and the Convention. That applied both to Islamic wills and to intestate succession, and the mufti had no jurisdiction in relation to public wills. The court held that since the testator was free to choose the type of will he wished to draw up in the exercise of his rights and therefore to draw up a public will in accordance with Article 1724 of the Civil Code, he was not obliged to follow Islamic law, which did not cover matters relating to such wills. Furthermore, the mufti had no jurisdiction over the testator's wishes, which could not be circumscribed. Otherwise, there would be discrimination on grounds of religion, which was unlawful under the general rules on prohibition of discrimination.
16 More specifically, the Court of Appeal noted that the decision taken by the deceased, a Greek citizen of Muslim faith belonging to the Thrace Muslim religious minority, to ask a notary to draw up a public will, choosing personally to decide how and to whom he would bequeath his property, fell within his legal right to dispose of his property in anticipation of his death, under the same conditions as other Greek nationals.

C *Proceedings in the Court of Cassation*

17 On 23 January 2012 the deceased's sisters lodged an appeal on points of law.
18 By judgment no. 1862/2013 of 7 October 2013 and on the basis of a provision of international law, namely Article 11 of the 1913 Treaty of Athens, and provisions of domestic law, namely section 4 of Law no. 147/1914, section 10 of Law no. 2345/1920 (enacted pursuant to the 1913 Treaty of Athens) and section 5(2) of Law no. 1920/1991 the Court of Cassation

allowed the appeal. It noted that section 10 of Law no. 2345/1920 (on the provisional Arch-Mufti and muftis serving Muslims residing in the territory) reproduced the contents of Article 11 § 8.1 of the Treaty of Athens, pursuant to which muftis exercised their jurisdiction over Muslims in the spheres of marriage, divorce, maintenance payments, guardianship, trusteeship, capacity of minors, Islamic wills and intestate succession. It emphasised that the law governing interpersonal relations among Greek nationals of Muslim faith, as laid down in the above-mentioned treaty ratified by Greece, was, pursuant to Article 28 § 1 of the Constitution, an integral part of Greek domestic law and prevailed over any other legal provision to the contrary. Examining the reasoning of the Court of Appeal's judgment, it concluded that that court's determination of the case had breached the relevant legislative provisions, because the law applicable to the deceased person's estate had been the Islamic law of succession, which formed part of domestic law and applied specifically to Greek nationals of Muslim faith. It noted that the estate in question belonged to the category of property held "in full ownership" (mulkia) – public land which had belonged to the Ottoman administration, the full ownership of which had been transferred to private individuals and which had been governed by Sharia law during the Ottoman occupation – and that, consequently, the impugned public will had to be deemed invalid and devoid of legal effect on the grounds that Sharia law recognised no such institution.

19 The Court of Cassation remitted the case to the Thrace Court of Appeal.

D *Proceedings in the Court of Appeal following remittal of the case*

20 By judgment no. 183/2015 of 15 December 2015 the Court of Appeal set aside the judgment delivered by the Rodopi Court of First Instance on 1 June 2010. In line with the Court of Cassation's judgment, it held that the relevant legislative provisions had been intended to protect Greek nationals of Muslim faith, constituted a special body of law and did not breach the principle of equality secured under Article 4 of the Constitution or the right of access to a court as guaranteed by Article 6 of the Convention. It pointed out that the law applicable to the deceased's estate had been Sharia law, because the property bequeathed belonged to the "mulkia" category, and that consequently the public will at issue was devoid of legal effect because Sharia law did not recognise any such institution. It emphasised that the judgments of the Court of Cassation were binding on the courts to which cases were remitted as regards the legal issues determined by those judgments. It therefore considered itself bound by the Court of Cassation's judgment of 7 October 2013 and could not overrule it, thus being unable to allow a request by the applicant to seek a preliminary ruling from the Court of Justice of the European Union concerning the interpretation of section 5(2) of Law no. 1920/1991 and of Article 45 of the Treaty of Lausanne. Since an appeal on points of law was lodged against that judgment, it was not immediately enforceable.

E Proceedings in the Court of Cassation concerning the Court of Appeal's judgment after remittal of the case

21 On 8 February 2016 the applicant appealed on points of law against the judgment of the Court of Appeal, and the hearing in the Court of Cassation was scheduled for 11 January 2017. She put forward a number of grounds of appeal.

22 In her first ground of appeal she submitted that the impugned judgment had been insufficiently reasoned as regards one specific point which she considered to have had a decisive influence on the outcome of the proceedings, namely that it had ignored the question whether her husband had been a "practising Muslim", which was a precondition for the application of the special body of law.

23 The applicant's second ground of appeal was that section 5(2) of Law no. 1920/1991 and certain Articles of the Civil Code had been incorrectly interpreted and applied. She submitted that the impugned judgment had extended the scope of the provisions creating a separate body of law for Greek nationals of Muslim faith to members of the Muslim community who did not faithfully adhere to Islamic doctrine.

24 The applicant argued in conclusion that those grounds of appeal had not been encompassed in the legal issue determined by judgment no. 1862/2013 of the Court of Cassation. She pointed out that that judgment had concerned Greek nationals of Muslim faith in general and had not addressed the matter of the law applicable to non-practising members of the Muslim community.

25 In her additional observations, the applicant contended that the case, which concerned the drawing up of a public will, a possibility afforded to all Greek citizens regardless of religious considerations, fell outside the mufti's jurisdiction. The specific provisions concerning the Muslim minority could not, in her submission, be applied without violating the individual rights of Muslims as guaranteed under the Greek Constitution, as well as by Article 6 § 1 of the Convention and Article 1 of Protocol No. 1.

26 By judgment no. 556/2017 of 6 April 2017 the Court of Cassation dismissed the appeal on points of law. It did not refer to the Convention in its reasoning.

27 As regards the applicant's first ground of appeal, it declared it inadmissible, finding that it was based on the extent of the deceased's religious sentiment as a Muslim, a criterion that had no legal effect. It added that the deceased's Greek nationality did not preclude the application of Sharia law.

28 As regards the second ground of appeal, the Court of Cassation held that the Court of Appeal's judgment had contained sound reasons, in line with the Court of Cassation's judgment no. 1862/2013. It emphasised that the Court of Appeal had assessed the facts of the case in the light of substantive law and had given sufficient reasons for its determination of the fundamental issue of recognising the invalidity of the will.

29 That judgment marked the end of the proceedings in respect of the property located in Greece.
30 As a result of the whole proceedings, the applicant was deprived of three-quarters of the property bequeathed.

F *Proceedings in the Istanbul Civil Court of First Instance*

31 In 2011, meanwhile, the testator's sisters had applied to the Istanbul Civil Court of First Instance for the annulment of the will, in accordance with the principles of private international law enshrined in the Turkish Civil Code. They submitted that the will was contrary to Turkish public policy. Hearings were held on 9 February and 26 May 2016, but the court adjourned its consideration of the case on the grounds that the applicant still had to appeal on points of law against judgment no. 183/2015 of the Thrace Court of Appeal. The new hearing in the case was scheduled for 28 September 2017, and then adjourned until 18 January 2018. By the date of the present judgment the Court had yet to be informed of the progress of those proceedings.

(…)

3 *The Court's assessment*

(A) PRELIMINARY REMARKS AND METHOD FOLLOWED

122. The present case concerns the applicant's right to inherit under a will made in her favour, in accordance with the Civil Code, by a Greek testator of Muslim faith. Whereas the applicant's husband had decided, in a will drawn up in accordance with civil law before a notary, to bequeath his whole estate to her, the Court of Cassation considered that the Islamic law of succession should be applied to her case. This had the consequence of depriving the applicant of her rights under the will made by her husband, which was rendered without any legal effect. The Court has decided (see paragraph 86 above) to consider the case solely under Article 14 of the Convention read in conjunction with Article 1 of Protocol No. 1. In assessing this complaint the Court will first of all address the question of the applicability of Article 14 of the Convention read in conjunction with Article 1 of Protocol No. 1. It will then seek to establish whether the applicant, as the beneficiary of a will made in accordance with the Civil Code by a testator of Muslim faith, in this case her husband, was in an analogous or relevantly similar situation to that of a beneficiary of a will made in accordance with the Civil Code by a non-Muslim testator, and whether she was treated differently. Finally, should both those questions be answered in the affirmative, the Court will have to determine whether there was any objective and reasonable justification for the difference in treatment.

(B) APPLICABILITY OF ARTICLE 14 OF THE CONVENTION READ IN
CONJUNCTION WITH ARTICLE 1 OF PROTOCOL NO. 1

(i) General principles 123. The Court has consistently held that Article 14 of the Convention complements the other substantive provisions of the Convention and the Protocols thereto. Article 14 has no independent existence since it has effect solely in relation to "the enjoyment of the rights and freedoms" safeguarded thereby. Although the application of Article 14 does not presuppose a breach of those provisions – and to this extent it is autonomous – there can be no room for its application unless the facts at issue fall within the ambit of one or more of them. The prohibition of discrimination enshrined in Article 14 thus extends beyond the enjoyment of the rights and freedoms which the Convention and the Protocols thereto require each State to guarantee. It applies also to those additional rights, falling within the general scope of any Convention Article, for which the State has voluntarily decided to provide (see, among many other authorities, E.B. v. France [GC], no. 43546/02, §§ 47-48, 22 January 2008; Carson and Others v. the United Kingdom [GC], no. 42184/05, § 63, ECHR 2010; İzzettin Doğan and Others v. Turkey [GC], no. 62649/10, § 158, 26 April 2016; Biao v. Denmark [GC], no. 38590/10, § 88, 24 May 2016, and Fábián v. Hungary [GC], no. 78117/13, § 112, 5 September 2017).

124. Furthermore, the concept of "possession" in the first sentence of Article 1 of Protocol No. 1 has an autonomous meaning which is not limited to ownership of material goods and is independent from the formal classification in domestic law: certain other rights and interests constituting assets can also be regarded as "property rights", and thus as "possessions" for the purposes of this provision (see Parrillo v. Italy [GC], no. 46470/11, § 211, CEDH 2015 and the references therein).

125. In each case the issue that needs to be examined is whether the circumstances of the case, considered as a whole, conferred on the applicant title to a substantive interest protected by Article 1 of Protocol No. 1 (ibid., § 211; see also Brosset-Triboulet v. France [GC] no. 34078/02, § 65, 29 March 2010 and Fabris v. France [GC], no. 16574/08, § 51, ECHR 2013).

126. The fact that the domestic laws of a State do not recognise a particular interest as a "right" or even a "property right" does not necessarily prevent the interest in question, in some circumstances, from being regarded as a "possession" within the meaning of Article 1 of Protocol No. 1 (see Brosset-Triboulet, cited above, § 71). A proprietary interest recognised by domestic law – even if it is revocable in certain circumstances – can constitute a "possession" for the purposes of Article 1 of Protocol No. 1 (see Beyeler v. Italy [GC], no. 33202/96, § 105, ECHR 2000-I).

127. Finally, the Court reiterates that in cases concerning a complaint under Article 14 in conjunction with Article 1 of Protocol No. 1 that the applicant has been denied all or part of a particular asset on a discriminatory ground covered by Article 14, the relevant test is whether, but for the alleged discrimination,

the applicant would have had a right, enforceable under domestic law, in respect of the asset in question (see Fabris, cited above, § 52; see also, mutatis mutandis, Stec and Others v. the United Kingdom (dec.) [GC], nos. 65731/01 and 65900/01, § 55, ECHR 2005-X).

(ii) Application of those principles in the present case 128. In the present case, it should be established whether the facts of the case, that is to say the applicant's inability to inherit under a will made in her favour, in accordance with the Civil Code, fall within the ambit of Article 1 of Protocol No. 1.

129. The Court has already dealt with cases where, following a death in a family, close relatives had automatically acquired inheritance rights over the estate, pursuant to the relevant law (see Mazurek v. France, no. 34406/97, § 42, ECHR 2000-II, and Merger and Cros v. France, no. 68864/01, § 32, 22 November 2004). The present case, however, concerns the acquisition of inheritance rights as a result of a will drawn up in accordance with the Civil Code.

130. In the instant case, it should be noted that by a decision of 10 June 2008 (see paragraph 10 above) the Komotini Court of First Instance approved the will and that on 6 April 2010 the applicant accepted her husband's estate by notarised deed. The Treasury was notified of that deed. The applicant then registered the property transferred to her with the Komotini Land Registry, paying the corresponding registration fees. The Rodopi Court of First Instance and the Thrace Court of Appeal adjudicated the challenge brought by the deceased's sisters by validating the will, which the testator had freely chosen to draw up in accordance with the relevant provisions of the Civil Code. The only reason why the applicant did not have the inheritance certificate provided for in Article 1956 of the Civil Code was that the deceased's sisters had challenged the validity of the will as soon as it had been approved by the Komotini Court of First Instance (see paragraph 11 above). Thus, the applicant would have inherited her husband's whole estate had the testator not been of the Muslim faith.

131. In those circumstances, the Court considers that the applicant's proprietary interest in inheriting from her husband was of a sufficient nature and sufficiently recognised to constitute a "possession" within the meaning of the rule laid down in the first sentence of the first paragraph of Article 1 of Protocol No. 1 (see mutatis mutandis, Fabris, cited above, § 54).

132. Consequently, the applicant's proprietary interest falls within the ambit of Article 1 of Protocol No. 1 and of the right to respect for property guaranteed therein, which is sufficient to render Article 14 of the Convention applicable.

(C) COMPLIANCE WITH ARTICLE 14 OF THE CONVENTION READ IN CONJUNCTION WITH ARTICLE 1 OF PROTOCOL NO. 1

(i) General principles 133. In order for an issue to arise under Article 14 there must be a difference in the treatment of persons in analogous or relevantly similar situations (see, among many other authorities, Konstantin Markin v. Russia [GC], no. 30078/06, § 125, ECHR 2012; X and Others v. Austria [GC], no.

19010/07, § 98, ECHR 2013; Khamtokhu and Aksenchik v. Russia [GC], nos. 60367/08 and 961/11, § 64, 24 January 2017, and Fábián, cited above, § 113). In other words, the requirement to demonstrate an analogous position does not require that the comparator groups be identical.

134. However, not every difference in treatment will amount to a violation of Article 14. Only differences in treatment based on an identifiable characteristic, or "status", are capable of amounting to discrimination within the meaning of Article 14 (see Fábián, cited above, § 113 and the references therein). In this context, the Court reiterates that the words "other status" have generally been given a wide meaning in its case-law (see Carson and Others, cited above, § 70) and their interpretation has not been limited to characteristics which are personal in the sense that they are innate or inherent (see Clift v. the United Kingdom, no. 7205/07, §§ 56–59, 13 July 2010). For example, a discrimination issue arose in cases where the applicants' status, which served as the alleged basis for discriminatory treatment, was determined in relation to their family situation, such as their children's place of residence (see Efe v. Austria, no. 9134/06, § 48, 8 January 2013). It thus follows, in the light of its objective and nature of the rights which it seeks to safeguard, that Article 14 of the Convention also covers instances in which an individual is treated less favorably on the basis of another person's status or protected characteristics (see Guberina v. Croatia, no. 23682/13, § 78, ECHR 2016 and Škorjanec v. Croatia, no. 25536/14, § 55, 28 March 2017 and also Weller v. Hungary, no. 44399/05, § 37, 31 March 2009).

135. The Court also reiterates that in the enjoyment of the rights and freedoms guaranteed by the Convention, Article 14 affords protection against different treatment, without an objective and reasonable justification, of persons in similar situations. For the purposes of Article 14, a difference of treatment is discriminatory if it "has no objective and reasonable justification", that is, if it does not pursue a "legitimate aim" or if there is not a "reasonable relationship of proportionality" between the means employed and the aim sought to be realised (see Fabris, cited above, § 56).

136. The Contracting States enjoy a certain margin of appreciation in assessing whether and to what extent differences in otherwise similar situations justify a different treatment. The scope of this margin will vary according to the circumstances, the subject matter and its background (see Stummer v. Austria [GC], no. 37452/02, § 88, ECHR 2011).

137. As to the burden of proof in relation to Article 14 of the Convention, the Court has held that once the applicant has demonstrated a difference in treatment, it is for the Government to show that the latter was justified (see Khamtokhu and Aksenchik, cited above, § 65; Vallianatos and Others v. Greece [GC], nos. 29381/09 and 32684/09, § 85, ECHR 2013 (extracts); and D.H. and Others v. the Czech Republic [GC], no. 57325/00, § 177).

(ii) Application of those principles to the present case

(A) WHETHER THERE WAS AN ANALOGOUS OR RELEVANTLY SIMILAR SITUATION AND A DIFFERENCE IN TREATMENT   138. The first task is to ascertain whether the applicant, a married woman who was a beneficiary of her Muslim husband's will, was in an analogous or relevantly similar situation to that of a married female beneficiary of a non-Muslim husband's will.

139. The Court notes that during his lifetime the applicant's husband, who was likewise a member of the Thrace Muslim community, had drawn up a notarised public will in accordance with the provisions of the Civil Code, bequeathing his entire estate to his wife. It is beyond doubt that she expected, as any other Greek citizen would have done, that on her husband's death his estate would be settled in accordance with the will thus drawn up.

140. However, by a judgment of 7 October 2013 the Court of Cassation overturned the Thrace Court of Appeal's judgment of 28 September 2011 upholding the judgment of the Rodopi Court of First Instance. The Court of Appeal had held that since the testator was free to choose the type of will he wished to draw up in the exercise of his rights, and therefore to draw up a public will in accordance with Article 1724 of the Civil Code, he was not obliged to follow Islamic law, which did not cover matters relating to such wills (see paragraph 15 above). The Court of Cassation, however, found that the Court of Appeal had infringed the law on the grounds that the law applicable to the deceased's estate had been the Islamic law of succession, which was part of domestic law and which, in Greece, applied specifically to Greek Muslims. More particularly, it held that the estate in question belonged to the mulkia category, as a result of which the public will in issue was voided of all legal effect. In so ruling, the Court of Cassation placed the applicant in a different position from that of a married female beneficiary of the will of a non-Muslim husband. In that connection, the Court also notes that several international bodies have highlighted this issue (see paragraphs 71–77 above).

141. In conclusion, the applicant, as the beneficiary of a will made in accordance with the Civil Code by a testator of Muslim faith, was in a relevantly similar situation to that of a beneficiary of a will made in accordance with the Civil Code by a non-Muslim testator, and was treated differently on the basis of "other status", namely the testator's religion.

(B) *WHETHER THE DIFFERENCE IN TREATMENT WAS JUSTIFIED* 142. The Court reiterates that its role is not to rule on which interpretation of the domestic legislation is the most correct, but to determine whether the manner in which that legislation has been applied has infringed the rights secured to the applicant under Article 14 of the Convention. In the instant case its task is thus to decide whether there was objective and reasonable justification for the difference in treatment in question, which had its basis in the application of domestic law (see, among many other authorities and mutatis mutandis, Fabris, cited above, § 63, and Pla and Puncernau v. Andorra, ECHR 2004-VIII, § 46).

– Pursuit of a legitimate aim

143. The Government submitted that the settled case-law of the Court of Cassation pursued an aim in the public interest, that is to say the protection of the Thrace Muslim minority. Although the Court understands that Greece is

bound by its international obligations concerning the protection of the Thrace Muslim minority, in the particular circumstances of the case, it doubts whether the impugned measure regarding the applicant's inheritance rights was suited to achieve that aim. Be that as it may, it is not necessary for the Court to adopt a firm view on this issue because in any event the impugned measure was in any event not proportionate to the aim pursued.

– Proportionality of the means used to the aim pursued

144. It remains to examine the question of the proportionality of the difference in treatment complained of to that aim.

145. The Court notes first of all that the application of Sharia law to the estate in issue had serious consequences for the applicant, depriving her of three-quarters of the inheritance.

146. The Court of Cassation and the Government justified that measure primarily on the basis of Greece's duty to honour its international obligations and the specific situation of the Thrace Muslim minority. The Court notes at the outset that the Court of Cassation applied Islamic inheritance law in the circumstances of the present case on the basis of a provision of international law, namely Article 11 of the 1913 Treaty of Athens, and provisions of domestic law, namely section 4 of Law no. 147/1914, section 10 of Law no. 2345/1920 (enacted pursuant to the 1913 Treaty of Athens) and section 5(2) of Law no. 1920/1991 (see paragraph 18 above).

147. In its case-law, the civil bench of the Court of Cassation held that the status established for Greek Muslims had not been revoked by the enactment of the Civil Code in 1946, and that section 4 of Law no. 147/1994 had been repealed only in so far as it concerned the Jewish community, and not the Muslim community. It added that although Law no. 1920/1991 had repealed section 10(1) of Law no. 2345/1920, it had incorporated the contents of that provision in its own section 5(2). It held that the aforementioned legislative provisions had been intended to protect Greek Muslims, constituted a special law applicable to interpersonal relations and were not contrary to Article 4 § 1 (principle of equality) and Article 20 § 1 (right to judicial protection) of the Constitution or to Article 6 § 1 of the Convention (see paragraph 45 above).

148. The main consequence of the approach adopted by the Court of Cassation in inheritance cases since 1960 and followed by certain lower courts, to the effect that inheritance matters involving members of the Muslim minority should be governed by Sharia law, is that notarised wills drawn up by Greek nationals of Muslim faith are devoid of legal effect because Sharia law only recognises intestate succession, except in the case of Islamic wills.

149. The Court reiterates that it is primarily for the national authorities, notably the courts, to resolve problems of interpretation of domestic legislation. Unless the interpretation is arbitrary or manifestly unreasonable, the Court's role is confined to ascertaining whether the effects of the interpretation are compatible with the Convention (see Radomilja, cited above, § 149). This also applies where domestic law refers to rules of general international law or international agreements (see Waite and Kennedy v. Germany [GC], no. 26083/94, § 54, ECHR 1999-I and Korbely v. Hungary [GC], no. 9174/02, § 72, ECHR 2008).

150. At the outset, the Court notes that in the instant case the Court of Cassation based the application of the Sharia law on the nature of the estate, that is to say property "held in full ownership". However, as the Court understands it, the concept of mulkia is a concept of Islamic law which is only relevant where the deceased's estate is being settled by a mufti under Sharia law (see paragraph 18 above). In the Court's view, the justification which Greece derives from Sharia law or from its international obligations is not persuasive, for the following reasons.

151. The Court notes that there can be no doubt that in signing and ratifying the Treaties of Sèvres and Lausanne Greece undertook to respect the customs of the Muslim minority. However, in view of the wording of the provisions in question (see paragraphs 64–65 above), those treaties do not require Greece to apply Sharia law. Indeed, the Government and the applicant agreed on that point. More specifically, the Treaty of Lausanne does not explicitly mention the jurisdiction of the mufti, but guarantees the religious distinctiveness of the Greek Muslim community, which was excluded from the population exchange provided for in that treaty and was expected to remain in Greece, where the large majority of the population was Christian. Nor did the treaty confer any kind of jurisdiction on a special body in relation to such religious practices. It cannot be overlooked, moreover, that during the hearing the Government stated that the provisions of the Treaty of Athens concerning the protection of the rights of minorities and those of the Treaty of Sèvres were no longer in force, as indeed they had already accepted in the case of Serif v. Greece (no. 38178/97, § 40, ECHR 1999-IX).

152. The Court also notes that section 5(2) of Law no. 1920/1991, which lists, inter alia, the mufti's area of competence in inheritance matters, refers solely to Islamic wills and intestate succession, and not to the jurisdiction of muftis over other types of inheritance. As is common in Greece, the notary whose services were called upon by the applicant's husband agreed to draw up the will as requested by the latter (see paragraph 9 above).

153. The Court further notes that – as was the situation in the present case – there are divergences in the case-law of the courts as regards, in particular, the question whether the application of Sharia law is compatible with the principle of equal treatment and with international human rights standards. Such divergences exist among courts of the same judicial branch, as well as between the Court of Cassation and the civil courts (see paragraphs 51–53 above) and between the Court of Cassation and the Supreme Administrative Court (see paragraph 44 above), but also within the Court of Cassation itself (see paragraph 47 above). The divergences create legal uncertainty, which is incompatible with the requirements of the rule of law (see, mutatis mutandis, Baranowski v. Poland, no. 28358/95, § 56, ECHR 2000-III, and Beian v. Romania (no. 1), no. 30658/05, § 39, ECHR 2007-V (extracts), thus undermining the Government's main argument as set out above (see paragraph 146 above).

154. Moreover, the Court can but note that several international bodies have expressed their concern about the application of Sharia law to Greek Muslims in Western Thrace and the discrimination thus created, in particular against women and children, not only within that minority as compared with men, but also in relation to non-Muslim Greeks. Thus, the Council of Europe Commissioner for Human Rights, in his report on the rights of minorities in Greece, noted that the application of Sharia law to matters concerning family law and inheritance was incompatible with the international undertakings entered into by Greece, particularly after its ratification of the post-1948 international and European human rights treaties, including those relating to the rights of the child and women's rights. He recommended that the Greek authorities interpret the Treaty of Lausanne and any other early twentieth-century treaty in compliance with the obligations flowing from the international and European human rights instruments (see paragraph 75 above). Other international bodies have made similar findings (see paragraphs 70–73 and 76–77 above).

155. The Court reiterates that according to its case-law, freedom of religion does not require the Contracting States to create a particular legal framework in order to grant religious communities a special status entailing specific privileges. Nevertheless, a State which has created such a status must ensure that the criteria established for a group's entitlement to it are applied in a non-discriminatory manner (see İzzettin Doğan and Others, cited above, § 164).

156. Moreover, it cannot be assumed that a testator of Muslim faith, having drawn up a will in accordance with the Civil Code, has automatically waived his right, or that of his beneficiaries, not to be discriminated against on the basis of his religion. A person's religious beliefs cannot validly be deemed to entail waiving certain rights if that would run counter to an important public interest (see Konstantin Markin, cited above, § 150). Nor can the State take on the role of guarantor of the minority identity of a specific population group to the detriment of the right of that group's members to choose not to belong to it or not to follow its practices and rules.

157. Refusing members of a religious minority the right to voluntarily opt for and benefit from ordinary law amounts not only to discriminatory treatment but also to a breach of a right of cardinal importance in the field of protection of minorities, that is to say the right to free self-identification. The negative aspect of this right, namely the right to choose not to be treated as a member of a minority, is not limited in the same way as the positive aspect of that right (see paragraphs 67–68 above). The choice in question is completely free, provided it is informed. It must be respected both by the other members of the minority and by the State itself. That is supported by Article 3 § 1 of the Council of Europe Framework Convention for the Protection of National Minorities which provides as follows: "no disadvantage shall result from this choice or from the exercise of the rights which are connected to that choice". The right to free self-identification is not a right specific to the Framework Convention. It is the "cornerstone" of international law on the protection of minorities in general. This applies especially to the negative aspect of the right: no bilateral or multilateral treaty

or other instrument requires anyone to submit against his or her wishes to a special regime in terms of protection of minorities.

158. Lastly, the Court notes that the present case highlights the fact that Greece is the only country in Europe which, up until the material time, applied Sharia law to a section of its citizens against their wishes. This is particularly problematic in the present case because the application of Sharia law caused a situation that was detrimental to the individual rights of a widow who had inherited her husband's estate in accordance with the rules of civil law but who then found herself in a legal situation which neither she nor her husband had intended.

159. In that regard, the Court notes that in the member States of the Council of Europe, Sharia law is in general applied as a foreign law within the framework of private international law. Outside that framework, only France has applied Sharia law, to the population of the territory of Mayotte, but that practice ended in 2011. As regards the United Kingdom, the application of Sharia law by the Sharia councils is accepted only in so far as recourse to it remains voluntary (see paragraph 83 above).

160. The Court notes with satisfaction that on 15 January 2018 the law abolishing the special regulations imposing recourse to Sharia law for the settlement of family-law cases within the Muslim minority came into force. Recourse to a mufti in matters of marriage, divorce or inheritance is now only possible with the agreement of all those concerned (see paragraph 57 above). Nonetheless, the provisions of the new law have no impact on the situation of the applicant, whose case was decided with final effect under the old system in place prior to the enactment of that law (see, mutatis mutandis, Söderman v. Sweden [GC], no. 5786/08, § 107, ECHR 2013).

161. In conclusion, having regard to the foregoing considerations, the Court finds that the difference of treatment suffered by the applicant, as a beneficiary of a will drawn up in accordance with the Civil Code by a testator of Muslim faith, as compared to a beneficiary of a will drawn up in accordance with the Civil Code by a non-Muslim testator, had no objective and reasonable justification.

162. In the light of the foregoing, the Court dismisses the Government's objection as to the applicant's lack of victim status, and finds that there has been a violation of Article 14 of the Convention read in conjunction with Article 1 of Protocol No. 1 to the Convention.

II Application of Article 41 of the Convention

163. Article 41 of the Convention provides:

> "If the Court finds that there has been a violation of the Convention or the Protocols there to, and if the internal law of the High Contracting Party concerned allows only partial reparation to be made, the Court shall, if necessary, afford just satisfaction to the injured party."

164. The applicant claimed 967,686.75 euros (EUR) in respect of pecuniary damage resulting from the violation of Article 1 of Protocol No. 1. In support of her claim she produced documents from the Greek tax authorities for the property located in Greece and expert reports drawn up in Turkey for the relevant property there. She also claimed EUR 30,000 in respect of non-pecuniary damage resulting from the violation of Articles 6 and 14 of the Convention. She claimed EUR 8,500 in respect of costs and expenses.

165. The Government contended that the applicant's claims in respect of pecuniary damage were vague, unsubstantiated and excessive. They submitted that the expert reports presented by the applicant had been drawn up by a firm of foreign experts and concerned property which was not located in Greek territory and had not formed the subject of the proceedings in the Greek courts. Those proceedings had concerned a total of six properties, all located in Komotini, but the applicant had not demonstrated that she had sustained any pecuniary damage: she had simply referred to the property tax (ΕΝΦΙΑ) which she had paid (totalling EUR 373.76). Moreover, the amount on the basis of which the tax authorities had calculated the tax payable had been EUR 42,000, corresponding to the applicant's share of the estate. As regards the sum claimed in respect of non-pecuniary damage, the Government argued that it was not in conformity with the relevant case-law of the Court. Lastly, they submitted that the applicant's claim in respect of costs and expenses was likewise vague, unsubstantiated and excessive.

166. In the circumstances of the case, the Court finds that the question of the application of Article 41 of the Convention is not ready for decision. That question must accordingly be reserved in whole and the subsequent procedure fixed, having due regard to any agreement which might be reached between the respondent State and the applicant (Rule 75 § 1 of the Rules of Court). The Court gives the parties three months for that purpose.

FOR THESE REASONS, THE COURT UNANIMOUSLY

1   Joins to the merits the Government's preliminary objection as to the applicant's lack of victim status, and dismisses it;
2   Declares the application admissible;
3   Holds that there has been a violation of Article 14 of the Convention read in conjunction with Article 1 of Protocol No. 1;
4   Holds that the question of the application of Article 41 of the Convention is not ready for decision; accordingly,

   (a) reserves the said question in whole;
   (b) invites the applicant and the respondent Government to submit, within three months from the date of notification of this judgment, their written observations on the matter and, in particular, to notify the Court of any agreement that they may reach;
   (c) reserves the further procedure and delegates to the President of the Court the power to fix the same if need be.

Section 2

Framework Convention for the Protection of National Minorities

> [*Adopted by the Committee of Ministers of the Council of Europe on 10 November 1994 and entered into force on 1 February 1998*]
> (...)

Article 5

1 The Parties undertake to promote the conditions necessary for persons belonging to national minorities to maintain and develop their culture, and to preserve the essential elements of their identity, namely their religion, language, traditions and cultural heritage.
2 Without prejudice to measures taken in pursuance of their general integration policy, the Parties shall refrain from policies or practices aimed at assimilation of persons belonging to national minorities against their will and shall protect these persons from any action aimed at such assimilation.

Article 6

1 The Parties shall encourage a spirit of tolerance and intercultural dialogue and take effective measures to promote mutual respect and understanding and co-operation among all persons living on their territory, irrespective of those persons' ethnic, cultural, linguistic or religious identity, in particular in the fields of education, culture and the media.
2 The Parties undertake to take appropriate measures to protect persons who may be subject to threats or acts of discrimination, hostility or violence as a result of their ethnic, cultural, linguistic or religious identity.

Article 7

The Parties shall ensure respect for the right of every person belonging to a national minority to freedom of peaceful assembly, freedom of association, freedom of expression, and freedom of thought, conscience and religion.

Article 8

The Parties undertake to recognise that every person belonging to a national minority has the right to manifest his or her religion or belief and to establish religious institutions, organisations and associations.
(...)

Article 12

1 The Parties shall, where appropriate, take measures in the fields of education and research to foster knowledge of the culture, history, language and religion of their national minorities and of the majority.
2 In this context the Parties shall inter alia provide adequate opportunities for teacher training and access to textbooks, and facilitate contacts among students and teachers of different communities.
3 The Parties undertake to promote equal opportunities for access to education at all levels for persons belonging to national minorities.
(…)

Article 17

1 The Parties undertake not to interfere with the right of persons belonging to national minorities to establish and maintain free and peaceful contacts across frontiers with persons lawfully staying in other States, in particular those with whom they share an ethnic, cultural, linguistic or religious identity, or a common cultural heritage.
2 The Parties undertake not to interfere with the right of persons belonging to national minorities to participate in the activities of non-governmental organisations, both at the national and international levels.

A Right to profess and practise religion or belief

A.1. ADVISORY COMMITTEE ON THE FRAMEWORK CONVENTION FOR THE PROTECTION OF NATIONAL MINORITIES, Compilation of Opinions of the Advisory Committee relating to Article 8 of the Framework Convention for the Protection of National Minorities (3rd cycle), *13 May 2016.*

Azerbaijan Opinion adopted on 27 May 2010, Article 8 of the Framework Convention Manifestation of religious belief, Recommendations from the two previous cycles of monitoring.

In the previous monitoring cycles, the Advisory Committee invited the authorities to ensure that legislative provisions related to the freedom of religious beliefs and the importation of religious literature did not undermine the right of persons belonging to national minorities to manifest their religion. In addition, the Advisory Committee urged the authorities to ensure that persons belonging to national minorities could freely manifest their religious beliefs individually or in community with others, including as regards non-traditional religious communities.

Present situation

The Advisory Committee notes that, following amendments to the Law on Freedom of Religion in 2009, a number of further restrictions have been imposed on religious communities. Apart from a requirement for all communities to re-register in order to continue functioning, higher fines have been introduced for disseminating religious literature without prior authorisation or carrying out religious activities such as worship in places other than where registered. The authorities explain that the re-registration exercise is only a formality and does not alter the legal status of the community concerned. However, the Advisory Committee was officially informed during its visit that the authorities had the right to abolish all organisations that had not re-reregistered, although it had never used that right.

The Advisory Committee is concerned by this lack of legal certainty for communities that have not been able to reregister, even following application to the courts. In addition, the Advisory Committee learned of lengthy and unpredictable proceedings and the closure of mosques or churches by local authorities in cases where the re-registration had not been completed. According to the authorities, 576 communities had been re-registered in July of 2012, out of some 900 applications.

The Advisory Committee notes that Muslim communities have to go through a double registration process, as, in addition to the procedure described above, their applications have to go first through the Caucasian Spiritual Board of Muslims. The process is reportedly particularly difficult for communities belonging to the Sunni faith, including those of persons belonging to national minorities such as the Lezgin and Avar, as approval of their applications appears to be selectively delayed or denied by the Board. While the Lezgin Mosque in Baku was de-registered and asked to re-register under a different name (see comments under Article 5 above), most of the mosques that were closed or since 2009 have reportedly been Sunni mosques, including the so-called Albanian mosque in Ganja. The Advisory Committee also heard reports of persons being arrested for praying 'at unauthorised places', including in private homes, and of being forced to sign statements that they would not meet for joint prayers. Even cases of forced shaving of beards of certain Muslims by the police have been reported. In addition, the Advisory Committee is concerned by reports regarding difficulties experienced by members of the Georgian Orthodox Church seeking to import small amounts of religious literature for worship and educational purposes. In December 2010, women were banned from wearing headscarves in schools and universities which reportedly led to a considerable number of drop-outs. This development is reported to have affected in particular some of the more pious national minority communities.

While the Advisory Committee acknowledges widespread anxiety among the population towards non-traditional religious groups and possible extremist tendencies and appreciates the efforts of the authorities to monitor religious activities, it cautions that all registration procedures have to be implemented fairly and transparently and with due regard to the fundamental right to manifest one's religious belief, including in community with others. In this regard, it notes with regret reports that the study of Islam has been considerably reduced, which, according to some observers, has led to lack of understanding and tolerance towards the beliefs of some, including non-traditional, communities in society, and contributes to the creation of inter-religious tension as well as miscommunications between different branches of one faith.

Recommendation

The Advisory Committee calls on the authorities to take resolute steps to ensure that persons belonging to all national minorities can freely express and manifest their religious beliefs, individually or in community with others, and that the ongoing re-registration exercise is implemented fairly and transparently. All rejections must be open to swift and effective legal redress.

B Right to association

B.1. ADVISORY COMMITTEE ON THE FRAMEWORK CONVENTION FOR THE PROTECTION OF NATIONAL MINORITIES, **Compilation of Opinions of the Advisory Committee relating to Article 8 of the Framework Convention for the Protection of National Minorities (3rd cycle),** *13 May 2016.*

Russian Federation Opinion adopted on 24 November 2011, Article 8 of the Framework Convention, Religious associations, Recommendations from the two previous cycles of monitoring.

In the previous monitoring cycles, the Advisory Committee invited the authorities to ensure that procedures used at regional and local levels to register religious associations complied with federal norms governing freedom of religion and association.

It also regretted difficulties reported by some groups, particularly Muslims, as regards obtaining permission to build places of worship and repossessing such places.

Present situation

The Advisory Committee regrets that persons who belong to religions and beliefs other than the Russian Orthodox Church reportedly face a number of difficulties with regard to their right to manifest their religion or belief and to establish religious organisations. In particular, it is worried by allegations brought to its attention during the visit that persons belonging to national minorities and affiliated with "non-traditional" religious groups, such as Baptists and Pentecostalists, have in some instances faced obstacles in the registration of their associations. This is particularly the case for persons belonging to indigenous peoples of the North and Far East who belong to these religious communities. Additionally, the Advisory Committee notes that an Expert Board was set up in February 2009 within the Ministry of Justice with a view to examining applications for registration of new religious groups, in particular to see whether they qualify as religious organisations and to check whether they could be accused of "extremism".

The Advisory Committee finds it essential that this body carries out its tasks in a non-discriminatory manner, so that it does not discourage religious organisations from freely exercising their rights.

The Advisory Committee also notes that there is a lack of places of worship for persons belonging to some national minorities and to some religious groups in particular, such as Protestants and Muslims. It was informed during its visit in Tyumen and Moscow that tense discussions had taken place around the issue of building mosques in these cities and that, as a result of the opposition of some segments of the population, the planned mosques have not yet been built. Similar difficulties have been encountered in other cities, while agreements on the building of mosques were reached in a few places, such as Barda (Perm Krai), Syktyvkar and Vladivostok.

Moreover, minority representatives have informed the Advisory Committee that religious communities other than the Russian Orthodox Church sometimes face difficulties in the process of restitution of religious property currently under way. They report in particular delays in the restitution process of protected federal or municipal buildings. These difficulties can aggravate the shortage of places of worship. Moreover, the Advisory Committee is concerned that in some areas, such as the city of Kaliningrad, a large number of properties were transferred to the Russian Orthodox Church, even though they had never belonged to it before. These properties included places of worship of other religious organisations, such as Lutheran and Catholic churches.

The Advisory Committee is concerned by reports indicating a multiplication of racist insults and attacks against persons wearing Muslim clothes, in particular women wearing a hijab and men wearing a beard (see also remarks under Article 6 on Islamophobia above). These hostile manifestations infringe the freedom to manifest one's religion or belief, as protected by Article 8 of the Framework Convention.

Recommendations

The Advisory Committee urges the authorities to ensure that "non-traditional" religious organisations can register without undue obstacles as religious organisations and that federal norms governing freedom of religion and belief and association are fully respected. The Advisory Committee invites the authorities to take further steps to ensure that persons belonging to minorities and practising Islam have adequate access to places of worship, especially in places where they live in substantial numbers. Decisions on the building or allocation of new places of worship should be taken in close and timely consultation with the representatives of the groups concerned. The Advisory Committee calls on the authorities to ensure that the process of restitution of properties to religious communities is carried out in a non-discriminatory manner and to ensure that persons belonging to national minorities, and practising religions others than the Russian orthodoxy, are not at a disadvantage.

C Right to education

C.1. ADVISORY COMMITTEE ON THE FRAMEWORK CONVENTION FOR THE PROTECTION OF NATIONAL MINORITIES, Compilation of Opinions of the Advisory Committee relating to Article 8 of the Framework Convention for the Protection of National Minorities (4th cycle), *18 September 2017.*

Cyprus Adopted on 18 March 2015, Article 8 of the Framework Convention, Religious education and the right to manifest one's belief

Present situation

According to its Constitution, Cyprus has no official religion. At the same time, the predominance of Greek-Orthodox Christianity manifests itself in the observation of Orthodox holidays, the presence of Orthodox icons in schools, as well as the practice of organising confessions to Orthodox priests in the course of religious education classes in some schools. The Advisory Committee welcomes the fact that the syllabus for religious education at all schools has been adjusted as of the school year 2011/2012, focussing less on the Greek Orthodox faith and including more elements aimed at familiarising students with other religious beliefs and broader ethical questions. While members of minority communities have welcomed this development and more students appear willing to attend public schools as a result, Greek Orthodoxy is still established as the predominant religion in practice, as most teachers of religious classes adhere themselves to that faith, and there is resistance in some schools to pursuing a genuine approach of embracing diversity that treats all cultures equally. Religious education still forms a mandatory part of the public-school curriculum, including at the schools attended mainly by students of minority background, while additional classes with religious education specific to the minorities continue to be taught on an optional basis.

A circular from the Ministry of Education issued in October 2014 clarified that Maronite, Armenian and Latin pupils could be exempted from religious education in elementary schools, provided that a justification is given, indicating the students' differing religion. As the circular further indicated that in secondary schools, 'Non-Christians' may be exempted from religious education, students of Armenian, Maronite or Latin background at secondary schools have faced difficulties, as teachers have pointed out that the circular did not apply to them. The Ministry of Education is reportedly in the process of issuing a second, clarifying circular to ensure that students belonging to the Armenian, Maronite and Latin minorities may be excused from religious education at elementary and secondary school levels. According to its interlocutors, the Advisory Committee understands however that most parents prefer their children to take part in the religious classes as they do not wish them to be left without supervision during school hours or to feel like outsiders in the class. It considers in this context that all children who do actively attend religious education should be treated equally and evaluated based on merit, irrespective of their personal religious belief.

The Advisory Committee welcomes the government efforts to promote the right of persons belonging to the Armenian, Maronite and Latin groups to manifest their beliefs including by visiting places of worship in areas outside the government control. It notes with particular interest the efforts of the Grand Mufti of Cyprus and the Archbishop of the Greek Orthodox Church of Cyprus, as well as the Maronite Archbishop, the Armenian Archbishop and the Latin Catholic Priest, under the auspices of the Swedish Embassy, to promote the right of all persons to have full access to their places of worship, without restrictions, including by jointly declaring all cases of vandalism or looting as unacceptable. The Advisory Committee expects that these important developments (see also comments on Article 6) will benefit all persons belonging to minorities in their right to manifest their religion, including the Roma, who, the Advisory Committee understands, mainly practice the Alevi faith.

With regard to the oath that military recruits need to take when joining the army, the Advisory Committee welcomes the information that members of the three communities, who, given their Christian creed take the oath, while Non-Christians are asked to sign a declaration, have been allowed since August 2014 to manifest their specific Christian belief during the oath ceremony.

Recommendation

The Advisory Committee encourages the authorities to pursue their approach of broadening the curriculum followed in religious education classes towards other religious and broader ethical questions and ensure that the new syllabus is appropriately applied in schools. It further encourages their efforts to promote the rights of all persons to manifest their distinct beliefs including by facilitating access to the various places of worship as far as possible.

3 Organization for Security and Co-operation in Europe (OSCE)

Section 1

Conference for Security and Co-operation in Europe, Helsinki Decisions, 10 July 1992

(...)
High Commissioner on National Minorities
23. The Council will appoint a High Commissioner on National Minorities. The High Commissioner provides "early warning" and, as appropriate, "early action" at the earliest possible stage in regard to tensions involving national minority issues that have the potential to develop into a conflict within the CSCE area, affecting peace, stability, or relations between participating States. The High Commissioner will draw upon the facilities of the Office for Democratic Institutions and Human Rights (ODIHR) in Warsaw.

Conference on Security and Co-operation in Europe, Budapest Summit Declaration, 21 December 1994

(...)
VIII. The Human Dimension
(...)
2. Human rights and fundamental freedoms, the rule of law and democratic institutions are the foundations of peace and security, representing a crucial contribution to conflict prevention, within a comprehensive concept of security. The protection of human rights, including the rights of persons belonging to national minorities, is an essential foundation of democratic civil society. Neglect of these rights has, in severe cases, contributed to extremism, regional instability and conflict. The participating States confirmed that issues of implementation of CSCE commitments are of legitimate and common concern to all participating States, and that the raising of these problems in the co-operative and result-oriented spirit of the CSCE was therefore a positive exercise. They undertook to encourage implementation of CSCE commitments through enhanced dialogue, implementation reviews and mechanisms. They will broaden the operational framework of the CSCE, in particular by enhancing the Office for Democratic Institutions and

Human Rights (ODIHR), increasing its involvement in the work of the Permanent Council and mission activity, and furthering co-operation with international organizations and institutions active in human dimension areas.

(...)

Commitments and cooperation
National minorities

21. The participating States confirm their determination consistently to advance the implementation of the provisions of the Final Act and all other CSCE documents relating to the protection of the rights of persons belonging to national minorities. They commend the work of the HCNM in this field.

22. The participating States welcome the international efforts to improve protection of the rights of persons belonging to national minorities. They take note of the adoption, within the Council of Europe, of a Framework Convention on the Protection of National Minorities, which builds upon CSCE standards in this context. They stressed that the Convention is also open – by invitation – to signature by States which are not members of the Council of Europe and they may consider examining the possibility of becoming parties to this Convention.

A Definition of national minorities

A.1. OFFICE OF THE OSCE HIGH COMMISSIONER ON NATIONAL MINORITIES, **The Ljubljana Guidelines on Integration of Diverse Societies,** *7 November 2012.*

Introduction

(...)

The term "national minority", as used in the Guidelines, refers to a wide range of minority groups, including ethnic, religious, linguistic and cultural communities, regardless of whether these groups are recognized as such by the States where they reside and irrespective of the designation applied to or claimed by them. In addition, "minority" is often used as a shorthand term for "persons belonging to national minorities". This does not imply that all principles, minority rights and policy options presented in the document apply to every situation in the same way. It is clear that, while basic human rights standards apply to all, good integration policies will need to be tailored to some extent to meet the challenges and needs of different minority groups and different circumstances. The content of integration policies may depend on such factors as the numbers involved, the length of settlement and geographic concentration, and the particular social, economic and cultural needs, among other considerations. In addition, the fact that many individuals have multiple identities that may be asserted in different ways, times and contexts must also be recognized when developing integration policies.

B Right to profess and practise religion or belief

B.1. OSCE Office for Democratic Institutions and Human Rights (ODIHR), Guidelines on the Legal Personality of Religious or Belief Communities, 2014.

Part 1. The freedom of religion or belief and permissible restrictions in general

1. The freedom of religion or belief is a fundamental right, as recognized in international instruments[1] and OSCE commitments.[2] International standards specify that everyone has the right to freedom of thought, conscience and religion.[3] This right includes the freedom to manifest one's religion or belief, either alone or in community with others, in public or in private, through worship, teaching, practice and observance.[4]

2. The terms "religion" and "belief" are to be broadly construed.[5] A starting point for defining the application of freedom of religion or belief must be the self-definition of religion or belief, though of course the authorities have a certain competence to apply some objective, formal criteria to determine if indeed these terms are applicable to the specific case. There is a great diversity of religions and beliefs.[6] The freedom of religion or belief is therefore not limited in its application to traditional religions and beliefs or to religions and beliefs with institutional characteristics or practices analogous to those traditional views.[7] The freedom of religion or belief protects theistic,

---

1. The International Covenant on Civil and Political Rights (ICCPR), art. 18; the European Convention on Human Rights (ECHR), art. 9; the American Convention on Human Rights (ACHR), art. 12; and the EU Charter of Fundamental Rights, art. 10.
2. Concluding Document of the Vienna Meeting (Third Follow-up Meeting to the Helsinki Conference), Vienna, (hereafter: Vienna 1989), para. 11, 16, 17 and 32; 1990 Document of the Copenhagen Meeting of the Conference on the Human Dimension of the CSCE (hereafter: Copenhagen 1990), para. 9.4; CSCE Budapest Document 1994: Towards a Genuine Partnership in a New Era (hereafter: Budapest 1994), para. 27; Document of the Eleventh Meeting of the Ministerial Council, Maastricht, 2003 (hereafter: Maastricht 2003), para. 9.
3. ICCPR, art. 18 (1); ECHR, art. 9 (1); ACHR, art. 12 (1); Copenhagen 1990, para. 9.4; EU Charter of Fundamental Rights, art. 10.
4. ICCPR, art. 18 (1); ECHR, art. 9 (1); ACHR, art. 12 (1); Copenhagen 1990, para. 9.4.
5. UN Human Rights Council, Report of the Special Rapporteur on freedom of religion or belief, 22 December 2011, A/HRC/19/60 (hereafter: UN SR Report on Recognition), para. 38; Joint Opinion on the Law on Freedom of Religious Belief of the Republic of Azerbaijan by the Venice Commission and the OSCE/ODIHR, CDL-AD(2012)022, adopted by the Venice Commission at its 92nd Plenary Session (Venice, 12–13 October 2012), para. 34.
6. UN SR Report on Recognition, para. 31.
7. United Nations Human Rights Committee, General Comment 22 (UN Doc. HRI/GEN/1/Rev.1 at 35 (1994)), para. 2; Joint opinion on the draft law on freedoms of conscience and religion and on the laws making amendments and supplements to the criminal code, the administrative offences code and the law on the relations between the Republic

non-theistic and atheistic beliefs, as well as the right not to profess any religion or belief.[8]

3   The freedom of religion or belief is closely linked to other human rights and fundamental freedoms, such as, in particular, the freedom of expression,[9] the freedom of assembly and association[10] and the right to non-discrimination.[11]

4   The freedom to have or to adopt a religion or belief of one's choice, which includes the right to change one's religion or belief,[12] may not be subject to any limitations.[13]

---

of Armenia and the Holy Armenian Apostolic Church of the Republic of Armenia by the Venice Commission and the OSCE/ODIHR, CDL-AD(2011)028, adopted by the Venice Commission at its 88th Plenary Session (Venice, 14–15 October 2011), paras. 22–24; Interim joint opinion on the law on making amendments and supplements to the law on freedom of conscience and religious organisations and on the laws on amending the criminal code; the administrative offences code and the law on charity of the Republic of Armenia by the Venice Commission and OSCE/ODIHR, CDL-AD(2010)054, adopted by the Venice Commission at its 85th Plenary Session (Venice, 18–18 December 2012), para.43; ECtHR 15 June 2010, *Grzelak v. Poland*, Application no. 7710/02, para. 85; ECtHR 25 May 1993, *Kokkinakis v. Greece*, Application no. 14307/88, para. 31; and ECtHR 18 February 1999, *Buscarini and Others v. San Marino*, Application no. 24645/94, para. 34.

8 United Nations Human Rights Committee, General Comment 22 (UN Doc. HRI/GEN/1/Rev.1 at 35 (1994)), para. 2; Interim joint opinion on the law on making amendments and supplements to the law on freedom of conscience and religious organisations and on the laws on amending the criminal code; the administrative offences code and the law on charity of the Republic of Armenia by the Venice Commission and OSCE/ODIHR, CDL-AD(2010)054, para. 46–47.

9 See, for example, Report of the Special Rapporteur on freedom of religion or belief, Asma Jahangir, and the Special Rapporteur on contemporary forms of racism, racial discrimination, xenophobia and related intolerance, Doudou Diène, further to Human Rights Council decision 1/107 on incitement to racial and religious hatred and the promotion of tolerance, 20 September 2006, UN Doc. A/HRC/2/3, paras. 40–43.

10 ECtHR 26 October 2000, *Hasan and Chaush v Bulgaria*, Application no. 30985/96, para. 62.

11 Opinion on Act CCVI of 2011 on the right to freedom of conscience and religion and the legal status of churches, denominations and religious communities of Hungary, CDL-AD(2012)004, adopted by the Venice Commission at its 90th Plenary Session (Venice, 16–17 March 2012), para. 19.

12 ECHR, art. 9 (1); Copenhagen 1990, para. 9.4; United Nations Human Rights Committee, General Comment 22, para. 5; Joint Opinion on the Law on Freedom of Religious Belief of the Republic of Azerbaijan by the Venice Commission and the OSCE/ODIHR, CDL-AD(2012)022, adopted by the Venice Commission at its 92nd Plenary Session (Venice, 12–13 October 2012), para. 31.

13 ICCPR, art. 18 (2); ACHR, art. 12 (2); UN Human Rights Committee, General Comment 22, para. 8; Joint Opinion on the Law on Freedom of Religious Belief of the Republic of Azerbaijan by the Venice Commission and the OSCE/ODIHR, CDL-AD(2012)022, adopted by the Venice Commission at its 92nd Plenary Session (Venice, 12–13 October 2012), paras. 28 and 30.

5   The freedom to manifest a religion or belief may only be limited if each of the following criteria is fulfilled:

   A   The limitation is prescribed by law;[14]
   B   The limitation has the purpose of protecting public safety, (public) order, health or morals,[15] or the fundamental rights and freedoms of others;[16]
   C   The limitation is necessary for the achievement of one of these purposes and proportionate to the intended aim;[17] and
   D   The limitation is not imposed for discriminatory purposes or applied in a discriminatory manner.[18]

(...)

II The freedom to manifest religion or belief in community with others

International human rights law protects a wide variety of community manifestations of religions and beliefs. The freedom to manifest a religion or belief consists of the freedom of worship and the freedom to teach, practise and observe one's religion or belief. There may be considerable overlap between these types of manifestations.

13. The freedom to worship includes, but is not limited to, the freedom to assemble in connection with a religion or belief[19] and the freedom of communities to perform ritual and ceremonial acts giving direct expression to their religion or belief,[20] as well as various practices integral to these freedoms, including the

---

14 ICCPR, art. 18 (3); ECHR, art. 9 (2); ACHR, art. 12 (3); Copenhagen 1990, para. 9.4; ECtHR 30 June 2011, *Association les Temoins de Jehovah v. France*, Application No.8916/05, para. 66–72.
15 The United Nations Human Rights Committee has observed that "the concept of morals derives from many social, philosophical and religious traditions; consequently, limitations on the freedom to manifest a religion or belief for the purpose of protecting morals must be based on principles not deriving exclusively from a single tradition" (UN Human Rights Committee, General Comment 22, para. 8).
16 ICCPR, art. 18 (3); cf. ECHR, art. 9, which limits the number of grounds for limitations to "the interests of public safety, for the protection of public order, health or morals, or for the protection of the rights and freedoms of others"; cf. ACHR, which limits the number of grounds for limitations to "public safety, order, health, or morals, or the rights or freedoms of others".
17 ICCPR, art. 18 (3); art. 12 ACHR; cf. ECHR, art. 9 (2) ("necessary in a democratic society in the interest of...").
18 United Nations Human Rights Committee, General Comment 22, para. 8.
19 UN General Assembly, Declaration on the Elimination of All Forms of Intolerance and of Discrimination Based on Religion or Belief, 25 November 1981, A/RES/36/55, para. 6 (a).
20 UN Human Rights Committee General Comment 22, para. 4.

building and maintenance of freely accessible places of worship,[21] the use of ritual formulae and objects and the display of symbols.

14. The freedom to observe and practise includes, but is not limited to, ceremonial acts, but also such customs as the observance of dietary regulations,[22] the wearing of distinctive clothing or head coverings,[23] participation in rituals associated with certain stages of life[24] and the use of a particular language customarily spoken by a group in practising their religion,[25] as well as the freedom to establish and maintain appropriate charitable or humanitarian institutions and the observance of holidays and days of rest.[26]

15. The freedom to practise and teach religion or belief includes, but is not limited to, acts integral to the conduct by religious groups of their basic affairs, such as the right to organize themselves according to their own hierarchical and institutional structures[27] and the right to select, appoint and replace their personnel in accordance with their respective requirements and standards, as well as with any freely accepted arrangement between them and their state;[28] the freedom to establish seminaries or religious schools;[29] the freedom to train religious personnel in appropriate institutions;[30] the right to make, acquire and use to an adequate extent the necessary articles and materials related to the rites or customs of a religion or belief;[31] the right of religious communities, institutions and organizations to produce, import and disseminate religious publications and materials;[32] the right of each individual to give and receive religious education in the language of their choice, whether individually or in association with others, in places suitable for these purposes,[33] including the liberty of parents to ensure the religious and moral education of their children in conformity with their own convictions;[34] the right to solicit and receive voluntary financial and

---

21 Vienna 1989, para. 16.4; UN Declaration on the Elimination of All Forms of Intolerance and of Discrimination Based on Religion or Belief, para. 6 (a).
22 UN Declaration on the Elimination of All Forms of Intolerance and of Discrimination Based on Religion or Belief, para. 6 (h).
23 UN Human Rights Committee General Comment 22, para. 4.
24 Ibid.
25 Ibid.
26 Ibid.
27 Vienna 1989, para. 16.4.
28 Vienna 1989, para. 16.4; UN Declaration on the Elimination of All Forms of Intolerance and of Discrimination Based on Religion or Belief, para. 6 (g); UN Human Rights Committee General Comment 22, para. 4.
29 UN Human Rights Committee General Comment 22, para. 4.
30 Vienna 1989, para. 16.8.
31 UN Declaration on the Elimination of All Forms of Intolerance and of Discrimination Based on Religion or Belief, para. 6 (d).
32 Vienna 1989, para. 16.10; UN Declaration on the Elimination of All Forms of Intolerance and of Discrimination Based on Religion or Belief, para. 6 (c) and (d).
33 Vienna 1989, para. 16.6.
34 Vienna 1989, para. 16.7.

other contributions from individuals and institutions;[35] and the freedom to establish and maintain communications with individuals and communities in matters of religion and belief at the national and international levels,[36] including through travel, pilgrimages and participation in assemblies and other religious events.[37]

C Right to legal personality

C.1. OSCE OFFICE FOR DEMOCRATIC INSTITUTIONS AND HUMAN RIGHTS (ODIHR), Guidelines on the Legal Personality of Religious or Belief Communities, 2014.

(...)

19. Under international human rights law, a refusal by the state to accord legal personality status to an association of individuals based on a religion or belief amounts to an interference with the exercise of the right to freedom of religion or belief, read in the light of the freedom of association.[38] The authorities' refusal to register a group, or to withdraw its legal personality, have been found to affect directly both the group itself and also its presidents, founders or individual members.[39] A refusal to recognize the legal personality status of religious or belief

---

35 Vienna 1989, para. 16.4; UN Declaration on the Elimination of All Forms of Intolerance and of Discrimination Based on Religion or Belief, para. 6 (f); Opinion on the Draft Law on the insertion of amendments on Freedom of Conscience and Religious Organisations in Ukraine, CDL-AD(2006)030, adopted by the Venice Commission at its 68th Plenary Session (Venice, 13–14 October 2006), para. 34.
36 UN Declaration on the Elimination of All Forms of Intolerance and of Discrimination Based on Religion or Belief, para. 6 (i).
37 Vienna 1989, para. 32.
38 ECtHR 1 October 2009, *Kimlya and Others v. Russia*, Application nos. 76836/01 and 32782/03, para. 84; ECtHR 10 June 2010, *Jehova's Witnesses of Moscow and others v. Russia*, Application no. 302/02, para. 101; ECtHR 17 February 2004, *Gorzelik and Others v. Poland*, Application no. 44158/98, para. 52 and ECtHR 1 July 1998, *Sidiropoulos and Others v. Greece*, Application no. 26695/95, para. 31; Opinion on Legal Status of Religious Communities in Turkey and the Right of the orthodox Patriarchate of Istanbul to use the adjective "Ecumenical", CDL-AD(2010)005, adopted by the Venice Commission at its 82nd Plenary Session (Venice, 12–13 March 2010), para. 6 & 9; Joint opinion on the draft law on freedoms of conscience and religion and on the laws making amendments and supplements to the criminal code, the administrative offences code and the law on the relations between the Republic of Armenia and the Holy Armenian Apostolic Church of the Republic of Armenia by the Venice Commission and the OSCE/ODIHR, CDL-AD(2011)028, para. 64; OSCE/ODIHR and Venice Commission, Guidelines for Review of Legislation Pertaining to Religion or Belief, 2004 (hereafter: 2004 Guidelines), para. 8.
39 ECtHR 10 June 2010, *Case of Jehova's Witnesses of Moscow and others v. Russia*, Application no. 302/02, para. 101; ECtHR 15 January 2009, *Association of Citizens Radko and Paunkovski v. the former Yugoslav Republic of Macedonia*, Application no. 74651/01, para. 53; ECtHR 19 January 2006, *The United Macedonian Organisation Ilinden and Others v. Bulgaria*, Application no. 59491/00, para. 53; ECtHR 3 February 2005, *Partidul Comunistilor (Nepeceristi) and Ungureanu v. Romania*, Application no. 46626/99, para.27 and ECtHR 31 August 1999, *APEH Üldözötteinek Szövetsége and Others v. Hungary* (Dec.), Application no. 32367/96.

communities has, therefore, been found to constitute an interference with the right to freedom of religion or belief[40] as exercised by both the community itself as well as its individual members.[41]

20. The right to legal personality status is vital to the full realization of the right to freedom of religion or belief. A number of key aspects of organized community life in this area become impossible or extremely difficult without access to legal personality. These include having bank accounts and ensuring judicial protection of the community, its members and its assets;[42] maintaining the continuity of ownership of religious edifices; the construction of new religious edifices; establishing and operating schools and institutes of higher learning; facilitating larger-scale production of items used in religious customs and rites; the employment of staff; and the establishment and running of media operations.[43]

D Right to education

D.1. OSCE HIGH COMMISSIONER ON NATIONAL MINORITIES (HCNM), The Hague Recommendations regarding the Education Rights of National Minorities & Explanatory Note, *October 1996*.

(...)

Explanatory note to the Hague recommendations regarding the education rights of national minorities

General introduction

The Universal Declaration of Human Rights of 1948 broke new ground in that it was the first international instrument to declare education to be a human right.

---

40 UN Human Rights Committee 21 October 2005, *Sister Immaculate Joseph and 80 Teaching Sisters of the Holy Cross of the Third Order of Saint Francis in Menzingen of Sri Lanka v. Sri Lanka*, communication 1249/2004, para. 7.2.
41 ECtHR 10 June 2010, *Jehova's Witnesses of Moscow and others v. Russia*, Application no. 302/02, para. 101; ECtHR 31 July 2008, *Religionsgemeinschaft der Zeugen Jehovas and Others v. Austria*, Application no. 40825/98 paras.79–80, and ECtHR 13 December 2001, *Metropolitan Church of Bessarabia v. Moldova*, Application no. 45701/99, para. 105.
42 ECtHR 10 June 2010, *Jehova's Witnesses of Moscow and others v. Russia*, Application no. 302/02, para. 102; ECtHR, *Kimlya and others v. Russia*, Application nos. 76836/01 and 32782/03, para. 85; ECtHR 31 July 2008, *Religionsgemeinschaft der Zeugen Jehovas and Others v. Austria*, Application no. 40825/98 para. 66; ECtHR 13 December 2001, *Metropolitan Church of Bessarabia v. Moldova*, Application no. 45701/99, para. 118; ECtHR 3 April 2008, *Koretsky and Others v. Ukraine*, Application no. 40269/02, para. 40 and ECtHR 16 December 1997, *Canea Catholic Church v. Greece*, paras. 30 and 40–41; Opinion on the Draft Law regarding the Religious Freedom and the General Regime of Religions in Romania adopted by the Venice Commission at its 64th plenary session (Venice, 21–22 October 2005), CDLAD(2005)037-e, para. 23; Opinion on the legal status of Religious Communities in Turkey and the right of the Orthodox Patriarchate of Istanbul to use the adjective "Ecumenical", CDL-AD(2010)005, para. 68.
43 UN SR Report on Recognition, para. 46.

Article 26 of the Declaration refers to elementary education as compulsory. It engages States to make technical and professional education generally available and higher education accessible on the basis of merit. It also makes clear that the objective of education should be the full development of the human personality and the strengthening of respect for human rights and fundamental freedoms. Article 26 goes on to say that education shall promote understanding, tolerance and friendship among nations, racial or religious groups and contribute to the maintenance of peace. It also makes clear that parents have a prior right to choose the kind of education that shall be given to their children. The provisions of article 26 are reiterated with greater strength in the context of treaty law and in greater detail in article 13 of the International Covenant on Economic, Social and Cultural Rights.

Article 26 sets the tone of openness and inclusiveness for the subsequent international instruments which have emerged over time and have confirmed and further elaborated the right to education both generally and with reference to minorities specifically.

- Article 27 of the International Covenant on Civil and Political Rights.
- Article 30 of the Convention on the Rights of the Child.

The above mentioned articles guarantee the right of minorities to use their language in community with other members of their group. The articles below, for their part, provide guarantees relating to the possibility for national minorities of learning their mother tongue or learning in their mother tongue.

- Article 5 of the UNESCO Convention Against Discrimination in Education.
- Paragraph 34 of the Document of the Copenhagen Meeting of the Conference on the Human Dimension of the CSCE.
- Article 4 of the UN Declaration on the Rights of Persons Belonging to National or Ethnic, Religious and Linguistic Minorities.
- Article 14 of the Framework Convention for the Protection of National Minorities.

To varying degrees, all of these instruments declare the right of minorities to maintain their collective identity through the medium of their mother tongue. This right is exercised, above all, through education. These same instruments, however, underline that the right to maintain the collective identity through the minority language must be balanced by the responsibility to integrate and participate in the wider national society. Such integration requires the acquisition of a sound knowledge of both that society and the State language(s). The promotion of tolerance and pluralism is also an important component of this dynamic.

The international human rights instruments that make reference to minority language education remain somewhat vague and general. They make no specific reference to degrees of access nor do they stipulate which levels of mother tongue education should be made available to minorities and by what means. Such concepts as "adequate opportunities" to be taught the minority language or to receive instruction in this language, as outlined in article 14 of the Council of Europe's Framework Convention for the Protection of National Minorities, should be considered in the light of other elements. These include the necessity of beneficial conditions facilitating the preservation, maintenance and development of language and culture as outlined in article 5 of the same Convention or the requirement to take the necessary measures to protect the ethnic, cultural, linguistic and religious identity of national minorities as stipulated in paragraph 33 of the Document of the Copenhagen Meeting of the Conference on the Human Dimension of the CSCE.

Irrespective of the level of access which may be afforded by States, it should not be established in an arbitrary fashion. States are required to give due consideration to the needs of national minorities as these are consistently expressed and demonstrated by the communities in question.

For their part, national minorities should ensure that their demands are reasonable. They should give due consideration to such legitimate factors as their own numerical strength, their demographic density in any given region (or regions), as well as their capacity to contribute to the durability of these services and facilities over time.

The spirit of international instruments

Over the years there has been an evolution in the manner in which the rights of minorities have been formulated in international standards. Such passive formulae as "... persons belonging to minorities shall not be denied the right ..." as expressed in the International Covenant on Civil and Political Rights (1966) have given way to a more positive, proactive approach such as "... States will protect the ethnic, cultural, linguistic and religious identity of national minorities ..." as contained in the Document of the Copenhagen Meeting of the Conference on the Human Dimension of the CSCE (1990). This progressive change of approach would indicate that a restrictive or minimalistic interpretation of the instruments is not in line with the spirit in which they have been formulated. In addition, the level of access must be established in conformity with the underlying principles of equality and non-discrimination as these are formulated in articles 1 of The Charter of the United Nations and in article 2 of The Universal Declaration of Human Rights and as reiterated in most international instruments. Consideration must also be given to the conditions specific to each State.

(...)

Public and private institutions

Article 27 of the International Covenant on Civil and Political Rights refers to the right of minorities to use their language in community with other members of their group. Article 13 of the International Covenant on Economic, Social and Cultural Rights guarantees the right of parents to choose for their children schools other than those established by public authorities. It also guarantees the right of individuals and bodies to establish and manage alternative educational institutions as long as these conform to minimum educational standards as laid down by the State. Article 13 of the Framework Convention for the Protection of National Minorities refers to the right of minorities to establish and manage their own educational institutions, although the State has no obligation to fund these institutions. Paragraph 32 of the Copenhagen Document imposes no obligation on the State to fund these institutions, but it does stipulate that these institutions may "seek public assistance from the State in conformity with national legislation".

The right of national minorities to establish and manage their own institutions, including educational ones, is well grounded in international law and must be recognized as such. Although the State has the right to oversee this process from an administrative perspective and in conformity with its own legislation, it must not prevent the enjoyment of this right by imposing unreasonable administrative requirements which might render it practically impossible for national minorities to establish their own educational institutions.

Although there is no formal obligation for States to fund these private establishments, these institutions should not be prevented from seeking resources from all domestic and international sources.

Minority education at primary and secondary levels

International instruments relating to minority language education declare that minorities not only have the right to maintain their identity through the medium of their mother tongue but that they also have the right to integrate into and participate in the wider national society by learning the State language. In view of the above, the attainment of multilingualism by the national minorities of OSCE States can be seen as a most effective way of meeting the objectives of the international instruments relating to the protection of national minorities as well as to their integration. The recommendations relating to primary and secondary schooling are meant to serve as a guide in the development of minority language education policy and in the provision of related programmes. The approach proposed is suggested by educational research and constitutes a realistic interpretation of relevant international norms.

The effectiveness of this approach depends on a number of factors. First there is the extent to which this approach strengthens the weaker minority mother tongue by using it as the medium for teaching. Another factor is the extent to which bilingual teachers are involved in the entire process.

Yet another factor to be considered is the extent to which both the minority and the State language are taught as subjects throughout the 12 years of schooling and finally the extent to which both languages are used as a medium of education in an optimal way in different phases of the child's education.

This approach strives to create the space that is required for the weaker minority language to thrive. It is in marked contrast with other approaches whose objective is to teach the minority language or even to carry out minimum instruction in the minority language only with a view to facilitating an early transition to teaching exclusively in the State language.

Submersion-type approaches whereby the curriculum is taught exclusively through the medium of the State language and minority children are entirely integrated into classes with children of the majority are not in line with international standards. Likewise, this applies to segregated schools in which the entire curriculum is taught exclusively through the medium of the minority mother tongue, throughout the entire educational process and where the majority language is not taught at all or only to a minimal extent.

Minority education in vocational schools

The right of persons belonging to national minorities to learn their mother tongue or to receive instruction in their mother tongue as formulated in paragraph 34 of the Copenhagen Document should imply the right to vocational training in the mother tongue in specific subjects. In the spirit of equality and non-discrimination, OSCE States should ensure access to such training where the desire for it is made evident and the numbers justify it.

On the other hand, the capacity of the State to plan and control its economic and educational policies should not be diminished. The ability of graduates of minority language vocational training schools also to function professionally in the State language, would be an advantage. It would enable them to work both in the region in which the minority in question is concentrated as well as anywhere else in the State. At a time of transition to the market economy which presupposes the unfettered movement of goods, services and labour, such a limitation can make it difficult for the State to facilitate opportunities for employment and overall economic development. Therefore, vocational training in the mother tongue of national minorities should ensure that the students concerned also acquire appropriate training in the State language(s).

D.2. OSCE-ODIHR, ADVISORY **C**OUNCIL OF **E**XPERTS ON **F**REEDOM OF RELIGION OR BELIEF**, Toledo Guiding Principles on Teaching about Religions and Beliefs in Public Schools,** *2007.*

(...)

Minority rights

In developing and implementing programmes related to teaching about religions and beliefs, attention needs to be paid to the rights and distinctive needs of minority groups in the larger community served by a particular school. This may include national or ethnic minorities with students in the school, or simply smaller religious or belief communities that have pupils in the relevant school. Efforts should be made to ascertain the distinctive needs of all such national or ethnic minorities, smaller religious communities, and migrants and new minorities.

In this regard, a number of points articulated in the Hague Recommendations, prepared under the auspices of the HCNM, are highly relevant. While these recommendations were developed with a primary focus on the issues of national ethnic minorities, they have obvious relevance to issues of concern to religious communities, whether or not they are ethnic minorities as well. Indeed, the fact that the right to freedom of religion or belief is involved, in addition to any other rights that ethnic minorities might be able to assert, adds to the significance of these recommendations.

A number of points made by the Hague Recommendations have relevance to teaching about religion. First, "States should consistently adhere to the fundamental principles of equality and non-discrimination" (Recommendation No. 2). Discrimination might arise in a programme for teaching about religions and beliefs at any stage in the development or implementation of the programme. If it does, rights are violated. Second, it is important to remember that the "relevant international obligations and commitments constitute international minimum standards. It would be contrary to their spirit and intent to interpret these obligations and commitments in a restrictive manner" (Recommendation No. 3). Third, "States should approach minority education rights in a proactive manner" (Recommendation No. 4). Fourth, just as importance and value should be attached "to the highlighting of minority histories, cultures and traditions," so attention should be paid to the teaching of the "histories, cultures and traditions" of religious communities that are present in a particular school (Recommendation No. 19). Fifth, "States should create conditions [...] [allowing national minorities] to participate, in a meaningful way, in the development and implementation of policies and programmes related to minority education" (Recommendation No. 5). Curriculum content "should be developed with the active participation of bodies representative of the minorities in question" (Recommendation No. 20). Any programme will need to make selections and choices, but inaccurate or disrespectful coverage should be subject to challenge and correction, and sound justifications for selections should be available. Finally, in accordance with a variety of international instruments, "the right of minorities to maintain their collective identity" should be respected" (Recommendation No. 1).[44]

E Right to participation

E.1. OFFICE OF THE OSCE HIGH COMMISSIONER ON NATIONAL MINORITIES, The Ljubljana Guidelines on Integration of Diverse Societies, 7 November 2012.

(...)

---

44 The Hague Recommendations Regarding Education Rights of National Minorities and Explanatory Note, October <>www.osce.org/documents/hcnm/1996/10/2700_en.pdf>.

c. Participation in cultural and religious life

41. States should create the conditions for persons belonging to minorities to effectively participate in the cultural life of their own community and of wider society. Freedom of religion and belief, and opportunities for voluntary participation in the religious life of a community, should be ensured, including through mutual accommodation, as appropriate. States should seek to implement policies and legislation that aim at inclusion on an equal footing of all members of society in cultural life. In addition to ensuring equal opportunities, such policies are important to prevent alienation and exclusion of minority groups, which can fuel radicalization and polarization and lead to conflict.

State policies should respect and, where relevant, support the preservation, enhancement and transmission to future generations of communities' cultural and religious heritage in all its forms. This may include cultural and religious practices, representations, expressions, knowledge and skills, objects and artefacts, and buildings and the spaces associated with them. To this end, it is essential that minority representatives are effectively involved in all stages of elaborating, implementing and monitoring relevant policies and legislation. Integration of society requires that persons belonging to minorities are effectively granted the right to preserve and develop their own cultural heritage and identity, as well as the right to take part and interact in the cultural life of the wider society, in a spirit of tolerance and intercultural dialogue.[45]

It is essential that the fundamental right of persons belonging to minorities to decide their own cultural issues does not result in their isolation. In this regard, permanent and ongoing intercultural dialogue among and between all minority groups and between minorities and majorities should be fostered, including through raising all residents' awareness of and exposure to all other cultures in their society. Cultural policies should not be confined to preserving and promoting traditional cultures, but also aim to simultaneously foster a plurality of cultural and artistic expressions, promote equal access to contemporary culture in all its forms and encourage interaction and intercultural exchange.

At the same time, while the right to participate in and develop one's own culture can be facilitated and supported by the State, culture itself is independent of the State. States should not establish an official "State culture" that encompasses and defines the contents of culture. Rather, cultural policy should observe the principles of pluralism, participation, democratization and decentralization. Processes of decentralization, including non-territorial self-governance (cultural-autonomy) arrangements, can play an important role in creating the conditions necessary for persons belonging to minorities to participate effectively in cultural life.[46]

---

[45] UN Declaration on Minorities, article 2(1); FCNM, articles 5, 6 and 15; and the Declaration on Intercultural Dialogue and Conflict Prevention, adopted by the Conference of the European Ministers of Culture on 22 October 2003.

[46] Commentary on Participation, paragraph 67.

Within a pluralistic cultural context, integration policies should take into account the varied cultural needs of different groups, including migrants[47] and indigenous peoples.[48]

In designing policies, States should be aware that for many communities, cultural identities, belief systems and religious practices are inextricably linked. Everyone has the right to freedom of thought, conscience and religion. This includes the freedom to have or to adopt a religion, belief or non-belief of one's choice. It further includes the freedom, either individually or in community with others, and in public or private, to manifest one's religion or belief through worship, observance, practice and teaching.[49] Freedom to manifest religion and belief, including public worship, can only be subject to limitations prescribed by law. These are only legitimate if they relate to specified public-interest grounds and are reasonable and proportional to the end sought.[50]

States should take appropriate measures to protect persons who may be subject to threats or acts of discrimination, hostility or violence as a result of their culture, religion or belief. State authorities and public officials have the responsibility to avoid negative rhetoric or actions that target specific cultural or religious communities.

Furthermore, undue limitations to full participation in cultural and religious affairs should be avoided. Such limitations may include excessive requirements for the registration of cultural or religious organizations and places of worship or for the acquisition of planning permission for religious or cultural buildings. They may also include disproportionate limitations on the public display of cultural or religious symbols and clothing. Public authorities should not impose any undue restrictions on what language(s) can be used during cultural or religious events. They may legitimately require, for example, that cultural associations and/or religious organizations translate official and administrative documents into the State or official language(s), including, where relevant, when recording legal civil acts for which they have authority.[51]

F Right to access to justice

F.1. OSCE HIGH COMMISSIONER ON NATIONAL MINORITIES, The Graz Recommendations on Access to Justice and National Minorities, *November 2017.*

Introduction

(...)

---

47 International Convention on the Protection of the Rights of All Migrant Workers and Members of Their Families, 1990, article 31.
48 UN Declaration on the Rights of Indigenous Peoples, 2007, article 1.
49 In general: Universal Declaration of Human Rights, article 18; ICCPR, article 18(1); and ECHR, article 9. For minorities in particular: ICCPR, article 27; FCNM, articles 7 and 8; and Copenhagen Document, paragraph 32.
50 ICCPR, article 18(3) and ECHR article 9(2).
51 Oslo Recommendations, Explanatory Note to Recommendation 5.

The concept of equality before the law entails a responsibility on the part of the State to not only refrain from violating the rights of citizens based on, inter alia, gender, ethnic identity, religion (or belief), language, disability, age or sexual orientation, or national and social origin (embodied primarily in the principle of non-discrimination), but also to take positive measures to ensure that persons belonging to minorities can effectively obtain a remedy if their rights have been violated or need enforcing. Indeed, one cannot speak of equal access to justice if, for instance, persons belonging to national minorities do not understand the judicial system, do not know their rights or cannot get suitable legal advice or afford legal representation, or even fear the judiciary and avoid it. These Recommendations are therefore informed by the State's dual obligation to not discriminate against persons belonging to national minorities seeking access to justice and to prevent indirect discrimination by taking positive measures to facilitate such access.

Because the HCNM approaches access to justice for national minorities from a conflict prevention perspective, it is important to underline that access to justice should include access to a remedy if it is found that an individual's rights, including the right to equal treatment, have been violated or need to be enforced. These Recommendations therefore not only address issues related to access to courts, but also to other mechanisms, such as national human rights institutions, that can secure an effective remedy for complainants – including persons belonging to national minorities – whose individual rights have been violated. The Ljubljana Guidelines suggest that ensuring effective access to remedies could include establishing and supporting effective independent bodies, such as ombudspersons or national human rights institutions.[52] In addition, the Oslo Recommendations point out that independent and effective national human rights institutions can often provide quicker and less expensive recourse than the courts.[53]

It should also be emphasized that persons belonging to minority communities may face what is sometimes referred to as compound discrimination; for example, both on a linguistic and gender basis. States should factor this into the policies that the State adopts to ensure access to justice for persons belonging to national minorities. Moreover, to achieve equal protection and prevent discrimination, certain categories of persons within minority groups may require special and positive measures to ensure that they can effectively access justice on an equal footing with other members of society. In line with the OSCE's Action Plan for the Promotion of Gender Equality, particular attention will be given throughout these Recommendations to measures that States should implement to ensure that women belonging to national minorities also have effective access to justice.

---

52 HCNM (2012) Ljubljana Guidelines, explanatory note to Guideline 21.
53 HCNM (1998) The Oslo Recommendations Regarding the Linguistic Rights of National Minorities, explanatory note to Recommendation 16.

The Graz Recommendations on Access to Justice and National Minorities

1. Access to justice for persons belonging to national minorities should be underpinned by the principles of the rule of law, non-discrimination and equality, including gender equality, the right to a fair hearing within a reasonable time by an independent and impartial body established by law, the right to legal assistance and the right to an effective remedy.
2. Measures to guarantee access to justice for national minorities should be broader than providing access to courts. States should establish, strengthen and fund independent human rights institutions that can secure effective remedies for all complainants, including persons belonging to national minorities.
3. States should ensure that when persons belonging to national minorities engage with judicial and national human rights institutions and take part in proceedings, they are able to do so in a language they understand, and preferably in their language, as well as in an environment that is respectful of their identity.
4. States should make legal assistance available to national minorities in a way that addresses the obstacles they face in accessing justice.
5. The composition of courts, tribunals, prosecution offices, law-enforcement agencies, correctional services, enforcement agencies (or bailiffs) and human rights institutions, should aim to reflect the diversity of the population at all levels.
6. To facilitate access to justice for national minorities, States should ensure that law-enforcement agencies work to build trust with minority communities and enforce the law in an impartial and non-discriminatory manner, free of prejudice and gender bias.
7. Victim support services and witness protection measures should be sensitive to the needs of persons belonging to national minorities, and of minority women in particular.
8. States should ensure that court orders and judgments affecting persons belonging to national minorities are executed effectively, impartially and within a reasonable time.
9. States should ensure that persons belonging to national minorities held in detention or imprisoned are treated with humanity and respect for their identity.
10. States should, as a matter of urgency, provide effective redress to persons belonging to national minorities who have suffered serious human rights violations as a result of inter-ethnic conflict.

(...)

7. *Victim support services and witness protection measures should be sensitive to the needs of persons belonging to national minorities, and of minority women in particular.*
(...)

In the course of criminal proceedings, persons belonging to minority communities may be called to provide testimony. By doing so, they can put themselves and their families at risk of retaliation and may be in need of protection before, during and after trial. Witnesses and their families may require police protection or even to enter witness protection programmes, which can include relocation. Achieving a satisfactory level of protection for witnesses from minority communities may be particularly difficult given their specific socio-economic, cultural and linguistic circumstances. For instance, a balance needs to be found between respect for outward cultural and religious symbols associated with minority communities and the need for protecting the identity of witnesses originally from that community. States should make sure that every possible effort is made to address the challenges related to the protection of witnesses belonging to minority communities to avoid hindering the pursuit of justice.

(...)

9 *States should ensure that persons belonging to national minorities held in detention or imprisoned are treated with humanity and respect for their identity.*

(...)

The closed environment of prisons and (to a lesser extent) police detention can amplify the discrimination and stigmatization that national minorities may already face in society at large. Minority women may be particularly at risk on account of their membership of a minority community and their gender. Generally, persons belonging to national minorities risk being subjected to one or a combination of the following while in prison or detention: worse treatment or conditions than those for other groups; an unwillingness to communicate with them in a language they understand and preferably in their language; a failure to respect religious and cultural habits, even when these comply with international human rights standards; physical and psychological abuse; enhanced searching and interview protocols; systematic classification into higher security arrangements (such as solitary confinement); and unwarranted disciplinary punishments in prison. States should put measures in place to ensure that detainees and inmates from minority communities are granted access to justice and that the reasons for their detention and imprisonment, as well as their treatment while in custody, can be challenged effectively before a court or with a national human rights institution. States should also collect disaggregated data on their prison population and, if warranted, devote resources to understand the causes of minority overrepresentation in prisons.[54]

(...)

---

54 See OSCE (2003) Decision No. 566 Action Plan on Improving the Situation of Roma and Sinti within the OSCE Area, paragraph 18.

II. IMPRISONMENT

(...)

Independent bodies (such as national human rights institutions, civil society organizations, national preventative mechanisms and the ICRC) should provide ongoing monitoring of possible discrimination in the prison environment, and a complaints mechanism should be available to minority prisoners.

Legal assistance should be made available to prisoners in a language they understand, and preferably in their language. All prisoners, including minority prisoners, should be allowed to observe the tenets of their religion, including dietary requirements. Their culture and, where relevant, their language should not be belittled, and they should be allowed to communicate with their families in their language. Symbols that are offensive to minorities and can provoke tensions with other groups should be eliminated (see Recommendation 3). Special vocational programmes should be designed for minority prisoners, including minority women, to support their rehabilitation and enhance their self-sufficiency. Care should be taken to make sure that minority prisoners are incarcerated in facilities and prison areas where they will not be at risk because of their status as minorities, and close to their communities. Consideration should be given to allow minority prisoners to serve their sentence in areas where national minorities are concentrated geographically.

G Right to access to media

G.1. OFFICE OF THE OSCE HIGH COMMISSIONER ON NATIONAL MINORITIES, The Tallinn Guidelines on National Minorities and the Media in the Digital Age & Explanatory Note, February 2019.

Introduction

(...)

The present Guidelines continue this line of thematic work by the HCNM in a very important policy area – the media and use of information technologies. The media and information technologies can play an instrumental role in preventing or igniting conflicts involving or affecting national minorities, which is a central concern for the HCNM. The media and information technologies can also make influential contributions to conflict resolution and peacebuilding and reconciliation processes. In addition, the Guidelines seek to clarify minority rights in a specific area – freedom of expression and the media – and their relevance to conflict prevention. They address specific challenges shared by OSCE participating States, namely how to operationalize the right to freedom of expression in diverse societies by providing guidance on creating and sustaining structures and processes for a pluralistic discussion between and within communities of majorities and minorities in the digital age. The media and more generally communication technologies play an increasingly important role in conflict cycles; they are often abused to stoke tension, but can also serve as an influential tool to foster dialogue and understanding.

Information and communication, and the technologies which enable them, can facilitate democratic deliberation, participation in public debate and public affairs, and integration of diverse societies in the broad sense of the Ljubljana Guidelines. They can also have important transnational and international dimensions. The right to seek, receive and impart information and ideas exists regardless of frontiers, and it is crucial that this right is guaranteed by States in their mutual relations. This right should be guaranteed to everyone, including in respect of access to the media, without discrimination based on ethnic, cultural, linguistic or religious grounds.[55] Moreover, the participating States have committed to make information available that will assist the electronic mass media in taking into account, in their programmes, the ethnic, cultural, linguistic and religious identities of national minorities.[56]

The present Guidelines also draw inspiration from the Bolzano/Bozen Recommendations, which are concerned with national minorities in inter-State relations, because the transnational and international dimensions to freedom of expression are essential for many national minorities who wish to maintain effective cultural, linguistic, political and other ties with their "kin-" or neighbouring States.[57] Moreover, States' active involvement with these matters has proved to be tension prone, often requiring the HCNM's intervention to support efforts to foster an enabling approach to minorities' access to the media and communication platforms from neighbouring States, while balancing this against other legitimate aims. Thus, the present Guidelines acknowledge the complementary roles of the media in advancing the goal of societal cohesion within States, while ensuring that the human rights to freedom of expression and cultural rights are not limited by State borders.

Pluralistic democratic society requires ample space for interaction, deliberation and debate on matters of importance and interest to the population. Such spaces should be inclusive: all members of society, including national minorities, should be able to access those spaces without discrimination and participate effectively

---

55 See ICCPR, Article 2.
56 See: Report of the CSCE Meeting of experts on national minorities, Geneva, 1991. See also, The Bolzano/Bozen Recommendations on National Minorities in Inter-State Relations (The Bolzano/Bozen Recommendations), Recommendation 14; The Guidelines on the use of Minority Languages in the Broadcast Media (the Broadcast Media Guidelines), Guideline 13.
57 "This term has been used to describe States whose majority population shares ethnic or cultural characteristics with the minority population of another State. [...] In addition, "kin" is regarded as one of the essentially contested concepts that lacks agreed scientific or legal definition. For these reasons, the term "kin-State" [...] is referred to only sparingly." See: The Bolzano/Bozen Recommendations on National Minorities in Inter-State Relations (the Bolzano/Bozen Recommendations), p. 3.

in the deliberation that takes place in them. Inclusive deliberative spaces allow different groups in society to interact with each other, to explore and develop their identities and articulate their views, and to share information and perspectives. These activities can play instrumental roles in enhancing understanding and reducing intolerance and mutual distrust in diverse societies and thereby strengthen societal integration, cohesion and stability. They can also provide valuable safeguards against societal tensions and conflicts.

As well as being inclusive, these deliberative spaces must be pluralistic. They must allow for robust public debate and the expression of wide-ranging viewpoints and perspectives, including those which are critical of the State or any member of society, from majorities or minorities alike, or which may even be considered offensive by some. This principle is well-established in European and international human rights law, but it bears recalling because it is often downplayed in practice in the heat of political discussion. The exercise of the right to freedom of expression is moreover governed by certain duties and responsibilities. Everyone participating in public debate – members of majority and minority communities alike – must abide by those duties and responsibilities. "Everyone" refers to both natural and legal persons, i.e. individuals as well as media organizations, internet intermediaries, civil society organizations, etc. Such duties and responsibilities include avoiding gratuitous insults and negative stereotyping of individuals, groups or communities.

(...)

The Tallinn Guidelines on National Minorities and the Media in the Digital Age

I ENABLING ENVIRONMENT FOR FREEDOM OF EXPRESSION AND MEDIA FREEDOM

1. States should take all appropriate measures to ensure that everyone, including persons belonging to national minorities, can exercise the right to freedom of expression in a practical and effective manner in the digital age. This includes the right to seek, receive and impart information, regardless of frontiers, in the languages and through the media of their choice.
2. States should take all appropriate measures to fulfil their positive obligation to create an enabling environment for robust, pluralistic public debate in which everyone, including persons belonging to national minorities, can participate effectively and express their opinions, ideas and identities without fear.
3. States should put in place effective systems of legal and practical protection to guarantee the safety and security of everyone wishing to participate in public debate. This requires the effective enforcement of legislation penalizing threats and violence against journalists and other media actors and the prosecution of the perpetrators of such abuses. The systems of protection must be fully applicable and accessible to persons belonging to national

minorities and sensitive to their needs, including gender-specific needs. Such systems could include specialized mechanisms of protection, as needed.

4   State and/or public officials should not undermine or threaten journalists and other media actors, or incite hatred towards or discrimination against them, on the grounds of belonging to a national minority or for reporting on national minority issues. Nor should they attack the integrity of journalists or of other media actors by making deliberately false accusations against them, and thereby jeopardizing their safety. They should moreover publicly and unequivocally condemn all threats and violence against journalists and other media actors, irrespective of the source of those threats and acts of violence.

5   States should take all appropriate regulatory and other measures to ensure that key features of an enabling environment for freedom of expression, the media and public debate are safeguarded in law, policy and practice. Those features include a law and policy framework for equality and non-discrimination; a system of protection for national minorities and their rights; an effective freedom of information regime; pluralism in an evolving media environment; and a culture of independence in the media sector, including in respect of national regulatory bodies and the operation of public service, commercial, community and other media.

6   If they have not already done so, States are encouraged to draw up, adopt and implement clear policy to ensure the effective realization of the right to freedom of expression in the digital age for everyone, including persons belonging to national minorities, women and men. The process of developing such policy should involve the effective participation of a wide range of stakeholders, including representatives of national minority groups, independent national media regulatory authorities, the media, internet intermediaries, civil society (including women's groups) and academia. States should ensure equal participation of women and men in these processes.

II MEDIA ENVIRONMENT

7   States should develop and deploy a range of measures to ensure that persons belonging to national minorities can take full advantage of the unprecedented opportunities to seek, receive and impart information and ideas of all kinds, regardless of frontiers, in the present media environment. The abundance of information and media does not, however, diminish existing State obligations to: – Ensure the effective access of persons belonging to national minorities to such expressive opportunities and informational resources; and – Support and/or facilitate the production of content by and for national minorities, including in their own languages, and the dissemination of such content across a range of platforms.

8   States should ensure that universal service obligations governing the communications sector are fully implemented in practice, including for national minorities and other communities residing in rural and geographically isolated areas, or which are otherwise marginalized. Such obligations include

the provision of electronic communications services of a specified quality at an affordable price, as well as a stable and reliable connection to the public communications network through (mobile) telephony and internet.

9   States should ensure that everyone – of all ages and genders and from all walks of life – can develop the set of skills that enable them to access, understand, critically analyse, evaluate, use and create media content, including online media and digital content. To achieve this aim, States should take effective measures to promote media and information literacy, including in the languages of national minorities.

10 States should adopt necessary and effective measures to encourage or, as appropriate, require internet intermediaries based within their jurisdiction to apply human rights due diligence throughout their operations and to take account of any particular implications for the rights of national minorities while doing so, including the elimination of all forms of online violence against women. All such measures – by States and internet intermediaries alike and which may include self- and/or co-regulatory mechanisms – should be fully in line with evolving interpretations of international and European human rights law, including the rights to non-discrimination, privacy and data protection, and be informed by relevant technological and regulatory developments.

11 Internet intermediaries should be allowed to, and encouraged to, offer their services in the languages of national minorities. They should also be encouraged to devise and implement strategic plans and concrete measures to enhance the availability, accessibility, prominence and findability of content produced by national minorities, including in minority languages, online. Intermediaries which use algorithm-based search or recommendation systems should be encouraged to provide greater transparency in respect of how those systems work and how they impact on minority content. They should also provide for improved levels of individual autonomy over the personal data and preferences that they use, including those which can lead to their identification (or not) as persons belonging to national minorities.

III PLURALISM AND DIVERSITY

12 States are encouraged to adopt a range of measures to support initiatives by the media to foster intercultural dialogue by offering content, programmes and services for all of society and thereby sustain shared points of reference. States should support the production of content by national minorities and its widespread dissemination across different platforms. Any measure taken to provide such support should not interfere with the editorial and operational independence of the media.

13 States may use regulatory or other measures to promote the use of particular languages in the media, including the State/official language(s) or other languages, for instance to foster societal cohesion and integration or to ensure a common language of communication, provided the goals are legitimate and

clearly stated and the regulation is proportionate to those goals. States may similarly promote the languages of national minorities, which are an essential component of their identity. Any measures to promote the use of particular languages in the media should seek to balance and provide reasonable and fair accommodation of the needs and interests of different linguistic groups in society.

14 Language quotas for public (digital) broadcasting are permissible if they comply with international and European human rights and media law, in particular as regards their proportionality to their stated objectives. They must furthermore not have the purpose or effect of unfairly restricting the use of other languages, especially national minority languages. The imposition of rigid language quotas on private broadcasters may conflict with freedom of expression and should be avoided by employing other approaches to foster a shared communication space. These safeguards for pluralism and diversity should also govern any language quotas that are applied to music or film. Language quotas should not apply to advertising.

15 States may require public service media, and encourage the audiovisual media generally, to make reasonable arrangements for the translation of media content in the State/official language(s) into the languages of national minorities, and vice-versa, in order to enhance the linguistic accessibility of both types of content throughout society and thereby help to foster intercultural dialogue. Any such requirements for public service media should be set out clearly in legislation and be proportionate to the aim pursued. Minority language audio-visual linear media should not in any case be subject to undue or disproportionate requirements for subtitling, dubbing, post-synchronization or any other forms of translation.

16 Public service announcements should be translated into the languages of national minorities, as appropriate, and disseminated in an equitable and non-discriminatory manner through a range of media, including minority media.

17 States should take effective measures to guarantee pluralism in the evolving media environment and to ensure that persons belonging to national minorities can access a wide range of media providing content that corresponds to their needs and interests, including in their own languages. These could include measures to promote such content and to ensure its visibility and findability.

18 States should take effective measures, including regulatory measures, as required, to prevent concentrations of media ownership and control which threaten media pluralism and the availability of national minority media services and content, including in the languages of national minorities.

19 States should introduce legislation and/or amend existing legislation to guarantee the independence and sustainability of public service media and allow them to fulfil their mandate to serve all sections of society, including national minorities, by providing diverse high-quality programming and services across a range of platforms. Such legislation should provide for, or

at least facilitate, the effective participation of national minorities in public service media activities at various levels, such as content-production, editorial decision-making and supervisory activities.

20 States are encouraged to introduce legislation and/or amend existing legislation to recognize the distinct nature of not-for-profit community media, which can be run by or otherwise serve national minority communities. Such legislation should guarantee the independence of community media and allow them to fulfil their objective to provide members of the communities they serve, including national minorities, with the opportunities and training that enable them to produce their own media content and to participate fully in the operation and management of their own media.

21 States may explore the potential for commercial media to provide pluralistic content and, in particular, national minority content, including in the languages of national minorities, and develop appropriate measures to incentivize the promotion of such content.

22 States should adopt specific legislative and other support measures to facilitate the independent and stable operation of a range of media at regional or local levels, including in geographical areas with national minority populations and/or in national minority languages.

23 States should not impede or restrict the ability of persons belonging to national minorities to access media established in other countries which serve the interests of national minorities. The ability to access such media does not diminish States' obligation to facilitate and support the development and effective operation of media serving national minorities in their own jurisdictions. States should moreover seek to prevent, or at least mitigate, the adverse effects for national minorities of copyright agreements that result in geo-blocking of media content.

24 Independent national media regulatory authorities should develop mechanisms to enable women and men belonging to national minorities to participate effectively in all areas of their work that are relevant to such groups. States are encouraged to consider introducing or strengthening, as appropriate, the structured representation of persons belonging to national minorities in independent national media regulatory authorities. Appropriate mechanisms should be adopted to ensure gender balance within these authorities.

25 Licensing schemes for (digital) radio and television should be based on predetermined, public, clear, transparent and equitable criteria. States should include, in appropriate ways, the service of national minority communities, including shared and dedicated channels and/or channels or programming in the languages of national minorities, among those criteria. Licensing schemes should be administered in a fair and non-discriminatory manner by designated independent authorities that adhere to clear procedures supported by appeal mechanisms.

26 States should explore, use and develop the potential of licensing schemes for (digital) radio and television to promote minority media, including in

minority languages, in each type of radio and television service. Such provisions could include special status for "minority" or "community" media meeting particular criteria, which could entitle them to, for instance and as appropriate, concessionary licence fees or less onerous technical specifications, fiscal obligations or regulatory reporting requirements.

27 States should require independent authorities charged with implementing licensing processes to issue information and guidance on the opportunities and requirements for minority media within existing licensing schemes. The information and guidance should be issued in the State/official language(s) and in the languages of national minorities and they should be publicized in appropriate ways.

28 Network operators, including cable, IPTV and satellite, as well as multiplex operators, should be allowed to, and encouraged to, include national minority channels, including in the languages of national minorities, in their (basic) packages. States may consider using fair and proportionate must-carry regulations to ensure that public service broadcasting or national minority channels are included in the (basic) packages of cable network or multiplex operators, for instance.

29 When licensing multiplex services and electronic programme guides, States should provide a legislative basis for appropriate accommodation of, and due prominence for, minority media channels, including in minority languages.

30 States should endeavour to incentivize the production, dissemination and promotion of national minority content, including in minority languages, and especially online. Media support schemes should take appropriate measures to cater adequately for the needs and interests of persons belonging to national minorities. To this end, existing schemes to promote general interest or pluralistic content, or particular types of independent media or content, could emphasize the need for content corresponding to the needs and interests of national minorities, including in their own languages, and especially online. Portions of the funds available under existing schemes could be earmarked for those purposes. The establishment of dedicated funding schemes is also encouraged.

IV MEDIA, INFORMATION TECHNOLOGIES AND CONFLICT PREVENTION

31 States and State or public actors should refrain from disseminating, supporting or endorsing in any way disinformation, propaganda or inflammatory discourse which aim to, or are likely to, undermine friendly relations among States and/or the sovereignty of other States; obstruct integration in other States, and/or generate hostility towards particular groups, including national minorities. Internet intermediaries should uphold human rights principles, respect human rights online, and voluntarily accept and apply all international human rights and women's rights instruments in the digital environment.

32 States may restrict or prohibit expression only in strict accordance with international or European human rights law. This means that any restriction on the right to freedom of expression must be provided by law and be a necessary and proportionate measure to achieve a stated, legitimate aim. Any prohibition of expression under domestic law must clearly correspond to, and be fully in compliance with, relevant specific provisions of international law. States should refrain from using vague or blanket terms for types of expression as a basis for content regulation, restriction or prohibition.

33 For offensive or harmful types of expression which do not have sufficient gravity or intensity to legitimately be restricted under international law, alternative responses are called for, such as counter-speech; intercultural dialogue, including via the media and social media; and education and awareness raising activities. Internet intermediaries should commit to eradicating online gender-based violence and allocate resources for information and educational campaigns to prevent ICT-facilitated violence against women and girls. States should support such initiatives and encourage the media, without encroaching on their editorial independence, and internet intermediaries, to do so as well.

34 States should encourage the media and internet intermediaries to foster intergroup dialogue and understanding in ways that are appropriate to their roles, functions and capacities, especially in the contexts of conflict prevention and conflict resolution. The media and internet intermediaries are governed by certain duties and responsibilities whenever they exercise their right to freedom of expression.

35 States must not jam broadcast signals, block websites, web-based services (including social media services) or applications or IP-addresses from within or outside their jurisdiction, save in compliance with international human rights law and pursuant to an order by an independent court or other independent, impartial and authoritative body.

36 Internet intermediaries should not be held liable for third-party content disseminated through their services or networks which they have not altered or edited, except when they have or reasonably ought to have knowledge of the illegal nature of particular content or they have refused to obey an independent and authoritative court order requiring them to block or remove illegal content and they have the technical capacity to do so. Nor should internet intermediaries be obliged to conduct general monitoring of content to ascertain the nature of third-party content disseminated through their services or networks.

37 States should require internet intermediaries to adopt and effectively implement clear and transparent policies and procedures governing the removal of illegal content disseminated by users through their services or networks. Those procedures should be subject to due process, including adequate oversight and effective appeal mechanisms, and ultimately be subject to independent judicial review and remedies. To deal with cases of online and

ICT-facilitated violence, in particular against women and girls, internet intermediaries should put in place complaint mechanisms that are easily accessible, including from linguistic and technical perspectives, user-friendly and easy to find.

(...)

The public has the right to receive information and ideas on matters of general interest to society and the media have the task of imparting such information and ideas.[58] Politics, current affairs, health matters, religion, culture and history are all examples of topics that are of interest to the public, unlike individuals' strictly private relationships or family affairs. The media disseminate information and ideas widely – often with explanation and contextualization – and thereby inform public opinion. Similarly, by selecting, framing and analysing issues, the media, in particular journalistic and news media, are capable of influencing public opinion and political agendas. It is essential that this task of disseminating information and ideas also covers matters of interest to national minorities. The targeting of national minorities is, however, not enough: when content for minorities is actually produced by the minorities themselves, including in their own languages, it is more likely that the content will satisfy their informational needs. The participation of persons belonging to national minorities in the production of such news and information, including in their own languages, should therefore be encouraged.

---

58 *The Sunday Times v. the United Kingdom* (No. 1), 26 April 1979, Para. 65, Series A No. 30; Human Rights Committee, GC 34, Para. 13 and Human Rights Committee, Communication No. 1334/2004, *Mavlonov and Sa'di v. Uzbekistan*.

4 European Union

Section 1

Charter of Fundamental Rights of the European Union

[*The text of the Charter has been solemnly proclaimed in 7 December 2000 and re-proclaimed in 12 December 2007 in sight of the signature of Treaty of Lisbon*]

CHAPTER III
EQUALITY
Article 21

Non-discrimination

1   Any discrimination based on any ground such as sex, race, colour, ethnic or social origin, genetic features, language, religion or belief, political or any other opinion, membership of a national minority, property, birth, disability, age or sexual orientation shall be prohibited.
2   Within the scope of application of the Treaty establishing the European Community and of the Treaty on European Union, and without prejudice to the special provisions of those Treaties, any discrimination on grounds of nationality shall be prohibited.

Article 22

Cultural, religious and linguistic diversity

The Union shall respect cultural, religious and linguistic diversity.

Treaty on European Union

> [Treaty of Lisbon amending the Treaty on European Union and the Treaty establishing the European Community, signed at Lisbon, 13 December 2007]

Article 2

The Union is founded on the values of respect for human dignity, freedom, democracy, equality, the rule of law and respect for human rights, including the rights of persons belonging to minorities. These values are common to the Member States in a society in which pluralism, non-discrimination, tolerance, justice, solidarity and equality between women and men prevail.

Article 49

Any European State which respects the values referred to in Article 2 and is committed to promoting them may apply to become a member of the Union. The European Parliament and national Parliaments shall be notified of this application. The applicant State shall address its application to the Council, which shall act unanimously after consulting the Commission and after receiving the consent of the European Parliament, which shall act by a majority of its component members. The conditions of eligibility agreed upon by the European Council shall be taken into account.

The conditions of admission and the adjustments to the Treaties on which the Union is founded, which such admission entails, shall be the subject of an agreement between the Member States and the applicant State. This agreement shall be submitted for ratification by all the contracting States in accordance with their respective constitutional requirements.

Treaty on the functioning of the European Union

> [Treaty of Lisbon amending the Treaty on European Union and the Treaty establishing the European Community, signed at Lisbon, 13 December 2007]

Article 10

In defining and implementing its policies and activities, the Union shall aim to combat discrimination based on sex, racial or ethnic origin, religion or belief, disability, age or sexual orientation.
(...)

Article 17

1 The Union respects and does not prejudice the status under national law of churches and religious associations or communities in the Member States.
2 The Union equally respects the status under national law of philosophical and non-confessional organisations.
3 Recognising their identity and their specific contribution, the Union shall maintain an open, transparent and regular dialogue with these churches and organisations.

Article 19

1 Without prejudice to the other provisions of the Treaties and within the limits of the powers conferred by them upon the Union, the Council, acting unanimously in accordance with a special legislative procedure and after obtaining the consent of the European Parliament, may take appropriate action to combat discrimination based on sex, racial or ethnic origin, religion or belief, disability, age or sexual orientation.
2 By way of derogation from paragraph 1, the European Parliament and the Council, acting in accordance with the ordinary legislative procedure, may adopt the basic principles of Union incentive measures, excluding any harmonisation of the laws and regulations of the Member States, to support action taken by the Member States in order to contribute to the achievement of the objectives referred to in paragraph 1.

A Non-discrimination

A.1. EUROPEAN PARLIAMENT'S COMMITTEE ON CIVIL LIBERTIES, JUSTICE AND HOME AFFAIRS, **Towards a comprehensive EU protection system for minorities,** *August 2017.*

(…)

3 Minority Rights Protection in the EU Legal System Key findings

Non-discrimination on the basis of nationality has been a key part of the EU legal framework since 1957.

The Lisbon Treaty, coming into force in 2009, brought new and important changes to the legal framework of minority rights. Article 2 TEU articulates for the first time "respect for human rights including the rights of persons belonging to minorities", a value on which the Union is founded, and the Charter brought a right to respect for cultural, religious and linguistic rights.

'Protection of minorities' is a key element of Copenhagen criteria, and it has consistently been applied to countries of the 2004 and later enlargements. Yet minority protection is not subsequently followed up once a country joins the

EU, as the European Commission officially 'loses' competence on the matter of national minorities.

Three directives are central: the Racial Equality Directive (2000/43), the Equal Treatment Directive (2000/78) and the Citizens' Rights Directive (2004/38). Their application has been widespread regarding discrimination on the ground of nationality but less developed in respect of minority rights.

A convergence of the EU's Fundamental Charter and European Convention on Human Rights changed EU Member States' approach, in particular on minority and Roma rights, from a matter of non-discrimination in respect of an individual to minority rights.

3.1. What are the EU's approaches to minority protection and the rights of minority groups?

This subsection of the study examines the present EU approaches to minority protection from the perspective of Union citizenship, free movement and fundamental rights protection. It places the discussion within the broader conceptual framework of a triangular relationship between the rule of law, democracy and fundamental rights outlined in section 1 above. This section investigates the various pieces making up the wider EU framework on minority protection in light of the changing paradigm of minority rights. The gaps arising between the non-discrimination and minority rights approaches raise a central question: Should EU citizens of a minority background be protected differently, depending on the country they live in? The answer, according to the current state of EU law, is yes. Action in respect of discrimination has been a key part of EU law since the European Economic Community Treaty entered into force in 1957. The establishment of a common market was based first on the principle of non-discrimination on the ground of nationality. This has worked particularly well in all areas – goods, persons, services and capital, although in this study it is only people who are at issue. The principle that all EU nationals coming within the scope of EU law are entitled to the same treatment as nationals of the state has been effective in diminishing discrimination against EU nationals who are not citizens of the host Member State – mobile EU citizens. There is a fundamental difference between minority rights and non-discrimination, in particular non-discrimination on the basis of nationality. There is greater convergence between minority rights and non-discrimination on other grounds such as ethnicity. But to understand the development of minority rights in the context of EU principles regarding discrimination it is necessary to examine the principle of non-discrimination on the basis of nationality, as it is the starting point in EU law. Furthermore, ethnic and other minorities who enjoy EU citizenship may be able to benefit from the prohibition on discrimination on the basis of nationality notwithstanding that as citizens of one Member States they do not constitute a minority in the context of this study.

Non-discrimination on the basis of nationality was something of a novelty in 1957. As studied in section 2 above, international instruments such as the ECHR did not explicitly prohibit discrimination on this ground. Instead, discrimination was prohibited only on the basis of (Article 14) "sex, race, colour, language, religion, political or other opinion, national or social origin, association with a national minority, property, birth or other status".

The idea that discrimination on the basis of nationality should also be unlawful was new. The extension of the non-discrimination provision in the ECHR to nationality would not take place until 1996 (*Gaygusuz v Austria*).[1] EEC law also included a prohibition on discrimination on the basis of sex from 1957, which would be extremely important in providing equality for women in a period during which discrimination on the basis of gender was still common in national legislation.

The prohibition of discrimination on the basis of nationality has served many EU citizens very well as they moved around the EU in search of work and better living conditions. It served as the foundation for the provision in Regulation (EEC) No. 1612/68 on the rights of EU migrant workers, which required equal treatment for EU workers in all areas of social and tax advantages.[2] The CJEU took workers' entitlement to equal treatment very seriously and developed its jurisprudence in a way that protected EU workers from discrimination in all social and tax matters, which, some Member States argued, were tangential to the free movement of workers and thus should not be covered by the prohibition.[3]

The changes to EU law brought about by the Maastricht Treaty entering into force in 1993 included the creation of citizenship of the Union, a status held by every national of a Member State. This was followed by a new Treaty basis for non-discrimination, which entered into EU law with the Amsterdam Treaty in 1999. The grounds of prohibited discrimination were sex, racial or ethnic origin, religion or belief, disability, age or sexual orientation (Article 13 TFEU).

The entry into force of the Amsterdam Treaty in 1999 and the necessity to develop the rights of EU citizens opened the way for three directives to be adopted to give effect to the new rights (at least according to the classification by the Commission): Directive 2000/43/EC149[4] (hereinafter the Racial Equality Directive) implementing the principle of equal treatment between persons irrespective of racial or ethnic origin; Directive 2000/78/EC[5] establishing a general framework for equal treatment in employment and occupation (hereinafter the Equal Treatment Directive); and Directive 2004/38/EC[6] on citizens' rights (hereinafter the

---

1 *Gaygusuz v Austria*, 39/1995/545/631, Council of Europe: European Court of Human Rights, 23 May 1996 <>www.refworld.org/cases,ECHR,3ae6b6f12c.html>.
2 Article 7(2) Regulation (EEC) No 1612/68 of the Council of 15 October 1968 on freedom of movement for workers within the Community, OJ L 257, 19.10.1968, pp. 0002–0012 (now repealed).
3 For a full investigation of the development of this jurisprudence see: Martin, D. and E. Guild. *Free Movement of persons in the European Union*. London: Butterworths, 1996.
4 Council Directive 2000/43/EC of 29 June 2000 implementing the principle of equal treatment between persons irrespective of racial or ethnic origin, OJ L 180, 19.7.2000, pp. 22–26. (http://eur-lex.europa.eu/legalcontent/EN/TXT/HTML/?uri=CELEX:32000L0043&from=EN).
5 Council Directive 2000/78/EC of 27 November 2000 establishing a general framework for equal treatment in employment and occupation OJ L 303, 2.12.2000.
6 Directive 2004/38/EC of the European Parliament and of the Council of 29 April 2004 on the right of citizens of the Union and their family members to move and reside freely within the territory of the Member States amending Regulation (EEC) No 1612/68 and repealing Directives 64/221/EEC, 68/360/EEC, 72/194/EEC, 73/148/EEC, 75/34/EEC,

Citizens' Rights Directive). This directive is relevant notwithstanding the fact that it sets out the rights of EU citizens – as will be shown below, the right to move and reside in another Member State on the basis of EU citizenship can be an important mechanism to exercise minority rights that are not recognised in the home state or where the home state has failed to protect minority rights.

This legislation, while appearing at times when the enlargement of the EU was being planned for 2004, was fairly autonomous from it (with the exception of the Citizens' Rights Directive). In 2008 a proposal was made for a 'Horizontal Equal Treatment Directive' – a Council Directive on implementing the principle of equal treatment between persons irrespective of religion or belief, disability, age or sexual orientation outside the labour market.[7] At the time of writing this proposal, requiring unanimity in the Council and the consent of the European Parliament, was still pending in the Council. The next key development was the legal force given to the EU Charter of Fundamental Rights by the Lisbon Treaty in 2009, which is dealt with more in detail below.

The prohibition on nationality discrimination was never presented as an issue regarding minority rights. Indeed, until the prospect of enlargement of the EU to the Central and Eastern European countries appeared on the EU horizon, minority rights were considered a purely internal matter of each Member State and the diversity of approaches to be a matter of national cultural perspectives. The inclusion in the Amsterdam Treaty of a new provision prohibiting discrimination on a wider range of grounds – sex, racial or ethnic origin, religion or belief, disability, age or sexual orientation (Article 19 TFEU) – was an enormous innovation brought about by pressure from civil society and it launched the EU into a much wider range of activities regarding discrimination.

Non-discrimination is the first and traditional EU approach to minority protection

Article 3(3) TEU states that the aim of the Union includes combating social exclusion and discrimination, and promoting social justice and protection, equality between women and men, solidarity between generations and protection of the rights of the child. Article 10 TFEU states that the foundation of the EU is representative democracy and that every citizen is entitled to participate in the democratic life of the Union. The Charter of Fundamental Rights clarifies the right of equality first as one before the law (Article 20) and second as the right to non-discrimination on grounds of sex, race, colour, ethnic or social origin, genetic features, language, religion or belief, political or any other opinion, membership of a national minority, property, birth, disability, age or sexual orientation.[8]

75/35/EEC, 90/364/EEC, 90/365/EEC and 93/96/EEC (OJ L 158, 30.4.2004). (http://eurlex.europa.eu/legal-content/EN/TXT/?uri=celex:32004L0038R(01)).

7 European Commission, Proposal for a Council Directive on implementing the principle of equal treatment between persons irrespective of religion or belief, disability, age or sexual orientation, COM/2008/0426 final – CNS 2008/0140, Brussels, 2008.

8 S. Peers et al., eds., *The EU Charter of Fundamental Rights: A Commentary* (Bloomsbury Publishing 2014). See Chapter 21.

Following the logic of individual rights, the Racial Equality Directive, the Equal Treatment Directive and the Citizens' Rights Directive start from the position of the individual and his or her right to non-discrimination. This is also the case for the pre-Lisbon measure, the Framework Decision on racism and xenophobia,[9] which requires the Member States to criminalise public incitement of violence or hatred against a group of persons defined on the basis of race, colour, descent, religion or belief, or national or ethnic origin (including through dissemination of material and publicly condoning, denying or grossly trivialising crimes of genocide, crimes against humanity and war crimes). Once again, the logic is to identify and publish the individual for perpetrating the act of discrimination.

This logic results in individual rights – provisions of the Treaties that prohibit discrimination and secondary legislation, which gives effect to the principle. The adoption of this legislation then shifts the implementation of non-discrimination to national authorities to transpose the relevant EU obligations and to ensure their application. The end point of this approach is legal challenges by individuals or organisations claiming to be the victims of discrimination on prohibited grounds and ultimately the interpretation of EU law by the Court of Justice.

Thus, The EU legal system has added its own specific tools or layers of protection, chiefly embodied in the EU Charter of Fundamental Rights and a set of secondary legislation instruments on non-discrimination and on combatting racism and xenophobia. When implementing EU law, and as part of their broader activities as members of the EU complying with Article 2 TEU values, EU Member States must comply with these standards too.[10]

The second approach is that of minority rights

This framework tends towards the collective – often represented by struggles regarding cultural, religious and linguistic rights. The EU appears to have been less confident about this approach until 2009, when it was incorporated into EU law with the Charter of Fundamental Rights, in particular its Article 22 and its wide obligation of respect for cultural, religious and linguistic diversity. This legal step took place only a year before the so-called 'French Roma affair', which placed the (then) EU Commissioner at loggerheads with the (then) French president regarding the expulsion of Bulgarian and Romanian nationals from France in 2010, marking a turning point in the EU's engagement with this alternative approach.[11]

The minority rights approach can be derived from the EU Charter. Article 22 of the Charter requires the Union to respect cultural, religious and linguistic diversity. However, the key issue regarding this obligation of respect is the EU issue of

---

9 Framework Decision on combating certain forms and expressions of racism and xenophobia by means of criminal law OJ L 328, 6.12.2008.
10 A. Arnull, *The European Union and its Court of Justice* (Oxford European Union Law Library 2006) 364–366.
11 S. Carrera, *Shifting Responsibilities for EU Roma Citizens: The 2010 French Affair on Roma Evictions and Expulsions Continued* (CEPS 2013).

competence. Member States are free to reject a minority rights approach, which Article 22 supports so long as the area under consideration is outside the scope of EU law. Respect for cultural, religious and linguistic diversity only arises where the EU has competence, such as on consumer protection or working conditions, and where an issue of respect for cultural, religious or linguistic rights arises. Below is the recent case law of the CJEU considered on the respect for cultural and religious rights regarding working conditions (and its ECtHR counterpart).

(…)

While the spark that ignited a juridical approach to minority protection within the competence of the EU was in respect of one EU minority – Roma – its value for other minorities is key. Instead of focusing on the individual and his or her treatment by state (or private) actors as discriminatory vis-à-vis a control group (the majority, however defined) the entitlement of a minority to enjoy their group rights became an issue. Still, this minority rights approach has not been successfully transposed to claims regarding cultural and religious freedom in either the CJEU or the ECtHR regarding the issue of headscarves, niqabs and burqas – all elements of women's clothing related to cultural and religious minority status.

The adoption of an EU Framework for National Roma Integration Strategies, now in the form of national action plans on Roma integration, has been the main manifestation of the development of this complementary approach.[12] The Commission's report of 7 April 2010, "Roma in Europe: The implementation of the European instruments and policies for Roma inclusion – Progress report" is the first comprehensive attempt at using the second approach, that of minority rights.[13]

The Lisbon Treaty coming into force in 2009 brought new and important changes to the legal framework of minority rights. Article 2 TEU states for the first time that "respect for human rights including the rights of persons belonging to minorities" is a value on which "the Union is founded". The references to pluralism, non-discrimination and tolerance as values that must prevail reinforce the new direction.

The Lisbon Treaty has also been important for minority inclusion through the legal force provided to the EU Charter of Fundamental Rights. Article 21 of the EU Charter repeats the traditional prohibition on discrimination but includes as a prohibited ground membership of a national minority. Article 22 of the Charter extends protection at least in the form of respect for cultural, religious and linguistic diversity. The arrival of other group rights, such as social rights, in the field of EU 'hard' law has prepared the way for a reconsideration of how minority rights can be more than just 'soft' guidance, but also take enforceable legal form

---

12 Communication from the Commission to the European Parliament, the Council, the European Economic and Social Committee and the Committee of the Regions, An EU Framework for National Roma Integration Strategies up to 2020 COM(2011)173. (http://eur-lex.europa.eu/legalcontent/EN/TXT/?qid=1444910104414&uri=CELEX:52011DC0173).

13 European Commission. Communication on the social and economic integration of the Roma in Europe. COM/2010/0133 final, 2010. (http://eur-lex.europa.eu/legalcontent/EN/TXT/?qid=1444909812175&uri=CELEX:52010DC0133).

available to groups and individuals. These developments have been flanked by a very substantial change in direction in the ECtHR on minority rights as regards Roma in particular, which began to take shape in the mid-2000s.[14] The association of EU law through the EU Charter with the ECHR and its jurisprudence has made this development particularly important for the EU.

(...)

3.3 What is the added value of Union citizenship, freedom of movement and the EU Charter of Fundamental Rights to minority protection?

This subsection will focus on the added value of Union citizenship through free movement of persons and the Charter to minority protection. As can be seen from the analysis of EU legislation, the Charter and the jurisprudence of the CJEU and the ECtHR, the most substantial impact that they have had on minority rights has been in respect of one particular minority – Roma.

This section will first deal with Roma and then examine the added value of EU citizenship for cultural, religious and linguistic minorities. The EU Charter provides in Article 22 that the Union shall respect cultural, religious and linguistic diversity. The text of the explanatory note on Article 22 states that it is based on Article 6 TFEU, Article 151(1) and (4) EC Treaty now replaced by Article 167(1) and (4) TFEU and Article 3 TEU. It is also inspired by Declaration No. 11 of the Final Act of the Amsterdam Treaty, now taken over in Article 17 TFEU.

(...)

3.3.2 Religious minorities and focus on Muslims

The TFEU does not establish any specific competence of the EU in the field of religion other than as regards non-discrimination. However, Article 17 TFEU does require the EU to respect the status under national law of churches and religious, as well as philosophical and non-confessional organisations.[15] The EU's scope is limited to the status of religious organisations and associations under national law. Article 167(4) TFEU could require the EU to take into account the impact of EU law on religious diversity. The Article 13 TFEU obligation that the EU respect Member States' customs regarding religious rites, cultural traditions and regional heritage relates to animal welfare and national concerns about religious beliefs (see also Protocol 35 TFEU on abortion in Ireland).[16] Similarly, the Treaty basis for

---

14 H. O'Nions, *Minority rights protection in international law: The Roma of Europe* (Routledge 2016); F. Ippolito and S. Iglesias Sanchez (eds), *Protecting Vulnerable Groups: The European Human Rights Framework* (Bloomsbury Publishing 2015); B. Bowring, 'Case-Law of the European Court of Human Rights Concerning the Protection of Minorities, July 2012 to August 2014' [2015] European Yearbook of Minority Issues Online 197.
15 S. Peers et al., eds., *The EU Charter of Fundamental Rights: A Commentary*, cit.
16 Ibid.

respect of linguistic diversity has been characterised as 'thin' by academics.[17] It is a form of cultural expression (see also Article 22 of the Charter).

There are EU efforts in addressing hate crimes and hate speech against religious minorities, including Islamophobia and anti-Semitism. Nevertheless, the overall EU role on religious minority protection should be assessed critically. Recently, CJEU has considered two cases[18] of discrimination on the grounds of religion in the area of employment. Both cases related to female employees wearing hijabs who were fired after refusing to remove them. In the *Achbita v G4S Secure Solutions case*, the company had a neutrality rule. Thus, the Luxembourg court found that such a rule could constitute not direct, but rather indirect discrimination on the ground of religion, but it was proportionate to the company's image and freedom to run the business.[19] The judgement raises interesting questions about the balancing of individual rights with what is strictly necessary, as on the other hand people wearing comparable items simply for fashion would not be found in non-compliance with the neutrality rule, and hence not fired.

In the *Bougnaoui and ADDH v Micropole SA case*, on the other hand, the firm had no such policy and it was rather clients' wishes not to be served by a design engineer wearing an Islamic headscarf.[20] In the latter case, the Luxembourg court found a breach with the Equal Treatment Directive.[21]

A comparison between the CJEU and ECtHR reasoning in a similar case, *Eweida, and others v UK*,[22] finds a "lack of emphasis or weight which it places on the value of a diverse, tolerant and plural society and on the individual's right to manifest his or her religion"[23] Such CJEU case-law could have adverse impacts on highly visible religious minorities, such as Muslim women wearing headscarves or Sikh men wearing turbans in finding and keeping the employment.

(…)

4 Challenges and Promising Practices in Effective Minority Rights Protection in Selected Countries

(…)

4.1. What are the key challenges in compliance with minority protection and non-discrimination standards?

(…)

---

17 See for instance R. Crauford Smith in S. Peers et al., eds., *The EU Charter of Fundamental Rights: A Commentary*, cit.
18 European Court of Justice, *Bougnaoui and ADDH v Micropole SA*, Case C-188/15 Judgement of 14 March 2017 and *Achbita v G4S Secure Solutions*, Case C-157/15, Judgement of 14 March 2017.
19 *Achbita v G4S Secure Solutions*, Case C-157/15, Judgement of 14 March 2017.
20 *ADDH v Micropole SA*, Case C-188/15 Judgement of 14 March 2017.
21 Council Directive 2000/78/EC establishing a general framework for equal treatment in employment and occupation.
22 *Eweida, Chaplin & ors v UK*, Applications 48420/10, 59842/10, 51671/10 and 36516/10, Chamber decision 15 January 2013.
23 S. QC Jolly, ' "Achbita & Bougnaoui: A Strange Kind of Equality" Blog Article' 15 March 2017 <>www.cloisters.com/blogs/achbita-bougnaoui-a-strange-kind-of-equality>.

Religious minorities

The cross-country comparative review in the area of religious minorities (see Annex 3) highlights the intersectionality of minority protection grounds. In many of the countries under assessment it is difficult in practice to distinguish between discrimination based on grounds of race, ethnicity or national minority origin and discrimination based on religion, as antisemitism and Islamophobia often include aspects of both. In addition, the laws have traditionally favoured the 'majority religion'. Such national laws give rise to dilemmas about applicable tax law, burial rites and applications for building new places of worship, which may discriminate against religious minorities (see Annex 3). At the EU level, mainly civil society warns about the rise of reported Islamophobic incidents and hate crimes related to so-called 'refugee and security crises', for instance in the Brexit debate in the UK.[24] The phenomenon takes shape in "increasing anti-Muslim remarks in public discourse by far-right and even mainstream political leaders, and attacks on mosques throughout Europe".[25] Discrimination of Muslim women in employment is of particular concern as well as overly broad CJEU interpretation of 'religious neutrality' rules, forbidding the display of religious symbols.[26] The CJEU decisions, according to some focus group discussion participants, raised more questions than answered and created "a negative case law".

B Right to profess and practise religion or belief

B.1. COUNCIL OF THE EUROPEAN UNION, EU Guidelines on the promotion and protection of freedom of religion or belief, 24 June 2013.

I Introduction

A REASON FOR ACTION

1   The right to freedom of thought, conscience, religion or belief,[27] more commonly referred to as the right to freedom of religion or belief (FoRB) is a fundamental right of every human being. As a universal human right, freedom of religion or belief safeguards respect for diversity. Its free exercise directly contributes to democracy, development, rule of law, peace and stability. Violations of freedom of religion or belief may exacerbate intolerance and often constitute early indicators of potential violence and conflicts.

---

24 European Network Against Racism, 'Briefing, Islamophobia in Europe: Recent Developments' January 2017 <>www.enar-eu.org/IMG/pdf/islamophobia_data_2016.pdf>.
25 Ibid.
26 *Bougnaoui and ADDH v Micropole SA*, Case C-188/15 Judgement of 14 March 2017 and *Achbita v G4S Secure Solutions*, Case C-157/15, Judgement of 14 March 2017.
27 See article 18 of the UDHR and article 18 of the ICCPR.

2   All persons have the right to manifest their religion or belief either individually or in community with others and in public or private in worship, observance, practice and teaching, without fear of intimidation, discrimination, violence or attack. Persons who change or leave their religion or belief, as well as persons holding non-theistic or atheistic beliefs should be equally protected, as well as people who do not profess any religion or belief.
3   Violations or abuses of freedom of religion or belief, committed both by state and non-state actors, are widespread and complex and affect people in all parts of the world, including Europe.

B PURPOSE AND SCOPE

4   In promoting and protecting freedom of religion or belief, the EU is guided by the universality, indivisibility, inter-relatedness and interdependence of all human rights, whether civil, political, economic, social or cultural.
5   In line with universal and European human rights standards,[28] the EU and its member States are committed to respecting, protecting and promoting freedom of religion or belief within their borders.
6   With these Guidelines, the EU reaffirms its determination to promote, in its external human rights policy, freedom of religion or belief as a right to be exercised by everyone everywhere, based on the principles of equality, non-discrimination and universality. Through its external policy instruments, the EU intends to help prevent and address violations of this right in a timely, consistent and coherent manner.
7   In doing so, the EU focuses on the right of individuals, to believe or not to believe, and, alone or in community with others, to freely manifest their beliefs. The EU does not consider the merits of the different religions or beliefs, or the lack thereof, but ensures that the right to believe or not to believe is upheld. The EU is impartial and is not aligned with any specific religion or belief.
8   The Guidelines explain what the international human rights standards on freedom of religion or belief are and give clear political lines to officials of EU institutions and EU Member States, to be used in contacts with third countries and with international and civil society organisations. They also provide officials with practical guidance on how to seek to prevent violations of freedom of religion or belief, to analyse cases, and to react effectively to violations wherever they occur, in order to promote and protect freedom of religion or belief in the EU's external action.

---

28 In Europe, freedom of religion or belief is notably protected by Article 9 of the European Convention on Human Rights and Article 10 of the EU Charter of Fundamental Rights. See Annex for a non-exhaustive list of international norms and standards.

C DEFINITIONS

9 Freedom of religion or belief is enshrined in Articles 18 of both the Universal Declaration of Human Rights (UDHR) and of the International Covenant on Civil and Political Rights (ICCPR), which should be read in the light of the UN Human Rights Committee's General Comment n°22. Under international law, FoRB has two components:

(a) the freedom to have or not to have or adopt (which includes the right to change) a religion or belief of one's choice, and
(b) the freedom to manifest one's religion or belief, individually or in community with others, in public or private, through worship, observance, practice and teaching.

10 In line with these provisions, the EU has recalled that "freedom of thought, conscience, religion or belief, applies equally to all persons. It is a fundamental freedom that includes all religions or beliefs, including those that have not been traditionally practised in a particular country, the beliefs of persons belonging to religious minorities, as well as non-theistic and atheistic beliefs. The freedom also covers the right to adopt, change or abandon one's religion or belief, of one's own free will".[29]

Right to have a religion, to hold a belief, or not to believe

11 Theistic, non-theistic and atheistic beliefs, as well as the right not to profess any religion or belief are protected under article 18 ICCPR.[30] The terms "belief" and "religion" are to be broadly construed and the article's application should not be limited to traditional religions or to religions and beliefs with institutional characteristics or practices analogous to those of traditional religions. States should not restrict the freedom to hold any religion or belief. Coercion to change, recant or reveal one's religion or belief is equally prohibited.
12 Holding or not holding a religion or belief is an absolute right and may not be limited under any circumstances.[31]

Right to manifest one's religion or belief

13 Article 18 of the ICCPR recognises the right of people to "manifest" their religion or belief, alone or in community with others, both publicly and privately. This freedom to manifest religion or belief e.g. in worship, observance, practice and teaching, potentially "encompasses a broad range of

---

29 Council Conclusions on Freedom of religion or belief, 16 November 2009.
30 See General Comment n°22.
31 Not even in time of public emergency – see article 4.2 of the ICCPR.

acts",[32] whose close and direct link with a religion or belief must be looked at on a case-by case basis.

14   As opposed to the freedom to have a religion, to hold a belief or not to believe, the freedom to manifest one's religion or belief may be subject to limitations, but "only to such limitations as are prescribed by law and are necessary to protect public safety, order, health or morals or the fundamental rights and freedoms of others".[33] These limitations must be in accordance with international standards and must be strictly interpreted. Limitations for other reasons, such as national security, are not permitted. Based on article 18.3 of the ICCPR and as developed in General Comment 22, any limitations must meet with the following criteria: they must be established by law, not applied in a way that vitiate the rights guaranteed in article 18, only applied for those purposes for which they were prescribed, directly related and proportionate to the specific need for which they were designed, and not imposed for discriminatory purposes or applied in a discriminatory manner. Where restrictions are justified on the basis of a need to protect public morals, such restrictions must be based on principles not deriving exclusively from a single tradition, as the concept of morals derives from many social, philosophical and religious traditions. Furthermore, any such limitations must be understood in the light of universality of human rights and the principle of non-discrimination.[34]

II   Operational guidelines

(...)

4   *Connection with the defence of other human rights and with other EU guidelines on human rights*

25. Freedom of religion or belief is intrinsically linked to freedom of opinion and expression, freedom of association and assembly as well as to other human rights and fundamental freedoms all of which contribute towards the building of pluralistic, tolerant, and democratic societies. Expression of a religious or non-religious belief, or of an opinion concerning a religion or belief, is also protected by the right to freedom of opinion and expression enshrined in Article 19 of the ICCPR.

26. Certain practices associated with the manifestation of a religion or belief, or perceived as such, may constitute violations of international human rights standards. The right to freedom of religion or belief is sometimes invoked to justify

---

32   See indicative examples of paragraph 4 of the General Comment n°22.
33   See art 18.3 ICCPR.
34   See General Comment n°34.

such violations. The EU firmly opposes such justification, whilst remaining fully committed to the robust protection and promotion of freedom of religion or belief in all parts of the world. Violations often affect women, members of religious minorities, as well as persons on the basis of their sexual orientation or gender identity.

27. In dealing with possible violations, use will be made of existing EU human rights guidelines, notably the guidelines on the promotion and protection of rights of the child, on violence against woman and girls and combating all forms of discrimination against them, on human rights defenders, on torture and on the death penalty, as well as the forthcoming EU guidelines on the enjoyment of all human rights by LGBTI persons, and on freedom of expression on line and off line.

B Priority areas of action

(...)

2 Freedom of expression

31. Freedom of religion or belief and the freedom of expression are interdependent, interrelated and mutually reinforcing rights, protecting all persons – not religions or beliefs in themselves – and protecting also the right to express opinions on any or all religions and beliefs. Censorship and restrictions on the publication and distribution of literature or of websites related to religion or belief are common violations of both of these freedoms, and impair the ability of individuals and communities to practice their religion or belief. Limitations to the right to express opinions on religion or belief are a source of great vulnerability for people belonging to religion or belief minorities, but also affect majorities, not least persons holding non-traditional religious views. Taken together, freedom of religion or belief and freedom of expression play an important role in the fight against all forms of intolerance and discrimination based on religion or belief.

32. In the event that violence is threatened or carried out, or restrictions are imposed in connection with an expression of opinions on religion or belief, the EU will be guided by the following principles:

a   When critical comments are expressed about religions or beliefs and such expression is perceived by adherents as being so offensive that it may result in violence towards or by adherents, then:

    o   If there is a prima facie case that this expression constitutes hate speech, i.e. falls within the strict scope of article 20 paragraph 2 of the ICCPR (which prohibits any advocacy of religious hatred that constitutes incitement to discrimination, hostility or violence), the EU will denounce it, and demand that it be investigated and tried by an independent judge.

- o If this expression does not rise to the level of incitement prohibited under article 20 of the ICCPR, and is thus an exercise of free speech, the EU will:
    - i. Resist any calls or attempts for the criminalisation of such speech;
    - ii. Individually or jointly with States or regional organisations, endeavour to issue statements calling for no violence to be committed and condemning any violence committed in reaction to such speech;
    - iii. Encourage state and other influential actors, whether religious or non-religious, to speak out and to engage in constructive public debate concerning what they see as offensive speech, condemning any form of violence;
    - iv. Recall that the most effective way to combat a perceived offense from the exercise of freedom of expression is the use of freedom of expression itself. Freedom of expression applies online as well as offline.[35] New forms of media as well as information and communications technology provide those who feel offended by criticism or rejection of their religion or belief with the tools to instantly exercise their right of reply.
- o In any case, the EU will recall, when appropriate, that the right to freedom of religion or belief, as enshrined in relevant international standards, does not include the right to have a religion or a belief that is free from criticism or ridicule.[36]

b When faced with restrictions to freedom of expression in the name of religion or belief, the EU will:
- o Recall that restrictions to freedom of expression shall only be such as are prescribed by law and are necessary to safeguard the rights or reputation of others, or for the protection of national security or of public order (ordre public) or of public health or morals,[37] and that no national security restriction is permissible for freedom of religion and belief.[38]
- o Defend the fact that sharing information about religions or beliefs and engaging in persuasion on these matters is protected under international law, provided that such persuasion is neither coercive nor impairs the freedom of others.
- o Recall at all appropriate occasions that laws that criminalize blasphemy restrict expression concerning religious or other beliefs; that they are often applied so as to persecute, mistreat, or intimidate persons belonging to religious or other minorities, and that they can have a serious inhibiting effect on freedom of expression and on freedom of religion or belief; and recommend the decriminalisation of such offences.
- o Forcefully advocate against the use of the death penalty, physical punishment, or deprivation of liberty as penalties for blasphemy.

---

35 See UN Human Rights Council resolution 20/8.
36 See paragraph 19 of the conclusions of the Rabat Plan of Action on incitement to hatred, 5 October 2012.
37 Article 19.3 ICCPR.
38 Article 18.3 ICCPR. See also General Comments No. 22 and 34.

o   Recall that international human rights law protects individuals, not Religion or Belief per se. Protecting a religion or belief may not be used to justify or condone a restriction or violation of a human right exercised by individuals alone or in community with others.

(...)

6 Manifestation of religion or belief

40. Individuals, have the right to decide for themselves whether and how they wish to manifest their religion or belief. Limitations to this freedom have to be strictly interpreted.[39] Manifestation of one's religion or belief can take many forms. This includes the right of children to learn about the faith/belief of their parents, and the right of parents to teach their children in the tenets of their religion or belief. It also includes the right to peacefully share one's religion or belief with others, without being subject to the approval of the state or another religious community. Any limitation on freedom of religion or belief, including regarding places of worship and state registration of religious or belief groups, must be exceptional and in compliance with international standards.

41. Frequent restrictions by States include the denial of legal personality to religious and belief communities, the denial of access to places of worship/meeting and burial, the punishment of unregistered religious activity with exorbitant fines or prison terms, or the requirement for children from religious and belief minorities to receive confessional education in the beliefs of the majority. Several states do not recognize the right to conscientious objection to military service as part of the legitimate exercise of the freedom of religion or belief, deriving from article 18 of the ICCPR.[40] Abuses by non-state actors include the destruction of places of worship, the desecration of burial grounds, forced observance of religious norms and acts of violence.

Section 2

Charter of Fundamental Rights of the European Union

Article 18

Right to asylum

The right to asylum shall be guaranteed with due respect for the rules of the Geneva Convention of 28 July 1951 and the Protocol of 31 January 1967 relating to the status of refugees and in accordance with the Treaty establishing the European Community.

---

39 See developments on limitations in the "Definitions" chapter of these guidelines.
40 See General Comment No. 22.

Treaty on the functioning of the European Union

> [*Treaty of Lisbon amending the Treaty on European Union and the Treaty establishing the European Community, signed at Lisbon, 13 December 2007*]
>
> (...)

Title V

Area of freedom, security and justice

Chapter 1

General provisions

Article 67

1. The Union shall constitute an area of freedom, security and justice with respect for fundamental rights and the different legal systems and traditions of the Member States.
2. It shall ensure the absence of internal border controls for persons and shall frame a common policy on asylum, immigration and external border control, based on solidarity between Member States, which is fair towards third-country nationals. For the purpose of this Title, stateless persons shall be treated as third-country nationals.

Chapter 2

Policies on border checks, asylum and immigration

Article 77

1. The Union shall develop a policy with a view to:
   (a) ensuring the absence of any controls on persons, whatever their nationality, when crossing internal borders;
   (b) carrying out checks on persons and efficient monitoring of the crossing of external borders;
   (c) the gradual introduction of an integrated management system for external borders.
2. For the purposes of paragraph 1, the European Parliament and the Council, acting in accordance with the ordinary legislative procedure, shall adopt measures concerning:
   (a) the common policy on visas and other short-stay residence permits;
   (b) the checks to which persons crossing external borders are subject;

(c) the conditions under which nationals of third countries shall have the freedom to travel within the Union for a short period;
(d) any measure necessary for the gradual establishment of an integrated management system for external borders;
(e) the absence of any controls on persons, whatever their nationality, when crossing internal borders.

3 If action by the Union should prove necessary to facilitate the exercise of the right referred to in Article 20(2)(a), and if the Treaties have not provided the necessary powers, the Council, acting in accordance with a special legislative procedure, may adopt provisions concerning passports, identity cards, residence permits or any other such document. The Council shall act unanimously after consulting the European Parliament.

4 This Article shall not affect the competence of the Member States concerning the geographical demarcation of their borders, in accordance with international law.

Article 78

1 The Union shall develop a common policy on asylum, subsidiary protection and temporary protection with a view to offering appropriate status to any third-country national requiring international protection and ensuring compliance with the principle of non-refoulement. This policy must be in accordance with the Geneva Convention of 28 July 1951 and the Protocol of 31 January 1967 relating to the status of refugees, and other relevant treaties.

2 For the purposes of paragraph 1, the European Parliament and the Council, acting in accordance with the ordinary legislative procedure, shall adopt measures for a common European asylum system comprising:

(a) a uniform status of asylum for nationals of third countries, valid throughout the Union;
(b) a uniform status of subsidiary protection for nationals of third countries who, without obtaining European asylum, are in need of international protection;
(c) a common system of temporary protection for displaced persons in the event of a massive inflow;
(d) common procedures for the granting and withdrawing of uniform asylum or subsidiary protection status;
(e) criteria and mechanisms for determining which Member State is responsible for considering an application for asylum or subsidiary protection;
(f) standards concerning the conditions for the reception of applicants for asylum or subsidiary protection;
(g) partnership and cooperation with third countries for the purpose of managing inflows of people applying for asylum or subsidiary or temporary protection.

3   In the event of one or more Member States being confronted by an emergency situation characterised by a sudden inflow of nationals of third countries, the Council, on a proposal from the Commission, may adopt provisional measures for the benefit of the Member State(s) concerned. It shall act after consulting the European Parliament.

Article 79

1   The Union shall develop a common immigration policy aimed at ensuring, at all stages, the efficient management of migration flows, fair treatment of third-country nationals residing legally in Member States, and the prevention of, and enhanced measures to combat, illegal immigration and trafficking in human beings.
2   For the purposes of paragraph 1, the European Parliament and the Council, acting in accordance with the ordinary legislative procedure, shall adopt measures in the following areas:

   (a) the conditions of entry and residence, and standards on the issue by Member States of long-term visas and residence permits, including those for the purpose of family reunification;
   (b) the definition of the rights of third-country nationals residing legally in a Member State, including the conditions governing freedom of movement and of residence in other Member States;
   (c) illegal immigration and unauthorised residence, including removal and repatriation of persons residing without authorisation;
   (d) combating trafficking in persons, in particular women and children.

3   The Union may conclude agreements with third countries for the readmission to their countries of origin or provenance of third-country nationals who do not or who no longer fulfil the conditions for entry, presence or residence in the territory of one of the Member States.
4   The European Parliament and the Council, acting in accordance with the ordinary legislative procedure, may establish measures to provide incentives and support for the action of Member States with a view to promoting the integration of third-country nationals residing legally in their territories, excluding any harmonisation of the laws and regulations of the Member States.
5   This Article shall not affect the right of Member States to determine volumes of admission of third-country nationals coming from third countries to their territory in order to seek work, whether employed or self-employed.

Article 80

The policies of the Union set out in this Chapter and their implementation shall be governed by the principle of solidarity and fair sharing of responsibility, including its financial implications, between the Member States. Whenever necessary, the Union acts adopted pursuant to this Chapter shall contain appropriate measures to give effect to this principle.

Directive 2011/95/EU of the European Parliament and of the Council on standards for the qualification of third-country nationals or stateless persons as beneficiaries of international protection, for a uniform status for refugees or for persons eligible for subsidiary protection, and for the content of the protection granted (recast), 13 December 2011

Chapter I

General provisions

Article 2

Definitions

For the purposes of this Directive the following definitions shall apply:
(...)

(d) 'refugee' means a third-country national who, owing to a well-founded fear of being persecuted for reasons of race, religion, nationality, political opinion or membership of a particular social group, is outside the country of nationality and is unable or, owing to such fear, is unwilling to avail himself or herself of the protection of that country, or a stateless person, who, being outside of the country of former habitual residence for the same reasons as mentioned above, is unable or, owing to such fear, unwilling to return to it, and to whom Article 12 does not apply;

Article 10

Reasons for persecution

1   Member States shall take the following elements into account when assessing the reasons for persecution:
(...)
   (b) the concept of religion shall in particular include the holding of theistic, non-theistic and atheistic beliefs, the participation in, or abstention from, formal worship in private or in public, either alone or in community with others, other religious acts or expressions of view, or forms of personal or communal conduct based on or mandated by any religious belief;
   (...)
   (d) a group shall be considered to form a particular social group where in particular: – members of that group share an innate characteristic, or a common background that cannot be changed, or share a characteristic or belief that is so fundamental to identity or conscience that a person should not be forced to renounce it, and – that group has a distinct

identity in the relevant country, because it is perceived as being different by the surrounding society.

Depending on the circumstances in the country of origin, a particular social group might include a group based on a common characteristic of sexual orientation. Sexual orientation cannot be understood to include acts considered to be criminal in accordance with national law of the Member States. Gender related aspects, including gender identity, shall be given due consideration for the purposes of determining membership of a particular social group or identifying a characteristic of such a group;

> (e) the concept of political opinion shall, in particular, include the holding of an opinion, thought or belief on a matter related to the potential actors of persecution mentioned in Article 6 and to their policies or methods, whether or not that opinion, thought or belief has been acted upon by the applicant.

A Right to Asylum

A.1. EUROPEAN ASYLUM SUPPORT OFFICE (EASO), country guidance Afghanistan, *June 2019*.

(...)

> 2.17. Ethnic and religious minorities

In the context of Afghanistan, ethnicity and religion are often interlinked. This chapter focuses on some ethnic and/or religious minorities:

> 2.17.1. Individuals of Hazara ethnicity
> 2.17.2. Shia, including Ismaili
> 2.17.3. Hindus and Sikhs
> 2.17.4 Baha'i
> 2.17.1. Individuals of Hazara ethnicity

Common analysis

This profile includes people who belong to the Hazara ethnicity. Mostly, persons of Hazara ethnicity are of Shia religion and the two profiles should be read in conjunction.

The majority of the Hazara population inhabits the Hazarajat. Hazara are also well represented in most cities, including Kabul.

The Hazara ethnicity can usually be recognised by their physical appearance.

COI summary

Since the fall of the Taliban regime, the Hazara have improved their position in society and the Afghan Constitution includes the Hazara as one of the people that comprise the nation of Afghanistan [Conflict targeting, 1.2.10.1]. There is no information of mistreatment by the State [Conflict targeting, 2.5].

Attacks by insurgent groups, in particular by ISKP, have significantly affected the Hazara population in 2018. Attacks by ISKP targeted places where Hazara/Shia gather, such as religious commemorations or political demonstrations, and sites in Hazara-dominated neighbourhoods in large cities, including Kabul and Herat. Such attacks could be related to their religion (see the profile on Shia). Among other reasons, the ISKP also reportedly targets the Hazara due to their perceived closeness and support for Iran and the fight against the Islamic State in Syria [Conflict targeting, 1.2.10.3; Security situation 2019, 1.2.2, 2.1, 2.13].

There are instances of Hazara civilians being abducted or killed while travelling along the roads. In reported incidents where Hazara road passengers were singled out and killed or abducted, other reasons could often be identified, such as non-political communal disputes or the individual being an ANSF member, having a job in the government or the NGO sector, etc., linking these incidents to other profiles [Conflict targeting, 1.2.10.2].

Risk analysis

The acts to which individuals under this profile could be exposed are of such severe nature that they would amount to persecution (e.g. killing, abduction, sectarian attacks).

Being a Hazara in itself would normally not lead to the level of risk required to establish well-founded fear of persecution. In most cases where a well-founded fear of persecution is substantiated, it would be related to circumstances falling under other profiles included in this guidance, such as the profiles on Shia, including Ismaili, Members of the security forces and pro-government militias, Government officials, including judges, prosecutors and judicial staff; and those perceived as supporting the government, etc. The individual assessment should also take into account risk-impacting circumstances, such as the area of origin and area of work (depending on the actor of persecution), profession, political activism, etc.

Nexus to a reason for persecution

Available information indicates that persecution of this profile may be for reasons of (imputed) religion (see profile on Shia), (imputed) political opinion (e.g. links to the government, perceived support for Iran), and/or race (ethnicity).

2.17.2. *Shia, including Ismaili*

Common analysis

This profile includes people who belong to the Shia religion. In Afghanistan, 10 to 15 % of the population are Shia Muslim. The majority of these Shia ethnic Hazara and the two profiles should be read in conjunction.

COI summary

The Shia community is disproportionately represented among civilian casualties in Kabul and Herat. There are reports of attacks against the Shia, especially on places where Shia gather, such as mosques, and during religious commemorations and political demonstrations [Conflict targeting, 1.2.10.2].

In 2018, the majority of ISKP attacks on religious sites reportedly targeted Shia communities. The territorial control of the ISKP is limited, however they have been able to carry out attacks in different parts of the country [Security situation 2019, 1.2.2, 2.1, 2.13; Conflict targeting, 1.2.10.3, 1.5.1.1].

Instances of discrimination against the Shia community are reported [Conflict targeting, 1.2.10.2, 2.5].

Risk analysis

The acts to which individuals under this profile could be exposed are of such severe nature that they would amount to persecution (e.g. sectarian attacks). When the acts in question are (solely) discriminatory measures, the individual assessment of whether or not discrimination could amount to persecution should take into account the severity and/or repetitiveness of the acts or whether they occur as an accumulation of various measures.

Not all individuals under this profile would face the level of risk required to establish well-founded fear of persecution. The individual assessment of whether or not there is a reasonable degree of likelihood for the applicant to face persecution should take into account risk-impacting circumstances, such as: area of origin (areas where ISKP has operational presence), participation in religious practices, political activism, etc.

Nexus to a reason for persecution

Available information indicates that persecution of this profile is for reasons of religion.

Chronological index of institutional documents and judgements

(Numbers in black refer to chapters and sections. Numbers in brackets indicate pages. Letters in italics indicate the right of reference. Letters with rounded font numbers identify the individual legal materials.)

1979 FRANCESCO CAPOTORTI (Special Rapporteur of the Sub-Commission on Prevention of Discrimination and Protection of Minorities), *Study on the Rights of Persons Belonging to Ethnic, Religious and Linguistic Minorities* (ST/HR(05)/H852/no.5), 1979, **I, 1**, (32), *a*, (59), *b*, (92), *c*, (105), *e*, a.1, b.1, c.1, e.1.

1985 JULES DESCHÊNES (Special Rapporteur of the Sub-Commission on Prevention of Discrimination and Protection of Minorities), *Proposal concerning a definition of the term "minority"* (E/CN.4/Sub.2/1985/31), 1985, **I, 1**, (41), *a*, a.2.

1993 UN HUMAN RIGHTS COMMITTEE (HRC), *CCPR General Comment No. 22: Article 18 (Freedom of Thought, Conscience or Religion)* (CCPR/C/21/Rev.1/Add.4), 30 July 1993, **I, 1**, (69), *b*, (94), *c*, b.2, c.2.

1994 UN HUMAN RIGHTS COMMITTEE (HRC), *CCPR General Comment No. 23: Article 27 (Rights of Minorities)* (CCPR/C/21/Rev.1/Add.5), 8 April 1994, **I, 1**, (52), *a*, (70), *b*, (95), *c*, (104), *d*, a.3., b.3, c.3, d.1.

1996 OSCE HIGH COMMISSIONER ON NATIONAL MINORITIES (HCNM), *The Hague Recommendations regarding the Education Rights of National Minorities & Explanatory Note*, October 1996, **III, 1**, (202), *d*, d.1.

2000 EUROPEAN COURTS OF HUMAN RIGHTS, Case of *Serif c. Greece* (Application no. 38.178/97), 14 March 2000, **II, 1**, (162), *a*, a.1.

2001 UN HUMAN RIGHTS COMMITTEE (HRC), *Sister Immaculate Joseph and 80 Teaching Sisters of the Holy Cross of the Third Order of Saint Francis in Menzingen of Sri Lanka v. Sri Lanka* (CCPR/C/85/D/1249/2004), Communication No. 1249/2004, 4 April 2001, **I, 1**, (74), *b*, b.4.

2002 UN REFUGEE AGENCY (UNHCR), *Guidelines on International Protection: "Membership of a particular social group" within the context of Article 1A(2) of the 1951 Convention and/or its 1967 Protocol relating to the Status of Refugees* (HCR/GIP/02/02), 7 May 2002, **I, 2**, (115), *a*, a.1.

2004 UN REFUGEE AGENCY (UNHCR), *Guidelines on International Protection: Religion-Based Refugee Claims under Article 1A(2) of the 1951 Convention and/or the 1967 Protocol relating to the Status of Refugees* (HCR/GIP/04/06), 28 April 2004, I, 2, (117), *a*, a.2.

2005 UN COMMISSION ON HUMAN RIGHTS, SUB-COMMISSION ON THE PROMOTION AND PROTECTION OF HUMAN RIGHTS, *Commentary of the Working Group on Minorities to the United Nations Declaration on the rights of persons belonging to national or ethnic, religious and linguistic minorities* (E/CN.4/Sub.2/AC.5/2005/2), 4 April 2005, I, 5, (134), *a*, (137), *b*, (138), *c*, (140), *d*, (153), *e*, a.1., b.1, c.1, d.1, e.1.

2007 UN HUMAN RIGHTS COMMITTEE, *Gareth Anver Prince v. South Africa* (CCPR/C/91/D/1474/2006), Communication No. 1474/2006, 14 November 2007, I, 1, (82), *b*, b.5.

OSCE-ODIHR, ADVISORY COUNCIL OF EXPERTS ON FREEDOM OF RELIGION OR BELIEF, *Toledo Guiding Principles on Teaching about Religions and Beliefs in Public Schools*, 2007, III, 1, (206), *d*, d.2.

COMMITTEE ON THE ELIMINATION OF DISCRIMINATION AGAINST WOMEN (CEDAW), *Concluding Comments of the Committee on the Elimination of Discrimination Against Women: Greece* (CEDAW/C/GRC/CO/6), 2007, I, 3, (122), *a*, a.1.

2009 UN HUMAN RIGHTS COUNCIL (HRC), *Recommendations of the second session of the Forum on Minority Issues on minorities and effective political participation* (A/HRC/13/25), 12 and 13 November 2009, I, 5, (143), *d*, d.2.

2010 UN OFFICE OF THE HIGH COMMISSIONER FOR HUMAN RIGHTS (OHCHR), *Minority Rights: International Standards and Guidance for Implementation* (HR/PUB/10/3), 2010, I, 1, (53), *a*, (100), *c*, a.4, c.5; I, 5, (136), *a*, (150), *d*, (153), *e*, a.2, d.3, e.2.

UN HUMAN RIGHTS COMMITTEE (HRC), *Fatima Anderson v. Denmark* (CCPR/C/99/D/1868/2009), Communication n. 1868/2009, 7 September 2010, I, 1, (96), *c*, c.4.

2012 UN OFFICE OF THE HIGH COMMISSIONER FOR HUMAN RIGHTS (OHCHR), *Promoting and Protecting Minority Rights. A Guide for Advocates* (HR/PUB/12/7), 2012, I, 4, (126), *a*, a.1; I, 5, (154), *f*, f.1.

OFFICE OF THE OSCE HIGH COMMISSIONER ON NATIONAL MINORITIES, *The Ljubljana Guidelines on Integration of Diverse Societies*, 7 November 2012, III, 1, (196), *a*, (207), *e*, a.1, e.1.

2013 UN SECRETARY GENERAL, *Guidance note of the Secretary General on racial discrimination and protection of minorities*, March 2013, I, 5, (156), f, f.3.

COUNCIL OF THE EUROPEAN UNION, *EU Guidelines on the Promotion and Protection of Freedom of Religion or Belief*, 24 June 2013, IV, 1, (232), *b*, b.1.

SPECIAL RAPPORTEUR ON FREEDOM OF RELIGION OR BELIEF – INDEPENDENT EXPERT ON MINORITY ISSUES – SPECIAL RAPPORTEUR ON THE SALE OF CHILDREN, CHILD PROSTITUTION AND CHILD

PORNOGRAPHY – SPECIAL RAPPORTEUR ON TRAFFICKING IN PERSONS, ESPECIALLY WOMEN AND CHILDREN – CHAIR-RAPPORTEUR OF THE WORKING GROUP ON THE ISSUE OF DISCRIMINATION AGAINST WOMEN IN LAW AND IN PRACTICE – SPECIAL RAPPORTEUR ON VIOLENCE AGAINST WOMEN, ITS CAUSES AND CONSEQUENCES, *Special procedures of the Human Rights Council, Communication 29 May 2013 – Iraq* (IRQ 2/2013), I, 4, (127), *b*, b.1.

FORUM ON MINORITY ISSUES, *Note by the Independent Expert on minority issues, Rita Izsák, on guaranteeing the rights of religious minorities* (A/HRC/FMI/2013/2), 3 October 2013, I, 5, (136), (156), a, f, a.3., f.2.

FORUM ON MINORITY ISSUES, *Recommendations of the Forum on Minority Issues at its sixth session: Guaranteeing the Rights of Religious Minorities* (A/HRC/25/66), 26 and 27 November 2013, I, 1, (57), *a*, a.5.

2014 UN OFFICE OF THE HIGH COMMISSIONER FOR HUMAN RIGHTS (OHCHR), *The inclusion of religious minorities in consultative and decision-making bodies*, 2014, I, 1, (57), *a*, a.6.; I, 5, (151), *d*, d.4.

OSCE OFFICE FOR DEMOCRATIC INSTITUTIONS AND HUMAN RIGHTS (ODIHR), *Guidelines on the Legal Personality of Religious or Belief Communities*, 2014, III, 1, (197), *b*, (201), *c*, b.1., c.1.

2016 ADVISORY COMMITTEE ON THE FRAMEWORK CONVENTION FOR THE PROTECTION OF NATIONAL MINORITIES, *Compilation of Opinions of the Advisory Committee relating to Article 8 of the Framework Convention for the Protection of National Minorities (3rd cycle)*, 13 May 2016, II, 2, (189), *a*, (191), *b*, a.1, b.1.

2017 EUROPEAN PARLIAMENT'S COMMITTEE ON CIVIL LIBERTIES, JUSTICE AND HOME AFFAIRS, *Towards a comprehensive EU protection system for minorities*, August 2017, IV, 1, (225), *a*, a.1.

ADVISORY COMMITTEE ON THE FRAMEWORK CONVENTION FOR THE PROTECTION OF NATIONAL MINORITIES, *Compilation of Opinions of the Advisory Committee relating to Article 8 of the Framework Convention for the Protection of National Minorities (4th cycle)*, 18 September 2017, II, 1, (193), *c*, c.1.

OSCE HIGH COMMISSIONER ON NATIONAL MINORITIES, *The Graz Recommendations on Access to Justice and National Minorities*, November 2017, III, 1, (209), *f*, f.1.

2018 EUROPEAN COURTS OF HUMAN RIGHTS, GC, Case of *Molla Sali c. Greece* (Application no. 20.452/14), 19 December 2018, II, 1, (173), *b*, b.1.

2019 FERNAND DE VARENNES (Special Rapporteur on Minority Issues), *Report of the Special Rapporteur on Minority Issues* (A/74/160), 15 July 2019, I, 1, (57), *a*, a.7.

OFFICE OF THE OSCE HIGH COMMISSIONER ON NATIONAL MINORITIES, *The Tallinn Guidelines on National Minorities and the Media in the Digital Age & Explanatory Note*, February 2019, III, 1, (213), *g*, g.1.

EUROPEAN ASYLUM SUPPORT OFFICE (EASO), *Country Guidance Afghanistan*, June 2019, **IV**, **2**, (244), *a*, a.1.

2020 UN HUMAN RIGHTS COUNCIL (HRC), *Freedom of religion or belief. Report of the Special Rapporteur on freedom of religion or belief* (A/HRC/43/48), 27 February 2020, **I**, **3**, (123), *a*, a.2.

FERNAND DE VARENNES (Special Rapporteur on Minority Issues), *Report of the Special Rapporteur on Minority Issues, Effective promotion of the Declaration on the Rights of Persons Belonging to National or Ethnic, Religious and Linguistic Minorities* (A/75/211), 21 July 2020, **I**, **1**, (58), *a*, a.8.

Chronological index of legal sources

(Numbers in black refer to chapters and sections. Numbers in brackets indicate pages. Clear numbers refer to articles of legal sources contained in this code. When the code refers to the legal text in full, no reference to the articles is included.)

1950 European Convention on Human Rights, [*Signed at Rome on 4th November 1950*], II, 1, (161), 9–10–14.
1952 Protocols 1. Enforcement of certain Rights and Freedoms not included in Section I of the Convention, [*Paris 20th March 1952*], II, 1, (162), 1.
1951 Convention relating to the Status of Refugees [*Adopted by the United Nations Conference of Plenipotentiaries on the Status of Refugees and Stateless Persons, held at Geneva from 2 to 25 July 1951*], I, 2, (109), 1–3–4.
1966 Protocol Relating to the Status of Refugees, [*Protocol was taken note of with approval by the Economic and Social Council in resolution 1186 (XLI) of 18 November 1966 and was taken note of by the General Assembly in resolution 2198 (XXI) of 16 December 1966. In the same resolution the General Assembly requested the Secretary-General to transmit the text of the Protocol to the States mentioned in article V thereof, with a view to enabling them to accede to the Protocol. Entry into force 4 October 1967, in accordance with article VIII*], I, 2, (112).

International Covenant on Civil and Political Rights, [*Adopted and opened for signature, ratification and accession by General Assembly resolution 2200A (XXI) of 16 December 1966 – entry into force 23 March 1976, in accordance with Article 49*], I, 1, (27), 4-18-20-24-26-27.

Optional Protocol to the International Covenant on Civil and Political Rights, [*Adopted and opened for signature, ratification and accession by General Assembly resolution 2200A (XXI) of 16 December 1966 entry into force 23 March 1976, in accordance with Article 9*], I, 1, (29).
1979 Convention on the Elimination of All Forms of Discrimination against Women, [*Adopted by United Nations General Assembly in 18 December 1979*], I, 3, (121), 1–2–3.
1989 Convention on the Rights of the Child, [*Adopted and opened for signature, ratification and accession by General Assembly resolution 44/25 of*

20 November 1989 entry into force 2 September 1990, in accordance with article 49], **I, 4,** (125), 30-32-34.

1992 Declaration on the Rights of Persons Belonging to National or Ethnic, Religious and Linguistic Minorities, [*Adopted by General Assembly resolution 47/135 of 18 December 1992*], **I, 5,** (131), 1-2-3-4-5-6-7-8-9.

Conference for Security and Co-operation in Europe, Helsinki Decisions, 10 July 1992, **III, 1,** (195), par. 23.

1994 Conference on Security and Co-operation in Europe, Budapest Summit Declaration, 21 December 1994, **III, 1,** (195), par. 2-21-22.

1998 Framework Convention for the Protection of National Minorities, [*Adopted by the Committee of Ministers of the Council of Europe on 10 November 1994 and entered into force on 1 February 1998*], **II, 2,** (188), 5-6-7-8-12-17.

2000 Charter of Fundamental Rights of the European Union, [*The text of the Charter has been solemnly proclaimed on 7 December 2000 and re-proclaimed in 12 December 2007 in sight of the signature of Treaty of Lisbon*], **IV, 1,** (223), **2,** (239), 21-22-18.

2007 Treaty on European Union, [*Treaty of Lisbon amending the Treaty on European Union and the Treaty establishing the European Community, signed at Lisbon, 13 December 2007*], **IV, 1,** (224), 2-49.

Treaty on the functioning of the European Union, [*Treaty of Lisbon amending the Treaty on European Union and the Treaty establishing the European Community, signed at Lisbon, 13 December 2007*], **IV, 1,** (224), **2,** (240), 10-17-19, 67, 77, 78, 79, 80.

2011 Directive 2011/95/EU [*of the European Parliament and of the Council on standards for the qualification of third-country nationals or stateless persons as beneficiaries of international protection, for a uniform status for refugees or for persons eligible for subsidiary protection, and for the content of the protection granted (recast), 13 December 2011*], **IV, 2,** (243), 2-10.

Index of rights and principles

(Numbers in black refer to chapters and sections. Numbers in brackets indicate pages. Letters in italics indicate the right of reference. Letters with rounded font numbers identify the individual legal materials.)

Principle of non-discrimination

FRANCESCO CAPOTORTI (Special Rapporteur of the Sub-Commission on Prevention of Discrimination and Protection of Minorities), *Study on the Rights of Persons Belonging to Ethnic, Religious and Linguistic Minorities* (ST/HR(05)/H852/no.5), 1979, **I, 1**, (92), *c*, c.1.

UN HUMAN RIGHTS COMMITTEE (HRC), *General Comment No. 22: The right to freedom of thought, conscience and religion: Art. 18* (CCPR/C/21/Rev.1/Add.4), 30 July 1993, **I, 1**, (94), *c*, c.2.

UN HUMAN RIGHTS COMMITTEE (HRC), *CCPR General Comment No. 23: Article 27 (Rights of Minorities)* (CCPR/C/21/Rev.1/Add.5), 8 April 1994, **I, 1**, (95), *c*, c.3.

COMMITTEE ON THE ELIMINATION OF DISCRIMINATION AGAINST WOMEN (CEDAW), *Concluding Comments of the Committee on the Elimination of Discrimination Against Women: Greece* (CEDAW/C/GRC/CO/6), 2007, **I, 3**, (143), *a*, a.1.

UN HUMAN RIGHTS COMMITTEE (HRC), *Fatima Anderson v. Denmark* (CCPR/C/99/D/1868/2009), Communication n. 1868/2009, 7 September 2010, **I, 1**, (96), *c*, c.4.

UN OFFICE OF THE HIGH COMMISSIONER FOR HUMAN RIGHTS (OHCHR), *Minority Rights: International Standards and Guidance for Implementation* (HR/PUB/10/3), 2010, **I, 1**, (100), *c*, c.5.

UN OFFICE OF THE HIGH COMMISSIONER FOR HUMAN RIGHTS (OHCHR), *Promoting and Protecting Minority Rights. A Guide for Advocates* (HR/PUB/12/7), 2012, **I, 5**, (154), *f*, f.1.

FORUM ON MINORITY ISSUES, *Note by the Independent Expert on minority issues, Rita Izsák, on guaranteeing the rights of religious minorities* (A/HRC/FMI/2013/2), 3 October 2013, **I, 5**, (156), *f*, f.2.

UN SECRETARY GENERAL, *Guidance note of the Secretary General on racial discrimination and protection of minorities*, March 2013, **I**, **5**, (156), f, f.3.

EUROPEAN PARLIAMENT'S COMMITTEE ON CIVIL LIBERTIES, JUSTICE AND HOME AFFAIRS, *Towards a comprehensive EU protection system for minorities*, August 2017, **IV**, **1**, (225), *a*, a.1.

UN HUMAN RIGHTS COUNCIL (HRC), *Freedom of religion or belief. Report of the Special Rapporteur on freedom of religion or belief* (A/HRC/43/48), 27 February 2020, **I**, **3**, (123), *a*, a.2.

Right to access to media

OFFICE OF THE OSCE HIGH COMMISSIONER ON NATIONAL MINORITIES, *The Tallinn Guidelines on National Minorities and the Media in the Digital Age & Explanatory Note*, February 2019, **III**, **1**, (213), *g*, g.1.

Right to access to justice

OSCE HIGH COMMISSIONER ON NATIONAL MINORITIES, *The Graz Recommendations on Access to Justice and National Minorities*, November 2017, **III**, **1**, (209), f, f.1.

Right to association

UN COMMISSION ON HUMAN RIGHTS, SUB-COMMISSION ON THE PROMOTION AND PROTECTION OF HUMAN RIGHTS, *Commentary of the Working Group on Minorities to the United Nations Declaration on the Rights of Persons Belonging to National or Ethnic, Religious and Linguistic Minorities* (E/CN.4/Sub.2/AC.5/2005/2), 4 April 2005, **I**, **5**, (153), *e*, e.1.

UN OFFICE OF THE HIGH COMMISSIONER FOR HUMAN RIGHTS (OHCHR), *Minority Rights: International Standards and Guidance for Implementation* (HR/PUB/10/3), 2010, **I**, **5**, (153), *e*, e.2.

ADVISORY COMMITTEE ON THE FRAMEWORK CONVENTION FOR THE PROTECTION OF NATIONAL MINORITIES, *Compilation of Opinions of the Advisory Committee relating to Article 8 of the Framework Convention for the Protection of National Minorities (3rd cycle)*, 13 May 2016, **II**, **2**, (191), b, b.1.

Right to asylum

UN REFUGEE AGENCY (UNHCR), *Guidelines on International Protection: "Membership of a particular social group" within the context of Article 1A(2) of the 1951 Convention and/or its 1967 Protocol relating to the Status of Refugees* (HCR/GIP/02/02), 7 May 2002, **I**, **2**, (115), *a*, a.1.

UN REFUGEE AGENCY (UNHCR), *Guidelines on International Protection: Religion-Based Refugee Claims under Article 1A(2) of the 1951 Convention and/*

or the 1967 Protocol relating to the Status of Refugees (HCR/GIP/04/06), 28 April 2004, **I**, **2**, (117), *a*, a.2.

EUROPEAN ASYLUM SUPPORT OFFICE (EASO), *Country Guidance Afghanistan*, June 2019, **IV**, **2**, (244), *a*, a.1.

Right to culture

UN HUMAN RIGHTS COMMITTEE (HRC), *CCPR General Comment No. 23: Article 27 (Rights of Minorities)* (CCPR/C/21/Rev.1/Add.5), 8 April 1994, **I**, **1**, (104), *d*, d.1.

UN COMMISSION ON HUMAN RIGHTS, SUB-COMMISSION ON THE PROMOTION AND PROTECTION OF HUMAN RIGHTS, *Commentary of the Working Group on Minorities to the United Nations Declaration on the Rights of Persons Belonging to National or Ethnic, Religious and Linguistic Minorities* (E/CN.4/Sub.2/AC.5/2005/2), 4 April 2005, **I**, **5**, (140), *d*, d.1.

Right to education

FRANCESCO CAPOTORTI (Special Rapporteur of the Sub-Commission on Prevention of Discrimination and Protection of Minorities), *Study on the Rights of Persons Belonging to Ethnic, Religious and Linguistic Minorities* (ST/HR(05)/H852/no.5), 1979, **I**, **1**, (105), *e*, e.1.

OSCE HIGH COMMISSIONER ON NATIONAL MINORITIES (HCNM), *The Hague Recommendations regarding the Education Rights of National Minorities & Explanatory Note*, October 1996, **III**, **1**, (202), *d*, d.1.

OSCE-ODIHR, ADVISORY COUNCIL OF EXPERTS ON FREEDOM OF RELIGION OR BELIEF, *Toledo Guiding Principles on Teaching about Religions and Beliefs in Public Schools*, 2007, **III**, **1**, (206), *d*, d.2.

UN OFFICE OF THE HIGH COMMISSIONER FOR HUMAN RIGHTS (OHCHR), *Promoting and Protecting Minority Rights. A Guide for Advocates* (HR/PUB/12/7), 2012, **I**, **4**, (126), *a*, a.1.

ADVISORY COMMITTEE ON THE FRAMEWORK CONVENTION FOR THE PROTECTION OF NATIONAL MINORITIES, *Compilation of Opinions of the Advisory Committee relating to Article 8 of the Framework Convention for the Protection of National Minorities (4th cycle)*, 18 September 2017, **II**, **1**, (193), *c*, c.1.

Right to existence

UN COMMISSION ON HUMAN RIGHTS, SUB-COMMISSION ON THE PROMOTION AND PROTECTION OF HUMAN RIGHTS, *Commentary of the Working Group on Minorities to the United Nations Declaration on the Rights of Persons Belonging to National or Ethnic, Religious and Linguistic Minorities* (E/CN.4/Sub.2/AC.5/2005/2), 4 April 2005, **I**, **5**, (134), *a*, a.1.

UN OFFICE OF THE HIGH COMMISSIONER FOR HUMAN RIGHTS (OHCHR), *Minority Rights: International Standards and Guidance for Implementation* (HR/PUB/10/3), 2010, I, 5, (136), *a*, a.2.

FORUM ON MINORITY ISSUES, *Note by the Independent Expert on minority issues, Rita Izsák, on guaranteeing the rights of religious minorities* (A/HRC/FMI/2013/2), 3 October 2013, I, 5, (136), *a*, a.3.

Right to free self-identification

EUROPEAN COURTS OF HUMAN RIGHTS, GC, Case of *Molla Sali c. Greece* (Application no. 20.452/14), 19 December 2018, II, 1, (173), *b*, b.1.

Right to legal personality

OSCE OFFICE FOR DEMOCRATIC INSTITUTIONS AND HUMAN RIGHTS (ODIHR), *Guidelines on the Legal Personality of Religious or Belief Communities*, 2014, III, 1, (201), c, c.1.

Right to maintain religion or belief

SPECIAL RAPPORTEUR ON FREEDOM OF RELIGION OR BELIEF – INDEPENDENT EXPERT ON MINORITY ISSUES – SPECIAL RAPPORTEUR ON THE SALE OF CHILDREN, CHILD PROSTITUTION AND CHILD PORNOGRAPHY – SPECIAL RAPPORTEUR ON TRAFFICKING IN PERSONS, ESPECIALLY WOMEN AND CHILDREN – CHAIR-RAPPORTEUR OF THE WORKING GROUP ON THE ISSUE OF DISCRIMINATION AGAINST WOMEN IN LAW AND IN PRACTICE – SPECIAL RAPPORTEUR ON VIOLENCE AGAINST WOMEN, ITS CAUSES AND CONSEQUENCES, *Special procedures of the Human Rights Council, Communication 29 May 2013 – Iraq* (IRQ 2/2013), I, 4, (127), *b*, b.1.

Right to participation

UN COMMISSION ON HUMAN RIGHTS, SUB-COMMISSION ON THE PROMOTION AND PROTECTION OF HUMAN RIGHTS, *Commentary of the Working Group on Minorities to the United Nations Declaration on the Rights of Persons Belonging to National or Ethnic, Religious and Linguistic Minorities* (E/CN.4/Sub.2/AC.5/2005/2), 4 April 2005, I, 5, (140), *d*, d.1.

UN HUMAN RIGHTS COUNCIL (HRC), *Recommendations of the second session of the Forum on Minority Issues on minorities and effective political participation* (A/HRC/13/25), 12 and 13 November 2009, I, 5, (143), *d*, d.2.

UN OFFICE OF THE HIGH COMMISSIONER FOR HUMAN RIGHTS (OHCHR), *Minority Rights: International Standards and Guidance for Implementation* (HR/PUB/10/3), 2010, I, 5, (150), *d*, d.3.

Index of rights and principles 257

OFFICE OF THE OSCE HIGH COMMISSIONER ON NATIONAL MINORITIES, *The Ljubljana Guidelines on Integration of Diverse Societies*, 7 November 2012, III, 1, (207), e, e.1.

UN OFFICE OF THE HIGH COMMISSIONER FOR HUMAN RIGHTS (OHCHR), *The inclusion of religious minorities in consultative and decision-making bodies*, 2014, I, 5, (151), *d*, d.4.

Right to profess and practise religion or belief

FRANCESCO CAPOTORTI (Special Rapporteur of the Sub-Commission on Prevention of Discrimination and Protection of Minorities), *Study on the Rights of Persons Belonging to Ethnic, Religious and Linguistic Minorities* (ST/HR(05)/H852/no.5), 1979, I, 1, (59), *b*, b.1.

UN HUMAN RIGHTS COMMITTEE (HRC), *CCPR General Comment No. 22: Article 18 (Freedom of Thought, Conscience or Religion)* (CCPR/C/21/Rev.1/Add.4), 30 July 1993, I, 1, (69), *b*, b.2.

UN Human Rights Committee (HRC), *CCPR General Comment No. 23: Article 27 (Rights of Minorities)* (CCPR/C/21/Rev.1/Add.5), 8 April 1994, I, 1, (70), *b*, b.3.

EUROPEAN COURTS OF HUMAN RIGHTS, Case of *Serif c. Greece* (Application no. 38.178/97), 14 March 2000, II, 1, (162), *a*, a.1.

UN HUMAN RIGHTS COMMITTEE (HRC), *Sister Immaculate Joseph and 80 Teaching Sisters of the Holy Cross of the Third Order of Saint Francis in Menzingen of Sri Lanka v. Sri Lanka* (CCPR/C/85/D/1249/2004), Communication No. 1249/2004, 4 April 2001, I, 1, (74), b, b.4.

UN COMMISSION ON HUMAN RIGHTS, SUB-COMMISSION ON THE PROMOTION AND PROTECTION OF HUMAN RIGHTS, *Commentary of the Working Group on Minorities to the United Nations Declaration on the Rights of Persons Belonging to National or Ethnic, Religious and Linguistic Minorities* (E/CN.4/Sub.2/AC.5/2005/2), 4 April 2005, I, 5, (138), c, c.1.

UN HUMAN RIGHTS COMMITTEE (HRC), *Gareth Anver Prince v. South Africa* (CCPR/C/91/D/1474/2006), Communication No. 1474/2006, 14 November 2007, I, 1, (82), *b*, b.5.

COUNCIL OF THE EUROPEAN UNION, *EU Guidelines on the Promotion and Protection of Freedom of Religion or Belief*, 24 June 2013, IV, 1, (), *b*, b.1.

OSCE OFFICE FOR DEMOCRATIC INSTITUTIONS AND HUMAN RIGHTS (ODIHR), *Guidelines on the Legal Personality of Religious or Belief Communities*, 2014, III, 1, (197), b, b.1.

ADVISORY COMMITTEE ON THE FRAMEWORK CONVENTION FOR THE PROTECTION OF NATIONAL MINORITIES, *Compilation of Opinions of the Advisory Committee relating to Article 8 of the Framework Convention for the Protection of National Minorities (3rd cycle)*, 13 May 2016, II, 2, (191), *b*, b.1.

Bibliography

Agarin T. and Brosig M. (ed), *Trajectories of Minority Rights Issues in Europe* (Routledge 2015).
Annicchino P., 'The Persecution of Religious and LGBTI Minorities and Asylum Law: Recent Trends in the Adjudication of European Supranational Courts' [2015] European Public Law 571.
Arnull, A., *The European Union and its Court of Justice* (Oxford European Union Law Library 2006).
Atrey S., *Intersectional Discrimination* (Oxford University Press 2019).
Bagley T. H., *General Principles and Problems in the International Protection of Minorities* (Imprimeries Populaires 1950).
Barten U., 'Article 27 ICCPR. A First Point of Reference' in Ugo Caruso and Rainer Hofmann (eds), *The United Declarations on Minorities* (Brill 2015) 46.
Bielefeldt H., Ghanea N., and Michael Wiener (eds), *Freedom of Religion or Belief. An International Law Commentary* (Oxford University Press 2016).
Bowring B., 'Case-Law of the European Court of Human Rights Concerning the Protection of Minorities, July 2012 to August 2014' [2015] European Yearbook of Minority Issues Online 197.
Bretscher F., *Protecting the Religious Freedom of New Minorities in International Law* (Routledge 2020).
Capotorti F., *Study on the Rights of Persons Belonging to Ethnic, Religious and Linguistic Minorities* (ST/HR(05)/H852/no.5 1979).
Capotorti F., 'Les développements possibles de la protection internationale des minorités' [1986] Le Cahiers de droit 239.
Carrera S. and others, 'Towards a Comprehensive EU Protection System for Minorities' 2017 <www.ceps.eu/system/files/ProtectionSystemForMinorities.pdf>.
Carrera, S., *Shifting Responsibilities for EU Roma Citizens: The 2010 French Affair on Roma Evictions and Expulsions Continued* (CEPS 2013).
Cismas I., *Religious Actors and International Law* (Oxford University Press 2014).
Davidson J. S., 'The Procedure and Practice of the Human Rights Committee under the First OP to the ICCPR' [1991] Canterbury Law Review 337.
Deschênes J., *Proposal Concerning a Definition of the Term 'Minority'* (E/CN.4/Sub.2 1985).
Eide A., 'The Council of Europe's Framework Convention for the Protection of National Minorities', in Kristin Henrard and Robert Dunbar (eds), *Synergies in Minority Protection Synergies in Minority Protection. European and International Law Perspectives* (Cambridge University Press 2009) 119.

Eskridge W. N. Jr and Fretwell Wilson R. (eds.), *Religious Freedom, LGBT Rights, and the Prospects of Common Ground* (Cambridge University Press 2018).
Ferrari D., *Il concetto di minoranza religiosa dal diritto internazionale al diritto europeo. Genesi, sviluppo e circolazione* (Il Mulino 2019).
Fields A. B., *Rethinking Human Rights for the New Millennium* (New York University Press 2003).
Fields A. B., 'Human Rights as a Holistic Concept' [1992] Human Rights Quarterly 1.
Fokas E., 'The Legal Status of Religious Minorities: Exploring the Impact of the European Court of Human Rights' [2018] Social Compass 25.
Ghanea N. and Xanthaki A. (eds), *Minorities, Peoples and Self-Determination: Essays in Honour of Patrick Thornberry* (Martinus Nijhoff Publishers 2005).
Henrard K., 'The European Court of Human Rights, Ethnic and Religious Minorities and the Two Dimensions of the Right to Equal Treatment: Jurisprudence at Different Speeds?' [2016] Nordic Journal of Human Rights 157.
Henrard K. and Dunbar R., 'Introduction' in Kristin Henrard and Robert Dunbar (eds), *Synergies in Minority Protection. European and International Law Perspectives* (Cambridge University Press 2009) 8.
Ippolito F. and Iglesias Sanchez S. (eds), *Protecting Vulnerable Groups: The European Human Rights Framework* (Bloomsbury Publishing 2015).
Jolly QCS., ' "Achbita & Bougnaoui: A Strange Kind of Equality" Blog Article' 15 March 2017 <www.cloisters.com/blogs/achbita-bougnaoui-a-strange-kind-of-equality>.
Krishnaswami A., *Study of Discrimination in the Matter of Religious Rights and Practices* (United Nations publication, Sales No. 60, XIV.2).
Lerner N., 'The evolution of Minority Rights in International Law' in Catherine Brölmann et al. (eds), *Peoples and Minorities in International Law* (Martinus Nijhoff Publishers 1993).
MacNaughton G., 'Decent Work for All: A Holistic Human Rights Approach' [2011] American University International Law Review 441.
O'Halloran K., *Human Rights, Religion and International Law* (Routledge 2019).
O'Nions H., *Minority Rights Protection in International Law: The Roma of Europe* (Routledge 2016).
Peers S. et al., (eds), *The EU Charter of Fundamental Rights: A Commentary* (Bloomsbury Publishing 2014).
Ramphal S., 'Human Rights Today: Must the Few be More than the Many?' in B. Whitaker (ed), *Minorities – A Question of Human Rights?* (Pergamon Press Ltd 1984).
Sampat-Mehta R., *Minority Rights and Obligations* (Herpell's Press 1973).
Sonneveld S., *Conference Summary: Freedom of Religion and Belief and Sexuality* (Ani Zonneveld 2016).
Tavani C., *Collective Rights and the Cultural Identity of the Roma. A Case Study of Italy* (Martinus Nijhoff Publishers 2012)
Thomas S., *Diplomacy and Religion* (Oxford University Press 2017).
Uddin Khan B. and Rahman M. M., *Protection of Minorities: Regimes, Norms and Issues in South Asia* (Newcastle upon Tyne 2012) 1 ss.
Ventura M., 'Non discriminazione e tutela delle diversità e delle minoranze' in *Europa. Un'utopia in costruzione* (Istituto della Enciclopedia Italiana 2018) 140.
Wolfrum R., 'The Emergence of "New Minorities" as a Result of "Migration"' in Catherine Brölmann, René Lefeber, and Marjoleine Zieck (eds), *Peoples and Minorities in International Law* (Martinus Nijhoff Publishers 1993).

Name index

Agarin, T. 1
Althammer, R. 92
Anderson, F. vii, xx, 90, 96, 248, 253
Annicchino, P. 6
Arnull, A. 229
Atrey, S. 1

Bagley, T. H. 36
Barten, U. 2
Belden Fields, A. 6
Bielefeldt, H. 1
Boodoo, C. 91
Bowring, B. 231
Bretscher, F. 22
Brölmann, C. 1
Brosig, M. 1

Capotorti, F. 2, 3, 4, 6, 10, 32, 45, 46, 47, 51, 53, 54, 59, 92, 105, 155, 247, 255, 257
Carrera, S. 16, 229
Caruso, G. 2
Cismas, I. 23
Crauford Smith, R. 232

Danning, L. G. 71
Davidson, J. S. 86
Dawod, S. I. 127, 128, 130, 131
Deschênes, J. v, xviii, 4, 41, 247
De Varennes, F. vi, xix, 57, 58, 249, 250
Doğan, İ. 15
Dunbar, R. 14, 18

Eide, A. 18, 141
Eskridge, W. N. 2

Faure, L. 100
Ferrari, D. 1, 22
Fokas, E. 15
Fretwell Wilson, R. 2

Gaygusuz, C. 227
Gelle, M. H. 97
Ghanea, N. 1

Hasan, F. S. 198
Henrard, K. 14, 15, 18
Hofmann, R. 2

Iglesias Sanchez, S. 231
Ippolito, F. 231

Jama, A. M. 99

Kazantzis, G. 100
Ker, A. 49
Khan, B. U. 3
Kitok, I. 71, 73
Kokkinakis, M. 75, 168, 170, 198
Krishnaswami, A. 60

Lefeber, R. 2
Lerner, N. 1

MacNaughton, G. 6
Molla Sali, M. xii, xxvii, 15, 16, 173, 249, 256

O'Halloran, K. 1
Ominayak, B. 71, 73
O'Nions, H. 231

Peers, S. 228, 231, 232
Prince, G. A. vii, xx, 82, 84, 128, 248, 257

Rahman, M. M. 3

Sampat-Mehta, R. 50
Serif, I. xii, xxvi, 15, 162, 184, 247, 257
Sonneveld, S. 23

Tavani, C. 18
Thomas, S. 23
Toonen, N. 98, 100

Ventura, M. 20

Whitaker, B. 45
Wiener, M. 1

Wingrove, N. 170
Wolfrum, R. 2

Xanthaki, A. 1

Zieck, M. 2
Zwaan-de Vries, F. H. 71

Subject index

Advisory Committee on the Framework Convention for the protection of national minorities xii, xxvii, xxviii, 18, 151, 191, 249, 254, 255, 257
Advisory Council of Experts on Freedom of religion or Belief xiii, xxix, 206, 248, 255
affirmative action 101, 102
affirmative measures 102
agnostic 9, 22, 57, 58
anti-discrimination 104, 154
association (right to) xi, xii, xxv, xxxviii, xxxi, 153, 191, 254
asylum (right to) viii, xiv, xxi, xxx, xxxi, 26, 115, 239, 244, 254
atheist 9, 22, 57, 58, 118, 198, 234, 235, 243

belief vi, viii, ix, x, xi, xii, xiii, xix, xxii, xxiii, xxvi, xxvii, xxviii, xxix, xxx, xxxi, 1, 8, 9, 10, 12, 13, 15, 16, 19, 20, 23, 26, 27, 28, 54, 55, 57, 58, 59, 61, 62, 64, 66, 67, 69, 70, 75, 76, 80, 81, 82, 84, 89, 90, 91, 94, 95, 105, 108, 117, 118, 119, 120, 121, 123, 124, 127, 130, 138, 139, 140, 151, 156, 161, 162, 167, 174, 175, 185, 188, 189, 190, 191, 192, 193, 194, 197, 198, 199, 200, 201, 202, 206, 207, 208, 209, 210, 223, 224, 225, 227, 228, 229, 231, 233, 234, 235, 236, 237, 238, 239, 243, 244, 248, 249, 250, 254, 255, 256, 257

citizens xviii, 4, 16, 42, 43, 48, 51, 52, 55, 56, 67, 68, 71, 72, 132, 143, 145, 175, 177, 186, 201, 210, 226, 227, 228, 229
civil society xxiv, 88, 89, 144, 147, 148, 149, 154, 158, 195, 213, 215, 216, 228, 233, 234

conflict xi, xxv, xxix, 12, 22, 68, 127, 137, 138, 145, 152, 160, 195, 208, 210, 211, 213, 214, 218, 220, 221, 245, 246
conscientious objection xix, 65, 239
conversion 3, 76, 140
Council of Europe xi, xxvi, 1, 14, 15, 17, 18, 25, 26, 47, 151, 161, 185, 186, 188, 196, 227, 252
cultural rights 12, 73, 103, 104, 203, 204, 214
culture (right to) vii, xxi, xxiii, xxxi, 104, 255

definition v, viii, xiii, xvii, xviii, xxii, xxviii, 1, 2, 3, 4, 5, 6, 9, 10, 11, 17, 20, 25, 26, 32, 33, 34, 35, 37, 38, 39, 41, 42, 44, 45, 46, 47, 49, 50, 51, 52, 53, 54, 57, 99, 109, 112, 115, 116, 117, 118, 129, 142, 157, 196, 197, 214, 242, 247
democratic society xxvi, 84, 87, 102, 153, 161, 167, 168, 169, 170, 171, 172, 199, 214
discrimination (principle of non): discrimination against minority women viii, 122; discrimination against women viii, ix, xxii, 26, 101, 102, 121, 122, 127, 129, 248, 249, 251, 256; discrimination based on religion or belief 69, 80, 95, 117, 120, 130, 156, 199, 200, 201, 237; discrimination based on sexual orientation 155; discrimination on the basis of gender 124, 227; indirect discrimination 92, 101, 104, 210, 232; intersectional discrimination 1, 13, 145; multiple discrimination 1, 13, 54, 155, 158; non-discrimination on the basis of nationality 225, 226; positive discrimination 102; racial

Subject index 263

discrimination xi, xxvi, 13, 16, 38, 96, 97, 99, 101, 102, 103, 104, 135, 138, 140, 155, 156, 157, 158, 159, 160, 198, 248, 254
diversity xxix, xxx, 4, 18, 22, 23, 24, 43, 57, 94, 103, 135, 136, 137, 142, 143, 144, 146, 147, 150, 193, 197, 211, 217, 218, 223, 228, 229, 230, 231, 232, 233
dominant groups 9, 34, 54, 55
dominant minority groups 38
dominant religion 120

education (right to) viii, ix, xii, xiii, xxi, xxii, xxviii, xxix, xxxi, 105, 126, 193, 202, 203, 255
equality vii, ix, xxi, xxii, xxx, 1, 4, 20, 47, 52, 59, 61, 70, 71, 76, 82, 84, 88, 93, 94, 95, 101, 102, 121, 122, 123, 124, 126, 132, 133, 152, 156, 157, 158, 160, 174, 176, 183, 204, 206, 207, 210, 211, 216, 223, 227, 228, 229, 232, 234
ethnic minority 46, 123
European Court of Human Rights 15, 26, 47, 48, 75, 98, 227, 231
European Parliament's Committee on Civil Liberties, Justice and Home Affairs xiv, 225, 249, 254
existence: protection of 156; right to ix, xxiii, 10, 134, 255

family 28, 44, 63, 123, 128, 130, 160, 165, 166, 170, 180, 181, 185, 186, 222, 227, 242
Forum on Minority Issues vi, ix, x, xi, xviii, xxiii, xxiv, xxv, 8, 9, 23, 57, 102, 136, 143, 149, 150, 156, 160, 248, 249, 253, 256
freedom of expression xxix, 72, 81, 161, 172, 188, 198, 213, 214, 215, 216, 218, 221, 237, 238
freedom of religion or belief viii, ix, xiii, xiv, xxii, xxviii, xxix, xxx, 1, 12, 13, 16, 19, 23, 123, 124, 127, 130, 139, 151, 197, 198, 201, 202, 206, 207, 233, 234, 235, 236, 237, 238, 239, 248, 250, 254, 255, 256, 257
freedom of thought, conscience and religion vii, xx, 16, 27, 59, 60, 94, 117, 161, 167, 170, 188, 197, 209
free self-identification (right to) xii, xxvii, xxxi, 173, 185, 256

gender equality ix, xxii, 123, 126, 160, 210, 211

High Commissioner for Human Rights vi, vii, ix, x, xi, xviii, xix, xxi, xxii, xxiii, xxiv, xxv, 9, 10, 12, 13, 53, 57, 100, 126, 136, 148, 150, 151, 153, 154, 155, 248, 249, 253, 254, 255, 256, 257
High Commissioner on National Minorities xiii, xiv, xxix, 19, 26, 141, 195, 196, 202, 207, 209, 247, 249, 254, 255, 257
Human Rights Committee v, vi, vii, vii, xviii, xix, xx, xxi, 3, 4, 42, 50, 52, 69, 70, 74, 79, 80, 82, 86, 89, 91, 92, 94, 95, 96, 98, 99, 101, 104, 117, 118, 130, 157, 197, 198, 199, 200, 202, 222, 247, 248, 253, 257

identity of minorities ix, xxiii, 39, 151; identity of religious minorities xxiii, 7, 137; promotion xxiii, xxiv, xxv, 103, 131, 135, 136, 137, 138, 140; protection xxiii, xxiv, xxv, 137, 138, 140
indigenous populations xviii, 42, 51, 54
individual rights 5, 47, 73, 177, 186, 210, 229, 232
Islam 58, 76, 98, 128, 190, 192
Islamophobia 17, 192, 232, 233
intolerance 60, 61, 62, 64, 65, 76, 80, 104, 105, 117, 120, 130, 137, 138, 156, 160, 198, 199, 201, 215, 233, 237

justice (right to access to) xiii, xxix, xxxi, 209, 254

legal personality (right to) xiii, xxviii, xxxi, 201, 202, 256
LGBTI 6, 237
linguistic minority 5, 13, 36, 41, 46, 54, 58, 72, 139, 157, 158

majority 4, 9, 11, 15, 17, 18, 31, 37, 38, 41, 44, 45, 46, 47, 49, 50, 52, 53, 54, 55, 61, 62, 65, 69, 75, 77, 78, 84, 87, 93, 94, 116, 120, 138, 146, 147, 148, 159, 170, 184, 189, 206, 214, 215, 224, 230, 233, 239, 244, 246
marriage xix, 61, 62, 63, 123, 124, 130, 165, 176, 186
media (right to access to) xiv, xxix, xxxi, 213, 254
minority children ix, xxii, 126, 127, 206
minority education xiii, xxix, 127, 206, 207
Muslim minority 15, 16, 124, 127, 165, 170, 177, 182, 183, 184, 186

national minorities xii, xiii, xiv, xviii, xxvii, xxviii, xxix, 8, 9, 10, 17, 18, 19, 20, 26, 46, 47, 51, 135, 139, 141, 142, 151, 185, 188, 189, 190, 191, 193, 195, 196, 202, 203, 204, 205, 206, 207, 209, 210, 211, 212, 213, 214, 215, 216, 217, 218, 219, 220, 222, 226, 247, 248, 249, 252, 254, 255, 257
non-citizens xviii, 43, 55, 56, 143
non dominant position 4, 5, 9, 13, 52, 53, 54, 55, 158
non dominant situation 46, 52

Organization for Security and Co-operation in Europe xii, xxviii, 196
OSCE High Commissioner on National Minorities xiii, xiv, xxix, 19, 141, 196, 202, 207, 209, 247, 248, 249, 254, 255, 257

participation (right to) x, xiii, xxiv, xxix, 140, 207, 256
particular groups 101, 220
particular social group viii, xxi, 11, 109, 115, 116, 118, 243, 244, 247, 254
Permanent Court of International Justice 47
persecution xiv, xv, xxx, xxxi, 6, 11, 58, 70, 95, 103, 110, 111, 116, 117, 118, 120, 121, 243, 244, 245, 246; fear of xxii, 110, 119, 246; religious 11
personal status xix, 63, 64, 160, 165
pluralism xxix, 20, 55, 123, 134, 135, 170, 171, 203, 208, 216, 217, 218, 224, 230
positive action 102, 103, 136
positive measures xi, xxv, 72, 73, 88, 144, 145, 152, 156, 210
predominant group 35, 61
predominant religion 69, 95, 193
property (right to respect for) 180

racism 104, 160, 198, 229
Refugee Claims (religion-based) viii, xxii, 11, 117, 118, 120, 248, 254
religious bodies 76, 81
religious diplomacy 2
religious holiday 168, 171
religious minority vii, 1, 2, 3, 4, 6, 8, 10, 11, 13, 14, 15, 16, 17, 18, 21, 25, 26, 46, 49, 58, 60, 89, 91, 120, 124, 151, 152, 155, 175, 185, 230, 232
right of persons belonging to religious minorities xix, 59, 60, 65, 67, 68, 69, 105, 106; to administer the affairs of their own religious communities 68; to establish educational institutions 106; not to be compelled to participate in the activities of other religions 60, 67

Secretary General xi, xxi, xxvi, 2, 13, 27, 30, 31, 32, 35, 37, 110, 112, 113, 114, 115, 156, 248, 251, 254
self-identification xii, xxvii, xxxi, 54, 55, 144, 157, 173, 185, 256
Sharia 174, 175, 176, 177, 183, 184, 185, 186
social groups vii, 6, 7, 9, 11
solidarity (sense of) 4, 52, 53
special measures 33, 34, 35, 38, 59, 60, 92, 101, 103, 135, 170
stateless persons xviii, 12, 13, 56, 109, 158, 159, 240, 243, 251, 252
Sub-Commission on Prevention of Discrimination and Protection of Minorities v, vi, vii, viii, xvii, xix, xx, xxi, 3, 10, 32, 33, 41, 53, 59, 61, 92, 105, 247, 253, 255, 257

tolerance 20, 44, 64, 94, 135, 138, 140, 188, 191, 198, 203, 208, 224, 230

xenophobia 104, 137, 138, 160, 198